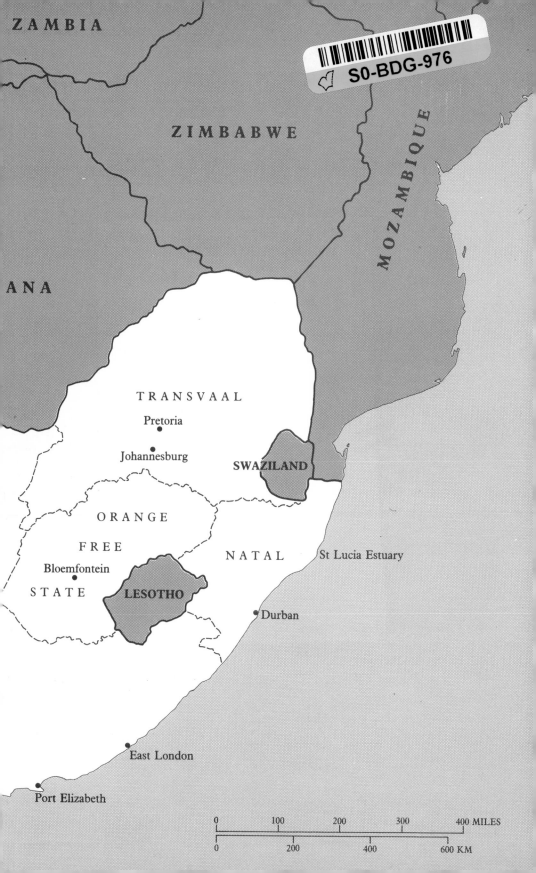

ZAMBIA

ZIMBABWE

MOZAMBIQUE

ANA

TRANSVAAL

Pretoria

Johannesburg

SWAZILAND

ORANGE

FREE

NATAL

St Lucia Estuary

Bloemfontein

STATE

LESOTHO

Durban

East London

Port Elizabeth

0	100	200	300	400 MILES

0	200	400	600 KM

Embargo Disimplemented
South Africa's Military Industry

sipri

Stockholm International Peace Research Institute

SIPRI is an independent international institute for research into problems of peace and conflict, especially those of arms control and disarmament. It was established in 1966 to commemorate Sweden's 150 years of unbroken peace.

The Institute is financed mainly by the Swedish Parliament. The staff, the Governing Board and the Scientific Council are international.

The Governing Board and Scientific Council are not responsible for the views expressed in the publications of the Institute.

Governing Board

Ambassador Dr Inga Thorsson, Chairman (Sweden)
Egon Bahr (Federal Republic of Germany)
Professor Francesco Calogero (Italy)
Dr Max Jakobson (Finland)
Professor Dr Karlheinz Lohs (German Democratic Republic)
Professor Emma Rothschild (United Kingdom)
Sir Brian Urquhart (United Kingdom)
The Director

Director

Dr Walter Stützle (Federal Republic of Germany)

sipri

Stockholm International Peace Research Institute
Pipers väg 28, S-171 73 Solna, Sweden
Cable: PEACERESEARCH STOCKHOLM
Telephone: 46 8/55 97 00

Embargo Disimplemented

South Africa's Military Industry

SIGNE LANDGREN

sipri

Stockholm International Peace Research Institute

OXFORD UNIVERSITY PRESS
1989

Oxford University Press, Oxford OIX2 6DP
Oxford New York Toronto
Delhi Bombay Calcutta Madras Karachi
Petaling Jaya Singapore Hong Kong Tokyo
Nairobi Dar es Salaam Cape Town
Melbourne Auckland
and associated companies in
Berlin Ibadan

Oxford is a trade mark of Oxford University Press

Published in the United States
by Oxford University Press, New York

British Library Cataloguing in Publication Data
Landgren, Signe
  Embargo disimplemented: South Africa's
  military industry.
  1. South Africa. Military equipment
  industries
  I. Title   II. Stockholm International Peace
  Research Institute
  338.4'7623'0968
  ISBN 0–19–829127–2

Library of Congress Cataloging in Publication Data
Landgren, Signe.
    Embargo disimplemented: South Africa's military industry / Signe
  Landgren.
      p.cm.
    'Sipri, Stockholm International Peace Research Institute.'
    Bibliography: p.
    Includes index.
    1. Munitions—South Africa.   I. Stockholm International Peace
  Research Institute.   II. Title.
    HD9743.S62L36 1988   382'.456234'0968—dc19   88–25255
    ISBN 0–19–829127–2

Set by Wyvern Typesetting, Bristol
Printed and bound in
Great Britain by Biddles Ltd.,
Guildford and King's Lynn

Preface

This case study of the buildup of South Africa's arms industry was undertaken along the traditional SIPRI line of interest in the spread of armaments. In addition, the purpose of the study was to investigate the functioning or the implementation of the arms embargo against South Africa. Twenty-five years of embargo experience provide a wealth of material for those engaged in the South African question as well as for those who take a general interest in the embargo method.

Moreover, the description of the various sectors of the South African arms industry provides an insight into the country's military capacity, which is of relevance to those evaluating the current conflict situation in the region.

A large number of experts provided valuable comments and material for the various chapters of the book. In particular, I wish to express my thanks to Dr Winrich Kühne of the Stiftung Wissenschaft und Politik at Ebenhausen who took the time to read and comment on the entire manuscript. I am also grateful to Dr Zdenek Cervenka and the library of the Scandinavian Institute for African Studies at Uppsala, and Mr Abdul Minty, Director of the World Campaign Against Nuclear and Military Collaboration with South Africa. Useful information was also gained from the International Seminar on the UN arms embargo against South Africa organized in May 1986 by the World Campaign and the UN Special Committee Against Apartheid.

Finally, I want to thank the SIPRI editor Gillian Stanbridge for both linguistic and scientific editing, and Miyoko Suzuki for the final word-processing.

Stockholm, June 1988   Signe Landgren

Contents

Part III.   The sectors of the military industry

Part IV.   Implementation and disimplementation

Appendices

List of tables and figures

Tables

Figures

Acronyms and abbreviations

AA	Anti-aircraft
AAM	Air-to-air missile
AC	Armoured car
ACDA	Arms Control and Disarmament Agency
ADE	Atlantis Diesel Engines
AEB	Atomic Energy Board
AEC	Atomic Energy Corporation
AECI	African Explosives and Chemical Industries
AFV	Armoured fighting vehicle
AIO	Action-Information Organization
Altech	Allied Technologies
ANC	African National Congress
APC	Armoured personnel carrier
Armscor	The Armaments Corporation of South Africa
ASEAN	Association of South-East Asian Nations
ASM	Air-to-surface missile
ASW	Anti-submarine warfare
ATM	Anti-tank missile
BOSS	Bureau of State Security
C^3I	Command, control, communications and intelligence
CBS	Columbia Broadcasting System
CBW	Chemical and biological weapons
CCL	Commodity Control List
CIA	Central Intelligence Agency
COCOM	Co-ordinating Committee
COIN	Counter-insurgency
CSIR	Council for Scientific and Industrial Research
DP	Data processing
EC	European Community
EEC	European Economic Community
Escom	South African Electricity Supply Commission
EW	Electronic warfare
FAC	Fast attack craft
FIDA	Feria Internacional del Aire
FN	Fabrique National (Belgium)
GDP	Gross domestic product
GEC	General Electric Co. (UK)

Genkor	General Mining Corporation
GNP	Gross National Product
Grinel	Grinaker Electronics
HF	High Frequency
IAEA	International Atomic Energy Agency
IAI	Israeli Aircraft Industries
IAR	Industriei Aeronautice Romane
IBM	International Business Machines
ICI	Imperial Chemical Industries
ICL	International Computers Ltd
ICV	Infantry combat vehicle
IDAF	International Defence and Aid Fund
IDC	Industrial Development Corporation of South Africa
IDR	International Defence Review
IISS	International Institute for Strategic Studies
IKL	Ingenieurkontor Lübeck
IMI	Israeli Military Industries
IR	Infra-red
Iscor	Iron and Steel Corporation
ITAR	International Traffic in Arms Regulations
ITT	International Telephone and Telegraph
LEW	Lyttleton Engineering Works
Magnis	Magirus Nissan
MAN	Maschinen-Fabrik Augsburg-Nürnberg
MARNET	Military Area Radio Network
MCTL	Military Critical Technologies List
MNR	Mozambican National Resistance (=RENAMO)
MPLA	Movimiento Popular de Libertaçao de Angola
MRI	Microelectronics Research Institute
MRL	Multiple rocket launcher
MW	Megawatt
NAC	National Accelerator Center
NATO	North Atlantic Treaty Organization
NCRL	National Chemical Research Laboratory
NEERI	National Electrical Engineeering Research Institute
NIAST	National Institute for Aeronautics and Systems Technology
NIDR	National Institute for Defence Research
NITR	National Institute for Telecommunications Research
NMERI	National Mechanical Engineering Research Institute
NP	National Party
NPRL	National Physical Research Laboratory

NPT	Non-Proliferation Treaty
NRIMS	National Research Institute for Mathematical Science
NRL	Naval Research Laboratory
Nucor	Nuclear Corporation
OAU	Organization for African Unity
OMC	Office of Munitions Control
PC	Patrol craft
PLO	Palestine Liberation Organization
PMP	Pretoria Metal Pressings
PRB	Poudreries Réunis de Belgique
PTBT	Partial Test Ban Treaty
PTI	Protea Telecommunications Industries
R	Rand
R&D	Research and development
RDT&E	Research, development, testing and Evaluation
RENAMO	Resistência Nacional Moçambicana (=MNR)
RPV	Remotely-piloted vehicle
RRE	Royal Radar Establishment
RRI	Rocket Research Institute
RSA	Republic of South Africa
SA	South Africa
SAAF	South African Air Force
SACP	South African Communist Party
SADF	South African Defence Forces
SAM	Surface-to-air missile
Samil	South African Military
SAN	South African Navy
SAP	South African Police
SAR	Search and rescue
Sasol	Suid-Afrikaanse Steenkool- Olie- en Gaskorporasie
SATO	South Atlantic Treaty Organization
SNEMCA	Société Nationale d'étude et de Construction de moteurs d'aviation
SPH	Self-propelled howitzer
SRC	Space Research Corporation (USA)
SRC-Q	Space Research Corporation, Quebec (Canada)
SRCI	Space Research Corporation International (Belgium)
SSM	Ship-to-ship missile
STC	Standard Telephone and Cables
Sub	Submarine
SWA	South West Africa (=Namibia)
SWAPO	South West African People's Organization

SWATF	South West Africa Territorial Force
SWU	Separate work units
TMA	Target-motion analysis
TNC	Transnational company
Ucor	Uranium Enrichment Corporation
UDI	Unilateral Declaration of Independence
UEC	United Electronics Corporation
UNITA	Uniâo Nacional para a Indepência Total de Angola
UPI	United Press International
USSR	Union of Soviet Socialist Republics
VHF	Very High Frequency

Part I.
Introduction

Chapter 1. South Africa as a case study

I. Purpose of the project

The Republic of South Africa stands out as the single 'most embargoed nation' in the world. International opposition to its apartheid policy and to its external policy in southern Africa has since 1963 been manifested in no fewer than four Security Council resolutions, prohibiting the *export* of armaments, military technology and nuclear technology, and also the *import* of armaments made in South Africa. But this trade has continued. Arms and, increasingly, production know-how, have continued to reach South Africa, coming from the very Western countries that agreed in the United Nations to abide by the arms embargo restrictions. This has enabled South Africa to build a modern, advanced, military-industrial complex on a scale which for the foreseeable future is unattainable by its poorer African neighbours. The establishment of a domestic arms industry has further meant that South Africa has changed from being exclusively an arms importer into being an arms exporting country in the international market. The central arms producing agency, the Armaments Corporation of South Africa (Armscor), claims to be the tenth largest arms producer in the Western world.[1] Finally, the continued trade in nuclear technology has created a nuclear weapon potential.

South Africa therefore presents a unique case study of how an arms embargo functions, which is the main purpose of this project. The questions to be pursued are *what* South Africa has been able to import in spite of the embargo, *how* it has been able to do so, and *why* the pressures to export and import military equipment turn out to be so much stronger than the impact of the arms embargo resolutions. South Africa's transition into becoming a militarily self-reliant power and a near-nuclear weapon power began in earnest when the first United Nations arms embargo was declared. This transformation has continued and gained momentum against a background of mounting obstacles to the import of armaments and military technology from the traditional suppliers. There has been a notable change in supplying nations, the type of equipment supplied and sought after, and supplying companies.

The story of South Africa's military buildup contains several aspects which are relevant in a broader context. First, the arms embargo method as a policy instrument remains a controversial issue in contemporary politics. In retrospect, looking at the various instances when arms embargoes have been practised, there is not one single case where the method has been described as efficient, relative to its stated purposes. Still, the method continues to be used, and will probably continue to be used in the future. Technically speaking, an arms embargo is one of the few sanctions with military implications available to individual states and to the United Nations, short of armed intervention. As such it still merits attention, instead of being categorically dismissed as 'inefficient'.

Secondly, the South African case provides insight into the general conventional arms race and presents examples of both the vertical and the horizontal spread of sophisticated armaments. The dynamics of this arms race has enabled a number of countries to occupy positions as regional big powers. Examples of such states include India, Pakistan, Israel, Argentina and Brazil. Like South Africa, all of them are counted as near-nuclear countries and ranked as leading Third World arms producers. The South African case is thus instructive for understanding the more general process of military industrialization. The account of South Africa's military industry in parts II and III of this study has been made as detailed as possible, in an effort to present a comprehensive picture of the use of foreign-supplied technology.

Thirdly, South Africa's military capacity is of interest in the more general context of the conflict in southern Africa, involving neighbouring Angola and Mozambique, the Namibian question and the rising internal unrest in South Africa itself, as well as geostrategic aspects with a bearing on the global East–West conflict. The situation in southern Africa has several times been described in the United Nations as constituting a threat to international peace and security. In particular, the continued supply of arms and military equipment to South Africa was determined by the Security Council in 1977 to constitute such a threat. This political background cannot be ignored but will be dealt with only insofar as it provides a key to understanding South Africa's determined effort to remain militarily superior in the region. The South African internal conflict between the White regime and its opponents *per se* is deemed to be outside the scope of this study.

II. The arms embargo method

Usage

The word 'embargo' first appeared at the beginning of the 17th century in connection with preventing commercial shipping in periods of conflict or war (from the Spanish *embargar*). Later the concept was widened to mean the prohibition of trade in certain types of goods, or trade in general. By definition, an embargo is a legal undertaking on a governmental level, as distinct from other types of boycotts. The Covenant of the League of Nations established economic and military sanctions as a means by which the organization could prevent international aggression. Arms embargoes were enacted on two occasions for this purpose, first against Paraguay in 1934 to stop its attack on Bolivia in the Chaco war, and secondly against Italy in 1935 to stop its invasion of Ethiopia.

The United Nations inherited this philosophy but has considerably increased its powers to use the embargo weapon. Article 41 of the United Nations Charter authorizes the use of sanctions to enforce the decisions of the Security

Council not only in cases of international aggression but also whenever a regime's actions are considered a *threat* to international peace.[2] However, arms embargoes have been used by the United Nations against only six countries: the People's Republic of China and North Korea in 1951, the Congo in 1960, Portugal in 1963, Rhodesia in 1965 and 1966, and finally South Africa in 1963, 1977 and 1984. These cases differ widely as to the duration of the embargo, the category of goods actually specified and the political circumstances. However, they all involve cutting off military supplies by means of international resolutions.

The embargo against China and North Korea was declared by the UN General Assembly, at the initiative of the United States, following upon China's intervention in the Korean war. As such it was just an illustration of the much broader UN commitment in Korea. The political background was extraordinary, and it has never been possible to use the arms embargo method again in major conflicts involving conflicting East–West interests within the framework of the United Nations. In the case of China and North Korea, the category of goods embargoed covered more than armaments. The General Assembly recommended:

that every state apply an embargo on the shipment to areas under the control of the Central People's Government of the People's Republic of China and of the North Korean authorities of arms, ammunition and implements of war, atomic energy materials, petroleum, transportation materials of strategic value, and items useful in the production of arms, ammunition, and implements of war.[3]

This embargo also represents an extension of the US prohibition of 1947 on exports of 'strategic goods' to the Soviet Union and Eastern Europe, later expressed in the so-called COCOM (Co-ordinating Committee) embargo which still remains in force today.[4]

Like the China embargo, the UN arms embargo against the Congo during the Congo crisis was just one facet of a much broader commitment. In July 1960, within 10 days of its independence, the Congolese Government asked for UN intervention with troops, since it was unable to cope with the mutiny of Belgian forces and the secession of the Katanga province. In September 1960, the UN General Assembly called upon all states to refrain from direct and indirect provision of arms and other materials of war and military personnel while the UN force remained in the Congo.

The other arms embargo cases mentioned above all represent Security Council actions involving agreement between the major powers that are permanent members of the Council.

The UN embargo against Portugal was declared in 1963 after a series of resolutions dealing with the situation in its African colonies. It was initiated by the 32 African nations in the General Assembly and resulted in a Security Council request to ban sales to Portugal of armaments for use in Angola, Mozambique and Guinea-Bissau. Like the embargo on arms exports to China and North Korea, this was a non-mandatory resolution.[5]

The only mandatory arms embargoes (that is, binding for all nations), declared by the United Nations are those against Rhodesia and South Africa. The Security Council Resolution of 1965 prohibiting shipments of arms and oil to Rhodesia was taken on British request. In 1966 it was extended to cover all trade, and it also became mandatory. The Rhodesia case to date remains the sole example of the use of mandatory general economic sanctions. As such, it continues to play a role in the South African context, insofar as general economic sanctions tend to be expected or demanded as the next logical step to follow upon the arms embargoes.

The first arms embargo against South Africa was formulated in Security Council Resolution 181 of 7 August 1963. It called for a voluntary cessation of all sales of armaments and other military equipment, and it was followed by resolution 182 of 4 December 1963, covering also equipment and materials for arms production in South Africa. These two were replaced by the mandatory embargo of 4 November 1977, declared in Resolution 418. In addition to prohibiting the sale of arms and material for arms production, the mandatory embargo also covers for the first time co-operation with South Africa in the manufacture and development of *nuclear* weapons.

The latest embargo is contained in the non-mandatory Security Council resolution 558 of 13 December 1984, requesting all nations to refrain from *importing* arms, ammunition and military vehicles produced in South Africa. (The full texts of the UN embargoes against South Africa are presented in appendix 2.)

While the collective use of the arms embargo method has thus been very limited, the reverse is the case with national use. First, following the outbreak or threat of war or internal conflicts, a number of nations in the industrialized world apply national arms embargoes against the belligerent states or parties to a conflict. The motivations differ, of course, according to the special political circumstances and according to which actors are involved. Explicit arms embargoes were declared, for example, by the UK and France against both Israel and the Arab states in 1955; the United States embargoed arms sales to both India and Pakistan in 1965; at the outbreak of the Nigerian civil war in 1967, formal embargoes were imposed by Belgium, Czechoslovakia, France, Italy and the Netherlands; and during the Falklands war in 1982, a number of the EC (European Community) countries declared an embargo on arms sales to Argentina, in addition to unilateral bans on such sales on the part of the UK and the United States.

In this context it may be said that the conceptual and practical difference between an explicit embargo and a ban, a boycott or a cutoff of arms sales is that an embargo signifies a stronger expression of policy. In particular, a collective arms embargo contains the message that the target regime is on its own and cannot expect further official military allies in a conflict. This is certainly how the South African authorities have interpreted the situation ever since the beginning of the 1960s.

Finally, it is of value to observe the relationship between economic sanctions and an arms embargo.

In the context of international trade an arms embargo amounts to selected economic sanctions, undertaken for political reasons. The efficiency of economic sanctions in general has been disputed, ever since the failure of the League of Nations' declared sanctions against Italy after the invasion of Ethiopia. In spite of the observed and debated negative or even counter-productive effects of the sanctions weapon since the 1930s, its use has paradoxically increased, in particular after 1970.[6] Hufbauer and Scott, using Keesing's Contemporary Archives for their data collection, have registered 86 examples of collective or national use of the sanctions weapon between 1945–82. Of these, 47 took place after 1970.[7]

The relation between an arms embargo and economic sanctions is also to be seen in the fact that the UN arms embargoes against South Africa of 1963, 1977 and 1984 were achieved only after a long history of demands in the UN not only for an *arms* embargo, but also for mandatory economic sanctions. (The demands began in 1946, the year India first began its trade boycott against South Africa.) Thus, for the large block of Third World states in the UN, the arms embargoes finally agreed to by the Western powers can actually be regarded as a compromise. This has been so, right up to the latest embargo—the 1984 embargo on arms imports from South Africa. When the Western powers finally agreed, it was done as an alternative to mandatory economic sanctions.

COCOM—a military embargo model

A US study of economic sanctions used for foreign policy goals covers 103 cases between 1914 and 1984, without making a distinction between strategic embargoes and general economic sanctions.[8] Of all these cases, only the multilateral but US-instigated and US-led 1948 COCOM strategic embargo against the USSR and Eastern Europe provides a basis for comparison with the South African case. Both the COCOM embargo and the UN embargo against South Africa are: (*a*) multilateral embargoes; (*b*) concentrated on military equipment (not covering all trade or amounting to general economic sanctions); and (*c*) long-lasting with no prospect of approaching an end.

What is interesting are the observable differences, however.

1. *Initiation* in the COCOM case was by the United States and *implementation* takes place in the United States and NATO countries. In the South African case, initiation resulted from pressure from the non-aligned states on the United Nations, not from countries involved in export of military *material* to South Africa, that is, countries which could actually implement the embargo.

2. *Definitions* of arms, military equipment and military technology are

detailed in the COCOM case and broadly follow the US Export Control List. In South Africa's case, there is no similar general definition of prohibited goods originating from one single and determined actor.

3. *Monitoring and punishment* in the COCOM case are unilaterally undertaken by the United States, which keeps a 'blacklist' of Western companies suspected of breaking the embargo; fines are the usual punishment, which may be extended to a total ban on business relations with the offender. In South Africa's case, no centralized monitoring agency exists at the national level in the respective supplying countries. Monitoring at the UN level has proved inadequate largely due to the absence of information-collecting national agencies, and the working of the embargo is being watched at the level of non-governmental organizations in the various countries. Punishment for breaking the embargo takes place under national legislation and is mostly directed against individual arms dealers.

In particular, the very fact that military equipment is defined in the COCOM case contradicts the argument that it is impossible to provide a detailed list of military equipment that should not be sold to South Africa. The COCOM list makes up a comprehensive catalogue of armaments and equipment for military use. (It numbers some 300 000 single items.) The US Department of Defense is responsible for the export directives on military *technology*, also applied by COCOM. These directives are presented in the Military Critical Technologies List, which is a 700-page document making up a virtually comprehensive description of modern armaments technology.

The list covers 18 militarily critical areas of technology, and is used as a reference work, not as a control mechanism in itself. In the United States it serves to modify the legal arms export implementation document—the Commodity Control List. The COCOM regulations use three criteria to prohibit export of products of 'significant contribution to the military potential' of the buyer: the first is whether the product is 'principally used in peacetime for the development, production or use of arms'; the second is whether the product provides technology 'of military significance'; and the third is whether the product is important 'to the buyer's military capacity'. The thrust of the COCOM undertaking is to prevent military exports to the socialist bloc, and no Western country has made use of the same criteria to prevent such exports to South Africa.

Efficiency

An arms embargo, like any other trade restriction, presents an enormous challenge to various powerful forces in society such as industry and commerce; it also provides a challenge to the international illegal arms market. Within international politics, it is a controversial issue. From the debates about South Africa in the UN and in various countries, it can be seen how the *efficiency* of the arms embargo has created highly emotional arguments between those who wanted the embargo and those who opposed it. The strongest advocates of the embargo on arms sales to South Africa were from the beginning the Third World countries and non-governmental organizations, followed by the Scandinavian countries. Those who were most reluctant, and vetoed all proposals for a mandatory embargo up to 1977, were those Western powers with the biggest financial connections with South Africa.[9]

Some claim that the most tangible effect of the arms embargo to date has been South Africa's buildup of its domestic arms industry. This is above all maintained by the South African authorities, and has been repeated on all possible occasions since 1963. For example, when the UN Security Council in December 1984 banned all arms purchases from South Africa, the South African delegate declared that the success of his country's arms industry could be directly attributed to the UN arms embargo: 'The outcome of the embargo was the creation of an efficient industry for the manufacture of arms of all types necessary for South Africa's self defense with the result that we are today self-sufficient in a number of important armaments sectors—and will be increasingly so tomorrow.'[10]

It is here regarded as a historical fact that the embargo did cause South Africa to create a domestic arms industry, since the National Party Government had no intention of letting its armed forces be disarmed. This process began from 1960, in anticipation of the danger of being cut off from the traditional British supplies.

Before 1963, South Africa spent 70 per cent of its military budget on arms procurement overseas, most of it from the UK. But by 1984, almost 100 per cent was spent within South Africa, for local arms production. This in itself illustrates the fact that the embargoes forced the buildup of a domestic armaments industry. The extent and level of this industry are further illustrated by Armscor's drive since 1982 to penetrate the world arms trade market. In 1981–82, South African arms exports were valued at US $23 million, while the stated target was US $150 million.

This embargo effect—to promote national production in a boycott situation—is by no means confined to South Africa. In fact, the same background is found behind all the largest emerging Third World or new arms producers—Argentina, Brazil, India, Israel, Pakistan and Taiwan. A recent example of this 'embargo reaction' is Chile, where the development of its aerospace industry in the 1980s owed its origins to the embargo applied by the British during the 1970s.[11] A less well-known example is the Rhodesian arms industry which grew up during the decade after UDI (the Unilateral Declaration of Independence) as a result of the cutoff of British arms supplies, and which is one reason why the Rhodesian forces could continue re-equipment.

When attempting to pass judgement on the degree to which an arms embargo has been effective, it is of use to distinguish between effectiveness in relation to the stated intentions behind the measure, and effectiveness of implementation.

All resolutions regarding South Africa tabled at the United Nations since

1946 (when India for the first time demanded economic sanctions to be undertaken against South Africa as a protest against racial discrimination of the Indian population there), represent international protest against the system of apartheid and a demand for its abolition. If it was hoped, or expected, that the arms embargo policy first implemented in 1963 would lead to the fall of the National Party Government in South Africa, it is clear that this effort has failed. If the arms embargo was viewed as one means among others to put pressure on South Africa, with the same purpose, the result seems less definite. The influence of political pressure is hard to establish with any accuracy: one school of thought may claim that outside pressure only serves to unite the target state, and that, in this case, international opposition has merely cemented what is called the 'laager mentality' among white South Africans. Another result might be found in a growing realization within, for example, the South African business community that the apartheid system no longer serves any purpose and is actually damaging the country's economy. It still remains impossible to say *which* forces will be most influential in bringing about change in South Africa, but it is rather premature to state that the embargo policy will have nothing at all to do with the future change.

The implementation of an arms embargo depends on the co-operation among all parties concerned, including non-signatories. Clearly, the mere number of actors involved and the nature of the Western market system render complete implementation impossible. In fact, when looking at all arms embargo cases to date, it can be seen that they all provide examples of what will here be called the methods of disimplementation.

At UN level, a 29-page report released in New York in 1985 reflects pessimism and disappointment on behalf of the advocates of the South African arms embargoes. 'Despite their positive results the embargoes do not appear to have achieved *their primary goals*, namely to induce the government of South Africa to eliminate apartheid and to reduce the threat of war in the region'.[12]

In this report, UN Secretary-General J. Pérez de Cuellar also states that the continued buildup of the military sector in South Africa suggests that while the embargoes are a necessary condition of a policy designed to eliminate apartheid, and to bring peace to the region, they are not sufficient to achieve those objectives. He also raises the question of the necessity of further international action to strengthen existing measures, without specifying what these actions might be.

Part IV of this study is related to the above passage in the UN report. It is an effort to summarize the existing loopholes of the UN arms embargo and the shortcomings in the supplying countries that do not adhere to their own embargo regulations.

The UN report of 1985 further stresses that in spite of the noted failure to pressure the South African Government to change its policies, the embargoes have had at least three desired effects: first, the embargo has from 1963 deprived South Africa of major weapon systems available to other arms importing nations of the world; secondly, it has from 1977 severely restricted

South African efforts to obtain the latest military technology; and thirdly, it has made it more difficult and more costly for South Africa to buy spare parts and components abroad. The study says clandestine trade has imposed extra costs which range from 20 per cent to 100 per cent.

The 1963 UN embargo on armaments to South Africa did bring important *changes* for its arms procurement policy, although these changes did not lead to the disarming of the regime. South Africa was cut off from the direct import of offensive armaments from its traditional suppliers, the UK, the United States and Canada. All efforts had to be concentrated on the buildup of a domestic arms production capacity through the import of production licences from alternative suppliers, primarily Italy and France. It remains to be seen how the arms embargo of 1977 will affect South African production capacity over time, considering the technical demands of the next generations of weapon systems. The latest foreign licences acquired for the production in South Africa of Israeli ship-to-ship missiles and fast gunboats, and for the French Mirage F-1 fighter, were, after all, concluded in 1973, well before the mandatory embargo. In addition, the production of the Mirage was actually stopped after 1977. Thus the process of stopping up the loopholes of the embargo seems to be slowly working, and may in the end leave only the illegal market open to South Africa. Whether that market can provide, for example, a fighter aircraft for the 1990s remains to be seen in a period when future arms projects pose great problems also to the leading arms producing countries of the world.

Thus, there is no clear-cut answer to the question of how efficient the arms embargo against South Africa is. The following statement represents a rather balanced summary of the effects of the arms embargo:

The intent of the arms embargo maintained by the United States and by many other countries has been both to express unequivocal opposition to South African apartheid and try to limit the growth of South Africa's military strength.

This policy has made clear and continues to make clear to South Africa the constraint to improved relations with the United States and other nations that a lack of progress toward change away from apartheid represents. It has achieved and continues to achieve that objective of those who implement it. It has also been a limiting factor to some extent in South Africa's efforts to expand its military strength. At the same time, the implementation of the embargo has coincided in time with, and in part been the motivating force in, an important augmentation of the productive capacity of South Africa's arms industry, to the point of near self-sufficiency in most fields. South Africa has thus not been deprived by the arms embargo of its basic tools of military power, although its access to many sophisticated weapons systems has been limited by the embargo.[13]

The story of how South Africa built up its military industry during the past 20 years is also an account of the disimplementation of the international arms embargo. But the embargo policy has not been terminated, and the story is not yet over.

III. The military industrialization process

South Africa in comparison

The military industrialization process can be summarized as a process whereby a given country transforms itself from being an arms importer into becoming an arms producer, and often also an arms exporter. Today's arms trade involves an increasing number of technology transfers rather than the mere sale of complete weapon systems. In particular, this trend is notable in Europe, but a number of Third World countries have embarked on the same road, beginning with Israel and India in the 1950s. South Africa purchased its first foreign licences for armaments production in 1960, and has since then always been ranked high among the leading new arms producing nations. According to a SIPRI study,[14] India and Israel were the leading Third World arms producers during the period 1950–84, accounting for 54 per cent of the production of *major weapon systems*[15] followed by a second group consisting of South Africa, Brazil and Taiwan, accounting for 26 per cent.

According to the same SIPRI study, by 1985 a total of only eight countries together accounted for over 90 per cent of the production of major weapon systems. The total number of Third World nations engaged in some form of domestic arms production remained relatively constant at just above 20 between 1970 and 1985.[16]

There are many examples of indigenous projects which for financial or technical reasons have been cancelled after several years' effort, as is indeed also the case in the industrialized world. The spread of military technology is thus more evident from the fact that a group of post-1945 arms producers have managed to build up and sustain domestic industries, than from a mere counting of projects and/or nations. It is the scale and scope of these new industries that are significant. Further, most of the armaments projects undertaken and successfully completed by these industries involve what is often called 'intermediate' technology.[17] The Third World producers/new producers cannot yet compete with the traditional arms producers in the production of armaments involving the most sophisticated technology. South Africa is in many respects a typical case among these new producers.

South Africa is *not* typical among the new producers insofar as it remains the sole nation that has been forced to use its domestic arms industries for import substitution over a comparatively long period, while all the other large armaments producers continue also to import weaponry.

Although all the new arms producing nations certainly operate under the influence of very different political, historical and economic conditions, their experience of the military industrialization process is broadly the same; technically, the acquisition of military production know-how advances via an identifiable set of stages towards the general goal of self-sufficiency in production (see figure 1.1). Further, the foremost motivation for wanting to achieve self-sufficiency in arms production is to lessen the degree of strategic

Figure 1.1. The military industrialization process

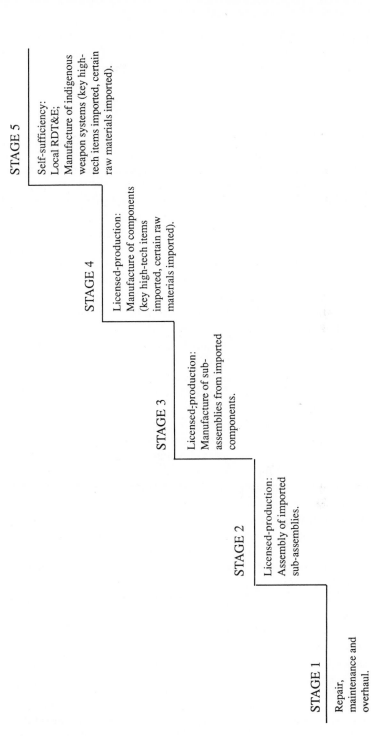

STAGE 5

Self-sufficiency:
Local RDT&E;
Manufacture of indigenous
weapon systems (key high-
tech items imported, certain
raw materials imported).

STAGE 4

Licensed-production:
Manufacture of components
(key high-tech items
imported, certain raw
materials imported).

STAGE 3

Licensed-production:
Manufacture of sub-
assemblies from imported
components.

STAGE 2

Licensed-production:
Assembly of imported
sub-assemblies.

STAGE 1

Repair,
maintenance and
overhaul.

dependence on foreign arms suppliers. Economic incentives, like the improvement of the balance of payments, the creation of jobs and the possibility of export earnings are also of importance, although of a secondary nature, at least for the leading regional powers such as South Africa.

Stages of development

The military industrialization process is initiated by setting up repair and overhaul and maintenance facilities for imported weapons. Then, instead of importing the next generation of a given system, a production licence is purchased. This involves assistance from the seller in the organization of the necessary infrastructure, actual production facilities, training and education. Production then develops step-wise; the experience and expertise gained at each stage are used as the basis for the next stage. First, samples of the weapons are delivered in complete form; a second batch is locally assembled from imported complete sub-assemblies; at a third stage components are imported to make up locally constructed sub-assemblies; fourth, certain raw materials are imported to enable local construction of components. Theoretically, the ideal of this model would be the local construction of the weapon from components from locally produced raw materials, and finally, to be able to proceed to local research and development of the next generation of the weapon system. In industrial publications and technical literature, the growing percentage of locally developed material is used to measure the degree of indigenization of arms projects.

The above is obviously a crude description of the mastering of the military industrialization process, and the final stages are in practice never reached for a variety of reasons. Still, it provides a useful way of measuring the spread of military know-how and is applicable where the import of foreign technology is involved. This has been pointed out, for example, by a South African defence industry expert, who describes the stage-wise mastering of technology as a movement from what he calls 'the first level' of industrial technology, meaning total dependence on imports, up to 'the fourth level', which is the stage where an indigenous R&D capacity has been reached.[18]

However, the South African arms industry had by 1988 still not reached this level of indigenous capacity. What had been achieved was rather a capacity to *retrofit, redesign* or *upgrade* weapon systems based on one or several different foreign arms.

Innovations in military technology as a result of an embargo situation are not unusual; besides South Africa, the Israeli arms industry provides many examples of a hybrid or derivative technology, or upgrading undertaken to circumvent the effects of restrictions in arms supplies from abroad:

Some of the most interesting developments in defence technology result from an 'isolation' situation, i.e. when a country, unable to purchase abroad the equipment it needs because of an international embargo or similar political problems, is forced to develop and produce on its own. The result is nearly invariably a system which, being tailored to specific requirements and specific industrial capabilities, is highly unconventional in design and performance.[19]

The concept of self-sufficiency

The concept of self-sufficiency is often used indiscriminately to mean any of the above technological achievements, even when the new local factory does no more than put together pre-produced sub-assemblies of a weapon. In reality, what is achieved is a degree of self-sufficiency, which varies greatly from one weapon category to the other, depending on the complexity of the technology involved. A dependence on access to foreign sources of military know-how in some sectors remains, and absolute self-sufficiency hardly exists today. In particular, modern armaments technology is so complex that monopoly over vital elements and key components can still be kept by a limited number of suppliers in the industrialized world. This can be attributed to the emergence of a 'division of labour' in armaments production globally, where the new arms producers in the Third World stop short of the acquisition of an R&D capacity within the most sophisticated sectors. It can be added that the demands of modern arms technology are such that self-sufficiency in its absolute sense does not exist even in technologically leading nations such as the United States. As one study has pointed out: 'Independent national design and production is a hypothetical variant which probably does not exist in the pure form'.[20] The now prevailing pattern is rather one of industrial interdependence between several nations, as pointed out in one of many recent defence industry studies:

The long-standing American supremacy in technology is dwindling. Large U.S. defense-oriented corporations are exhibiting a transnational mentality. . . . Recent sales have stressed the overseas transfer of manufacturing technology and equipment as well as engineering, training, and complete factories. In many cases the U.S. firm does not even obtain an equity position in these foreign plants. . . . In addition, *the United States is rapidly becoming dependent on foreign sources for many critical parts as well as for critical materials*.[21]

The South African press and other publications take all opportunities to present individual weapon systems as 'locally developed' and the arms industry as such as 'self-sufficient'. The following is representative of such sweeping judgements: 'Thanks to an oil embargo, South Africa is nearly self-sufficient, with the world's best process for producing oil from coal. Thanks to an arms embargo, South Africa, which was 60 per cent dependent on imported arms 20 years ago, is 90 per cent self-sufficient and a net arms exporter'.[22]

However, when looking at the *origins* of the individual projects, one sees that little would have been achieved without foreign technology. The production of sub-machineguns and modern rifles is based on Israeli and Belgian designs; the aircraft industry was established with French and British assistance and built around Italian and US designs; the naval industry and the construction of ship-to-ship missiles was based on Israeli know-how; the nuclear industry was based on technology sharing with the United States, France and FR Germany; military vehicles include a tank which was an upgraded British model and armoured cars which are based on French models, while the military truck industry was based on West German technology. Electronics and communication equipment production were sustained by multinational companies operating in the country, most of them British or US-based.

The official South African view of its self-sufficiency in armaments production during the past decade reflects the transition from a dependence on foreign licences to a search for foreign technical assistance and R&D collaboration. The Defence White Paper of 1977 says:

The RSA is fully self-sufficient in respect of armaments required for its internal protection. Although the same cannot be said in all respects as regards a conventional external threat, it can be mentioned that the RSA ensures its safety by negotiating licences for more sophisticated and expensive equipment, which, if necessary, could be put into operation in the country.[23]

After the mandatory embargo of 1977, however, it turned out to be impossible to negotiate any new licences for armaments, and the planned licensed production of the French Mirage F-1 fighter, for example, was prevented.

The Defence White Paper of 1982 presents Defence Minister M. Malan's definition of self-sufficiency without mentioning foreign licences: 'Self-sufficiency is the local ability to conceptualize products and produce these without direct assistance from abroad'. It lists the weapon categories where South Africa is self-sufficient as including artillery guns and rockets, artillery fire-control equipment, short-range guided missiles, mini-computers, mine detectors and mine-resistant vehicles, armoured vehicles, tactical telecommunications equipment, anti-personnel and anti-vehicle mines and small arms. Notably, this listing leaves out altogether the categories of aircraft and ships.

According to an interview with Armscor executive F. J. Bell in 1982, the first area where Armscor helped the South African Defence Forces (SADF) to become self-sufficient was in electronics and telecommunications; by 1975 most of such equipment needed was made locally.[24] He also mentioned specifically the development of land-mine resistant armour plating.

In 1985 Defence Minister Malan claimed: 'We are entirely self sufficient insofar as conception, design and development are concerned. What we still need from outside is not so much military equipment as such, *but tools and technical assistance.*' (Total self-sufficiency in *ammunition* production was announced in 1981.)[25]

But the Defence White Paper of 1984 refrains altogether from mentioning the word 'self-sufficiency' and instead points out the problem of obsolescent armaments and the need for indigenous research and development in the future:

A major problem is that some of the most reliable main armaments are obsolescent.

More modern armaments made available to our enemies contributed towards this process of obsolescence. With armaments development and manufacture continuous attempts are made to eliminate any possible gap between the phasing-out of the obsolete and the commissioning of new armaments. During the next decade the SA Defence Force will have to concentrate on the development, production and commissioning of a new generation of main armaments in order to meet the threat of the Soviet arms stockpile in certain neighbouring countries and to maintain the existing balance of power. This renewal programme will of necessity entail increased demands in respect of manpower, finances and sophistication in the next decade. These demands will have to be met, however, as a fully prepared SA Defence Force is an absolute prerequisite to ensure the security and survival of RSA and its people.[26]

This Defence White Paper, instead of listing those weapon categories where self-sufficiency was previously claimed, confines itself to listing items in production, described as examples of 'a sound armaments development'. These items are 'the R4 rifle, the G-5 gun, the Ratel infantry combat vehicle, mine-resistant vehicles, missiles and strike craft'.[27] Self-sufficiency has become tautological: what is being produced is what can be produced, or, in the words of Armscor Chairman P. G. Marais, 'Armaments development is a question of developing what is available'.[28]

Important weapon categories are still missing, notably fighter aircraft, submarines and heavier ocean-going ships. Interestingly, the same source also states that foreign technology may not be counted upon in future; a recognition of sorts that such technology *has* been available so far.

In order to meet future armaments needs without any foreign aid or technological inputs, research and development must not only be undertaken over a much wider spectrum, but should also be increasingly aimed at the long term. The result of several programmes will only be available at the end of the decade. Planning and budgeting in respect of these programmes are therefore extremely difficult.[29]

It is probably fully recognized by the South African authorities that the acquisition of such technology as that which enabled the construction of the G-5 and G-6 howitzers (involving the US/Canadian company Space Research Corporation in a deal which was widely publicized), will not be easily repeated for other new weapon systems.

To sum up the above discussion, South Africa is certainly self-sufficient enough in its armaments production to be able to supply its armed forces for their present tasks in Namibia and Angola, and internally. Through indigenous production, the *dependence* on foreign suppliers has been significantly changed. The sale of production know-how is an irreversible decision—even when licences are cancelled, the know-how acquired cannot be eliminated. Indeed, it is argued by sellers,[30] that such an action would only benefit South Africa—production will then continue within the country without any payments of licence fees to the seller. There are many examples of this, such as the continued production of the Israeli Uzi sub-machinegun after the licence was formally revoked in 1963.

Percentages of 'self-sufficiency'

Exact information on South Africa's self-sufficiency in terms of figures varies, depending on what is being counted, when and how. The following is a selection of disparate information, such as it exists.

One crude way to prove self-sufficiency is to point to the fact that the South African arms industry continues production for the SADF, replacing what previously had to be imported from overseas. Already in 1971 Defence Minister Botha claimed in a speech in Parliament that South Africa was 'close to self-sufficiency in arms procurement', stating that it 'has achieved such a measure of self-sufficiency that it does not need any armaments from the outside world for its *internal defence*'.[31] The distinction between weapons for internal and external defence is familiar from the vocabulary of such arms supplying nations as the UK and France in the context of embargo implementation.

Other distinctions give different statistics. According to the South African Government, at least 75 per cent of the armament orders in 1978 would be met by local industry, if naval craft were excluded.[32] When including ships, 57 per cent of all armaments were locally produced. At the same time, P. W. Botha said that only 45 per cent of the *budget* for arms procurement was spent inside South Africa. At a first glance incomprehensible, this particular statement is a good example of the use of percentages of both contents[33] and value to measure indigenization.

In 1983, Armscor Chairman P. G. Marais said in a television interview in South Africa that 74 per cent of all war material was now produced in South Africa. When asked if the remaining 26 per cent was being clandestinely acquired, the answer was yes.[34] A comparison over time was given by the SADF journal *Paratus* which said that in 1972 South Africa produced only about 30 per cent of the arms purchased by the SADF, compared to approximately 90 per cent by 1982.[35]

According to another report in *Paratus*, in the invasion of Angola in 1981, called Operation Protea, 94 per cent of the armaments used by the SADF were produced in South Africa.[36] By 1985, according to most sources, almost 100 per cent of *Army* needs were locally produced.

The above estimates have in common the actual numbers of armaments as the basis for their percentage calculations. The more usual basis is to estimate local content in terms of value, that is, to present the share of the defence budget spent on local production versus imports of arms, or military equipment. In 1974, for example, Defence Minister Botha told the South African Parliament that over one-third of the current defence budget was spent on arms purchases from overseas, and that this in turn depended on the high cost of the French weapon systems—such as Mirage fighters, which were being supplied in spite of the 1963 embargo. The rest of the budget for arms acquisition—less than two-thirds—was spent on the local arms industry.

In general, from about 1982, official South African Government or Armscor spokesmen have claimed that in terms of value 85 per cent of all arms are being produced in South Africa.

Another criteria for self-sufficiency was mentioned by Deputy Defence Minister H. J. Coetzee in an interview with the US journal *Newsweek*. In response to the question of what degree of self-sufficiency had been achieved, he said: 'That varies. Since 1977, it has gone as high as approximately 80 per cent, and then fallen again. *But we have certainly succeeded in providing for our needs*'.[37] This 'success' is precisely what has brought about the disappointment with the UN embargo effect within the UN, and in that context, the whole question about percentages of self-sufficiency, as well as the definition of self-sufficiency, remains rather academic.

However, another way of looking at the claims of self-sufficiency quoted above is that they are actually clear-cut cases of *disinformation*—the foreign technological aid and/or basis that is to be found behind the majority of the South African local weapon projects is not visible, whatever basis of calculation is being used. This foreign origin is described in part III below.

Notes and references

[1] *Paratus*, July 1982, p. 44, quoting Armscor managing director F. J. Bell (The name in Afrikaans is KRYGKOR—Krygstuigontwikkelingskorporasie); *Afrique Défense*, June 1982, quoting 'Recent study presented at House of Representatives', Washington; *Financial Times* (UK), 22 Dec. 1981: 'Armscor claims to be the West's tenth largest arms producer'.

[2] Charter of the United Nations, Chapter 7: 'Action with respect to threats to the peace, breaches of the peace, and acts of aggression'.

[3] UN Document A/1805, 18 May 1951.

[4] The Co-ordinating Committee, set up in Paris in 1949, later incorporated all NATO countries and Japan.

[5] The concepts of 'mandatory' and 'voluntary' are not used in the actual texts of United Nations resolutions. In principle, the wording 'decides' means a binding decision, while the wording 'recommends', 'requests' or 'calls upon' means a non-mandatory decision, where the individual nations may decide to follow the recommendation or not.

[6] *Economic Sanctions Against South Africa* (Africa Publications Trust: London, 1981); Kelly, J. A., *Sanctions and Southern Africa: A Bibliographical Guide* vol. 14, no. 3, (Africa Publications Trust: London, 1982), pp. 201–34; Dajani, M. S., *Economic Sanctions, Ideals and Experiences* (RKP: London, 1983); Doxey, M. P., *Economic Sanctions and International Enforcement* (Macmillan: London, 1980), 2nd ed.

[7] Hufbauer, G. C. and Scott, J. J., *Economic Sanctions Reconsidered: History and Current Policy* (Institute for International Economics: Washington, DC, 1985).

[8] Hufbauer and Scott (note 7), table 1.1, pp. 13–20.

[9] The same dividing line exists between those who regard the arms embargo as an absolute measure, and those who regard it as a compromise stopping short of general mandatory economic sanctions: 'In general it could be seen that the Western countries are satisfied with the decision (the 1977 mandatory arms embargo) and expect it to be effective in its own right. The African countries, speaking through the representative of Benin, on the other hand, are very cynical about the embargo and more concerned about the erosion of the earlier embargo and the need for complete isolation of South Africa. Evidently, their perspective is one of seeing the arms embargo as a minor concession': Wallensteen, P., 'South Africa and the politics of arms embargo', *Weapons against Apartheid? The UN arms embargo on South Africa*, Uppsala University, Department of Peace and Conflict Research, Analysis and Debate series, 12 June 1979, p. 53.

[10] Defence Marketing Services, Greenwich, *International Defense Intelligence*, vol. 7, no. 4 (28 Jan. 1985).

[11] 'Embargo set back for export industry', *Jane's Defence Weekly*, 22 Mar. 1986, p. 654.

[12] *Jane's Defence Weekly*, 28 Sep. 1985.

[13] *Enforcement of the United States Arms Embargo Against South Africa*, Hearing before the Subcommittee on Africa of the Committee on Foreign Affairs, House of Representatives, 97th Congress, second session, 30 Mar. 1982 (US Government Printing Office: Washington, DC, 1982); Prepared statement of William B. Robinson, Director, Office of Munitions Control, Bureau of Politico-Military Affairs, Department of State, p. 9.

[14] Brzoska, M. and Ohlson, T. (eds), *Arms Production in the Third World*, SIPRI (Taylor & Francis: London & Philadelphia, 1986).

[15] That is, excluding small arms, ammunition and military software.

[16] *The Arms Trade with the Third World*, SIPRI (Almqvist & Wiksell: Uppsala, 1971), p. 725, table 22; and *World Armaments and Disarmament, SIPRI Yearbook 1985* (Taylor & Francis: London & Philadelphia, 1985), pp. 334–5, table 10.2.

[17] Jones, R. W. and Hildreth, S. A., *Modern Weapons and Third World Powers*, Significant Issue Series, vol. 6, no. 4, Georgetown University (Westview Press: Boulder, CO, 1984), p. 3.

[18] Bell, F. J., executive general manager, Armscor 'The defence industry: private or state-owned? A sound balance for survival' in *Defence Today*, no. 89–90, 1985, p. 416.

[19] Bonsignore, E., 'The South African G-6 self-propelled howitzer', *NATO's Fifteen Nations*, Oct.–Nov. 1982, p. 100.

[20] Uddis, B., 'European perspectives on international collaborative ventures in aerosphere', ed. M. Edmonds, *International Arms Procurement*; 'New directions', in Edmonds, op. cit., chapter 7.

[21] Gansler, J. S., *The Defense Industry* (MIT Press: Cambridge, MA, 1980), pp. 6–7.

[22] *International Herald Tribune*, 26 Aug. 1985.

[23] White Paper on Defence 1977, Republic of South Africa, Department of Defence, p. 27.

[24] *The Star*, 13 Mar. 1982.

[25] *African Defence*, Oct. 1985, p. 35.

[26] *White Paper on Defence 1984*, Republic of South Africa, Department of Defence, p. 22.

[27] *White Paper on Defence 1984* (note 26).

[28] *Defence*, Jan. 1984, p. 24.

[29] *Defence* (note 28).

[30] This argument was made in connection with the discussion of the implementation of the UN embargo of 1977 which calls for a revoking of arms production licences sold before 1977.

[31] *The Times*, 7 May 1971.

[32] *Financial Times* (UK), 28 Oct. 1977.

[33] Contents is a term used to denote both raw materials and components..

[34] In de Villiers, D. and de Villiers, J., *PW (Biography of P. W. Botha)*, (Tafelberg: Capetown, 1984), p. 294 (in Afrikaans).

[35] *Paratus*, Nov. 1982, p. 19.

[36] *Paratus*, Nov. 1983, p. 23.

[37] 'South Africa's military build-up', *Newsweek*, 29 Sep. 1980, p. 17.

Chapter 2. Historical impediments to embargo implementation

I. Introduction

There are two sets of factors which from the outset made South Africa 'embargo resistant'. The first consists of resource factors, meaning South Africa's economic and military capacity such as it was at the time of the first UN embargo in 1963. The second is made up of political background factors such as geostrategy, Western dependence on strategic minerals from South Africa and South Africa's traditional position as a Western ally. Combined, all of these factors go a long way towards explaining why South Africa was no easy target for a military embargo from the West. At the same time, it should be emphasized that these factors were *historical* impediments to successful embargo implementation, and that arguments of the early 1960s are not necessarily still valid. The geostrategic importance of South Africa is seldom mentioned these days. In particular, the claim that the West is dependent on South African minerals and strategic resources is being increasingly challenged.

The continued viability of the South African economy, subject to partial sanctions and threatened by the prospect of general economic sanctions, is a controversial issue where opinions differ widely. The same is the case with the issue of the country's strategic resources. The purpose of the brief presentation here remains limited to the implications of South Africa's initial status as an economic and political asset to the West, since this enabled access also to military technology from the leading industrial powers.

II. Resource factors

Economic capacity

When exposed to the first UN embargo, South Africa was not a poor underdeveloped and militarily-weak country. Its per capita gross national product (GNP) was the highest in Africa and its gross domestic product (GDP) in 1985 of US $73 000 million was three times more than the *combined GDP* of all nine black-ruled states in the region.[1] Its international trade and its mining and manufacturing industries were highly advanced. Moreover, its military establishment, in existence since 1912, was not to be shaken by such a measure as a cutoff of foreign armaments supplies. On the contrary, the Army, Air Force and Navy proved themselves capable of handling the new situation by contributing to military R&D and co-operating with the arms industry in retrofitting and upgrading existing weapon systems.

The South African economy is based on its mineral resources. It was foreign capital, mainly British, which enabled development of the gold and diamond mines. Gold was discovered in the Witwatersrand in 1886. Although foreign investment 100 years later, in 1986, accounted for only a small proportion—3.8 per cent—of new fixed capital formation in South Africa, the South African Government acknowledges its strategic importance. For example, President P. W. Botha has stated that foreign investment was important: 'because it supplemented domestic savings to finance investment, favourably affected the balance of payments and often involved the transfer of technological know-how and sometimes the immigration of managers and highly qualified technical people'.[2]

By 1985, half the world's annual production of gold came from South African mines. South Africa remains the largest gold-producing nation in the world and is, in fact, the world's only gold-based economy. The Soviet Union occupies the second place, but mines on average just over one-third of South Africa's total.

South Africa is also the world's leading producer of vanadium (needed in modern aircraft construction), chromium (needed for elements of cruise missiles) and platinum. The latter is used for strengthening metal, especially in aircraft and in the manufacture of nitric acid which is used in explosives. Gold also has a direct military application—it is a vital component of military electronic equipment and turbine engines, as it never rusts, corrodes or decays. South Africa is also one of the world's largest producers of vermiculite, manganese, diamonds, titanium, antimony and fluorite, and is one of the largest steel and coal producers. Over 80 per cent of South Africa's exports are made up of such primary products, mostly minerals. Gold alone accounted in 1982 and 1983 for roughly 50 per cent of *all* exports, and 21 per cent of state revenues come from the gold-mining industry. This basis for South Africa's economy has inspired the epithet 'The Golden Armour' for its weapon arsenal, indicating how this arsenal is being paid for.[3]

The same resources also explain South Africa's role as one of the corner-stones of the multinational corporation system of the West. The ensuing global network of industrial and capital connections, international banking and foreign loans created the opportunities for South Africa's access to military information, technology and equipment. South Africa's integration in the Western economy is crudely illustrated in tables 2.1 and 2.2. The figures presented are from the early 1980s in order to reflect the situation which prevailed during the period when the arms industry was being established. The trend towards disinvestment, the pullout of the largest British and US companies and the increasing difficulties in obtaining foreign loans have changed this picture considerably. A report by the UN Commission on Transnational Corporations says that at the end of 1983 the total amount of direct foreign investment in South Africa was in the range of $15.5 billion to $17 billion.[4] In 1980 between 2000 and 2500 transnational companies were identified as having subsidiaries or associated companies or other investments in South Africa, as

Table 2.1.   Foreign companies in South Africa in 1980

Country	Number of companies
UK	1200
FRG	350
USA	340
France	50
Netherlands	50
Australia	35
Belgium	20
Italy	20
Switzerland	12
Sweden	10
Spain	6
Canada	5

Source: *Apartheid and Business*, Business International Multi-client Survey, Geneva, Oct. 1980, in *Apartheid, the Facts* (IDAF: London, June 1983), p. 82.

Table 2.2.   South Africa's major trading partners

Exports to South Africa		Imports from South Africa		Bilateral trade	
Countries	Rand million	Countries	Rand million	Countries	Rand million
FR Germany	1309	Switzerland	1542	USA	2646
Britain	1253	USA	1406	FR Germany	2219
USA	1240	Britain	964	Britain	2217
Japan	601	Japan	950	Japan	1724
France	471	FR Germany	910	Switzerland	1724
Italy	250	France	351	France	822
Switzerland	182	Italy	341	Italy	592
Netherlands	158	Belgium	328	Belgium	460
Belgium	131	Netherlands	212	Netherlands	370
Sweden	102	Hong Kong	185	Canada	268

Source: *Financial Mail*, Johannesburg, 4 July 1980.

shown in table 2.1. By 1984, this figure had changed to 1068 corporations according to UN information.[5] About one-third of these were based in the UK, while companies based in the USA and FR Germany each made up one-quarter of the total.

Further, information available from foreign governments, the United Nations and other international agencies shows that in 1983 more than 90 per cent of foreign investment in South Africa was accounted for by the UK, the United States, FR Germany, France and Switzerland.[6] Over the nine years between 1972 and 1980, South Africa borrowed a total of nearly $7 billion from banks based in the UK, USA, FR Germany, France, Switzerland and Belgium.[7]

Table 2.2 shows the largest trading partners in 1980 according to South African statistics. This excludes trade in armaments, oil, uranium, platinum and gold. All of these trading partners are not suppliers of military technology.

On the other hand, the major military suppliers as identified in chapters 3–12 below are the UK, the USA, France, Italy, FR Germany, Japan and Belgium, which are all among the largest trading partners. The notable exception is Israel, which does not appear in the trade figures but which stands out as the single most important supplier of military technology after 1977.

Military capacity

In 1963, South Africa was unchallenged as the leading military power in sub-Saharan Africa, although its forces were small compared to the situation today. But the Nationalist Government concentrated its efforts on building up the country's military power from 1948. During the 1950s, South Africa imported more major armaments than all the other nations of Sub-Saharan Africa combined. This military buildup has been reflected in the rise in military expenditure. Throughout the period after World War II, South Africa has been the largest military spender in sub-Saharan Africa, and second only to Egypt in the entire continent.

The weapons imported were traditionally almost exclusively of British origin. In 1955, a major re-equipment programme was initiated in connection with the handing over of the Simonstown naval base from the UK to South Africa. The air defence net was also expanded from 1955, and Sabre fighters were purchased from Canada and helicopters from the USA. When signing the Simonstown Agreement, the British Government insisted that explicit distinctions should be made between arms for external defence and arms for internal use, thereby initiating the formula later extensively used by the UK, France, Italy and other arms suppliers to circumvent the arms embargo. South Africa therefore began already in the latter half of the 1950s to produce arms and ammunition on a large scale. Table 2.3 shows the growth of military expenditure. Between 1961 and 1966, the rise was 500 per cent.

From 1970 to 1975 the increase in defence spending ran at about 30 per cent a year, and up to 1980 at about 20 per cent a year. More than half of the defence spending is devoted to landward defence. The foundation of the SADF is the Army; 80 per cent of all military personnel are soldiers involved in ground operations. Arms production *per se* absorbs the largest part of the defence budget.[8] In addition to published figures, there is also the Special Defence Account which allows for secret expenditure.

There are many other areas of expenditure which are excluded from the budget figure. For example the Department of Public Works pays for expenditure on SADF construction and property, the Department of Finance covers the considerable cost of the SWA (South-West Africa/Namibia) Territory Force, and the Department of Community Development covers the cost of housing military personnel. Examples of additional expenditure are the capital expansion of Armscor projects, the military R&D carried out by the Council for Scientific and Industrial Research (CSIR) and university departments and institutes; support for SADF Medical Services from the Department

Table 2.3. Military expenditure 1960–87[a]
Figures in rand million at current prices

Fiscal year	Defence budget	Special defence account	Total defence[b] spending
1960–61	44		
1961–62	72		
1962–63	129		
1963–64	157		
1964–65	210		
1965–66	229		
1966–67	255		
1967–68	256		
1968–69	252		
1969–70	271		
1970–71	257		
1971–72	321		325
1972–73	335		351
1973–74	472		502
1974–75	692	311	707
1975–76	970	596	1043
1976–77	1350	897	1407
1977–78	1654	1000	1940
1978–79	1899	799	1976
1979–80	1972	1189	2189
1980–81	1970	1160	(2300)
1981–82	2465	1330	(2800)
1982–83	2668	1754	(3400)
1983–84	3093	2024	(3800)
1984–85	3755	2224	(4300)
1985–86	4274	—	(4800)
1986–87[c]	5123	—	7500[d]
1987–88[c]	6680	—	—

[a] *Source*: Document A.1: 'South Africa's military capacity', presented at the International Seminar on the UN Arms Embargo Against South Africa, International Maritime Organisation, London, 28–30 May 1986. Yearly figures except 1986–87 and 1987–88 compiled from South African White Papers on Defence and press reports.

[b] Total defence spendings are conservative estimates and include additional appropriations and transfers.

[c] *Source*: *Resister*, London, no. 43, Apr.–May 1986.

[d] *Source*: *Africa Confidential*, London, 10 June 1987.

of Health and Welfare, and the secret funding of aid to UNITA and the Mozambican National Resistance (MNR). In addition, a so-called mini-budget later in the financial year provides extra military funding. According to UN reports, the South African Government's real defence expenditure is probably about 30–35 per cent higher than the official budget figure.[9]

Thus, South Africa has so far been able to sustain the increasing costs of its military establishment including the substantial rise in the prices of imported military equipment and know-how. Table 2.4 shows the military balance between the nations most involved in the conflict in southern Africa. It illustrates the increasing investment in new equipment and also the expansion of military manpower. At the same time it illustrates the militarization of the region. By 1988 South Africa remained the single largest military power—but was being increasingly challenged.

Table 2.4.   The military balance in southern Africa 1987 (1977)

Country	Armed forces[a]	Combat aircraft	Tanks	AFV	APC	Navy
Angola	53 000(31 500)	148(33)	540(205)	200(100)	255(165)	FAC 11(—)
Cuba	40 000[c] (15 000)					
	93 000(46 500)					
						PC 12(13)
Mozambique	32 000(20 000)	60(8)	250(40)	48(some)	200(some)	PC 27(—)
Zimbabwe	12 000					
Tanzania	650					
Malawi	400					
	45 050(20 000)					
Zimbabwe	47 000(104 550)	43(48)	43(—)	127(60)	65(some)	—
Total 1987	**185 050(66 500)[b]**	**251(89)**	**833(245)**	**375(160+)**	**520(165+)**	**50(13)**
South Africa	97 000(55 000)	336(362)	250(170)	3100(2110)	1500(500)	Sub 3(3)
SWATF	22 000					Frig 1(3)
						Dest —(1)
	119 000(55 000)					FAC 12(—)
						PC 39(2)

Source: *The Military Balance 1977–78* and *1987–88* (IISS, London). For Cuban figure see table 3 below.

[a] Reserve forces and para-military forces are excluded. The forces in 1977 are in brackets. South Africa would be capable of mobilizing a total force exceeding 800 000 men if all manpower available is included, i.e., also the forces of the so-called independent homelands.

[b] Excluding Rhodesia.

[c] Official figure given in Jan. 1988 for the first time (by Cuban Politburo member Jorges Risquet), quoted by AFP, Havana, 7 Jan. 1988.

The continuous wars along South Africa's borders have provided testing grounds for all types of weaponry, which is then upgraded and modified by the armaments industries in accordance with SADF specifications. These wars have also brought about a general militarization of South African society, including a change of structure to give the military a larger role in national politics. There is a growing number of studies dealing with the increasing role of the military in South Africa.[10]

The State Security Council represents the most important state body in security matters, and brings politicians, the SADF and Armscor into close co-operation with each other.

The role of the SADF in South African society, first defined in the Defence Act of 1912, has throughout its history been intertwined with the role of the

South African Police (SAP). Its first use was actually to put down a miners' strike on the Witwatersrand in 1913. The army has since 1980 increasingly been used to quell demonstrations or other disturbances in black townships, and lately also in white areas. This is not to say that South Africa is a military-ruled state—but the military *influence* is growing: 'There is, it must be emphasized, a growing recognition of the importance of the military in the South African political equation, which corresponds to actual movements leading to greater military participation in political and social affairs in recent years'.[11]

III. Political factors

South Africa's strategic importance to the West

South Africa's strategic importance to the West was at its height during the cold war period and continued to attract attention in such instances as the Indian Ocean arms race, the collapse of the Portuguese colonial regime in southern Africa and the control of the southern sea lanes. One more recent example was the debate in the UK following the Falklands war when some experts deplored the fact that the UK was no longer in a position to use the South African Simonstown naval base for its war effort. In the context of the general East–West conflict, the southern African mineral resources became *strategic* resources. The official South African view of NATO's dependence on the country is exemplified in the following statement:

According to Soviet strategists, South Africa occupies a major place in world strategy, partly because of its geographic position and partly because of its role as a supplier of strategic minerals . . . Control of South Africa means control of the Southern Atlantic and the Indian Ocean . . . The Soviet Union's aim is to deny the NATO powers access to South African resources. The loss to the Western World of Southern Africa's minerals, port facilities and similar resources would be serious enough in itself, but were these riches to be added to the Soviet sphere, the USSR would obtain a staggering addition to its economic power.[12]

The strategic resources

South Africa is the world's leading producer, or second- or third-largest producer, of 12 metals, with the Soviet Union as the sole large-scale competitor for some of these.[13] These strategic metals are used in military sectors such as telecommunications, space, aviation, nuclear industries, optronics, chemicals and petrochemicals. Together, the Soviet Union and South Africa produce more than 90 per cent of the world's platinum, 60 per cent of the world's gem diamonds, 40 per cent of the industrial diamonds, and 80 per cent of the gold.[14] Table 2.5, based on South African statistics, illustrates this ranking order.

In the past, South Africa has been able to take optimal advantage of these hard facts. President P. W. Botha has occasionally threatened to embargo the

Table 2.5.   Production of some strategic metals in South Africa and the USSR (world rank order and percentage of world production)

| Product | South Africa | | USSR | |
	per cent	rank	per cent	rank
Vanadium	40	1	29	2
Chromium	34	1	23	2
Vermiculite	35	2	9	3
Manganese	20	2	39	1
Diamonds	20	3	28	2
Titanium	16	3	8	6
Antimony	13	3	12	4
Fluorite	9	3	11	2

Source: Minerals Bureau of South Africa (internal documents). Compiled in *Defence & Armament*, no. 44 (Oct. 1985), p. 14 ('Strategic Minerals. South Africa: One of the Hidden Facets of the Crisis', by A. Giraudo).

West, in response to the limited economic sanctions imposed on South Africa. In 1986, the Minister of Manpower, Mr P. du Plessis, even warned that South Africa may form a precious metal cartel with the Soviet Union if sanctions from the West increase.[15]

But, South Africa's value to the West as a supplier of rare strategic minerals is being increasingly challenged. In November 1985, *Financial Week*—one of South Africa's two main economic and financial magazines—carried an article called 'The myth of South Africa's strategic minerals', which said *inter alia* that: 'South Africa is potentially more vulnerable as a supplier than the world at large as a customer', and further, that: 'although South Africa contains a remarkable concentration of metals and minerals, none of them is found there exclusively, and that it is their price, rather than their exclusivity, that has given South Africa its present market advantage'.

In October 1986, 10 strategic minerals were excluded from the US import ban on South African products. However, an official State Department report at the same time denied that the existing pattern of minerals imports would give South Africa any political leverage:

The United States imports more than 50 percent of its needs for over two dozen minerals deemed of either strategic or critical importance to U.S. national defense. Three at the top of the list—chromium, manganese, and platinum—are obtained in large part from South Africa, and much of a fourth (cobalt) is exported from landlocked countries in the region through South Africa's transport system and ports.

Having viewed the strategic minerals issue through the prisms of the several competing schools of thought in the policy community, we are agreed that a minerals cutoff (either by counter-sanctions or by a breakdown of the South African economy and infrastructure) would have an undeniable impact on the United States. In some cases, we could be forced to increase imports from the Soviet Union. But we have concluded that the potential impact of such a denial is not sufficient cause to determine U.S. policy toward South Africa.[16]

South Africa has also been an important source of uranium for the UK, FR Germany, Israel and Taiwan—all of them important suppliers of military know-how.

The Cape Route

During the buildup period of its military industry, South Africa was also able to capitalize on its role as the guardian of the Cape Route. Each year some 25 000 merchant ships pass the Cape of Good Hope, transporting about 80 per cent of NATO oil needs from the Persian Gulf and about 70 per cent of mineral needs.[17] The strategic position of South Africa directly inspired the above-mentioned distinction between weapons for 'external defence' and weapons for 'internal defence' which constitutes one of the major loopholes in the arms embargo. Global strategic concerns also explain West European assistance to set up the modern radar network at Silvermine in South Africa for monitoring all sea traffic from India to the South Atlantic.

The South African view is that the Soviet threat to the Cape Route is a permanent factor and dates back to tsarist times:

The South African Navy's earliest beginnings can be traced to the Port Elizabeth Naval Volunteer Brigade which was raised in 1861 but seems to have merged with a volunteer artillery unit in the following year. On 30 April 1885 a part-time unit named the Natal Naval Volunteers was formed in Durban. These men manned the six-inch guns which were to defend Durban if the Russians, then as always, threatening Afghanistan, should decide on a piece of expansionism.[18]

This threat perception may have been shared by Western governments in the 1950s and 1960s but has waned since then. The US State Department report quoted above had the following to say about the Soviet threat in the area:

South Africa's position aside the sea-lanes around the Cape of Good Hope is frequently used as an argument in favor of South Africa's military importance, but the apparent consensus among U.S. defense planners is that these sea-lanes are under minimal threat and that the active collaboration of the South African Government would not significantly increase our ability to protect them.[19]

NATO and 'SATO'

South African governments for a long period kept trying to attract NATO interest in extending the organization's sphere south of the Tropic of Cancer. When this got no response from the Western powers, South Africa proposed the setting up of a corresponding 'SATO' (South Atlantic Treaty Organization). The suggested members in addition to South Africa included Australia, Argentina and Brazil. This too met with no serious response, as political conditions changed in the planned member countries. But as late as 1984, South African experts still discussed the possibility of a SATO organization that would include Argentina, Brazil, Uruguay and Chile.

These plans are of interest as a reflection of the frantic search for military partners, with the implications this would have had for military acquisition possibilities. As it is, just a few Latin American countries are of some use for the South African military industry, mostly as outlets for Armscor exports, or as transit for military imports. One example is the import via Paraguay of a Rheinmetall production line essential to the G-5 howitzer construction in South Africa.

South Africa's national strategy

The traditional economic and political ties with the West formed the basis for the South African perception of its role as the guardian of Western interests against the communist threat. Its national doctrine is expressed as the need to create 'a total strategy to meet a total onslaught'.

This doctrine was first formulated by the present Prime Minister P. W. Botha in 1975 (then Defence Minister), and it reflects South Africa's reaction to the collapse of the Portuguese colonial regime in 1974. The doctrine was elaborated in detail in the Defence White Paper of 1977 by Defence Minister Malan, who became the foremost spokesman and architect of South Africa's national strategy. This document remains a most informative source as to South Africa's *own* perception of its role in southern Africa and its strategic importance to the West, and presents the rise to power of Marxist regimes in Mozambique and Angola as proof of a Soviet threat to South Africa. The independence of Zimbabwe in 1980, also under a radical regime, further strengthened South Africa's threat perception of being encircled by hostile communist powers. By 1985, South African troops had been actively involved in what they called a counter-terrorist war in Angola and Namibia for more than a decade. (The cost of these border wars had been put at R2 million a day.)[20]

The 'onslaught' is attributed in the final analysis to the Soviet Union. The Defence White Paper of 1984 lists *all* opposition to the ruling party as proof of a grand design to take over the country; under the heading of 'Onslaught against the RSA' the Defence Minister says:

One of the major considerations of Soviet strategy in Africa is the control of the subcontinent's riches in strategic minerals and the denial of these to the West. . . . Indirect action in the form of a revolutionary onslaught serves to establish Soviet influence in Southern Africa. The South African Communist Party (SACP) and the African National Congress (ANC), which for all practical purposes has been integrated with the SACP and acts as its military wing, are the major elements of the Soviet plan to obtain control of the RSA. SWAPO plays a similar role in SWA[21] in the achievement of Soviet objectives in that region. Several world-wide and regional organizations, of which the United Nations (UN) and the Organization for African Unity (OAU) are the most important, also lend themselves to furthering USSR objectives in Southern Africa by joining in the propaganda onslaught against the RSA.[22]

Furthermore, Malan stated that this total strategy must be 90 per cent *political*.

The choice of investment projects in the defence industry closely reflects political developments in the region: emphasis was first put on the need for army equipment and counter-insurgency weapons during the 1960s. The failure of South Africa's incursion into Angola in 1975 revealed the weakness in conventional weaponry, in particular in long-range artillery to fight the Soviet- and Cuban-supplied MPLA (Movimiento Popular de Libertaçao de Angola) forces. This led to a new emphasis on the need for modern sophisticated weaponry, and over the years the SADF have found themselves increasingly engaged in conventional warfare in Namibia and in southern Angola, and in counter-insurgency operations. In particular, in Angola, where South Africa has helped to build up the anti-government UNITA (Uniâo Nacional para a Indepência Total de Angola) guerrillas into a semi-conventional force, it finds itself obliged to continue with this support against Soviet equipment which is often found superior to the ageing South African equipment. The 1982 Defence White Paper explicitly stated that serious consideration should be given to the possibility of a conventional war.

South Africa can be described as very typical among the emerging regional powers—it is a key actor in a conflict region, it is commonly regarded as the economic and military giant of the region, if not of the entire continent; it is economically linked to the West in many fields and it possesses important natural resources. Still, it is possible to state that South Africa's dominance is being challenged in each field, and that its government's policies are being increasingly challenged inside the country. One recent study of Third World powers presents the following general findings which can be applied also to South Africa:

Regional powers are those that by definition exercise more influence over their neighbours than vice versa. Local leviathans, to use Samuel Huntington's term, usually are thought to be crucial to regional stability. What they do with modern weapons then may hold one of the keys to the future of conflict. . . . Yet, a basic finding of the study is that all these regional powers are weaker than is commonly supposed, even by regional standards. Although for obvious reasons they usually do not broadcast their weaknesses, their own perceptions of threat and of their respective national capabilities add up to severe constraints and narrow choices in every case. Typically, these regional powers are more conscious of the limit of their role as regional powers than of their respective opportunities to assert regional influence.[23]

The consistent efforts by South Africa to acquire military hardware, coupled with its general mobilization of armed preparedness, reflects the ambitions of a typical regional major power, not just a security need. The military buildup may have consequences for Angola, Zimbabwe, Mozambique, Botswana, Lesotho and Namibia, all of which have had experience in becoming an 'Operational Area' for the SADF.

The buildup of military power can increase the scale, scope and intensity of regional conflict. Sophisticated weaponry not only facilitates a military option to conflict solution, but may thus widen the parameters of armed conflict. Given a constant South African reaction to the continuing influx of more sophisticated Soviet weaponry into Mozambique and Angola, the southern African military scene is certainly approaching a higher level of preparedness for outright conventional war. As one analyst points out:

> The trend toward greater military competence is certain to affect the level of conflict as military-political relationships between states are altered, and as more countries become capable of conducting modest military campaigns, the means to engage in armed conflict and to project power into neighbouring states is on the rise.[24]

The then Chief of the SADF, General K. Viljoen, said at an air strategy conference in Pretoria in 1985 that military air power of what he called 'not-so-friendly' countries to the north had increased by some 200 per cent since 1977. He proceeded to list Angola, Mozambique, Tanzania, Zambia and Zimbabwe among these countries, and also stated that some of them had expanded their total military forces threefold, and that at least 10 per cent of these forces included Cuban, Soviet and East German personnel.[25]

If added to this list, the incursions during 1985 in Botswana, Lesotho and Swaziland in pursuit of ANC bases and the Namibian campaign leave no 'friendly' countries in the region. South Africa still sees itself as the only reliable guarantor of Western interests in the region, although increasingly frustrated by Western anti-apartheid policy. It remains to be seen what influence, if any, the relaxation of superpower tension in the 'Gorbachev era' may have upon South African doctrine.

Notes and references

1 *Third World Affairs*, 1985.
2 *Survey of Race Relations 1983*, South African Institute of Race Relations, p. 109.
3 Shepherd, R., 'South Africa's Golden Armour', *National Reporter*, winter 1985.
4 *International Focus on Transnational Corporations in South Africa and Namibia*, UN Department of Public Information, Division for Economic and Social Information, New York, 1985.
5 *Resister*, no. 43, Apr.–May 1982.
6 MacLellan, E., '5 nations are found to account for 90% of all foreign investment in South Africa', *International Herald Tribune*, 8 Aug. 1985.
7 *Transnational Corporations in Southern Africa,* United Nations Commission on Transnational Corporations, UN Economic and Social Council, 9 July 1981.
8 *Rand Daily Mail*, 15 May 1982.
9 See note 7.
10 See for example, Frankel, P. H., *Pretoria's Praetorians—Civil-Military Relations in South Africa*, University of the Witwatersrand (Ohio Press: Cambridge, 1984); Grundy, K. W., 'The Rise of the South African Security Establishment—An Essay on the Changing Locus of State Power', The South African Institute of International Affairs, Bradlow Series, no. 1, Aug. 1983.
11 This development helps to explain the relative lack of opposition to the investments in the military sector of the economy, including the arms industry.
12 'Soviet aggression and bending of realities', *Paratus*, Jan. 1986, p. 31.
13 *Paratus* (note 12).
14 *Paratus* (note 12).
15 *African Defence*, Feb. 1986, p. 20.
16 *A US Policy Toward South Africa*, The Report of the Secretary of State's Advisory Committee on South Africa, Jan. 1987, United States Department of State, Publication 9537, Apr. 1987.
17 *Neue Züricher Zeitung*, 20 Dec. 1980.
18 'Naval Base Simon's Town celebrates 20 great years of independence', *Paratus*, Apr. 1982, p. 20.

[19] US Department of State (note 15).
[20] Interview with Marais, *Defence*, Jan. 1984, p. 24.
[21] SWA = South West Africa, official South African name for Namibia.
[22] White Paper on Defence 1984, p. 1.
[23] Jones, R. W. and Hildreth, S. A., *Modern Weapons and Third World Powers,* Significant Issue Series, vol. 6, no. 4, Georgetown University (Westview Press: Boulder, CO, 1984), p. 3.
[24] Thom, W. G., 'Subsaharan Africa's changing military environment', *Armed Forces and Society*, vol. 2, no. 1 (Fall 1984), p. 40.
[25] *African Defence*, Oct. 1985, pp. 34–5.

Part II.
The development of South Africa's military industry

Chapter 3. The historical background

I. Introduction

The South African armaments industry was created thanks to its access to Western technology (see appendix 4). The aircraft industry was initiated with Italian and British technology in the 1960s, proceeding to more sophisticated projects around French designs in the 1970s and 1980s. The armoured vehicle industry was basically built with French technology, and other military vehicles with West German technology. The small arms industry was established with the acquisition of production licences from Belgium, France, Israel and the UK. Warship and naval missile construction was made possible by Israel. The electronics and nuclear industries owe their origins to technology available through large multinational corporations based in the technologically more advanced Western nations.

II. 1912–39

The Union Defence Force was created in 1912, modelled on British tradition and dependent almost entirely on British equipment.

The last British Army forces were withdrawn in 1921, but South Africa's defence remained closely linked to that of the rest of the British empire. The Royal Navy retained its bases at Simonstown and Walvis Bay. During the 1930s, a shortage of defence funds restricted development of the armed forces, and the depression years from 1930 on brought further military spending cutbacks. In 1934, the naval services were temporarily closed down. During this period, virtually no indigenous armaments production took place, with one exception: in 1930, South Africa began the domestic production of certain types of military aircraft. But this effort too was affected by lack of funds, so that by the outbreak of World War II in 1939 the South African Air Force had an inventory consisting of obsolete aircraft ill-suited for combat tasks.

III. 1939–45

The effort during 1939–45 included armaments production on some scale for use by the South African troops on the Allied side, most importantly in the East African campaign against Italy, in North Africa, and for the protection of the Cape sea route. In 1940, when the supply route from Europe was cut off, the Industrial Development Corporation (IDC) was founded to plan, stimulate, and finance industrial development. The same year, 1940, an Advisory Committee on Defence Force Requirements was set up to handle all matters concerning the acquisition of armaments. The recommendations of this body led to the setting up of six armaments factories during the war years, where shells, cartridge cases and bombs were locally manufactured. Several types of infantry arms and even tanks of British design were assembled locally. With the help of British expertise, over 5000 armoured vehicles were produced during the war, as well as howitzers, mortars and ammunition. Some electronic equipment was also produced, mainly radar components.[1] During the same period sections of the African Explosives and Chemical Industries (AECI), an explosivies manufacturer owned by Imperial Chemical Industries (ICI) of the UK, were engaged in military production. These companies were privately owned and took up military production with active government encourage- ment, a stimulus that was to be renewed from 1961 on.

All the wartime factories were dismantled after 1945, with the exception of two: the Defence Ordnance Workshop (later to become Lyttleton Engineering Works) and the SA Mint .303 Ammunition Factory, which remained in operation as state-owned factories. The .303 ammunition was produced for the British Brownings in standard use with the SADF. But the wartime experience with armaments production by *private* industries is sometimes referred to by the South African authorities as a model even today. For example, the Chief of the Navy, Vice-Admiral Putter said in 1983 that the 'business entrepreneurship' that characterized these early industrial efforts had been of invaluable use for the later buildup of South Africa's arms production potential, particularly as re- gards the co-operation between private industry and the Defence Department.[2]

The experience during the war created a basis for later weapons technology development, as did the search for new minerals, first of all uranium. The South African Prime Minister, General J. Smuts, was appointed a Field Marshal and Counsellor on allied strategy to Churchill. Thus, he was in a position to inform the Allied Command in 1941 of the existence of uranium in South Africa as a by-product of the gold-mining industry. South Africa became an important uranium exporter to both the United States and the UK.[3]

This was the beginning of South Africa's development towards its present position as a supplier of strategic minerals to the West. In turn it explains South Africa's position as an attractive investment country for transnational com- panies, which has created access to the world's leading industrial centres, and thereby also access to companies which can provide military technology.

IV. 1945–61

In 1949, a Board of Defence Resources was created as a more permanent body to direct national armaments policy. It was superceded in 1951 by the Munitions Production Office, which was a section of the Department of Defence. One result was the establishment of South Africa's first rifle factory in 1953.

As early as 1945, the Council for Scientific and Industrial Research (CSIR) was founded to undertake military research and development, among other tasks. In 1954, military R&D was separated as a special task through the creation of the National Institute for Defence Research (NIDR), still under the CSIR.

What is worth noting about this pre-embargo period is that some of the most vital preconditions for domestic arms production were created well before the first embargo of 1963. When it became necessary to produce armaments, South Africa had a thriving steel industry, and an explosives industry serving the mines. An abundance of power was available from indigenous coal. A large number of skilled engineers and scientists were already working in the country.

The decision to establish the first defence research organization in close co-operation with general industrial research testifies to a wish to incorporate military industrialization into the general process. This was an expression of Afrikaner nationalism, which was able to make its imprint on the country following the election of the National Party (NP) into power in 1948. After a first period of concentration on the construction and systematic implementation of the policies of apartheid, the first NP Government turned its attention to the country's armed forces. Among other things, it undertook to eradicate the dominance of English-speaking whites within the country's armed forces and police.

Regarding weapons procurement, it was not yet an urgent issue to achieve independence from British supplies during the 1950s while South Africa was still a member of the Commonwealth. In this capacity, South Africa was able to receive nearly 80 war-surplus Vampire fighters and trainers from the UK in 1952–54, and some 200 Centurion tanks in 1955–59. The latter were to become the basic model for future indigenous tank construction. The situation regarding arms procurement during the 1950s was summarized by F. J. Bell, the executive general manager of Armscor since 1982, in a speech describing the evolution of the South African armaments industry:

So let us start at the beginning when there was nothing. Why was there nothing? Because of historic relations—and you cannot change history, history is a fact—there had developed a form of dependence by us on powers like the UK and the USA, and because of this, there was never a need and certainly no opportunity to develop an own defence industry—state or private. During 1961 it became clear that a start had to be made, and we should probably honour our ancestors for the foresight they had to start, and at the same time forgive them for not knowing exactly how and where to start.[4]

What was not foreseen in the 1950s was that some of the major arms systems supplied then would have to serve for a much extended lifetime, due to restrictions because of the arms embargoes.

This is particularly true in the case of warships and naval armaments. Under the Simonstown Agreement of 1955, the UK handed over the Simonstown naval base to South Africa and undertook to provide R50 million worth of naval vessels. These ships continued to constitute the bulk of South Africa's navy until the end of the 1970s, and included four anti-submarine warfare (ASW) frigates, a number of seaward defence vessels and coastal minesweepers. The last of the maritime reconnaissance HS Avro Shackleton bombers delivered from the UK in 1957 was, for example, retained in service until totally obsolete in 1985, all efforts to receive a more modern type having failed. Of five ex-British Ford class seaward defence vessels delivered between 1954 and 1962, four still remain in service. Of the 10 Ton-class ex-British minesweepers/hunters, eight remain in service. Similarly, some of the 36 Canadian Sabre-4 jet fighters delivered in 1956 were retained in service up to 1980, when they were finally officially withdrawn. These prolonged lifetimes for certain weapon systems reflect not only the embargo implementation, but also the enforced capacity of the South African arms industry to maintain and upgrade otherwise obsolete equipment. In addition, contacts with the Western computer industry were established in the early 1950s with the help of US-based multinational companies. IBM received its first order in 1952 from Pretoria's Division of Economics. The increasing use of computer equipment in South Africa has been closely linked to the consolidation and expansion of the white power structure.

Regional defence production

The efforts to break the military isolation brought upon South Africa by its expulsion from the Commonwealth were also reflected in the plans to achieve a common military production within the southern Africa region. These military industrialization plans proceeded up to the collapse of the Portuguese regime in 1974, and the partners were to have been first of all Rhodesia and Portugal, but also the independent black-ruled states. A degree of industrial co-operation was actually achieved only with Rhodesia. The Rhodesian arms industry which grew up as a result of the UK and UN embargo did not only involve a large South African input of material and other support, but also a certain output to South Africa. In Rhodesia, South African arms technicians were able to get direct experience of the conditions of wartime armaments development and production. The time span was too short for any major breakthrough, but one product of joint Rhodesian–South African design was the range of armoured transport cars described in chapter 6 below.

Notes and references

[1] Harrigan, A., 'The South African Military Establishment', *Military Review,* Oct. 1973.
[2] 'We are ready', interview with Chief of the Navy, Vice Admiral Putter, *Paratus,* vol. 34, no. 2 (Feb. 1983), pp. 18–20.
[3] *South Africa 1982, Official Yearbook of the RSA,* Department of Foreign Affairs and Information (Chris van Rensburg Publishing: Johannesburg, 1982), p. 49.
[4] 'The defence industry: private or state owned? A sound balance for survival', *Defence Today,* no. 89–90, 1985, p. 413.

Chapter 4. The organization and structure of the modern arms industry

I. Introduction

The structure necessary for the future military-industrial complex was established during the 1960s. The massacre at Sharpeville in March 1960 focused, for the first time, large-scale international attention on developments in South Africa. The same year, armed uprisals began in the Portuguese African colonies. Inside South Africa, black opposition to the white regime had manifested itself in protests against the pass law system for the non-white population; additionally the referendum held in 1960, which resulted in South Africa's change of status into a republic, brought out anti-apartheid opposition on the part of the other Commonwealth members, including increasingly frequent proposals for an arms embargo against South Africa. The South African Government reacted to the prospect of more open civil unrest and external threats by deciding to acquire more modern weaponry. In 1961 alone, no less than 127 licences for the local manufacture of military equipment were negotiated with overseas arms industries.[1] Among these were the Israeli Uzi sub-machinegun, sub-licensed from Belgium, and the NATO 7.62-mm standard gun, both of which continued in production even after the licences had been revoked.

In 1961, the newly declared Republic of South Africa was denied continued membership of the British Commonwealth and the prospect of a future arms embargo, or at least a cutoff of British weapons, seemed that much more likely. Several South African experts describe the year 1961 as the turning point. However, in view of the fact that negotiations for arms contracts in general need time, and even more so when the transfer of technology is involved, it may rather be assumed that planning for a future industry actually began somewhat earlier. The events during the last years of the 1950s—the unprecedented 'Defiance Campaign' led by the African National Congress (ANC) to protest against the pass laws for the black population, together with the external mounting protests against apartheid in the UN, the Commonwealth and elsewhere, and finally the Sharpeville massacre in March 1960—prompted the militarization of South African society, which is still in progress. It was in 1960 that for the first time after World War II, a massive programme was initiated aimed at the modernization of the defence force. This modernization also included an increase in domestic arms production capacity. The overall change into a more militarized society dates from the same period.

The arms embargo coincided with a South African interest in increasing its share of military production—the 1963 embargo alone did not *cause* a sudden investment in arms technology.

In parallel with the first substantive arms technology imports, several important weapons agreements were negotiated just before or during 1963 with South Africa's new arms suppliers—France and Italy. Between 1965 and 1969, France supplied 45 per cent of South Africa's total arms imports. France agreed to supply Mirage-3 fighters armed with air-to-surface missiles and Daphne submarines, and Italy undertook to sell the production rights for what in Italy was classified as an unarmed trainer, but in South Africa became the Impala counter-insurgency (COIN) fighter. It has also often been claimed that the Soviet Union, China, Czechoslovakia and other East European arms producers sold arms to South Africa after 1963 in order to benefit from the rocketing prices on embargoed equipment.[2] Some East European participation in clandestine arms deals has surfaced in connection with smuggling trials. Other weapons of Soviet origin have been intercepted by South African authorities. For example, it was confirmed in Pretoria that Armscor in 1979 appropriated 150 tonnes of Soviet arms on board a ship in Durban, destined for Uganda and for SWAPO (the South West African People's Organization) in Angola. Armscor took over these arms and offered to pay for them.[3] With the declaration of the 1963 embargo, and the ensuing national embargoes declared by all the relevant arms producing nations in the West during 1964, the South African options narrowed and investment in domestic arms production progressively began to become a forced path, rather than a choice.

II. Reorganizing the institutional structure

The most important organizational innovations in the 1960s concerned setting up new institutions to direct armaments production. In 1964, under the Armaments Act, the Armaments Production Board was established. In 1968, its name was changed to the Armaments Board and it was complemented by the setting up of a special production unit, the Armaments Development and Production Corporation (Armscor), under the Development and Production Act No. 57, of the same year.

In 1976, against an international background of mounting demands for a UN mandatory arms embargo against South Africa, a major reorganization of these institutions was undertaken. The Armaments Board was incorporated into Armscor, which from then on also took control over arms imports and exports. In 1978, a large part of military research carried out by the NIDR was transferred to Armscor. The restructuring and expansion of Armscor was made possible by a secret government grant of R1200 million. The result was a highly streamlined organization, exclusively geared to meet the needs of the SADF. According to the Armscor Chairman, P. G. Marais, the Armscor organization

is part of and exists only to render a service to the SADF. The aim, of course, is to procure and manufacture arms at the lowest possible cost . . . The Defence Force is responsible for determining new types of weapons that it requires to defend South Africa, and expansion of the existing lines. After these have been defined, we come into the picture. Through a joint committee they state their needs relative to the external threat, then we state our capabilities of meeting their needs within cost and time limits.[4]

Since 1982, arms *exports* promotion has become a major new task of the organization, and a special export department called Nimrod was set up the same year.

The big reorganization of Armscor that began in 1976 resulted in today's organization, which is often described as a 'super-corporate umbrella structure', encompassing the whole cycle of armaments production from initiation of research and development (R&D) through development and production to export promotion. According to F. J. Bell of Armscor, the transfer of all functions from the Armaments Board into a corporation signified a move towards greater flexibility and efficiency: 'In our system, a Corporation has much more freedom of action as well as authority than a Statutory Board, and could more effectively initiate and carry through the things that had to be done. One of these things was a new concept of procurement . . .'.[5] After the 1977 embargo, South Africa indeed needed a new concept of procurement, as the possibilities to purchase foreign licences were also being slowly blocked. (In retrospect, the more bureaucratic Armaments Board probably could not have emulated the highly innovative measures used by Armscor to clandestinely 'import' the technology needed for the G-5 howitzer.) The White Paper of 1979 expressed this perceived change by emphasizing that Armscor would now have to become 'technologically self-sufficient in order that, in the case of a more exclusive boycott of components and raw materials, available alternatives and substitutes can be utilized, and that new generations of advanced systems based on local components and raw materials can be developed'.[6]

In general, it is very difficult to find out details of licensed production contracts, concerning not just South Africa but technology trade as such. Two statements by high Armscor executives have disclosed some very important information in this context, namely, that the UN embargo of 1977 in South Africa's interpretation abrogated all existing licence agreements. This meant not only that South Africa no longer had to pay licence fees, but, far more importantly, that they were free to further exploit and redevelop technology already purchased without any need to consult the original foreign suppliers. F. J. Bell, executive manager of Armscor, described the new independence brought about by the arms embargo thus:

The licencer normally protects himself against future competition by making it virtually impossible for the licencee to exploit the technology while it is still relevant. By the time he is allowed to do this, legally, in terms of the licence, the technology is generally obsolete. *It so happened that what triggered the need for this quantum jump in technology (the 1977 embargo), also carried in itself the opportunity for doing so.* Not many of you are aware of the fact that Resolution 418 which instituted the arms embargo against South Africa, also decreed that all licence agreements shall be considered terminated. Industries could now exploit, without further legal constraints or twinges of conscience, the technology which they had established.[7]

In 1984, Armscor Chairman P. G. Marais said in an interview that South Africa would be able to produce helicopter engines. 'We do have quite a number of licences, even though they have been cancelled by the United Nations'.[8] This indicates that if a 'licence' means concrete plans and blueprints of a weapon system already in South African hands, Armscor feels free to use these for further development irrespective of the opinions of the licencers. The continued production of the originally French Eland armoured car, the development of the Skerpioen missile and the Kukri missile and so on could all serve as examples of Armscor 'innovations' of originally foreign licence-supplied technology.

In this context, it could also be speculated that the Mirage technology, in contrast to other weapons, must have been better protected by the French since this project was cancelled in South Africa after 1977.

The development stage in the military industrialization process which South Africa was forced to reach was the stage of adapting or *upgrading* existing technologies established under licence (see figure 1.1). This was expressed by F. J. Bell as follows: 'To move industrial technology from the second to the third level faster than the normal evolutionary process is possible with a determined state action. And the best motivation for not only a determined but substantial effort is a mandatory arms embargo. Believe me, it was a great help'.[9]

However, completely indigenous designs still have to be created before Armscor can claim they have reached the 'last stage' or self-sufficiency in arms production. In fact, the organization has been troubled by a set of industrial problems related to management and over-production. The launching of its export drive in 1982 is not only interpretable as a sign of 'success'. It could just as well testify to the common dilemma of modern arms industries—the costs inherent in armaments production demand a conquest of the international arms export market. The arms export efforts are further described in chapter 13.

III. The Armaments Board

The setting up of the Armaments Board can be seen as a sign of the seriousness with which the UN embargo of 1963 was met in South Africa. Its first task was to co-ordinate the arms acquisition activities of all parties involved—the Government, the SADF, private industry and the few state factories. The Armaments Board took over from the Department of Defence the actual running of the two state factories, the Lyttleton Engineering Works and the .303 ammunition factory, to improve efficiency. The *procurement* of armaments, which up to then had been handled by the SADF and the State Tender Board, was also transferred to the new organization for the same purpose.

The main new task was to ensure optimal utilization of industry. The principle of using private industry for arms production was, in general, confirmed but with important exceptions. New state factories were to be built for the production of weapons which were defined as either very strategic or where manufacture was uneconomic by normal business standards.

Other large state corporations already existed in areas of particularly strategic value. One early example is Sasol ('Suid-Afrikaanse Steenkool, Olie en Gaskorporasie') which handles the extraction of oil from coal and is one of the largest industrial projects in the world. Its first plant began to operate in 1955. Another example is Escom (the Electricity Supply Commission), which has co-operated in nuclear energy research since the late 1950s.

The definition of 'strategic' arms at the time included ammunition, guns, missiles, explosives, propellants, mines and bombs, according to Armscor manager F. J. Bell.[10] It may be of interest to observe that this list does not include aircraft or ships. In fact, aircraft manufacture was begun as a private undertaking in 1964, and was later transferred to state manufacture.

During the 1960s, South African arms production know-how was at the assembly stage, as expressed by F. J. Bell:

The second level is where our industry was in the middle 60s, and it was obvious that industry could only start military production at the level that they were used to. Consequently, the first activities were local assembly from imported kits of parts under the strict control and guidance of the licensor. Without them, we couldn't have got off the ground. For the first time industry was exposed, in the presence of the licensor, to quality control, quality management configuration control and all the many buzz words which most of them had never come across before. Risk was mainly by the State who had negotiated the licence agreements and consequently took the rap, and cost overruns, due to badly negotiated agreements or the inevitable pitfalls of technology transfer.[11]

IV. Armscor

The establishment of Armscor can be seen partly as a natural continuation of the move towards rationalization in arms production. Partly, it also resulted from a study of foreign arms industry establishments. Defence Minister P. W. Botha, who took a personal interest in the development of South Africa's arms production capacity, visited Portugal and France for the purpose of investigating the organization of armaments production. Actually, Armscor is a state corporation depending almost entirely on private enterprises, a blend described by Defence Minister Malan as 'unique in the Western world'. From the parliamentary debates it can be seen that from 1967 onwards it was first of all the French military industrial system that was used as the model for South Africa.

Armscor plays a central role in the highest military decision-making body, the Defence Council. In Act No. 57, amending the Armaments Act of 1964, referred to above, the tasks of Armscor were listed as follows: first, to take over all manufacturing facilities so far handled by the Armaments Board; to expand such facilities and set up new industries; and to handle all arms exports and imports. According to para. 4 of the Act, the corporation shall also 'carefully review all matters relating to raw materials necessary for the development or production of armaments, to the labour supply available for such development or production, to the rates of wages proposed to be paid and to the armaments required for export . . .'[12]

Armscor occupies an important place in South African defence planning and thus gets first-hand knowledge of what types of weaponry are needed. (See figure 4.1.)

Figure 4.1.   Armscor's place in South African defence planning

Source: *Financial Mail* (SA), 11 Sep. 1981.

Assets, work-force and financing

The Act also stipulated that the state was to be the sole shareholder, that the share capital of the corporation would be R100 million, and finally that Armscor was to be exempt from the Companies Act No. 46 of 1926, meaning that the activities were to be secret and the company files not made available to the public. Other sources refer to the initial capital of Armscor as R140 million.[13]

In 1982, *Paratus* stated that Armscor's total assets after the completion of an expansion programme amounted to R1300 million. This expansion programme had involved a new explosives and propellant installation at Wellington, and a new quick-fire installation at Elandsfontein, Pretoria. Armscor's total expenditure portfolio for FY 1981 was R1432 million and for FY 1982 R1540 million.[14]

The work-force grew from 12 000 in 1974 to a peak of 33 000 in 1984, after which it had to be reduced as the period of rapid growth came to an end. In 1986, Armscor's own payroll stood at 23 000.[15] This fast expansion made Armscor into one of the industrial giants of South Africa.

Within the state sector it ranked eighth by 1961, after *inter alia* Escom, Iscor, and the Reserve Bank. Armscor is still not equal to the largest private enterprises in South Africa—see table 4.1 for the rank order of selected large corporations according to a 1981 company comparison by total assets undertaken by the *Financial Mail* (Johannesburg).[16]

In addition to the number of employees at Armscor's own facilities comes the employees of about 3000 companies which are contractors and sub-contractors to Armscor. This gives a total of 80 000 employees in 1982. The

Table 4.1. Top South African companies in rank order

Companies	Assets Rand million	Activities
Anglo-American (private)	8118	Diamonds, gold, mining
Escom (state)	7562	Electricity
Iscor (state)	5063	Steel
Barlow Rand (private)	3238	Steel
Fed. Mynboo (private)	2525	Mining
Consolidated Gold (private)	1979	Mining
IDC (state)	1705	Industrial development
Armscor (state)	1157	Armaments and military equipment

Source: Financial Mail, 8 May 1981.

total number of employees involved with Armscor was approximately 103 000 in 1986.

According to Armscor Chairman P. G. Marais, the exact figure for total employment in the arms industries is difficult to state, since the components manufacturers (the subcontractors) do not work more than 35–40 per cent on armaments-related products. But if the figure of 80 000 is used, this still makes Armscor the third or fourth biggest single employer in South Africa.

(Just as is the case with other big enterprises in South Africa, Armscor has been eager to point out that it does not practice apartheid, but rather contributes to the creation of skilled black labour:

Among the thousands of employees in the armaments industry, there are many Blacks, whose contribution to the production of armaments is an important one. It is ARMSCOR's policy to promote good labour relations among all its employees, and perhaps this is one reason why almost every day, you can find long queues of Black people at the gates of ARMSCOR's subsidiaries, hoping to be employed by these companies.[17]

No percentages of black/white labour forces are known.)

Financing

Armscor is an autonomous corporation and is actually *not* solely dependent on government financing for running its subsidiaries. With its share capital and reserve funds, it obtains medium- and long-term loans from the South African capital market. For its daily activities Armscor uses the widest available range of banking facilities, and co-operates closely with the most important South African banks and financial institutions.

In 1981, for example, the South African press reported that Armscor had obtained a loan of R50 million from Union Acceptance, running for 15 years at an interest rate of 13.35 per cent plus 7 years at 13 per cent interest. It was also said that Armscor was scheduled to become a public company in the future.[18]

Barclays Bank, with one representative on the Defence Advisory Board, provides loans to the military industry, and so do the corporations Sasol and

Escom, either to Armscor subsidiaries or to the private companies involved with Armscor.

The Armscor expansion lasted from 1977 to 1981. The last of the big facilities put into operation in 1981 cost R90 million.

Organization

The Armscor organization consists of a head office and nine subsidiary companies. In addition, 600–800 private companies are involved with arms production; some 70 per cent of all military production is by the private industries. Of the remaining 30 per cent handled by the Armscor-owned industries, some of the work may be contracted out to private producers by the individual company. In 1976 the Defence Minister announced that Armscor sub-contracted as much as 80 per cent of its work to private companies.[19] (See figure 4.2.)

Figure 4.2.   Distribution of Armscor costs for weapons production

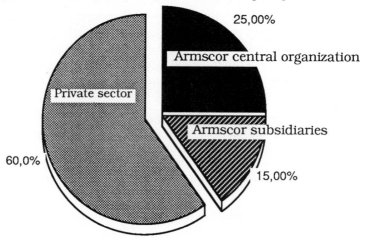

Source: *Financial Mail* (SA), 11 Sep. 1981.

The Board of Armscor includes the Chief of the SADF and the Director of General Finance as the sole state representatives. Armscor falls directly under the authority of the Minister of Defence, and is linked to the Defence Planning Committee. The 10-man board of directors is dominated by businessmen, entrepreneurs, financiers and scientists. The names of these directors are in principle kept secret, except in the case of Mr J. Maree of Barlow Rand. He was 'lent' to Armscor between 1979 and 1982 to reorganize the management system according to latest models. Armscor has gone through a thorough programme to reduce costs and to increase efficiency since the beginning of the 1980s. Throughout the entire Armscor organization the latest Japanese and US methods of quality control and quality engineering have been applied. According to a report in 1985, the US-designed management system that is claimed to have caused the post-war industrial revolution in Japan has been introduced into many of South Africa's arms producing companies. At Sandock-Austral, which produces ships and armoured vehicles, productivity was thereby increased by 50 per cent in three years, and the number of hours required for the production of a vehicle was cut by half. The workshop space needed for vehicle assembly was reduced by 50 per cent.[20]

Armscor attempts to ensure diversification of production in the private companies—the policy is that only 40 per cent of a given company's capacity is used for military equipment. For instance, Sandock-Austral, apart from its military production, does considerable civilian work on turbines and other equipment required by the mining industry in South Africa, as well as for export. On the other hand, *all* industries in South Africa can in times of crisis be requested to switch their production to 100 per cent military production. Old wartime legislation to this effect was revived with the passing of the National Supplies Procurement Act No. 89 of 1970. Foreign or multinational companies in South Africa also fall under this provision.

Armscor also has a policy to avoid duplication of any existing engineering or manufacturing plant in South Africa. If there are facilities that could produce the requirements, and if their owners are willing to co-operate, Armscor uses these facilities. P. G. Marais quoted the Ratel armoured car as an example: the entire construction was based on a German design, acquired by a private producer and produced in the private sector (Sandock-Austral).[21]

Military research and development

Military R&D began in earnest in South Africa in 1961, as stated by Prof. A. J. A. LeRoux, vice-president of the CSIR in Johannesburg: 'Defence research, which began little more than a year ago, has already achieved some striking successes and has saved the country hundreds of thousands of Rand in the know how and equipment which would otherwise have been bought overseas at tremendous cost'.[22]

The National Institute for Defence Research (NIDR)

The CSIR remains the central organization overseeing military research and development through its most important subsidiary, the NIDR. The NIDR directs defence research at universities, in addition to its own work, which is rarely publicized. The work on the Cactus missile in co-operation with French armaments industries in the 1960s was handled by the NIDR. Other than the NIDR, there are a number of CSIR affiliates engaged in military work.[23]

The National Institute for Aeronautics and Systems Technology (NIAST)

The NIAST performs strategic R&D in the field of aeronautics for South Africa's aviation industry, which almost exclusively produces military aircraft for the Air Force. The agency's work is classified and, unlike most other CSIR subsidiaries, it does not publish an annual report. The field of activities covers flight dynamics, aerodynamics, aircraft structures, propulsion, servomechanisms and digital and microwave systems.

The National Research Institute for Mathematical Sciences (NRIMS)

The NRIMS provides consulting services to other government agencies and performs a range of contract research. Many projects involve sensitive work and are classified due to their military and internal security applications. For example, one such project deals with computer graphics for image processing, a field with numerous military applications. In 1979, the institute worked on a military project for the Armscor company Infoplan concerning target acquisition, and in 1980 on a computer-aided design program for Lyttleton Engineering Works, also a major Armscor subsidiary.

The National Mechanical Engineering Research Institute (NMERI)

The NMERI worked in 1980 on a project to develop a new design for explosive shells. In another project the institute developed a 'shock response spectrum' to test the impact of nearby explosions on vehicles; in 1979 a breakthrough was made in the development of a new glass fibre helicopter blade to replace foreign imports. NMERI also maintains a wind tunnel for aerodynamic testing, all according to the annual reports of the institute.

The National Chemical Research Laboratory (NCRL)

The NCRL performs military-related work for the Air Force, ordnance development and testing. In 1980, the institute provided consulting services to the Hoedspruit Air Force Base.

The National Electrical Engineering Research Institute (NEERI)

NEERI works on R&D for the electronics industry, with substantial links to the SADF. High-ranking military officers and arms industry representatives are involved with the institute, such as the Executive Manager of the External Production Division of Armscor, the Director of Military Engineering for the SADF, the Chief of Air Staff Logistics, the manager of the Telecommunications, Radar and Computers Groups of Armscor, and the chief of the Signal Projects Division of the SADF.

Virtually all NEERI's contract work is classified. The institute's major contributions to the military-industrial complex have been the establishment of a small specialized integrated circuit production facility, research in large-scale integrated circuits, work in signal processing, and development of computer-aided design programmes.

The National Institute for Telecommunications Research (NITR)

According to its annual reports, the NITR performs long-term R&D in radio communications, and much of its work is classified as it relates to defence. Representatives of Armscor, the Telecommunications Office of the South African Army and local military electronics firms participate in NITR work.

The NITR has played an integral role in the development of South Africa's air defence system, and it also operates satellite-tracking facilities.

The National Physical Research Laboratory (NPRL)

This agency operates, in conjunction with the NITR, a radar facility and it does applied research in the optical sciences, high-pressure physics, acoustics and other fields. The NPRL facilities are at the disposal of several Armscor subsidiaries and other military producers. It has established a metallurgical laboratory for the South African Air Force and helped outfit it with technology acquired from overseas.

Nuclear research

Nuclear research is carried out at three institutes, the CSIR affiliates National Accelerator Centre (NAC), the Pretoria Cyclotron Group, and the independent Atomic Energy Board (AEB). The NAC and the Cyclotron Group serve as research and training centres for the growing nuclear industry. The Cyclotron Group also produces radioactive isotopes. The Atomic Energy Board was set up in 1957, and oversees nuclear research, generally believed to include also research in nuclear *weapons* technology.

A common feature for all the above-listed R&D agencies is their close collaboration with—and access to—Western technology and expertise, in particular US computer and electronics supplies, but also West German and British equipment.

Embargo restrictions have often failed to cover electronic and computer equipment due to its dual use in both civilian and military production. Furthermore, the access to this technology has been facilitated by the presence of multinational companies in South Africa.

R&D financing

By 1983, two per cent of the South African defence budget was spent on research and development.[24] This is approximately the same level of spending as in Canada, Switzerland, Italy, Japan and Norway, while Sweden spends over 6 per cent of its defence budget on R&D, and the leading military producers (France, the USA and the UK) all spend 11–13 per cent.[25] That considerable advances in the field of military R&D were achieved during the 1970s is evident from a comparison of the present situation with that in 1971. Then, South Africa was on a par with such countries as Spain, Portugal and Greece as to the proportion of GNP spent on R&D.[26]

Armscor itself in 1984 spent 5 to 6 per cent of its money on R&D. This figure was expected to rise over the next few years to 8–9 per cent as the company research tackled more complex equipment. The main thrust of the R&D is to modify existing weapon systems for the SADF.[27]

The upgrading and updating programmes are indeed very extensive, which is to be seen from the detailed descriptions of the various weapon projects in the following section of this study. In the Air Force, for example, emphasis lies on the upgrading of navigation and electronic warfare equipment and weapon systems, and a big programme has started for updating the Mirage fleet, in the absence of new indigenous designs and without access to a new foreign fighter aircraft. Both the Mirage and the Impala COIN fighter, the production of which has ceased, must be kept in service for many years to come. Likewise, for the Navy, present emphasis lies on upgrading and updating the weapon systems on the existing ships. A further development is being made of a ship-to-ship missile based on the existing Israeli-designed Skerpioen, and possibly, the French Exocet. The French-supplied Daphne submarines, like the fighters, will have to last for a very long time, pending replacement by a new design, possibly the West German Type 209.

In addition, each of Armscor's subsidiaries has its own R&D set-up, co-ordinated by a central R&D committee. The Atlas Aircraft Corporation's R&D section, for example, developed the Hide dispenser system from 1980 to be mounted on the Mirage fighters when foreign systems became unobtainable due to the arms embargo. In the field of military engines, local R&D has produced some 2000 South African-made components; 150 components producers were involved.

Armscor works very closely with the R&D staffs of all the relevant private companies. This implies that private industry actually finances a considerable part of South African military R&D, which is thus not visible in Government defence budgets.

Armscor's R&D is also financed by the Special Defence Account, of which all details are classified. In addition, Armscor charges universities and research institutes with the responsibility for research in specific areas. Bursaries are made available to university and technical students in engineering and related disciplines. Some 75 per cent of these students enter into the service of the Armscor group every year.[28] P. G. Marais has pointed out the development of the mine-proof vehicle as one of the successes of this involvement of the academic community in military research.[29] Research in other strategic areas also makes an input into military R&D. So, for example, Armscor has been able to significantly advance the science of detonics (explosives technology) to a point where it is claimed that South Africa now equals the US and Sweden. More than 40 propellants and 143 types of ammunition are being produced. This was achieved by drawing on the experience accumulated in the South African mining industry. The Armscor subsidiary Somchem was in 1984 advertising for scientists to work in missile research.[30]

Official information, or any other information about military R&D in South Africa, is hard to come by—it is significant that the section dealing with research in the official South Africa Yearbooks includes *nuclear* research but omits defence research altogether. The NIDR institute is not mentioned in the listing of research organizations in this source, which may testify to its importance for military R&D; neither is, of course, Armscor. The South African press has complained about this secrecy on various occasions: 'Even those examples probably do not reveal the full extent of security-related expenditure. Little is known, for example of the financing of Armscor—although this is undoubtedly at least partially self-funded . . .'[31]

On the burden of R&D expenditure, Armscor Chairman P. G. Marais has said, without mentioning any figures, that:

We can never again allow ourselves to get into the position we were in in 1965 or 1970, when the weapon systems of our Army were mostly old and antiquated things like the Bren guns, the Bredford trucks etc. Now, we have to keep up with whatever could be brought into Africa against us. . . . We have to keep up with whatever we think can be brought in against us and try to be ahead of it. That is the main reason for our heavy R&D programme. *We cannot get the technologies or go out and buy the armaments we require suddenly*. That is why we keep our best people on R&D.[32]

The Armscor subsidiaries

The state sector of the South African armaments industry has grown from the two World War II factories into nine (see table 4.2). As stated above, the production handled by these state enterprises is classified as the most strategic.

Some mergers took place after 1977, reflecting a trend similar to that of arms industries in the West in general: a movement towards greater concentration within larger companies. Telcast was incorporated into Atlas, and Eloptro into Kentron. Kentron was formed in 1978. The task of the new company was to bring together the existing V3A air-to-air missile production, the teams developing the V3B and its export version Kukri and also the teams working on

Table 4.2. The Armscor subsidiaries

Company	Product category	Projects
Atlas Aircraft Corp./Telcast	Aircraft and maintenance/ high technology alloys	Impala COIN fighter 1-3; Bosbok light trainer; Kudu light trainer: Mirage fighter assembly; Cheetah Mirage fighter
Infoplan	Computer services	
Kentron/Eloptro	Guided weapon systems/ optical equipment	V3B Kukri AAM; Skerpioen SSM
Lyttleton Eng. Works	Small arms and guns	G-5; G-6
Musgrave Manufacturers and Distributors	Commercial rifles; shotguns; handguns	
Naschem	Filling and manufacture of heavy calibre ammunition and air bombs	
Pretoria Metal Pressings	Small calibre ammunition	
Somchem	Propellants, explosives, rockets and projectiles	
Swartklip Products	Pyrotechnics and grenades	

other projects such as Valkiri. The essential complimentary industries also became closely affiliated to Kentron: the Somerset West propulsion and warhead plant, which had been set up in 1973, the Eloptro electro-optical plant, and the St Lucia test range.

The R&D share of Kentron's turnover was in 1983 reported to be R32 million, and its production range included optical and electro-optical observation equipment, fire control and missile guidance, work on air-to-air missiles (AAMs), surface-to-air missiles (SAMs) and ship-to-ship systems; plus RPVs (remotely-piloted vehicles) and target systems.[33]

There is also a programme for converting existing stocks of V3A missiles to V3B status. In addition, Kentron does service work on older missiles in the South African Air Force (SAAF), such as the Magics. Armscor has, for example, developed a new silicon nose transparency for the R-530 Magic's seeker head after the original article was found too weak for South African conditions.

The Kentron plant was completed after only a nine-month building programme. There were reports in 1984 that a study on upgrading the Cactus system had been initiated. In 1983 the Somchem factories outside Cape Town were expanded. This is where the double base solid-propellant rocket motors and warhead components for South African missiles are produced.

The private sector companies

As stated, the total number of military producers involved with Armscor varies according to how production is diversified between civilian and military equipment in the various industries. The Defence White Paper of 1977 said that Armscor distributed work to more than 1200 private contractors and subcontractors. In 1982, it was stated that Armscor's private sector was made up of 50 main contractors, 400 subcontractors for main components, plus 1500 firms producing related equipment.[34] Included among these companies were some 200 foreign transnational or foreign-owned industries.

Among the approximately 50 main private subcontractors supervised by Armscor are some of South Africa's largest industrial enterprises, some with a minority government ownership.[35] Two of the largest are the Dorbyl Group and Sandock-Austral.

Dorbyl works within metal engineering and shipbuilding and employs a work-force of 26 000 at 48 plants. Its annual turnover is R700 million. The Dorbyl Group includes the companies Dorbyl Heavy Engineering, Railway Products, Structural Engineering, Projects and Construction, Automative Products, and Marine. It makes up a good example of a large-scale industry with an important civilian sector, as does Sandock-Austral.

The Dorbyl works as they exist today were created in 1973, when two of South Africa's largest and most well-known engineering groups amalgamated. These were Dorman Long (Africa) and Vanderbijl Engineering Corporation. The new company was called Dorman Long Vanderbijl Corporation (Dorbyl).

Dorbyl has the largest shipbuilding complex in Africa, but its construction work has mainly been in the field of commercial vessels. The Dorbyl Group possesses a global network of industrial connections in various fields, which obviously has a bearing on the acquisition of military equipment and technology.

Sandock-Austral is organized in two main divisions; Armaments and Shipbuilding, and Industrial Engineering, and operates light plants. It is 62 per cent owned by the South African General Mining Corporation (also known as Genkor), and is the most advanced specialized engineering company in South Africa. The original Austral armaments plant was a subsidiary of the West German company Thyssen-Henschel. In 1968, General Mining bought Austral, which then possessed only one factory. In 1971, Austral was merged with the Barendz Shipyard in Durban to create the Sandock-Austral company. It was the sole supplier of armoured combat vehicles such as Eland and Ratel. Production has since been diversified, and military business by 1983 was 80 per cent of total production.[36]

Sandock-Austral expresses its capacity in advertisements thus: 'We *design, develop, manufacture and repair*: wheeled armoured vehicles, naval and commercial ships, commercial and industrial gearboxes, vacuum pumps and butterfly valves, mining equipment.'[37]

In 1984, a new company was set up by Sandock-Austral through merging with Renk AG (FR Germany) called Renk-South Africa. Renk holds 51 per cent of the shares, and the company produces special-purpose gears.[38]

A selection of important Armscor private subcontractors was published by *Paratus* in 1982. (See table 4.3.)

This blend of civilian-military production serves as a useful means when arranging the import of foreign components, material or designs—the buyer is not easily identified as connected to the South African Defence Forces or Armscor, and the goods are not identified as military equipment.

Before Armscor's export drive of 1982, information on the Armscor subsidiaries and the private sector companies was very scarce. The identities of the subsidiaries were not known. There are examples of Infoplan acting as a civilian importing agency, for instance, to circumvent the US arms embargo.

Future plans and problems

F. J. Bell has said that Armscor's planning horizon is 20 years, and that it is expected that the arms embargo will continue to the end of the century. Included in this 20-year plan are helicopters, fighter aircraft, submarines, corvettes, ship-to-ship missiles and anti-tank missiles, all said to be of local design.[39]

While the South Africans have an obvious vested interest in presenting Armscor as the most successful arms industry of the world, information about difficulties keeps appearing. Questions about the cost of armaments produc-

Table 4.3.   Selected private subcontractors to Armscor

Company	Product category	Projects
Dorbyl Group	Engineering; hulls for ships	
Sandock-Austral	Arms, shipbuilding, engineering	Eland APC; Ratel APC
ESD	Avionics, weapon electronics, digital systems, radar, radio communication	
Elmectron Industries	Generating sets	
Circon	Generating sets	
Protea Telecommunication Industries	Electronics; transformers; power supplies; field telephones	
Stromberg Safety Equipment	Army orders	
Trivetts-UEC	Ship electronics	
Van de Wetering Engineering	Engineering	
Magnis Truck Corp.	Military trucks	
Osprey Group	Aircraft components and instrumentation	
Messina	Engines for Samil trucks	
Perth Engineering	Engineering	
Deutz Dieselpower	Diesel engines	
Grinel	Military communications; electronic equipment	
Anderson Generator Manufacturers	Generators	

tion and about Armscor spending have constantly been asked by the opposition in the South African Parliament. In 1975, for example, Defence Minister Botha had to defend Armscor against criticism and suggestions that defence spending was 'entirely inflationary'.[40] He said that Armscor had brought the country to a point where the international weapons boycott had largely been 'neutralized'—Armscor had helped to develop know-how so that the most sophisticated weapons could be produced locally, and this was one of the reasons for the increased defence budget. But criticism continued, and over the years a series of measures were undertaken to improve Armscor performance.

Between 1982 and 1984, sales were stagnating and drastic staff cuts had to be made, affecting first of all the state enterprises. Armscor's staff of 30 000 in 1982 had been cut down to 23 000 by December 1984. Some private companies were closed down, while others were given more tasks by Armscor, which led to intra-industrial discontent and accusations of favouritism in the South African press. These reports also connected the difficulty of further expanding the arms industry directly with the growing effects of the 1977 UN arms embargo.[41]

In 1984, a special committee was set up by the Defence Minister to deal with Armscor's financial problems. The committee was headed by the Commander-in-Chief of the Army Lt. Gen. J. J. Geldenhuys, who was later to become the new Commander-in-Chief of the General Staff, and included the Armscor Chairman and private sector representatives.

The cuts have affected a wide cross-section of South African industry, including electronics, heavy engineering and construction companies. The Dorbyl Chairman confirmed that some 'reprogramming' had taken place in his company's contracts with Armscor.[42]

The price paid by Armscor to fulfil the demands of the Defence Department and the SADF must obviously have been very high. It was, for example, at one stage said that some communications equipment was costing South Africa *nine* times the price of imported equipment (if such had been available). With the never-ending border war (stretching along the Namibia/Angola border, Zimbabwe and Mozambique) costing an estimated R2 million per day, and the escalating costs of future military technology, it is obvious that finances are strained.[43] Another war cost estimate was given in 1986 in an interview with Gen. J. J. Geldenhuys, who said '. . . the Rhodesian war cost something on the order of $1 mn/per day, our war today against SWAPO costs us something like 1 million rand/per day . . .'[44]

In particular, costs due to losses in the unending wars along the country's borders are bound to be considerable: it has been reported, for example, that the SADF wrote off equipment and incurred expenses to the value of R32 million during the 1984/85 financial year. The biggest single item—R11.5 million—resulted from a collision which destroyed three aircraft and damaged two.[45]

The general economic problem

It was hoped that Armscor's mounting economic problems would be partially solved by arms exports. But these efforts have taken place against a background of increasing competition and growing general economic problems for South Africa.

The roots of the economic recession are manifold, but one important cause is identified as the drive towards self-sufficiency or the 'siege economy':

Self-sufficiency is a form of self-imposed isolation. As was clear on a limited scale in Zimbabwe, it provides jobs and prosperity in the short term, but stagnation in the long term. If a country is to thrive it must have access to the best bargains and the best markets in the world. If it protects its industries against international competition, it misses the bargains and prices itself out of the market . . . South Africans pay a premium on hundreds of different products in order to protect local manufacturers against foreign competition. But the cost is enormous. It can be determined by simple arithmetics and it runs to billions a year. But the benefits are not as easy to quantify or justify. Self-sufficiency in all products is not a prerequisite for prosperity, yet in South Africa the authorities are currently considering—or developing—local production facilities for high quality ball bearings, high pressure steam turbines, and enriched uranium. There are less than a dozen countries in the Western world which produce these items. . . . As the country approaches self-sufficiency, it becomes more easy to isolate and cut the jugular which carried the few items we must import still. For example, there is no sign so far that South Africa will make diesel fuel injectors. If these items were denied us, the heavy investment in the local diesel engine plant and the resulting high trade prices would have been in vain.[46]

Lobbies against apartheid have for decades pressed multinational companies to pull their money out of the country, and foreign capital itself has reacted to the political instability by cutting credit lines. This forced the Rand down from 85 US cents in March 1984 to just over 35 cents in August 1985.[47] In 1985, South Africa's Reserve Bank Governor appealed to the Government to accelerate the pace of change towards dismantling the apartheid system. This was communicated to South Africa through the Swiss National Bank, acting as mediator between South Africa and more than 300 foreign creditor banks, as the condition for re-scheduling the huge foreign debt repayments. On 1 September 1985, South Africa suspended capital repayments on US $14 000 million of short-term debts. Payments were to be delayed until 1990.

This situation obviously has an important bearing on the future of South Africa's military industry, where enormous investments will be needed—in particular in the high-technology sectors.

To fulfil its mandate to meet the country's armament needs, Armscor has had to adopt practices which according to one report must be 'a cost-accountant's nightmare'.[48] Unlike normal manufacturers, which do not invest in production facilities unless they are sure of profitable sales volumes, Armscor has been obliged to tool up for uneconomical short production runs of highly sophisticated weapon systems. It has also been forced to tie up resources in holdings of strategic stocks. Armscor holds up to *four years* supply of some items which are not available in South Africa, compared to civilian manufacturers who may hold a three-months' supply of materials and components. This is a direct embargo effect.

A shade of desperation crept through in a statement by Armscor manager F. J. Bell on the occasion of the opening of the Vehicle Test Centre at Elandsfontein in 1983: 'the arms embargo against South Africa is very real and the people who monitor it are highly efficient. So if what we are fighting for is worth it, then we will fight dirty if need be'.[49]

Notes and references

1 Barber, J., *South Africa's Foreign Policy, 1945–70* (Oxford University Press: Oxford, 1973), p. 192.
2 Thayer, G., *The War Business—The International Trade in Armaments* (Weidenfeld & Nicolson: London, 1969).
3 *South Africa Yearbook 1982*, p. 872.
4 P. G. Marais, quoted in *The Apartheid War Machine*, International Defence and Aid Fund, London, 1980, p. 14.

5 *Defence Today*, no. 89–90, 1985, p. 416.
6 Defence White Paper 1979.
7 'The defence industry: private or state-owned? A sound balance for survival', F. J. Bell, in a speech to French industrialists, published in *Defence Today*, no. 89–90 (Oct. 1985), pp. 415–16.
8 Commandant Piet Marais, Chairman of Armscor, *International Defense Review*, no. 10, 1984, p. 1567.
9 *Defence Today* (note 5), p. 416.
10 *Defence Today* (note 5), p. 413.
11 *Defence Today* (note 5), p. 415.
12 *Statutes of South Africa*, Act No. 57 (Government Printer: Pretoria, 1968), pp. 420–21.
13 Venter, A. J. 'South Africa's Military-Industrial Complex', *International Defense Review*, no. 12, 1971, p. 548.
14 *Paratus*, June 1982, p. 25. Armscor's assets in 1988 were worth R 1800m and its turnover was R 2200m, according to *South African Panorama*, May 1988, p. 1.
15 *Defense & Armament*, no. 47, Jan. 1986, p. 44.
16 Figures from: SA Reserve Bank and Johannesburg Stock Exchange, in *Financial Mail* (SA), 8 May 1981.
17 *Paratus*, Sep. 1979, p. 45.
18 *Rand Daily Mail*, 1 Apr. 1981.
19 *Militarisation and the Apartheid State*, NUSAS (Allies Press: Cape Town, 1982).
20 Dodd, N. L., *African Defence*, June 1985, pp. 51–2.
21 *Sunday Times* (SA), 11 July 1982.
22 *Flight*, 12 Dec. 1963.
23 The following information is taken from the report *Automating Apartheid—US Computer Exports to South Africa and the Arms Embargo*, NARMIC/American Friends Service Committee, Philadelphia, 1982.
24 Defence White Paper 1982.
25 *World Armaments and Disarmament: SIPRI Yearbook 1985* (Taylor & Francis: London, 1985), p. 289, average for 1981–84.
26 *Financial Mail* (SA), 13 Mar. 1971.
27 *Flight*, 22 and 29 Dec. 1984, p. 1682.
28 'KRYGKOR/ARMSCOR', *Paratus*, Special Supplement, Nov. 1982.
29 *Defence*, Jan. 1984, p. 24.
30 Advertisement in *Paratus*, Oct. 1984, p. 50.
31 *Financial Mail* (SA), 29 July 1983.
32 *International Defense Review*, no. 10, 1984, p. 1565.
33 Pretty, R. T., 'South African Kukri air-to-air missile', *Jane's Defence Review*, vol. 4, no. 6, 1983.
34 Interview with F. J. Bell, Armscor, *The Star*, 13 Mar. 1982.
35 The following data about private sector companies were published in *Paratus*: Armscor Special Supplement, Nov. 1982.
36 *Financial Mail* (SA), 17 June 1983.
37 *Paratus*, Jan. 1983, p. 94.
38 *Défense et Armements*, no. 35 (Nov. 1984).
39 *African Defence*, no. 33, May 1983, p. 29.
40 *Rand Daily Mail*, 24 Apr. 1975.
41 *Sunday Star*, (SA), 30 Dec. 1984.
42 *Financial Times* (UK), 22 Dec. 1981.
43 *Defence*, Jan. 1984, p. 24.
44 *Défense et Armements*, no. 47 (Jan. 1986), p. 51.
45 *Jane's Defence Weekly*, 22 Feb. 1986.
46 *Financial Mail* (SA), 1 May 1981.
47 The rand in mid-1988 was valued at 36 cents, approximately.
48 *Financial Mail* (SA), 12 Dec. 1983.
49 *Star Weekly*, 14 May 1983.

Part III.
The sectors of the military industry

Chapter 5. The aircraft industry

I. Introduction

French, British, Italian and Israeli participation and technology created the South African aircraft industry. In addition, a certain amount of US technology was acquired, through Italy. The first projects of the Atlas Aircraft Corporation were the counter-insurgency fighter Impala, of Italian origin but with a British engine, and the Kudu and Bosbok light planes, of Italian-US origin. Next came the assembly of the 48 Mirage F-1 fighters from France, and finally the redesign, most likely incorporating Israeli know-how, of the Mirage-3 fighter into the Cheetah, announced in 1986. The Alpha XH-1 prototype helicopter gunship likewise announced in 1986 as an 'indigenous' South African design, is better described as a redesigned Alouette-3 helicopter of French design. The developments at the Atlas works provide a good illustration of the stages of the military industrialization process. Atlas began with repair and maintenance facilities in 1965, simultaneously with the purchase of the first production licence, and was producing sophisticated redesigns in 1986. At the same time, this very development also illustrates the heavy reliance on foreign technology, as well as the limitations of the South African industry. The announced new designs are actually *redesigns,* although the input of South African R&D does, of course, testify to a higher level of sophisticated arms technology achieved over the years since 1965.

As will be seen from the account of individual projects presented below, the main task of the South African aircraft industry has been redesign, refitting, modification and upgrading work, rather than indigenous design. To date, Atlas has not presented one single aircraft which could be called indigenous.

On the one hand, this can be said to illustrate typical South African conditions—because of the embargoes, and because of the need to keep the South African Air Force aircraft in operational condition, constant upgrading has to be done. On the other hand, it is not unique for upgrading and modification to take the place of the import of new aircraft. Rather, extension of the service life of existing aircraft fleets has become very common for a number of air forces in the world. This is a reaction in small and medium-sized nations to the rising costs involved in new imports. For the Third World, or new producing countries, modification and upgrading is often the sole way to continue operating their own aircraft industries, since indigenous R&D projects turn out to be both financially and technically impossible. Israel remains the sole new producer to have designed a modern sophisticated fighter aircraft—the Lavi. But the cost escalation caused the Lavi project to be cancelled in 1987.

Most retrofit and upgrading work within aircraft industries is concentrated on avionics and armaments, which has also occupied the resources of Atlas Aircraft. Overhaul work has constantly been done on all parts of the SAAF aircraft, including hydraulic systems, navigational gyros and weapons. Many replacement parts are milled from scratch on digitally-controlled cutting machines, including five-axis machines for jet engine manufacture. Parts that cannot be made locally or obtained abroad are recovered by salvaging techniques, whereby the worn metal is built up. Atlas Aircraft reuses everything that can be re-used and an estimated 26 000 components leave the factory each month just in service and overhaul.

The SAAF cannot easily afford to scrap aircraft and helicopters.[1] Thus all military aircraft, once delivered to South Africa, go through extensive programmes to keep them in service far beyond normal service life. For example, the B-12 Canberra bomber aircraft delivered from Britain in 1962 and 1965, were still flying in 1979, at 15 per cent of their fatigue lives, having been extensively refitted.[2] The British-supplied Buccaneer naval bomber fleet, in service from 1965, was, 10 years later, still praised by the SAAF as 'one of the finest aircraft in the service', one that could not be replaced in the future.[3] The Buccaneers were eventually equipped also with a refined bomb-aiming system and the last of these aircraft remained in service until 1985 when they were finally grounded, having reached an insurmountable stage of obsolescence.

The Avro Shackleton long-range maritime patrol aircraft, of British 1954 design, reached their ultimate stage as late as 1984, and as in the Buccaneer case, no direct replacement has so far been possible due to the international embargoes. The SAAF tried to acquire first the US Lockheed Orion, then the British HS-748 or the Nimrod, and finally the French Breguet Atlantic, to replace Shackleton, but all these attempts failed. Then, a modification programme was undertaken on two of the state-owned air transport company's Safair freighters, the Lockheed L-100 Hercules. These two planes, once supplied as civilian aircraft to a civilian customer from the United States, will be leased by the Government to the SAAF to undertake maritime patrol duties. The Italian-supplied Piaggio P-166S Albatross is also undergoing an upgrading programme for the same purpose.[4]

In 1983, the purchase of a British-produced airship by a commercial Johannesburg travel agency caused the South African press to speculate on a possible future military use of *airships* in the maritime patrol role.

In 1986, yet another retrofit programme was begun by Atlas Aircraft according to SAAF specifications, which enabled something of a record artificial life for an aircraft: about 80 of the 130 second-hand US North American T-6 Texan trainers supplied in the 1950s from the UK entered an upgrading programme. This was to include the addition of modern instrumentation and avionics to extend their useful life by at least another decade. The SAAF remains the sole and last large-scale operator of this plane.[5] The machinery, the tooling and components for these extensive programmes have by necessity been acquired from overseas; this equipment escaped definition as military equipment and even less as armaments. Likewise, the very set-up of the Atlas Aircraft Corporation drew extensively on overseas assistance and expertise.

II. Establishment of the Atlas Aircraft Corporation

During 1963, a few small private companies were set up to undertake aircraft construction, such as Miles Aircraft (South Africa) in Cape Town, Pierre Emeraude and a few others. None of these first light-plane projects met with success, however.

In 1964, the South African Government decided on more substantive means to assist the formation of an aircraft industry, but still based on private initiative. The Government transferred 40 per cent of its peace-time maintenance service to private concerns: the Bonuskor group was asked to form the companies for this undertaking and two were registered the same year. One was the Atlas Aircraft Corporation of South Africa with an initial capital of £23.5 million, set up as the operating company in November 1964. The second was Bonaero Corporation with a controlling interest in Atlas. The other main shareholder in addition to Bonuskor was the Industrial Development Corporation (IDC).

Construction of the Atlas Aircraft factory was undertaken with advisory aid and plans drawn up by the French firm Sud-Aviation and began in 1965. The licence for the first aircraft to be produced, the jet trainer Impala-1, had already been purchased from Italy, and assembly could start in 1966.

In addition to the assembly plant, the Atlas works include an overhaul hangar, electrical, mechanical and hydraulic workshops, storehouses and three turbojet test houses. The deadline for the completion of the whole factory area was May 1967, by which time the Air Force was already operating some 15 Impalas.

Foreign assistance and participation was crucial to the establishment of this industry, as recognized by the South Africans themselves:

The task was a difficult one. The complexity of modern aircraft had increased beyond all comparison with any other aircraft ever built in South Africa. The manufacture of modern airframes and engines and the overhaul and maintenance of these aircraft demanded a level of skill and experience not available in South Africa in any appreciable measure. To satisfy the manpower requirements, extensive overseas recruiting was resorted to initially.[6]

The foreign assistance referred to above consisted of French consultants and advisors, over 1000 British aircraft engineers and technicians and Italian engineers, who helped set up the Impala production line. In addition, a Rolls Royce team reportedly aided the setting up of the engine assembly for the Impala.[7] According to one report, the deputy director and chief engineer of Israeli Aircraft Industries (IAI) also visited the Atlas Works in 1967, to discuss joint fighter production.[8] This seems too early to have been the start of technical co-operation for the Cheetah fighter. (This fighter, presented in 1986, is similar to the Israeli Kfir Mirage version.) Staff from Aermacchi remained with Atlas until 1982 and one out of ten Atlas employees are still foreigners. In 1986, the work force numbered 6100, and 250 apprentices per year were being trained.[9] By 1971, Atlas had a total staff of 3700 whites, and 500 non-whites, from 17 different nations.[10]

The organizational and financial problems were found too demanding for private industry, and the state took over the Atlas works in 1969, when Armscor acquired all the shares of the company. This was reportedly a relief for the private company. Government takeover of private companies has been rare in the South African arms industry history, and was explained in the following terms by Armscor:

The capital investment in high technology, high cost manufacturing and test equipment was out of all proportion to the turnover. Some machines were only used once a week . . . and because there was no previous experience in arms manufacture and related industrial activity, people with the required skill were not readily available. Training costs were sometimes prohibitively high to develop the necessary abilities. It was no wonder that the private industries to which the first requirements had been allocated— like aircraft production, high explosives, etc., were in fact relieved when the state decided to take them over.[11]

III. The Atlas Impala programme

Impala-1: 1966–74

The first priority for the Air Force was to get an armed trainer for counter-insurgency tasks, to replace the old Harvard planes. By 1961, when the Simonstown Agreement was re-negotiated with Britain, it became clear to the South Africans that this agreement would not include the sale of any equipment suitable for COIN duties. It was then decided to embark upon a domestic construction programme. First, the French Potez Magister trainer seemed to be the best choice, since there were fears in South Africa that the British engine powering the Italian MB-326 GB trainer would make this sale vulnerable to future British embargo restrictions. An industrial solution was eventually found to this problem, and the MB-326 was selected. In South Africa this became known as the Impala.

There was at the time no doubt that the plane was intended for COIN operations.

The total SAAF order for MB-326 is for 300 aircraft, of which only a very small proportion can conceivably be required for flying training in the modest-sized SAAF. It is evident, therefore, that the Verwoerd government intends to form a very conceivable counter-insurgency arm equipped with the type, and orders for arms and attack systems for installation in the South African MB-326s are expected to be forthcoming.[12]

This was never admitted by any of the parties involved in the deal, whether governments or industries. Aermacchi even denied in 1964 that any negotiations at all had taken place with South Africa.[13]

Nearly 20 years later it was no longer necessary to hide the main function of Impala, which by then had been in use in COIN operations for a long time: 'The Impala, being a light ground attack aircraft used in support of ground forces, is intended for counter-insurgency', said South African Air Force Commandant L. Lourens in 1982 at the inauguration of a Tactical Airfield Unit system in northern Natal.[14]

The licence for the production of the more advanced MB-326M was acquired from Aermacchi of Italy in 1963, before it began to implement the UN embargo. In any case, as a 'trainer' it was defined as non-lethal equipment, and was not covered by the embargo.

Italy delivered 16 finished aircraft, 10 in major component form, and 40 sub-assemblies, 66 aircraft in total. The first licence agreement was said to cover the production of an additional 200 aircraft, but the numbers involved have never been confirmed. In total, 14 planes were completed in 1966, and altogether, 151 planes of the Mark 1 version had been delivered by 1974, when the Mark 2 entered production.[15] About 60 of these were equipped for 'light strike duties', that is, for counter-insurgency tasks. This version can be armed with several alternative under-wing loads—two machineguns and two napalm tanks; or two air-to-surface missiles; or two 227 kg bombs and two rocket packs each with six 80-mm rockets. It incorporates US-designed avionics, and the British Rolls Royce Viper jet engine, sub-licensed by Britain to the Italian firm Piaggio, which in turn sub-licences it to South Africa. Total machine-tool investment to start up the Impala programme was reported at R 500 000.[16]

Impala-2: 1974–77

The usefulness of the 60 light-strike planes resulted in a second licence agreement, announced by Defence Minister Botha in 1971. Negotiations with Italy were completed in 1973, covering the acquisition of 100 advanced Aermacchi MB-326K light-strike planes, to be known as Impala-2. This is a single-seat ground attack aircraft powered by an improved version of the Viper engine, and it became widely used for COIN purposes in Angola and Namibia.

The licence programme was organized so that a first batch of six prototypes plus unassembled parts for 15 planes for assembly by Atlas were delivered in early 1974. The first Atlas-assembled planes flew in February 1974. Subsequently, 50 planes were built for the SAAF and put into use. This makes a total of 71 planes.

Figures given for the total number acquired vary, as for the Impala-1. According to one source, a total of 85 Impala-2s had been built by 1982, while unofficial information from the Italian industry puts the number at 100.[17] There is in addition some reason to assume that 50 planes were the Mark 2 version, and the remaining 50 were of an updated Mark 3 version, as described below.

The total number of Impalas of all versions in service by 1984 was given as 130 Mark 1 plus 70 Mark 2[18] and by 1985 130 Mark 1 plus 85 Mark 2.[19]

By 1981, approximately 90 per cent of the Impala-2 was of South African manufacture.[20] This would mean that the remaining 10 per cent of the equipment was still available from abroad.

Few details are known about the manufacture of equipment for Impala. However, in 1967, Marconi of the UK set up a new factory in South Africa to produce the radio compass for this plane. The Impala continued in production, together with its Rolls Royce engine, for as long as up to 1985, when it was officially announced that the line had closed. The reason given was that the requirements of the SAAF had been filled. The same year, information appeared to the effect that contrary to earlier assumptions, a third version had been in production in recent years, presumably with a higher degree of local content after the 1977 embargo.

Impala-3: 1978–85

The existence of this previously unknown third version was first described by Defence Minister Gen. M. Malan. Five to ten Mark 3s took part in an air raid on Maputo, Mozambique, in May 1983. The Mark 3 version was also confirmed in a book published in 1983 by a South African Air Force officer who had participated in several operations in Angola: 'From August 26, six Mark III Impala ground-attack fighters ready for long distance bombardment were based at Mpacha'.[21]

It is unlikely that the Impala-2 remained unchanged in production for 10 years, in particular when taking into account the striving to upgrade existing weapons in general. However, there are no details available as to the specifics of a third Impala version.

The fact that the production line finally closed down in 1985 allows for some speculation. First, it is plausible that the supply of certain components eventually stopped as the impact of breaking the embargo became politically more costly for the supplier. If this is the case, continued production could have been found too expensive even for the South Africans. Also, the production stop for Impala could have resulted directly from the failure to gain any export orders for the plane. At any rate, the Impala programme represents to date the most indigenous technology acquisition, and the longest continuous production effort in the field of military aircraft.

Rolls Royce Viper engine

Little is known about the details of the assembly in South Africa of the Rolls Royce engines used in the Impala aircraft. When the licence was first granted by the UK to Piaggio in Italy in 1960, the British Government insisted at first on inserting a clause prohibiting the export of planes with the Rolls Royce Viper engine to South Africa. This demand was later waived, as a result of pressure from both British and Italian industry, and was replaced by a clause prohibiting the re-export of the engine to Rhodesia.[22]

The Viper 632 turbojet, powering Impala-2, was developed in collaboration between Rolls Royce and Fiat of Italy, which gave Italian industry a greater opportunity to influence export regulations than otherwise. It started to be produced in 1974, and South Africa was one of the first states to receive it. The Italian licensee Piaggio was controlled by Fiat, which was in partnership with the Italian Government as owners of the Aeritalia company. Aeritalia was the Italian business partner that negotiated the Impala deal with South Africa. Thus, it does not seem credible, as was later claimed by Italy, that the Italian Government was ignorant of this deal.

There is no information on the local content of all the Rolls Royce engines that were assembled in South Africa. All that is known is that no indigenous aircraft engines have been designed and developed—a typical feature with regard to new aircraft industries.

According to *Jane's All the World's Aircraft*, the Rolls Royce Viper 540 turbojet was still being assembled in South Africa under sub-licence from Piaggio in 1983. That would mean that neither the UK nor Italy found it meaningful to revoke the licence. Rolls Royce components were not to be locally manufactured in South Africa under the 1973 agreement for the upgraded engine, but merely assembled under licence from imported components.

IV. The Atlas Bosbok and Kudu programme

Atlas Bosbok

In 1971, the production of light military aircraft by Atlas was announced by Defence Minister Botha. Two light-plane projects were undertaken. In 1973 a sales agreement was concluded with Aeritalia for 40 AM-3Cs—which became the Bosbok—to be delivered to the South African Army Air Corps as replacements for the aged Cessna-185s. Twenty Bosboks had entered service by mid-1975 in a liaison squadron of the Army Light Aircraft Command.

Aeritalia at the time firmly denied that the deal involved licensed production, but when delivery began in 1974, only eight planes were supplied complete. The remaining 32 were assembled by Atlas up to the end of 1975. South African authorities refer to this plane as locally developed.[23]

'Light planes' and 'trainers' are not defined as offensive weapons and thus are exempted from embargo restrictions. But the Bosbok filled a gap for the SAAF, for reconnaissance, forward air controlling and transport duties. It has a US Avco Lycoming GSO-480 engine, sub-licensed to Piaggio in Italy, and further sub-sub-licensed from Italy to South Africa. The first plane built for South Africa was displayed at the Turin Air Show in 1972.[24]

Atlas C4M Kudu

Development started at Atlas in 1971 on what was described by its general manager as a 'bush aircraft' for dual civil-military application. This project too was based on a licence agreement with Aermacchi for the production of 40 aircraft based on the Aermacchi-Lockheed AL-60 light-plane design. All sub-assemblies had been delivered by 1975.

Kudu uses the same engine as Bosbok and the same wing, but retains the fuselage of the parent AL-60 model. Subsequently, Atlas designed a larger fuselage able to carry eight persons.[25] The prototype made its first flight in February 1974. Like the Bosbok, this plane is claimed as a 100 per cent South African development when it is rather an early example of local adaptation of foreign-supplied know-how.[26] *Paratus* writes about 'the new Bosbok and Kudu aircraft, which have been designed and produced in South Africa specifically for this country's requirements'.[27] Even *Jane's All the World's Aircraft 1982–83* describes the Kudu as 'developed by Atlas', without mentioning the US and Italian contents.

It is a transport aircraft, in use with the Army Air Corps. It has an exceptionally low speed and can operate from unprepared surfaces. Like the Bosbok, the Kudu has proved highly suitable for operations in the border areas. Both plane types were still in extensive use in Namibia in 1986.[28]

Both the US design and the US engine incorporated into the Kudu ought reasonably to have involved a US veto on re-export from Italy to South Africa. There is no trace of any debate or discussion about this. Presumably, as in many other cases of technology transfer, the deals took place in secrecy and were completed long before they received any publicity. It is also an unsolved mystery how a US engine could be resold by Piaggio to South Africa.

V. Atlas-Mirage-3/F-1

Like the above described projects, negotiations for the licensed assembly of Mirage-3 and Mirage F-1 fighters were conducted in 1971. On 27 June 1971, it was announced that a deal had been concluded with Dassault and Société Nationale d'étude et de construction de moteurs d'aviation (SNECMA), ensuring French industrial and technical co-operation and training of South African staff in France. The licence provided for the manufacture of the entire F-1 aircraft, including the SNECMA engine and electrical equipment. South Africa also had the option of deciding what percentage of French-made parts to use as production experience progressed.

The first licence reportedly covered the assembly and progressive manufacture of 18 Mirage-3E bombers and 16 Mirage F-1C all-weather interceptors, plus 32 Mirage F-1A ground-attack fighters. Rumours had it that a total of 100 F-1s was to be achieved. In 1974 this plane was described as comparable to the US Phantom and the Soviet MiG-23. It could operate from rough runways and had a combat radius of 1000 km. The standard fixed armaments consisted of two 30-mm cannon and two Matra R-530 or Super-530 radar homing and infra-red (IR) homing air-to-air missiles. In addition it carried Matra Magic IR air-to-air missiles. The ground-attack version bears an AS-30 air-to-surface missile, or six 600-litre napalm tanks.

The Mirage F-1 was hailed as a formidable weapon in the southern African context, because it was designed—like the US Phantom—as a typical 'Third World plane', that is, for large-scale COIN operations from small airfields. This is how the planes were later used in South Africa.

With the acquisition of this aircraft the strike capability of South Africa was perceived to be utterly superior to that of its African neighbours. At this time, Angola and Mozambique did not possess more than a guerrilla warfare capacity, and were only on the verge of independence from Portugal.

This deal, widely publicized at the time, was presented in triumph as signalling a real breakthrough for the South African aircraft industry. According to H. F. Samuels, President of Armscor, the Mirage was considered to be the fighter of the future and would remain in production for a long time. The Defence White Paper of 1973 even claimed that the Mirage F-1 was already being built in South Africa—a claim which for all practical purposes was technologically impossible. The production of a jet fighter-interceptor armed with missiles did represent a technological advancement, but as it turned out, the triumph was premature. The Atlas Mirage programme did not advance beyond the stage of assembly before it was eventually halted by the 1977 mandatory embargo. From the outset, technical difficulties proved to be great—which was later acknowledged even by the South African authorities.

Atlas had some experience of maintenance, repair and overhaul work on the Mirage-3C fighter-interceptors and the Mirage-3E fighter-bombers which had been purchased in large numbers between 1964 and 1966. (In 1964, 16 Mirage-3Cs were delivered, followed by 20 Mirage-3Es in 1965–66.) This fleet now made up the main core of fighter aircraft in the South African Air Force. But the expansion and preparation work at the Atlas plant for the local Mirage programme took more than two years (under French guidance), and the factory was not ready until 1975. Moreover, tooling and preparation problems in France also led to a delay in the schedule. All the initial 48 F-1 planes were to have been delivered by 1974, but the first one was completed in France only at the end of that year.

In May 1976, the French Government categorically denied that any licence for the series production of the Mirage F-1 had been sold to South Africa. In January 1977, the Johannesburg newspaper *The Citizen* declared that South Africa was to build at least 100 F-1s. These 100 planes never materialized. 'Production' was confined to the assembly of sub-assemblies of the 48 originally contracted, which had all been shipped to South Africa well before the 1977 embargo; and to the last batch of 18 Mirage-3Es, ordered at the same time. On 18 April 1977, Atlas for the first time allowed a foreign journalist to photograph the Mirage-3 and F-1 assembly lines at the plant.[29]

France adhered to the 1977 embargo, and within a few years the impact was also noticeable on these locally assembled aircraft: in 1979 it was reported that for all practical purposes the Mirage F-1 fleet was grounded due to a lack of spare parts. This affected also the power-plant and the Cyrano-4 radar.[30] The Mirage-3 remains South Africa's main fighter. Here, the spare parts supply seemed to cause less problems, due to various factors described below, although French president Giscard d'Estaing announced in February 1977 that France would extend the embargo to cover the supply of spares for Mirage-3 (as well as for F-1, Alouette-3, Super Frelon, Transall C-160 and the tactical missiles already delivered).[31]

The 1977 embargo affected also industrial machinery for the Mirage project. In 1977, Atlas was capable of building six aircraft a month, using certain ready-made units from abroad. But the deliveries of these, mainly from France, officially came to a halt from 1 October 1977. Replacements were said to be possible from Taiwan and Israel, but nothing more has come forth about this, and the cancelling of the licensed Mirage project seems to prove that substitutes for the French supplies could not be obtained from any other source.[32]

The following report from 1984 can be seen as representative of the exaggerated South African claims of construction capacity, and of general Western speculations about future aircraft acquisitions:

The South Africans *can still build French Mirage fighters* under licence, but it is a 10-year-old model that will be less of a match for the more advanced aircraft now starting to be seen in other countries in the region. The *answer is likely to be increasingly close cooperation with Israel*. There are reports that South Africa may soon acquire more than 30 Israeli Kfir aircraft, and may work with the Israelis on the co-production of a more advanced fighter, the Lavi, scheduled to be operational in the early 1990s.[33]

In reality, the South Africans could never build the Mirage: Atlas' capacity only developed to the *assembly* stage of the plane. No new versions were constructed, and when the Cheetah design was finally announced one year later this programme still did not seem to envisage construction of new planes but an extensive retrofit of the existing Mirage-3s. Co-operation with Israel may have been undertaken, however, since all relevant sources have reported a marked similarity between the South African Cheetah and the Israeli Kfir fighter, both based on the French Mirage.

The likelihood of co-operation on the Israeli Lavi fighter seems dubious. By 1985, Israel was claiming full adherence to the mandatory embargo against South Africa, and was also heavily dependent on US funding of its Lavi project. That the US, in turn, would allow Israel to supply the Lavi technology to South Africa is just not credible. The Lavi project was finally cancelled in 1987.

Another type of know-how acquisition connected to the Lavi aircraft was reported in November 1987, first by the newspaper *Jerusalem Post*. After the cancelling of Lavi, South Africa reportedly offered huge salaries in an attempt to recruit aeronautical engineers and technicians from Israel. The newspaper said that Atlas Aircraft was trying to attract 600 experts from among the 3000 IAI staff due to lose their jobs after the costly high-technology Lavi project was halted in August. Foreign military attachés in Israel were quoted as saying that several South African engineers had been attached to the Lavi project over the years. IAI has no power to prevent its employees from signing contracts with Atlas. According to Israeli legislation, the Government can bar carriers of classified military information from visiting 'hostile countries'. South Africa is, however, not defined as such.

VI. Atlas 'Cheetah'—the 'new' fighter design

After 1977, there are several scattered statements published in South Africa which have tended to confirm that the embargo made it impossible for the SAAF to acquire a new jet fighter aircraft for the 1990s, and that Atlas would eventually have to embark on an indigenous design. In 1984, for example, the chief opposition defence spokesman in Parliament, Mr P. Myburgh, listed a new fighter aircraft among the big future problems for the South African arms industry.[34]

All outside observers agree on the need for a new fighter, but have tended to stress the necessity for foreign technological co-operation. This viewpoint is exemplified by the following source, which also actually predicts what later appeared as the Cheetah:

As an interim move, the SAAF is reportedly planning *to update its Mirage-3CZs* by the addition of canards and a new radar, but for longer-term replacement in the 1990s, it appears that South Africa will have no alternative but to develop an indigenous combat aircraft, probably in collaboration with another politically isolated partner such as Taiwan or Chile.[35]

This is, of course, speculation. Both Taiwan and Chile are among the decreasing number of nations in the world that keep any kind of military and diplomatic relations with South Africa. While Chile's arms industry is much less advanced than South Africa's, Taiwan seems to provide at least a technical basis for such speculation. In November 1985, an official government spokesman announced that Taiwan planned to build an advanced jet fighter aircraft that would be superior to US-supplied planes (no longer available for political reasons). Production would begin by the early 1990s.[36]

Meanwhile, pending a new jet fighter design, the updated Mirage was presented in mid-July 1986. In his statement on the occasion Defence Minister M. Malan intimated that the redesign was a new plane, saying:

Today we have taken a major step with regards to the defence of our country. The announcement by our State President of the *Cheetah—our very own fighter aircraft*—is indeed a meaningful event. It is an event every South African can be proud of. One which speaks of home-grown achievement of development . . . With the launch of the Cheetah aircraft, we are entering a new era of self-sufficiency and an enhanced operational capability for the South African Air Force. The Cheetah is indeed a modern, sophisticated and highly effective trump card in our military arsenal. Not only is it an ultra-effective *addition* to South Africa's Defence Force, but it is an extremely flexible and manoeuvrable asset.[37]

Prime Minister Botha also used the occasion to challenge the UN embargo policy: 'We will not allow ourselves to be humiliated and undermined in order to escape sanctions. We are not a nation of jelly fish'.[38]

But the displayed aircraft itself, as reported by other Western sources and indeed also by representatives of both the Atlas Aircraft Corporation and the SAAF, clearly showed that the Cheetah is, in fact, the long-awaited mid-life update of the Mirage-3 fleet.[39] One report also states that this updating of Mirage-3 was completed by Atlas in collaboration with the IAI.[40] The main work lies in the canard modification,[41] new navigation and attack systems, new performance levels, the replacement of many structural components and upgrading of light systems.[42] In sum, about 50 per cent of the old Mirage-3 is reconstructed and brought up to the same standard as the Israeli Kfir-2. The main difference is that the South African plane retains its French SNECMA-Atar 9 engine, while the Israeli plane uses a US General Electric J79 engine, which for embargo reasons is out of reach for South Africa. Some observers actually stated that the Cheetah was 'almost identical to the IAI Kfir TC-3'.[43] The basic similarity with the Israeli Kfir fighter, which is also an upgraded and modified Mirage-3, was in fact generally noted, and it seems likely that the Cheetah was developed with Israeli assistance. Already in 1981, the IAI showed a refit package for the Mirage-3C at the Paris Air Show, including canards, extra weapon pylons and new weapon delivery systems, at the price of US $2 million. It was claimed that such a modification increased the plane's airframe life by 32 per cent.[44]

Apart from Israel, both France and Switzerland were by 1985 carrying out the same type of canard modification and upgrading of their respective air forces' Mirage-3 fighters to extend their lifetimes. Chile also announced, in early 1984, a similar upgrading of its Mirage fighters, and confirmed that these modifications were made in co-operation with IAI. This could support the claim that the IAI agreed to provide canard modification also to Atlas Aircraft. Officially, the company denies any connections with South Africa, and the South Africans deny assistance from abroad.

Thus, the aircraft presented as proof of 'home-grown achievement of development' and as 'our very own fighter aircraft', is a 50 per cent reconstruction of the 24-year-old Mirage-3 and draws heavily on Israeli and French know-how. The French possibilities of interfering in a deal involving French military technology remain unknown, and often—as in this case—even undebated. If the French legislation were similar to that in the USA, France would, theoretically, have been able to prevent a range of equipment needed to maintain the Mirage fleet in South Africa from ever reaching the Atlas works through third countries.

Further, the redesign has not added any planes to the SAAF inventory, as claimed by the Defence Minister. It merely means that a number of the existing Mirage fleet will be modified to Cheetah standard. This fleet was by 1988 estimated at 40–45 aircraft still in service.[45] Other reports mention a total remaining number of 39 aircraft. However, of these, 15 are two-seat trainers, which would be less suitable for modification to the Cheetah fighter standard. That would leave a total number of some 24–30 fighters for the canard modification programme. So far, there are no reports that the 47 Mirage F-1 fighters in service have been updated. Production in South Africa of entirely new planes of the Cheetah configuration would probably have to involve the acquisition of more foreign know-how; for example, in the form of the Kfir-2 production line which was closed down in Israel in 1987. Such an acquisition in turn seemed more remote by 1988, as US pressure on Israel to cut off military exports to South Africa became more pronounced.

Alpha XH-1 combat helicopter

Second to a new fighter aircraft, the SAAF need for a new helicopter has constantly been emphasized, this being perhaps the most indispensable counter-insurgency weapon. After being announced on various occasions over a 20-year period by South African authorities, the 'indigenous combat helicopter', the Alpha XH, was finally demonstrated in prototype form in March 1986.

While the fighter development connection is more likely to have been Israeli, there appeared to be French know-how behind the combat helicopter—which was based on the Alouette-3. This would be logical, considering that the SADF helicopter fleet was entirely French-supplied, except for the five British Wasp naval helicopters supplied in 1971. Between 1961 and 1975, nearly 200 military helicopters were delivered from France, including Alouette-3, Super Frelon and Puma.

Reports that the 20 Puma helicopters were licence-assembled in South Africa have never been confirmed and were probably not correct. Additional deliveries of French helicopters seem to have been made clandestinely after the 1977 embargo, from commercial sources via third countries.[46] The Alouette-3 remains the most predominant type in SAAF service, with more than 100 still operational by 1988.

In 1983, Armscor spokesmen officially confirmed that the Atlas Aircraft works was preparing for a helicopter project, specifically aimed at maintaining air superiority in South West Africa (Namibia).[47] One year later, in 1984, the opposition defence spokesman announced his doubts about a South African helicopter project, saying that this would be too expensive and that 'it would be like re-inventing the wheel one thousand times'.[48] But Armscor Chairman P. G. Marais confirmed in an interview in 1984 that a *feasibility study* for an indigenous helicopter was under way and that South Africa was manufacturing an increasing range of spare parts for helicopters, thus adding to its base of technological know-how. He went on to say: 'It is difficult to say entirely designed in South Africa, because we would be using some of the best elements of what we already have. But we will have to end up by building them ourselves at some stage'.[49]

In 1985, Armscor Chairman P. G. Marais said that he did not see South Africa attempting helicopter *production* 'for another 10 years or so', although the matter would be receiving attention.[50] The same spokesmen, however, repeated in early 1986 that a feasibility study had begun on a helicopter project, and that an indigenous composite rotor blade had entered production during 1985. An indigenous helicopter engine was also reported to be at the planning stage. What Armscor had access to, in addition to the experience already gained by Atlas Aircraft in overhaul and maintenance and upgrading of the Alouette-3 fleet, probably also included French industrial assistance. In 1985, a French source reported that the company Aerospatiale had sent, in September of that year, a team of technicians 'to help Atlas start a combat helicopter project'.[51]

On 2 March 1986, the Atlas Aircraft works publicly showed a light helicopter prototype, called the Alpha XH-1. On that occasion, Air Force Chief General D. Earp declared that 'The Alpha is entirely locally designed to SAAF specifications, using what South African industry can provide'.[52] In connection with the first showing, it was also revealed that a SAAF contract had been placed with Atlas Aircraft in March 1981, and that development work had thus been going on in secret for five years.

The power-plant on the prototype was a gas turbine, presumably based on the Alouette-3 engine, which was originally licence-produced by Atlas. French know-how behind the Alpha prototype was immediately suspected: 'The Alpha XH-1 has a number of marked similarities to the Aerospatiale Alouette-3 from which it is believed to be largely derived'.[53]

Other sources also reported that the details of the helicopter made available on this occasion indicated that the design had been developed under a contract between Aerospatiale of France and Atlas Aircraft. This agreement may be similar to that signed between Aerospatiale and Industriei Aeronautice Romane (IAR) of Romania, which has developed a gunship version of the Alouette-3, known as the IAR 317 Airfox.[54] Flight trials of the Alpha were begun in February 1985.[55] According to these first reports, the Alpha has similar rotor, power-plant and transmission installations to the Alouette-3. It is also equipped with the same helmet-mounted sight that was developed for the Kukri missile but here used to fire the GA-1 gun. The Alpha prototype further has a locally developed airframe and systems fit. The engine, gearboxes and rotor systems include locally manufactured components. It was also stated that the production helicopter would have 100 per cent locally manufactured contents. The Commander-in-Chief emphasized that the Alpha prototype was to be regarded as a technology demonstration, to be further studied before a final production design was decided upon. He also said that the technologies explored in the XH-1 prototype would be applied to other future helicopters in South Africa. This raised the prospect of a future development of a more powerful attack helicopter, perhaps based on the French Pumas already in the SAAF inventory.[56]

A rather surprising allegation regarding foreign sources of supply for the Alpha was made by *Interavia* in 1986: 'Atlas at present manufactures the engine and transmission for the Alouette-3 and XH-1, but obtains the *rotor-head* from abroad, presumably from Yugoslavia or Romania, though Atlas will not comment on this'.[57] In South Africa, no mention is made of any foreign input: 'The Alpha XH-1 is a local development, blending a local design with local components and systems'.[58]

It should be stressed that neither Israeli co-operation with regard to the Cheetah Mirage version, nor French co-operation on the Alpha project, can be confirmed. But it is not likely that South Africa by pure 'coincidence' should suddenly be capable of indigenous designs so similar to existing projects in technologically advanced countries.

VII. Spare parts and engines

The Atlas Aircraft Corporation remains South Africa's sole aero-engine producer. Its first project was the licensed production from 1965 of the British Rolls Royce Viper-22-1 turbojet for the Atlas-built Impala counter-insurgency aircraft.

From 1975, Atlas Aircraft proceeded to manufacture also the Rolls Royce Viper 540 for the Impala-2 attack aircraft. Subsequently, yet another higher-thrust version, the Rolls Royce–Fiat joint development Viper 632–43 was sub-licensed to Atlas to be retrofitted to the Impala-2.[59] Likewise during the 1970s, as the import of complete helicopters from France proceeded, and the Mirage assembly began, Atlas reportedly purchased the production rights for both the helicopter engines and the Atar turbojet engine for the Mirages. When these licences apparently lapsed, or were revoked after 1977 as has been claimed, the tooling remained. This must have had an important significance for the future Cheetah and Alpha projects.

Lastly, what was claimed by Armscor as a breakthrough in indigenous engine technology was exhibited for the first time at the FIDA-86 arms exhibition in Chile when Atlas Aircraft presented a new indigenously developed small gas turbine engine, scaled for remotely-piloted vehicles (RPVs) and sea-skimming missiles. The engine is a four-stage axial flow engine with a 20-hour life. According to Atlas Aircraft officials, six test engines had been built and run, and the first test took place in 1983.

Atlas Aircraft by 1986 claimed the capacity to design and build advanced jet engines entirely within the country, with the exception of the need to import *titanium*. This has raised questions, since titanium is generally described as one of the strategic resources in South Africa's own possession.[60]

Apart from Atlas Aircraft, only one other South African aero-engine producer has been reported (in 1971). This was the Aeronautics Research

Unit, said to be developing a valveless pulse-jet engine at the time. No reports have appeared since then.[61]

Spare parts have reportedly presented a serious problem although manufacture has been undertaken by Atlas Aircraft for many years; but in 1979 it was announced that Atlas no longer needed to import any parts for the maintenance and repair of the large French helicopter fleet. Responsibility for spare parts supply seems to have been diversified to a certain extent. The SAAF Air Logistics Command has undertaken wider responsibilities for development and manufacture of spares and equipment, as well as overhauls and repairs. In 1985 a programme was begun to equip the SAAF's nine French-supplied C-160 Transall turbo-prop transports with new spare parts to extend their fatigue lives. The Air Logistics Command's inventory includes over 778 000 items, making it one of the largest in the southern hemisphere.[62]

VIII. Other aircraft producers

In addition to the abortive efforts at light-plane production mentioned above, a few other efforts at aircraft construction have been undertaken in South Africa.

In 1965, the Meyers-Jansen Aircraft Corporation was set up to assemble Maule and Meyers light planes from the USA for civil and military duties. The company changed its name to CR Jansen Aviation in 1970 when both planes were in production, supplied to the South African Police (SAP). Neither has attracted attention in connection with the embargo implementation, however.

Another early company was Rotorcraft Helicopters, which in 1970 produced a minicopter, also for the SAP, equipped with a Rolls Royce engine, and likewise not much featured in the embargo debate.[63] Rotorflight Helicopters of Cape Town was in 1985 reported to have started the manufacture of helicopters for the Air Force jointly with the Israeli Chemavir-Masok company.[64]

The AFIC was set up in 1967 to construct an Italian light plane known as AFIC RSA-200. Production took place at the Atlas works but was suspended in 1972, awaiting new manufacturing facilities. The plane was reportedly sold to several civilian customers. All light planes may be used by the Commando Air Force, under the SAAF.

Notes and references

[1] *Defense & Armament*, no. 47 (Jan. 1986), p. 45.
[2] *Flight International*, 1 Dec. 1979, p. 1821.
[3] *Rand Daily Mail*, 19 May 1975, quoting United Party spokesman on defence, Mr. V. Raw.
[4] *Paratus*, Dec. 1984.
[5] *Milavnews News Letter*, no. 291 (Jan. 1986).
[6] *South Africa Yearbook 1982*, p. 412.
[7] Douglas-Home, C., 'Contradiction in arms to South Africa policy', *The Times*, 24 Jan. 1969.
[8] Adams, J., *Israel and South Africa* (Quartet Books: London, 1984), p. 34.
[9] *Défense et Armements*, no. 47 (Jan. 1986).

[10] Venter, A. J., in 'South Africa's Military-Industrial Complex', *International Defense Review*, no. 12, 1971, p. 548.
[11] F. J. Bell, in *Defence Today*, no. 89–90, 1985, p. 414.
[12] *Flight International*, 16 Sep. 1965.
[13] *Milavnews News Letter*, no. 40 (Jan. 1965).
[14] *Paratus*, July 1982.
[15] *Milavnews Air Letter*, no. 282 (4 Apr. 1985), p. 175.
[16] *Milavnews News Letter*, Feb. 1968, p. 24.
[17] *Milavnews Air Letter*, no. 282 (Apr. 1985).
[18] *Flight International*, 2 Dec. 1984.
[19] *Milavnews Air Letter*, no. 282 (Apr. 1985).
[29] *Jane's All the World's Aircraft 1982–83* (Macdonald: London, 1983), p. 176.
[21] *Milavnews News Letter*, no. 264 (10 Jan. 1983).
[22] Legum, C., 'Rolls-Royce deal in South Africa', *Observer*, 23 Sep. 1973.
[23] *Paratus*, Nov. 1979, p. 21.
[24] *Paratus*, Dec. 1984, p. 43.
[25] *Flight*, 4 Mar. 1979.
[26] *Rand Daily Mail*, 18 June 1985: 'The C4M Kudu has been designed and built by Atlas Aircraft Company at Kempton Park'.
[27] *Paratus*, Nov. 1979.
[28] For example, as described in 'Bush war', *Flight International*, 1 Mar. 1986, indicating a thorough maintenance and refurbishing capacity.
[29] *Air et Cosmos*, 30 Apr. 1977.
[30] *Flight International*, 24 Mar. 1979, p. 886.
[31] *Milavnews News Letter*, no. 184 (Feb. 1977).
[32] *Neue Züricher Zeitung*, 29 Sep. 1977.
[33] Hornsby, M., reporting from the exercise in 1984 'Thunder Chariot', in *The Times*, 14 Sep. 1984: 'Pretoria shows off its military might in Northern Cape'.
[34] *Argus*, 21 May, 1984.
[35] *Milavnews News Letter*, no. 286, Aug. 1985.
[36] Ibid.
[37] *Paratus*, Aug. 1986, p. 4.
[38] 'Botha challenges sanctions with jet fighter' by Bernard Simon in Johannesburg, *Financial Times* (UK), 17 July 1986.
[39] Daly, M., 'South Africa's Cheetah', *Jane's Defence Weekly*, 26 July 1986, p. 92; and *Milavnews News Letter*, no. 298 (Aug. 1986), p. 21.
[40] Daly (note 39).
[41] The canard modification, in summary, adds more life to the Mirage-3 and less drag than the canardless delta configuration. The improved yaw stability permits a higher angle-of-attack. Overall manoeuvrability at low speed is much improved. See for example 'Canard Mirage on test', *Flight International*, 14 Dec. 1985, p. 38.
[42] Daly (note 39).
[43] *Flight International*, 16 Aug. 1986, p. 18.
[44] *Flight International*, 2 Mar. 1985, p. 8.
[45] *The Military Balance 1985/86* (IISS: London, 1986).
[46] *International Helicopter Magazine*, vol. 7, 1983, p. 23.
[47] *African Defence*, Oct. 1983, p. 33.
[48] Mr P. Myburgh, quoted in *Argus*, 21 May 1984.
[49] *International Defense Review*, Oct. 1984, p. 1567.
[50] *Jane's Defence Weekly*, 13 July 1985.
[51] *Le Quotidien*, Paris, 5 Nov. 1985.
[52] *Flight International*, 15 Mar. 1986, p. 2.
[53] *Defence*, Apr. 1986, p. 169.
[54] *Milavnews News Letter*, no. 294 (Apr. 1986).
[55] *Paratus*, Apr. 1986; *Defence*, Apr. 1986.
[56] *Flight International*, 22 Mar. 1986, p. 11.
[57] Lambert, M., 'The second world of armaments—Chile and South Africa at FIDA 86', *Interavia*, May 1986, p. 493.
[58] *Paratus*, Apr. 1986.

[59] *Flight International*, 19 June 1975; *Jane's All the World's Aircraft 1975/76*.
[60] *Jane's Defence Weekly*, 22 Mar. 1986, p. 515.
[61] *Aviation Week & Space Technology*, 15 Nov. 1971, p. 13.
[62] *Jane's Defence Weekly*, 26 Apr. 1986, p. 769.
[63] *Jeune Afrique*, no. 515 (17 Nov. 1970), p. 27.
[64] Adams, J., *The Unnatural Alliance—Israel and South Africa* (Quartet Books: London, 1984), p. 112.

Chapter 6. The armoured vehicle industry

I. Introduction

It is generally agreed by the South African authorities and outside observers that the South African armed forces need, above all, armoured vehicles and infantry weapons. The armoured vehicle industry has over the years come to represent the show-piece of South Africa's military production. Involving less complicated and more easily acquired and mastered technology than aircraft, the South Africans have been able to produce and develop a variety of vehicles for Army needs, making optimal use of foreign motor industry technology.

As in the other sectors of the defence industry, responsibility for R&D of various types of army equipment is given to different institutions. One such institution is the School of Armours at Bloemfontein, which has had R&D tasks for armour equipment since 1966. That year the school was separated from the School of Artillery and Armour.[1]

The armoured vehicle industry has been able to draw heavily on foreign technology. It has been easier to import vehicles from Europe as 'civilian' goods, and engines and electronic components continued to be imported after the 1963 and 1977 embargoes.[2] It is illustrative that by 1980, before the pullout of foreign companies had begun, the South African auto industry consisted of the following eight manufacturers: Ford and General Motors (USA), which were both suppliers to the SAP and the SADF and had been operating in South Africa since 1924 and 1926 respectively; Chrysler (USA); Toyota and Datsun-Nissan (Japan); British Leyland (UK); Volkswagen (FRG); and Alfa Romeo (Italy).

In 1983, Chrysler sold out to the Anglo-American-owned Sigma Motors, and in 1985 Ford merged its plant with Sigma Motors and reduced its stake to 40 per cent. General Motors and British Leyland have also handed over to South African ownership.

The list of military projects include the Eland armoured car, which began to be produced in 1966 (French licence); the Ratel armoured car of 1976 (West German technology); the Olifant upgraded tank of 1982 (UK Centurion); the much-publicized G-5 and G-6 self-propelled howitzer of 1982 and 1985 (incorporating technology from the US, Canada, Belgium and Sweden); and the mobile Valkiri 127-mm artillery rocket of 1980, modelled on the Soviet BM-21 system, first captured in Angola.

Before Rhodesia became independent in 1980, the South African Army intervened and participated for several years in the civil war between the forces of the Ian Smith regime and the national liberation forces. The Rhodesian experience greatly served the South African Army in the development and production of an entire series of unconventional vehicles, in addition to the major projects above. Most of these are high, wheeled vehicles with a V-shaped chassis designed for crew protection against anti-tank mines. These include the Buffel, Hippo, and Casspir armoured transport cars, the transport vehicle for the Army's Cactus SAM system and the South African Military (Samil) series of military truck/transport vehicles.

The Hippo was designed and from 1976 produced jointly with the Rhodesian arms industry.[3] The Rhodesians were reported to have designed and produced a wide variety of such specialized vehicles, while the South African Army concentrated on a few basic types, which are turned out in large numbers.

The Casspir armoured transport car led to the development of several derivatives: the Gemsbok mountain armoured car, the Bosbok transporter and the Duiker water tanker.

The Hippo was succeeded by a further development designated the Zebra transporter. For the further acquisition of more sophisticated armoured cars, the 1975 'Operation Savannah', the first invasion into Angola, became decisive. There, the South African artillery of World War II vintage met with Soviet tanks, armoured cars and long-range artillery. Subsequently, the Olifant tank, the Ratel long-range infantry combat vehicle, the Valkiri mobile rocket launcher, and the G-5 and G-6 self-propelled howitzers were developed.

II. Armoured cars

The Eland programme

In 1961, South Africa acquired a number of Panhard 245 AML-90 and AML-60 armoured cars from the French surplus inventory after the war in Algeria, offered by France on the international market. This armoured car had been designed during that war specifically for use against guerrilla forces. The AML-90 is armed with a 90-mm gun, and the AML-60 with a 60-mm mortar. Up to then, the South African Army had exclusively used British Saracen armoured cars, supplied in large numbers in 1956–60. But South Africa needed a much larger supply for COIN duties. The French armoured car was tempting because it was immediately available, considering the general political background in South Africa in 1961.

In 1963 the AML was selected for licensed production partly because it was believed to be better suited to the South African terrain and to COIN tasks, and partly because any licensed production of British armoured cars was out of the question by this time. But it was quickly found that local adaptations were necessary. South Africa had no previous experience of such production, and therefore the Government asked for tenders from private industry. Eventually, Sandock-Austral, which was producing mine equipment and pumps, was given the task of producing an improved version of the Panhard. The licence covered the armaments but not the engine. The car went into production in 1966, and was in 1970 designated Eland.

Private commercial interests seem to have played a great part in setting up the assembly line for the Eland. This involved West German assistance in return for a higher import quota for West German civilian cars to South Africa, in agreement with the French motor industry.[4] France avoided publicity at the time, and FR Germany obtained the military truck market in South Africa. In South Africa, Eland was produced with three interchangeable turrets; one 90-mm version, one 60-mm gun version and one 60-mm mortar version. All three are, in addition, armed with 7.62-mm machineguns. The maximum speed is 100 km/hour with a road range of 600 km or 15 hours in cross-country use.

In 1970, series production was announced of what was already designated as Eland-6, indicating the speed of local upgrading and adaptation undertaken on this vehicle. In 1972 a version of Eland with a local engine was on the drawing board. There is controversy about this engine—one source claims it originated in the USA.[5] Other modifications were also found necessary, since the original Panhard 245 was very useful in desert terrain but less so in the South African bushland. Larger wheels were constructed, driver mobility was enhanced, the turret was changed and the French 90-mm cannon was replaced by a South African-made cannon of the same calibre. No further details have been announced.

The information on indigenization differs, but it seems reasonable to assume that it has reached a high level. Some early difficulties with local production were reported. For example, the first 56 armoured cars were not accepted by the Army but were returned to the factory and completely disassembled, improved and tested again. By 1967 as much as 86 per cent of the Eland was manufactured in South Africa, the main part of the balance obviously being the imported engine. The Defence White Paper of 1973 claimed that the Eland was almost 100 per cent South African-made. In 1979, it was reported that 98 per cent of Eland contents were locally made.[6]

The type Eland Mark 7 has been reported in use in Namibia and Angola. A total of 1600 were built under licence, and there is reason to assume that the post-1977 production proceeded without further co-operation with French industry (based on the earlier-quoted statement by F. J. Bell that the 1977 embargo cancelled all existing licences for arms production). By 1983, the production of Eland had been halted, and succeeded by the Ratel type.[7] That production has stopped is also indicated by the fact that Eland was *not* among the equipment offered for export by Armscor in 1982. Eland was used in the first major operation of the SADF, the invasion of Angola, in 1975. It remains in full use, a new task being to escort the Valkiri rocket launchers.

A special armoured plate industry was also set up, and numerous sub-contractors were engaged in components and parts manufacture. Once this broad foundation for an armoured vehicle industry was established, further developments could be started.

The Ratel programme

While the Eland series was kept in production for 17 years, until its basic technology must have become quite dated in spite of local upgrading, Sandock-Austral was able to put a new infantry combat vehicle into production—the Ratel—in 1975. The Ratel was developed as the successor to the British Saracen ACs. It is a 6×6 wheeled vehicle, which incorporates some features from the Eland, notably the three interchangeable turrets with 90-mm guns, 60-mm mortars and French 20-mm guns. Its crew consists of a commander, a gunner, a driver and six infantrymen.

It is powered by a six-cylinder diesel engine, probably of South African manufacture, and has a road speed of 105 km/hour and a range of 14 hours cross-country. The tyres are produced in South Africa under licence from Polyair, Austria. They are shell proof and can be made napalm proof and also be driven for a period without air. It is unclear if the Ratel is armed with the earlier French-supplied Entac anti-tank missile. On the whole, few details have been publicly given about this vehicle. In 1985 it was reported that a long-range beam-riding anti-tank missile was in use with the Ratel.

Production began in 1976, and the designation was Ratel-20 infantry combat vehicle (ICV). During Operation Daisy in October 1981, Ratels penetrated more than 350 km into Angola in an offensive on a SWAPO command post.

A new logistic support version of Ratel was displayed as a prototype at the Piraeus arms exhibition in Greece in 1982. It was shown in South Africa for the first time in a demonstration for journalists in 1983, and production units participated in a military parade in Pretoria in 1984. The Log Ratel is 8×8 wheeled, mine-protected, and carries supplies for 14 days for one mechanized infantry unit. Its speed is 100 km/hour and it is developed for special cross-country ability. This version is powered by a V12 air-cooled diesel engine, presumably also made in South Africa. In 1985 a prototype was completed of a new version, the Ratel 81-mm mortar carrier.

Ratel is generally presented as the first South African-designed combat vehicle and as wholly indigenous. But, in fact, Ratel was developed in South Africa from a prototype designed by the West German company Büssing, later incorporated into the MAN (Maschinen Fabrik Augsburg-Nürnberg) concern. Büssing sold the same study to Belgium, where it was developed as the SIBMAS ICV. Thus, the basic similarity which has been observed between the South African and Belgian products is explained by their common origin.[8]

Armscor executive manager F. J. Bell has stated that Ratel is 90 per cent South African made. The origins of the 10 per cent imported contents are still unknown.[9]

AC-100 and AC-200

First reports of these two-wheeled armoured vehicles, based on the Ratel but representing extensive redesign, appeared in 1985. They were officially announced by Sandock-Austral in 1986.

The AC-100 was developed to form the basis for a complete family in both 4×4 and 6×6 configuration, with turrets similar to those installed on the Ratel—that is, for a 12.7-mm machinegun, 20-mm cannon, 60-mm mortar and 90-mm gun. In addition, a new turret was added, armed with a rapid fire 76-mm cannon and a 7.62-mm machinegun.

The AC-200 is a 6×6 mine-protected armoured support vehicle, at prototype stage in 1986. The programme included the development of a complete family of 4×4, 6×6 and 8×8 vehicles for logistics, recovery and technical support; armoured troop transport, ambulance and command post vehicles. Both the AC-100 and AC-200 are powered by V8 turbo-charged diesel engines. It was demonstrated that, wherever possible, proven—commercially available—components, such as the engine, transmission and axles have been used to keep life-cycle and procurement costs at a minimum. Apart from that, commercially available motor industry components include a considerable input of foreign technology, available from foreign subsidiaries operating in South Africa or directly imported—and outside any embargo lists.[10]

The Ingwe security vehicle, 1986

The Ingwe mine-proof 4×4 security vehicle was designed for both civil and military roles, primarily for private use in South Africa's border areas. Development was prompted by the laying of landmines by guerrillas. The Ingwe was also announced in 1986, by Sandock-Austral.

It is unclear if the Ingwe is identical to another new mine-proof armoured personnel carrier by Sandock-Austral, reported to be developed for export purposes and named as the Soetdoring troop transport vehicle (14 troops).[11]

III. Tanks

The Olifant main battle tank

To date, no new heavy or light tank has been designed in South Africa. As is the case with fighter aircraft and helicopters, this task has proved too demanding for all the new arms producers. Still, the main heavy equipment of any army is its tank force. South African authorities have kept referring to tank production in a series of premature statements over the years. For example, former Defence Minister P. W. Botha (in a defence debate in 1974), announced that construction of tanks would soon begin. At one time there were widespread reports that a French AMX tank was to be licence-produced, but this did not occur.

The first effort to develop an indigenous South African tank—the Semel—was stopped due to the international arms boycott. Apparently, two versions of the Semel were attempted, bearing the description of Semel-1 and Semel-2.

The confrontation with Soviet-supplied tanks in Angola further urged the South Africans to find another solution to its tank replacement problem. The solution was extensive upgrading of the Centurion-5 tank in service in South Africa since 1955, as in the case of the upgraded and redesigned Mirage. In 1982 the result, Olifant-1, was shown to military correspondents at the Temple military base. It had been so modified that it was described merely as bearing a relationship to the British Centurion Mark 13.[12]

The history of the maintenance of the ageing Centurion tank force includes the clandestine import of new engines and parts from the UK via Jersey, as well as the purchase through private agents of 41 second-hand Centurion-5s from Jordan in 1974, and 90 tanks of the same type in near-scrap condition from India in 1977. In 1978, Israel agreed to modernize 150 of the South African Centurions. The latter deal involved a Norwegian shipping company and led to a trial in Norway. The Army research centre was responsible for the Olifant programme. A recent study revealed that Defence Minister Botha himself initiated the Centurion upgrading, having failed to obtain any new licences from abroad.[13]

Two prototypes of Olifant were presented before the production model finally appeared in 1982. By 1983 it was said that South Africa possessed 250 Olifant tanks, which were being kept in reserve in case of a conventional attack on the Republic.[14] The number is not unreasonable—168 Centurions were delivered between 1955 and 1959 from the UK, and the total acquired second hand was 131, which makes an overall total of 299.

The 56-tonne Olifant-1 has been adapted to South African conditions and based to some extent on Israeli modifications to the same Centurion type.[15] In 1982, the Chief of the SADF, Gen. K. Viljoen, disclosed that when South Africa went into Angola in October 1975 to fight the Angolan Government's MPLA troops, a small force of modified Centurions was kept in reserve at Ruacana. This tank was still equipped with the outdated 84-mm guns.

The diesel engine used in the modified Centurions was apparently constructed around a Canadian model. It was revealed by the Canadian Broadcasting Corporation, CBC, in 1981, that the Canadian company Levy Auto Parts of Toronto had exported diesel engines to South Africa. The company rebuilds tank engines and transmissions for NATO use, and a former employee was quoted in the CBC report as saying that the engines were modified for South Africa in 1980. The engines were then broken down and labelled as truck parts for export.[16]

In the first biography of Prime Minister P. W. Botha, published in 1984, it is reported that the Indian Government was deliberately tricked into selling its 90 aged Centurions to South Africa in the belief that they were going to Mozambique. The tanks ended up at the Armscor workshop where they were stripped down to their chassis. Their old 86-mm guns were replaced by 105-mm guns linked to computerized sights, and the new South African-produced diesel engines were installed instead of the petrol engines. This resulted in increased range and performance. The metamorphosis resulted in a practically new tank: 'The Centurion does not recognize itself any more, it is now the Olifant,' says the biography.[17]

The history of the 105-mm gun goes back to 1971, when it was decided to replace the old British 20-pounder gun arming the Centurion tanks. The SADF wanted a more powerful 105-mm gun, which proved impossible to obtain because of the arms boycott. Local development was begun of an improved anti-tank projectile code-named the R2M2. In April 1976, an army order was placed for 4000 of the projectiles at a cost of R115 400. But the R2M2 project was finally cancelled in 1978 because the appearance of Soviet T-54 and T-55 tanks in Angola demanded a 105-mm gun. In 1977, in the words of Army Chief General K. Viljoen, 'the problem regarding the 105-mm gun was solved'. Official silence regarding South African designers and producers has fostered suspicion that the gun may have been produced from a foreign design, although there is no evidence that this is the case. However, the ammunition is being produced and offered for export, and the gun is arming the Olifant tank.[18]

The Olifant-1 has a top speed of 44 km/hour, an indigenous 12-cylinder diesel engine and a range of 200 km or 16 hours operating time. Olifant is not offered for export.

IV. Field artillery

Before 1975, the South African Army's towed field artillery and self-propelled weapons were all of World War II vintage. In Operation Savannah in Angola, the South Africans were outgunned. A mixed motorized column of South African and UNITA troops was approaching the major Angolan port of Moçamedes and was severed by the recently deployed so-called Stalin Organ (Red-eye) multiple rocket launcher fire, and Soviet field artillery. The only reinforcement the South Africans had was the aged British 25-pounder cannon locally known as the G-1, and the G-3 140-mm guns, also of British World War II design. This experience, which forced the South Africans to withdraw,[19] resulted in the development of the Valkiri rocket launcher and the G-5 and G-6 artillery pieces, which projects display two basic methods of absorbing foreign technology: imitation of captured weapons and investment abroad at the source of a foreign technology.

The Valkiri 127-mm MRL system

When the Valkiri multiple rocket launcher was introduced in 1980, foreign military experts immediately pointed out the similarity to both Taiwanese and Israeli projects.[20] Co-operation cannot be ruled out, but remains unconfirmed.

It is a fact that captured Soviet models have provided the inspiration to the military industries of South Africa and Israel. Independent construction based on these models is thus possible. But in view of the complexity of the Valkiri system it seems likely that some kind of industrial assistance came from Israel, if not from Taiwan. Taiwan is one of the few countries that throughout the period has kept cordial political and military contacts with South Africa.

In South Africa, the Valkiri is described as having 100 per cent local content.[21] Its origin is declared as being a Soviet BM-21 122-mm rocket launcher captured in Angola in 1976. Development work on Valkiri started in 1977. The R&D work was shared between Armscor, the South African Artillery and the missile-producing company Kentron. In 1980 Kentron was awarded the national prize of the Associated Scientific and Technical Societies of South Africa for the Valkiri development. The same year it was first displayed in a military parade, and series production started.

Valkiri fires an unguided rocket mounted on a Unimog truck platform. Each launch vehicle has three rows of eight rockets, equivalent to 24 rounds: the pre-fragmented warhead has a range of 22 km, considerably greater than the Stalin Organ.

Valkiri was presented as available for export at the Piraeus arms exhibition in 1982, where it was explained that it was intended to supplement the G-5 howitzer in the field and that it was a highly mobile system. On the road, the Valkiri looks like a normal light truck, since the launchers are lying on a flat bed. That bed is elevated when the system is being used, and contains 24 launcher tubes with one rocket in each. A single warhead's lethal area is 1500 m^2. Four men load the 24 rockets in 10 minutes, and the firing is one rocket per second. The normal resupply vehicle is a Samil-100 truck.

In his announcement introducing the Valkiri to the SADF arsenal, Prime Minister P. W. Botha—then still also Minister of Defence—praised the sophisticated technology incorporated into this weapon: the project team was confronted with the ballistic problems of launching a self-propelled rocket, not a dormant projectile. But this technology was not invented by South Africa— the fuse for Valkiri is powered by an internal wind turbine generator, developed for Armscor by the company Fuchs. Fuchs was initially the South African subsidiary of the French electronics firm Thomson-CSF.[22]

The G-5 towed self-propelled field howitzer

The G-5 towed field artillery piece and its derivative, the G-6, are the most publicized projects in the history of South Africa's arms industry to date. As was the case with the Valkiri, the project resulted from the first Angolan war, and the G-5 was, like the Valkiri and the Olifant, first displayed in the 1980 military parade.[23] It is the result of a clandestine technology acquisition with ingredients that would seem at home in the world of fiction, as is often the case with smuggling affairs (see figure 6.1).

The G-5 and G-6 are presented by South African industry and Western technical publications alike as one of the most modern (that is, lethal) artillery pieces in the world, unequalled by any current artillery in the NATO or Soviet inventories. It is also presented as designed and developed in South Africa. Armscor Chairman P. G. Marais said, for example, that the G-5 was a '100% South African produced system'.[24] It is *produced* locally, but the system draws heavily upon US, Belgian and Swedish design.

The acquisition of the basic technology needed for this field artillery was uncovered in 1977, by accident, and revealed by a BBC television team. As the story was subsequently unwrapped it came to involve a CIA agent, Israeli industrialists, the Belgian PRB (Poudreries Réunis de Belgique) munitions company and Mr G. Bull, head of the US-owned Space Research Corporation (SRC) in Canada and designer of the 155-mm field howitzer. In addition, the G-5 incorporates the Swedish-invented 'base-bleed' technology, sold by Bofors to the PRB of Belgium, which enables the increased range of the howitzer. Israel had acquired the SRC-designed field howitzers in 1972 and used them in the Yom Kippur war in 1973. Armscor first approached the Israelis, then through a CIA agent made contact with the SRC company in Quebec. Israeli Military Industries (IMI) was sub-contracted by SRC to supply Armscor with the propellant for the shells, which would be filled in Israel and then shipped to South Africa. Israel eventually pulled out of the affair, however. The South Africans managed instead to obtain all the necessary technology.

After a US Customs and Senate investigation in 1978, the Canadian branch of Space Research Corporation-Quebec (SRC-Q) was fined for breaking the embargo against South Africa. But by the time SRC-Q pleaded guilty to the smuggling of 33 000 howitzers, shells and howitzer parts to South Africa, the equipment was already there, and work on the development of the G-5 had begun. The transfer of military technology, although punished according to the law, was a *fait accompli*.

The G-5 is rather an extensive redesign and further development of the Space Research Corporation's GC-45 field howitzer. The GC-45 was designed and developed between 1975 and 1977 by the SRC in Canada, but its range was only 30 km. The Austrian company Voest-Alpine acquired the production licence for the GC-45, which then became the GHN-45. The South African G-5 also closely resembles the Austrian howitzer (now being exported in large numbers to Far East customers); and it resembles the Israeli M-68 howitzer and the Swedish FH-77. This resemblance is no coincidence, since all these models were built around—and draw upon—the same technological principles and innovation, in particular, the so-called base-bleed technology.[25]

After having found the company and the designer willing and capable of accomplishing a field howitzer design that answered to South African specifications, Armscor secured future access to SRC-Q co-operation by acquiring 20 per cent of the shares in the company's holdings. This is one of the most effective means to circumvent embargo restrictions, and there are a few other

90

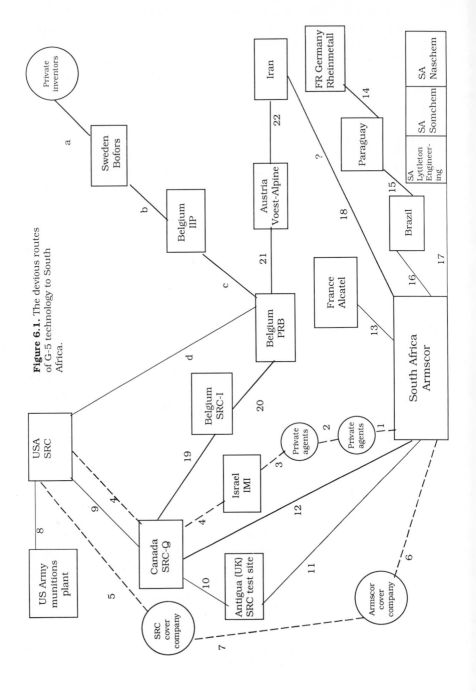

Figure 6.1. The devious routes of G-5 technology to South Africa.

Key:

a–d — Origins of G-5 technology: ERFB technology invented by Dr Bull is combined with base-bleed technology, patented in Sweden in 1969 and sold to SRC, USA, via Bofors, Sweden, and IIP and PRB, Belgium.

1–4 — In 1975 an Armscor request for a long-range howitzer is refused by the US State Department, whereupon a local CIA station puts Armscor in contact with Dr Bull, inventor of ERFB technology and owner of SR. The contacts are made via private arms dealers and Israeli IMI, which has previously imported ERFB ammunition.

5 — In preparation for the export of G-5 technology, Dr Bull sets up a cover company, Paragon Holdings, Barbados, and CTI, Canada.

6 — South Africa sets up a cover company, Colet Trading, Lichtenstein, and buys Space Capital, Netherlands.

7 — The G-5 deal is signed between Paragon Holdings and Colet Trading. Space Capital handles the Armscor purchase of 20% in SRC-Q plus patent rights for the G-5. CTI is an intermediary in the sale.

8 — The US Army munitions plant manufactures steel forgings for Space Research.

9 — Steel forgings are exported to SRC-Q, Canada, where they are manufactured into shells for the G-5.

10 — Shells are exported to Antigua for testing (with official destination Israel).

11 — Shells are exported further to South Africa on West German ships, with official destination Spain.

12 — Export of howitzer parts and other equipment. Cementation Engineering, Cape Town (UK Trafalgar Square Group) poses as the official buyer and the goods are labelled 'construction equipment'.

13 — Import from France of special lathes for G-5 production.

14–16 — Import from the FRG of a production line for shell filling, smuggled via Paraguay and Brazil.

17 — Production of G-5 howitzer starts at Armscor subsidiaries, 1979.

18 — Unconfirmed report of export of G-5 howitzer to Iran.

19–22 — Alternative route of G-5 technology to Iran: ERFB-BB technology is sold to Austria, which exports ERFB howitzer to Iran via Jordan.

Abbreviations:

BB: Base bleed (technology which increases the range of artillery).
ERFB: Extended-range full bore ammunition.
CTI: Canadian Technical Institute.
IIP: Industrial International Production.
IMI: Israeli Military Industries.
PRB: Poudreries Réunis de Belgique.
SRC: Space Research Corporation.
SRC-Q: Space Research Corporation—Quebec.
SRC-I: Space Research Corporation International (set up in Brussels to market the 155mm ERFB-BB howitzer).

such cases that have been revealed (for example South African participation in the French Exocet and Crotale missile programmes).

The G-5 155-mm gun has, thanks to the base-bleed ammunition technology, an unequalled range of over 40 km. It uses a 75 hp Magirus-Deutz-based power pack, produced in South Africa by the subsidiary to this West German truck company, which is used to move the gun into position, and to move the firing platform. The gun is towed by a heavy truck. The cannon itself is mounted on a six-wheeled carrier. It weighs 13.5 tonnes. Other South African features include a revised muzzle break, improved recoil mechanism, revised shot-seating arrangement, improved cradle with stronger dynamic balance arrangements, new firing-platform raising systems instead of the original telescopic system and strengthened trail legs. The G-5 has a crew of five to eight soldiers.

As part of its new export drive, Armscor in June 1982 showed the G-5 for the first time in South Africa, giving detailed performance specifications to military journalists. The cost of the development remains secret, however. The slow rate of introduction of the G-5 into Army use, as well as the slow development rate of the G-5, do indeed seem to reflect difficulties in getting enough export orders. The UN embargo of 1984 on *imports* of South African-made weaponry has probably aggravated the financial problems of these projects.

Several details of the G-5 production have been revealed. The first step is special steel tube fabrication by Iscor. Iscor became involved in product development in 1978. Its tasks include the initial sinking of the bore, external profiling, heat treatment, and stress relieving of G-5 barrels. The tube is then moved to a Pretoria factory for electronic testing. It also undergoes a deep-hole burning process in which the hole is drilled through the barrel. Security is tight, and only a few selected employees are allowed in this part of the factory.[26] The gun is then sent to Lyttleton Engineering Works (LEW) for final assembly. LEW completes machining of the bore and chamber. Production barrels are made from locally-produced refined steel.

Two G-5s were tested in the desert near Walvis Bay in Namibia for the first time in 1982, and the howitzer has since gone into production. By 1984, 40 were deployed with the South African Army.[27] In the absence of any official information on total requirement and deliveries, it appears that a total of almost 400 G-5 systems is needed.[28] The G-5 is to provide the main core of the South African Artillery Field Branch, and is presented by South African military sources as able to preserve its superiority over any enemy artillery until the year 2000. The performance of the G-5, and its follow-on G-6, led Defence Minister Malan to exclaim: 'With what we have we could go straight through to Cairo.'[29]

As to the alleged *nuclear* capability of the G-5 artillery, there may be some substance to the early statements by South African authorities. Armscor Chairman P. G. Marais, when the G-5 was publicly announced in 1982, said that 'South Africa has developed a "super-weapon" capable of carrying nuclear warheads'.[30] Two days later he denied this in a statement dismissing

US allegations that the G-5 was developed to fire nuclear warheads. P. G. Marais also said that Armscor had not received any request from the SADF to develop a gun with nuclear capacity.

However, the G-5 and the G-6 may in fact be capable as nuclear delivery systems, and this capacity is often claimed in Western technical literature. In fact, as early as 1980, *Newsweek* reported that 'South Africa has acquired one of the world's most deadly artillery systems—a 155 mm cannon capable of firing "nuclear bullets" that pack a 3-kiloton payload'.[31]

The existence of a nuclear shell for the G-5 remains unconfirmed. But in autumn 1987, reports appeared in the South African press of a new and effective use of this gun/howitzer in Angola as a substitute for bombing from the air.[32] The SADF uses the highly mobile G-5 artillery mainly to give fire support to the infantry and thus allows for economizing in the case of the Mirage fleet, armoured vehicles and infantry troops.

The G-6 Rhino wheeled self-propelled field howitzer

While the G-5 was developed to meet the South African Army's need for a long-range fire support weapon, the need for another highly-mobile weapon of the same type remained. Development of the wheeled G-6 was begun in the early 1980s, and this type was first shown in video and model form at the Piraeus arms exhibition in 1982.

Some SRC technological assistance was reported in the early stages of this project, including supply of a 6×6 wheeled Canadian cross-country logging vehicle. This was subsequently replaced by the South African Ratel chassis, upon which the G-5 ordnance was basically mounted. By 1983, two prototypes and two pre-series G-6s had been built and full series production was expected to begin in 1986.[33] It was reported to be in use with the Army in 1984.[34]

The R&D cost of the G-6 has been quoted as US $20 million. The superior performance claimed for this field artillery is firstly based on the fact that it is wheeled, not tracked, which previously was the rule for this type of artillery.[35] It has considerable mobility and is particularly useful in South African roadless terrain or in the so-called Operational Area, be it Namibia, Angola, Botswana, Lesotho or Mozambique. The total weight of the G-6 is 35 tonnes; its road speed is 90 km/hour, its cross-country speed is 35 km/hour and the range of action is 400–600 km. If so required it can also knock down trees and huts. It carries 44 shells and 50 charges in its racks.

As in the case of the G-5, Western sources keep stating that the G-6 can fire nuclear warheads.[36] The G-6 was presented to the press on 11 September 1982, at the Armscor vehicle testing grounds near Pretoria. When P. G. Marais was asked whether the G-6 would be equipped to fire nuclear projectiles, he replied that the United States had already developed a nuclear warhead round that could be fired by 155-mm guns. 'If necessary,' he said, 'the G-6 would also be given this capacity'.[37] But he stated that this was not its primary purpose, nor was it at present South African Government policy. He declared on the same occasion that South Africa had received no outside assistance in the development of the G-6 programme.

Among the South African innovations is a wedge-shaped nose assembly in front of the driver, used to clear bush as the G-6 proceeds across country. There were several early reports in 1982 to the effect that the G-6 was in fact *not* designed for South African use but rather intended for export.[38] But most later reports state that the G-6 was very thoroughly devised for South African Army needs for a long-distance intervention weapon.

In fact, the SRC-Q intended its original howitzer design for export to NATO. This was effectively stopped by the company's co-operation with South Africa.

Various reports criticize NATO's unwillingness to purchase the SRC-Q/Armscor/PRB technology:

A redirection on development of NATO artillery appears to be urgent. Already heavily committed to their own programmes (the M-198 for the USA, the FH-70 for UK, the FR Germany and Italy) the NATO countries have so far paid little or no attention to the very promising technologies pioneered by SRC-Q and developed by Armscor, PRB and Voest-Alpine. However, it appears very doubtful that this situation could, or should continue. The ERFB range of ammunition can be fired by other current Western 155mm gun/howitzers, but performs best when fired by long-barreled weapons of the GC-45 category.[39]

SRC-Q attempted a major international marketing activity for its new howitzer and several measures were taken to hide the South African involvement. In 1983 it was still being mentioned that prospects for export of the G-6 from South Africa might include licensed production in Israel, and licensed production in some Benelux countries for sale to Arab customers. One G-6 piece had reportedly been shipped to Europe. However, with the 1984 UN embargo on all arms imports *from* South Africa, it seemed that all chances that Armscor would manage to sell its G-6 to NATO were over. Rather, the majority of the world's arms developers find themselves following in the wake of Armscor's G-5, but with their own designs. Scattered reports that negotiations took place with *China* for sale of the G-6 or the G-5 also lack credibility.

Little is known about the foreign contents of the G-6, except that the prototypes built in 1982 contained a 'certain amount' of foreign-made components, which had been purchased through normal commercial channels; it was not classified as military equipment and hence not subject to the embargo. It was planned to replace as many of these components as possible with South African-made items for the series production of G-6.[40] One of these components may well be the power-plant, an air-cooled turbo-charged diesel engine, perhaps a Teledyne or a Deutz model. Armscor has not presented any details about the engine, which it would be expected to do if it had been of South African manufacture.

From 1983, Armscor started development of an ammunition carrier, based on the same chassis as the G-6. Later information on the G-6 has been scarce and the first ambitious plans seem to have been cut down to the more modest goal of supplying only the single armoured division of the South African Army. Neither series production nor actual deployment have so far been confirmed. In March 1988, the computerized G-6 artillery system was displayed again at the FIDA show in Chile.

G-5 and G-6 ammunition

Armscor has invested heavily in the establishment of new ammunition factories to ensure supply. The foundation was laid by the acquisition of an entire plant for the filling of shells from Rheinmetall in FR Germany, in a clandestine shipment via Paraguay and Brazil. The West German company was subsequently brought to trial for this sale. At the Naschem plant at Potchefstroom the 155-mm and 140-mm shells are being filled at an estimated rate of 80–100 rounds per hour. Naschem devoted over four years' work to the development of a process-control system, and the plant operates according to what is termed an upgraded NATO specification.[41]

Naschem is also engaged in the development of a white phosphorous round for the G-5, but responsibility for filling the other standard ammunition needs rests with Swartklip Products. Swartklip was due in April 1985 to start series production of a red phosphorous round.

Yet another company is involved in ammunition critical to the G-5— Somchem, which maintains two explosives and propellant manufacturing plants and a dynamic test facility in the Cape Province. The company is the principal contractor for the current six-zone propellant system. Somchem stated that its charge production capacity in 1985 ran at an annual 250 000, covering 140-mm and 155-mm requirements. Manufacture of charges for the G-5 began in 1980, and base-bleed unit deliveries began in 1981.[42] In this context, it is worth pointing out that no information has as yet appeared anywhere referring to possible production of *nuclear* ammunition.

V. Army trucks and specialized versions

In addition to the above-presented armoured vehicles and artillery, South Africa has managed to build up large military truck and transporter production. For army purposes, these vehicles are essential to provide logistics for armoured and other mechanized operations. After the first UN embargo in 1963, the SADF immediately initiated a survey of the current military vehicle position. It was found that at the time the SADF had over 200 types of military vehicles in service, many rather old and due for replacement. The recommendation of this survey was that the SADF required basically three new trucks, with load capacities of two, five and ten tonnes. From this base all the special purpose variants were to be developed.

The Military Vehicle Division of Armscor, formed in 1964, procured some 20 different types of truck, from Europe mostly, for testing. This first effort showed that no single model fully answered to the South African requirements. A second conclusion was that some form of standardized testing was needed, and this led to the design, development and construction of the large Armscor testing track and facilities at Elandsfontein, Pretoria. The complex cost R60 million.

South Africa then created new import rules to ensure local production participation and concluded licence agreements with Magirus-Deutz (later the Magirus Iveco/Fiat consortium) and Daimler-Benz of FR Germany. Magirus-Deutz established a local subsidiary in South Africa, where assembly of imported truck chassis took place.[43]

It was feared that the situation created by the embargo would lead to difficulties in the future, and the conclusion was, firstly, that the number of new types had to be drastically reduced and, secondly, that they had to be manu-factured in South Africa. The latter was also a security demand in the light of the worsening political situation—the need for counter-insurgency and special vehicles equipped to better suit the South African terrain was considered urgent. Daimler-Benz has sold 2500 Unimog trucks to South Africa since 1978, classified as intended 'for non-military use'. This type has become standard in the South African Army, shown in military parades equipped with multiple rocket launchers.

From 1970, Magirus-Deutz has delivered ostensibly civilian trucks to South Africa. The West German company delivered 5000 LKW chassis without engines to its subsidiary in South Africa. In 1978 when the UN embargo came into force in Europe, this firm was purchased by South Africa, and renamed Truckmakers Inc. The production of vehicles continued, with imported West German components.[44] One estimate was that by 1985, the South African Army possessed a total of 6000 Unimog trucks and 10 000 Magirus-Deutz trucks.[45]

Samil trucks

Three new trucks have been produced by Truckmakers: the Samil-20, Samil-50 and Samil-100. These trucks are of Magirus-Deutz and Unimog origins.

From 1981 a Mark-2 version of the first two types began to be produced, claimed to be 90 per cent indigenous.[46] The redevelopment was done with the aim of increasing local content. Specifically mentioned is the incorporation of the South African manufactured ADE water-cooled engine, allowing for the assumption that the pre-1981 engines were Deutz-designed. Work was under-way in 1985 to produce similar improvements to the Samil-100. In addition to the locally developed engine, the Samils have locally-built axles and gearboxes.

By 1983, well over 11 000 Samil trucks had been turned out, and they continue to be developed for export customers. In fact, the Samil first became known when it was presented for export at the Piraeus 1982 exhibition. The reviewers of Samil in Western technical literature on this occasion appeared as delighted as Armscor at the composition and performance of these vehicles:

> The SAMIL truck range is without doubt the successful outcome of a long chain of operational experience and expertise. The vehicles involved have all been system engineered to meet the very demanding requirements of the South Africa Defense Forces, down to the last detail. The SAMIL range is now 'combat proven' and in that process has proved to be extremely reliable, efficient and tough . . . *Political considerations apart*, the South Africans can be sure of markets for the SAMIL range. It would be nice to think that some SAMIL vehicles will end up in the workshops of Europe and elsewhere.[47]

The same source consistently presents enthusiastic market forecasts for South African weapons, disregarding *political* obstacles to such sales. For example, it stated: 'All Samil trucks have been produced to meet the exacting conditions prevalent in South Africa and that factor alone should make the MK-II Samils attractive to many other nations'.[48] (This eulogy on 'rugged trucks' from South Africa was composed in 1983. The next year, 1984, saw the UN embargo on imports of military equipment from South Africa, and the year after, 1985, saw an increasing campaign to boycott the import of any goods from South Africa.)

From the basic Samil types more than 70 variants have been developed and deployed with the Army, Air Force and Navy. Of these variations, the armoured personnel carrier derivatives have received most attention, for example the Buffel, based on a much-modified Unimog chassis, and the Bulldog, based on the Samil-20 chassis. These are mine-protected armoured personnel carriers used for general patrol. The Buffel is extensively used in the operational area.[49] They are often damaged by landmine explosions, and an elaborate repair network exists to resurrect all damaged cars. South African Army policy does not allow any Buffel to be written off. First, it is taken care of by the logistics support section of the 61 Base Workshop. The Army independently repairs the chassis, the engine and the gearbox. Then it is handed over to an SADF-commissioned firm, Off Highways Equipment Sales, who specialize in the repair of Buffels.

It is designed in such a way that all parts are replaceable. From the engine, chassis and below it consists of the original Unimog components. Its superstructure is locally designed and manufactured. One unique feature is the bullet-proof armour plating designed by Armscor. This plating cannot be wasted and is returned to the Army for reprocessing. There are reports that the formula for this new type of armour plate, said to be the finest today, was supplied by Israel, in return for steel from South Africa.[50]

Composite armours are among the widely advertised export .items of Armscor. In an interview, Armscor Chairman P. G. Marais stated that 'We have done a lot of development work on composite armours, and our own quality of ceramic tiles. They were developed here specially. We are moving away from traded vehicles'.[51]

Another APC is the Rhino troop carrier, also based on the Samil-20. There are several workshop trucks and container trucks, a recovery vehicle and a 10-tonne tanker based on the Samil-50, and a mine-resistant ambulance called Rinkhals. An artillery tractor based on the Samil-100 was constructed mainly for use with the G-5 155-mm howitzer.

In 1982, it was announced that a new truck called Sakom began production at Truckmakers for the military. The Sakom-50 10-tonne truck is a less sophisticated off-road type designed to the specifications of the SADF for long-range operations on the savannah. It is a 4×2 wheeled derivate of the Samil-50, of which it uses many parts. Also in 1982, Truckmakers announced a commercial range of lorries based on the military Samil design.[52]

To match the Samil trucks, about 80 different trailers have been constructed for various purposes. Among these are specialized vehicles for transporting up to 10 war dogs, and units for the embalming and carrying of corpses.[53]

Magnis trucks

In 1972, Nissan Motor Company of Japan invested US $2 million in South Africa to construct an engine plant. The actual work was conducted by Nissan Capital's subsidiary in the USA.

When the local South African subsidiary was merged with Magirus-Deutz of South Africa, a new local military truck designer was created, blending West German and Japanese know-how. It was called Magnis—a contraction of Magirus and Nissan. This enterprise evolved against a background of official Japanese protests on all occasions when Japan was mentioned among suppliers of military equipment to the South African armed forces.

A new range of heavy military trucks, designed and developed in South Africa for the Army, was unveiled in 1984. The new trucks are produced by Magnis Heavy Travel Corporation of Rosslyn, Pretoria. This means that 'the SADF is no longer dependent on a West German built truck for what is arguably the most important utility vehicle in the force'.[54]

Military jeeps

It is known that the British Leyland Landrover was being licence-produced as late as 1973, but there are no figures on total numbers produced or deployed.[55] Leyland in 1976 invested £20 million in South Africa for Landrover production and continued to export spare parts and knock-down vehicles for assembly for a long time. South African-assembled jeeps of this type were exported to Portugal and used by the Portuguese colonial army in Guinea-Bissau and Angola.

The Trax vehicle was designed and built in South Africa, originally intended for civilian use, but suitable for the Army as a replacement for the Landrover jeep. Its speed is 160 km/hour. The Trax-370 uses a Chrysler engine and Chrysler gearbox, and the Trax-200 uses a Peugeot engine. These engines are licence-produced in South Africa by the Sigma Motor Corporation, owned by the Anglo-American Corporation and Chrysler. In 1980, Sigma took over the previously entirely foreign-owned subsidiaries of Leyland (South Africa) and Peugeot-Citroen (South Africa). The Trax is equipped with a Racal (UK) radio communications system. Trax Interstate itself is 90 per cent South African-owned. In 1978 it offered its vehicle for sale at R7400.[56] In 1979, 19 multi-purpose jeeps were delivered to the Swaziland Army.

VI. Engines

After the 1977 arms embargo, South African attention was directed to another strategic industry, namely diesel engine production, and a decision was taken to achieve a local capacity in this field as well. It was foreseen that future import of such engines was in jeopardy, although they could be labelled 'civilian' equipment. The clandestine acquisition of new engines for the transformation of the second-hand Centurion tanks from India into the Olifant confirms that such import was indeed no longer an easy task. The engines were supplied by a private company in Canada to the UK, and from the UK via Jersey, labelled 'tractor parts', to South Africa.

The Atlantis Diesel Engines Works

The engine technology was eventually secured from FR Germany and the UK through the purchase of a production licence from Daimler-Benz (FRG) and Perkins Diesel (UK) in 1978. Perkins Diesel is a technical consultancy company, and a subsidiary of Canada's Massey-Ferguson, which in turn has a large US ownership.

The Atlantis Diesel Engines (ADE) works could then be set up, at a cost of R350 million, as an Armscor subsidiary. The plant was financed by the IDC of South Africa and pilot production began in 1980. Equipment and know-how were supplied by Daimler-Benz and Perkins and capacity was planned at 50 000 diesel engines per year. Since then. Atlantis has controlled practically the entire local market for diesel engines and has built 21 different types. It is of high strategic importance for the South African vehicle industry. Further diesel engine imports have been discouraged by the introduction of customs duties of up to 40 per cent.[57] This attempt to achieve self-sufficiency by creating a monopoly brought considerable opposition from the motor industry, whose representatives were apparently less worried than the authorities about the prospect of an embargo. Due to the high production costs, the Atlantis plant, first intended only for military needs, was extended to produce engines also for commercial vehicles. It is estimated that all local ADE engines add 20 per cent to the retail price of cars and carriers.[58]

At the same time as the diesel engine project, another ambitious project was begun with the aim of making South Africa self-sufficient in gearboxes and axles by the mid-1980s. The gearbox-axle project was undertaken by General

Mining, which built a new plant in the Johannesburg area. The technology was acquired from the big West German gearbox manufacturer Zahnradfabriken.

In 1979, the US company Eaton Corporation also showed interest in this project (many of the South African trucks imported from Japan use a gearbox from Eaton). Hence, Eaton had discussions with the South African Economic Development Corporation about the sale of licensed production rights and the erection of a gear and axle plant to complement the Atlantis facility. But eventually, the West German company won the order. Local and foreign criticism of these investments concentrated on the economic effects of creating such a monopoly: 'This may be the most expensive way of getting a strategic industry', argued one truck manufacturer.[59]

The sole competitor to Atlantis is Deutz Dieselpower, originally a subsidiary of the West German company Magirus-Deutz. Deutz has also produced diesel engines since 1969.

Related industry

Among related industries, Anderson Generators in Johannesburg produces a wide range of motor industry equipment, including petrol engines. It began working in 1939, and presents itself in its advertisements as 'proud to be associated with the South African Defence Force'.[60] Another new development presented in 1985 was Armscor's Kriek motorcycle, used by the Army in the COIN operations in northern Namibia.

Notes and references

[1] *Paratus*, Oct. 1982, p. 7.
[2] There is a general import replacement drive in South Africa for the entire motor industry, including the civilian car industry. The local programme that came into force in January 1980 stipulated that local contents for *all* motor cars should reach 66% by weight: *Financial Times* (UK), 26 May 1981.
[3] The existence of such an industry was known but very few details have emerged even after the creation of independent Zimbabwe, except that the industry was wholly private: F. J. Bell in *Defence Today*, no. 89–90, 1985, p. 412.
[4] *Observer Magazine*, 1 Apr. 1973: the story was never confirmed.
[5] *Defense & Armament*, no. 24 (Nov. 1983), p. 50.
[6] *Truppendienst*, Mar. 1979, p. 275.
[7] *Defense & Armament*, no. 24 (Nov. 1983), p. 50.
[8] *Défense et Armements*, no. 32 (July–Aug. 1984), p. 43.
[9] *Paratus*, July 1983, p. 5.
[10] *Jane's Defence Weekly*, 26 Apr. 1986.
[11] *Pacific Defence Reporter*, Oct. 1985, p. 39.
[12] *Citizen*, (SA), 11 Sep. 1982.
[13] de Villiers, D., and de Villiers, J., *PW* (Biography of P. W. Botha), (Tafelberg: Cape Town, 1984), (in Afrikaans).
[14] *Defense & Armament*, no. 24 (Nov. 1983), p. 50.
[15] *Citizen*, 11 Sep. 1982.
[16] *Cape Times*, 2 Dec. 1981.
[17] de Villiers (note 13), p. 295.
[18] de Villiers (note 13).

[19] The many reports about South African weapon inferiority and other military problems, logistics, long support lines and so on, conflict with statements by the South African military that they 'could have gone all the way to Luanda'. At any rate, parallel with military problems, the political situation became impossible since the expected US aid or even intervention on UNITA's side did not come forth. In this way, both a political and a military technological shock was received by the SADF.

[20] *Jane's Weapon Systems 1982–83* (Macdonald: London, 1983), p. 377.

[21] *Paratus,* June 1982, p. 8.

[22] *Paratus,* June 1982, p. 9.

[23] This occurred on the occasion of P. W. Botha's handing over the Defence Minister post to SADF Chief General M. Malan.

[24] *Guardian,* 29 Mar. 1982.

[25] This particular base-bleed technology was patented by two engineers of the Swedish Defence Research Institute in 1969. International sales rights were then sold to the Swedish Company Bofors. Bofors in turn sold the international rights to the Belgian PRB company, with which a co-operation agreement had existed for several years. Formally, the sales rights were sold to PRB's marketing subsidiary, International Industrial Products. PRB in turn was co-operating with the Space Research Company in Quebec. See figure 6.1 for an illustration of the industrial network behind the new howitzer technology.

For Swedish use, the PRB-developed base-bleed projectile is being re-purchased by Bofors for adaptation to the FH-77B howitzer. This is one of many current illustrations of how the European arms producers co-operate to cut the escalating costs of R&D in the arms technology needed for the 1990s.

[26] *The Rand Daily Mail,* 23 Apr. 1982.

[27] *Military Balance 1984–85* (IISS: London, 1985).

[28] *Defence Attaché,* no. 1, 1985, p. 32.

[29] 'Outgunning the enemy till the year 2000', *Paratus,* Feb. 1982, p. 13.

[30] *Sunday Times* (SA), 27 Mar. 1982.

[31] 'The global race for nuclear arms' *Newsweek,* 15 Sep. 1980, p. 22.

[32] Steenkamp, W., *Cape Times,* 7 Oct. 1987.

[33] *Military Technology,* no. 1, 1983.

[34] *The Military Balance 1983–84* (IISS: London, 1984).

[35] In 1983, the only other *wheeled* SP-howitzer in existence was a Czech model, as reported by the *International Defense Review,* no. 9, 1983, p. 1253.

[36] For example, *Soldat und Technik,* no. 3, 1983, p. 133, and *Defense & Armament,* no. 24 (Nov. 1983), p. 51.

[37] *Citizen* (SA), 13 Sep. 1982.

[38] *Financial Times* (UK), 14 Sep. 1982.

[39] *Military Technology,* no. 1, 1983, p. 11. See also *International Defense Review,* no. 6, 1982, p. 754.

[40] *Military Technology* (note 39), p. 16.

[41] 'ARMSCOR's latter-day Long Tom', *Defence Attaché,* no. 1, 1985, p. 32.

[42] *Defence Attaché* (note 41), p. 33.

[43] *Cape Times,* 10 Feb. 1982.

[44] The original deal, known in FR Germany as 'Projekt Schwalbe', is further described in *Der Spiegel,* no. 42 (2 Oct. 1981).

[45] *Frankfurter Rundschau,* 16 Aug. 1985.

[46] *Paratus,* July 1985, p. 33.

[47] Gander, T. J., 'SAMIL range of rugged military trucks', *Jane's Defence Review,* vol. 4, no. 4, 1983, p. 348.

[48] *Jane's Defence Weekly,* 27 July 1985, p. 187.

[49] *Paratus,* Nov. 1984.

[50] Adams, J.—*The Unnatural Alliance, Israel and South Africa* (Quartet Books: London, 1984), p. 111.

[51] Timmerman, K. R., *The South African Defense & Armament,* no. 47 (Jan. 1986), p. 42.

[52] In 1978 a special crack anti-terrorist unit known as the South West Africa Specialist Unit, SWASU, was formed to operate in bush conditions at the border. This unit uses horses, motorcycles and *dogs* to track down SWAPO guerrillas in the dark.

[53] The latter function is said to be 'particularly necessary in South African operational conditions': *Jane's Defence Review,* vol. 4, no. 4, 1983, p. 348.

[54] *Sunday Star* (SA), 18 Nov. 1984.
[55] Caiti, P., 'The heirs of the jeep', *Defence Today*, Feb. 1973, p. 71.
[56] *South Africa Digest*, 5 Dec. 1978.
[57] *Der Spiegel*, no. 42, 1981.
[58] *Financial Times* (UK), 26 May 1981.
[59] *The Star*, 14 Aug. 1980.
[60] Advertisement in *Paratus*, Oct. 1984, p. 51.

Chapter 7. The missile industry

I. Introduction

Throughout the 1970s, the South African missile industry seemed to be even more secret than the other branches of the defence industry. In retrospect, it can be said that the lack of information was not because of the need to cover up details of this high technology effort, but because of a long drawn-out lack of progress. The development history of the South African-produced air-to-air missile actually lasted from the first test shooting in 1968 to the presentation of the V3B Kukri at the arms exhibition in Piraeus in 1982—that is, over a period of 14 years. Ship-to-ship missile technology was acquired only with the licensed production of the Israeli fast attack boats from 1978 onwards. A more indigenous version is still under development, and work on an anti-tank missile is reported to be at the R&D stage. The sole successful missile project of the 1960s was the Cactus surface-to-air system, which was, however, produced by France with South African finance. (In France it was called Crotale.)

The foreign technology needed for the missile industry was acquired from FR Germany, France, Israel and possibly the United States, in that order.

The South African recognition of the general need for missile systems was illustrated by the establishment of the Rocket Research Institute (RRI) in 1964, which took on responsibility for R&D in the missile field. The RRI works under the CSIR. The initiation of rocket and missile research could take place due to a co-operation agreement with West German industry. The RRI itself was set up under the auspices of the University of Pretoria, drawing on expertise from the Max Planck Institute for Aeronomy and the Institute for Stratospheric Physics at Lindau/Harz. Two West German organizations were involved in early rocket construction in South Africa—the Herman Oberth Gesellshaft of Bremen and the Waffen und Luftrüstung. The latter was an umbrella organization for some 30 private West German firms involved in the rocket industry. It was dissolved in 1964 as it was in conflict with the Brussels Treaty of 1954, which limits military research in FR Germany.

The first concrete task of this institute was to organize the co-operation with France for the Cactus/Crotale SAM programme. According to Professor A. J. A. Le Roux, vice-president of the CSIR in Johannesburg, the new institute would also give South Africa a 'foothold in space and weather research'. He also stated that 'The Republic of South Africa has been forced by events in Africa to enter the missile field'.[1] The RRI was reported to use the Tsumeb test range, established with the help of West German companies, until the first South African test site was built at St Lucia in Natal in 1968, with the aid of an unspecified European company. The West German company Bölkow AG has been mentioned in connection with the first test firing of missiles at the St Lucia test range.[2] But the company involved in building the St Lucia test range *could* have been the French concern Sodetag. This company plays a major role in the French nulear tests in the Sahara and, in the 1960s, it commissioned the building of missile test ranges and satellite tracking stations; among the latter the Paardefontein tracking station near Pretoria.[3] Sodetag also played some part in channelling South African capital to the French Crotale/Cactus SAM programme in 1964. French participation came to be of vital significance for South Africa's mastering of missile technology, for both air-to-air missiles and ship-to-ship missiles. From 1978 there was also access to Israeli ship-to-ship missiles.

While the South African financing and participation in the French Crotale SAM system is well known and has been widely published since 1968, information indicates that South African scientists were also deeply involved in other French missile projects. It has been alleged that South Africa financed not only Crotale but also the Milan anti-tank missile, the Matra R-530 and R-550 Magic air-to-air missiles and the Exocet ship-to-ship missile.[4]

The information on Exocet was borne out by Prime Minister P. W. Botha in his biography published in 1984. This is of obvious relevance to later, unconfirmed information that South Africa will begin serious production of an Exocet-type ship-to-ship missile.[5]

It has also been said that the French industry developed the AS-20 and AS-30 air-to-surface missiles, exported to South Africa, according to South African requirements and specifications. The TCA (télécommande automatique) technique which is used in both missiles allegedly originated from South African requirements.[6]

In addition to the work of the RRI, research and development in missile technology is undertaken at the Armscor subsidiary Kentron Missiles, which was formed in 1978 to handle the Kukri and Valkiri projects. Seventy per cent of Kentron's products are classified, and it employs 260 engineers working full time on the various projects, including an anti-tank missile, an air-to-ground missile and a stand-off delivery system.

In 1973, a new missile research institute was set up under the NIDR—the Propulsion Division at Somerset West—with the task of conducting development up to the production stage of missiles and their warheads, propellants and propulsion systems. The division of labour amongst these institutions is not quite clear. The Tsumeb research centre may be linked to nuclear research, the RRI to space research and the NIDR division to conventional missile technology.

The missiles imported by South Africa included the French Matra R-530 and R-550 Magic air-to-air missiles, arming the Mirage fleet; the AS-20 and AS-30 air-to-surface missiles on Buccaneer bombers, the SS-11 anti-tank missiles; the Franco-German Milan and Entac ATMs for Eland armoured cars, Gabriel ship-to-ship missiles from Israel known as Skerpioen in South Africa and also, from the United States in 1956, 200 AIM-9 Sidewinder air-to-air missiles, originally to arm the 40 Canadian-supplied Sabre fighters.

II. Missile projects

Kukri

The South African air-to-air missile project, designed to replace Sidewinder, was code-named 'Voorslag' and planning started in 1964. In 1980, the Kentron company was awarded the prize of the Associated Scientific and Technical societies of South Africa for the development of the Kukri AAM (and also for the Valkiri rocket launcher, as described above).

Kukri was shown as available for export in Piraeus in 1982, and the same year it was being deployed with the Mirage fighters of the South African Air Force. Kukri's development history dates back to 1966.[7]

At the time of the establishment of the Rocket Research Institute in 1964 it was announced that the Institute was to be supplemented by a firing range within the Republic. In 1968, the St Lucia missile test range was built in Natal between Cape Vidal and the Mozambique border. The site was planned to service both the CSIR and the armaments production organizations as well as the Army, Navy and Air Force. Defence Minister P. W. Botha admitted when announcing these plans that overseas firms which had already planned several missile bases in Europe had been called in as consultants.[8]

The first tests of a guided air-to-air missile were conducted at the St Lucia range in December 1968. Officials of the CSIR regarded the firing as highly successful.[9] Nearly three years passed before the next reports appeared. In September 1971, the Defence Ministry, in a highly premature report, claimed the successful completion of a solid fuel Mach 2 AAM, which had now been tested from a Mirage fighter. Defence Minister P. W. Botha claimed the missile was 'better than those of most countries' and would be available for export. Between 1968 and 1971, South African scientists had gained access to French missile technology, and the original AAM concept, based on the cannibalization of the old AIM-9 Sidewinders, had been revised to include features from the Matra R-550 Magic dogfight missile. The 1971 AAM, known as the V3A, was reported ready for production in 1975. It is not known how many V3As were actually produced, but in 1982 it was reported that the AAM had been operational for a few years.[10] The V3 work was kept secret for a long period, and the designation V3A was revealed only in 1979.

In 1975 development of the improved V3B Kukri version was begun, to incorporate additional features specified by the South African Air Force. It entered production in 1979. Both the V3A and V3B are placed on the wing-tips of the Mirage fighters.

French assistance was reported in 1975, when the AAM was described as being very similar to the Matra Magic. This assistance came to an end in 1977, however, and after the public presentation of Kukri in 1982, Western technical expertise seemed rather united in the opinion that the South Africans were justified in claiming indigenous development. The Kukri is described as partly derived from the Magic, and partly resembling the Israeli Shafrir, but with notable differences.[11]

Technical sources are very impressed by the Kukri, which is described as a 'futuristic missile'. This refers first of all to the helmet sighting system, allowing for what is called a 'look-and-shoot' capacity. The missile sight operates through the pilot's helmet, and is connected to the movements of the pilot's right eye. The pilot only has to *look* at his target before firing a missile. The aircraft does not need to be turned. This free-launch target designation is a concept which in European aerospace industries is intended for the future advanced short-range AAMs of the 1990s.[12] In South Africa, compatibility with existing aircraft and weapon systems was maintained by making the V3A and V3B conform to the Sidewinder and Magic launchers. System improvements for the V3B included an upgraded motor and an increased helmet sight designation angle.

The diameter of the rocket motor for Kukri is 127 mm, as compared to the Sidewinder's 120 mm, and 160 mm for the Magic and Shafrir. This is the same as the motor employed in the Valkiri artillery rocket—also produced by Kentron. There is a full range of support equipment in production for the Kukri system, including a gas trolley, missile transit trolleys, assembly jigs, an IR-tester, a missile safety tester and a microprocessor-controlled first-line system-checking and diagnostic equipment. Work is reported on a lighter designator helmet to SAAF requirements, basically meaning the development of a helmet that fits each pilot individually. Presently the helmet is produced in two standard sizes, meaning that the pilots have to fit the helmet rather than the other way around.[13]

Work has also been reported on a third generation of the V3 which is assumed to be an all-aspect missile, although as yet unconfirmed.[14] In March 1988, a previously unknown infra-red air-to-air guided missile designated *Darter* was displayed at the FIDA show in Chile.

The Cactus SAM

Cactus/Crotale is an all-weather mobile air-defence SAM system mounted on three vehicles. It is also air-transportable. The Cactus project was included in the 1964 'arms-for-uranium' deal with France, which marked the entry of France as an alternative arms supplier, replacing the UK. This followed the cancellation of a number of South African arms orders by the Labour Government that came to power in Britain in 1964. The cancellations included the BAC Bloodhound SAM.

Cactus—in France called Crotale—was designed according to a South African concept; South African scientists participated in the development work in France. Initial R&D costs have been reported as Fr. 500 million.[15] From the outset, financing was provided entirely by South Africa, but as the programme proceeded the French Bank of Foreign Trade in 1968 credited Thomson-CSF and Hotchkiss Brandt with Fr. 352.5 million. Of this sum, Fr.

50 million was paid by the French Government. This credit was for study, development and production, and complementary research on the Cactus/Crotale plus its maintenance in South Africa.

In January 1967, radar equipment worth Fr. 5 million was delivered to South Africa for Cactus. The total value of the first South African consignment of Cactus, delivered in 1971, has been reported as Fr. 1 800 000.[16] When R&D work had been completed, total South African financing of the programme amounted to 85 per cent.

The existence of this programme was not revealed until 2 May 1969 when P. W. Botha made an announcement to Parliament. Later the same year P. W. Botha visited France to witness a test launching of the missile.[17] Even less was known about South African involvement and financing of other French and French–West German missile projects as described in the introduction above. This method of circumventing embargo restrictions—by investing and actively participating in a military project overseas—was apparently completely unforeseen by the international community advocating the 1963 arms embargo. It was obviously an efficient means of defying the embargo, avoiding the unfavourable mass media attention that smuggling cases bring once they are revealed.

In South Africa, the company Fuchs was planning to undertake production of Cactus at an initial value of R20 million. Fuchs was the local representative of Thomson-CSF. Meanwhile, Thomson-CSF undertook the training of South African scientists in France.[18] Since 1969, however, the name of this producer has not appeared again. Possibly, initial assembly of the French-supplied radars, launch system and firing units was indeed undertaken at Fuchs. The vehicles were, at any rate, later produced in South Africa (as mentioned in chapter 4).

Between 1968 and 1975, South Africa deployed a total of eight platoons of Cactus systems; eight acquisition vehicles, and 16 firing vehicles with 240 missiles.[19] By 1973, three batteries were deployed in the Transvaal along the Mozambique border. By 1985, total deployment was 54 Cactus systems with the Army.[20]

However, both deliveries from France after 1975 and actual production in South Africa remain a mystery. In 1976 Jordan's clandestine arms deal with South Africa took place, involving the delivery of Jordan's entire Tigercat SAM system, a total of 18 batteries with 54 units of British origin, now deployed with the South African Army together with Cactus. Speculations have it that Tigercat was imported because the performance of Cactus had been disappointing. This is not very likely, in view of the fact that the French Crotale version is one of the export successes of the French arms industry, sold to some 10 countries; it is also in use with the French Air Force.[21] The lack of further information after 1975 might rather imply that the original contract had been fulfilled and the 1977 embargo prevented further French assistance.

It is unlikely that the missiles were ever produced in South Africa, for as in the case of the Mirage-3 there are no South African claims of indigenous capacity. This silence takes on even more significance if one compares it with the first triumphant announcements made about the Cactus, when Defence Minister Botha said that 'South Africa has developed, with French assistance, a ground-to-air missile believed to be the most advanced and effective weapon of its kind in existence'.[22]

In fact, all work except that on the vehicle seems to have been undertaken in France: Matra was responsible for the development and manufacture of the Cactus missiles, and Thomson-CSF built the ground equipment, which was initially designed to be fitted into special Hotchkiss-Brandt all-terrain vehicles.

Although Botha stated in 1972 that Cactus would be available for export, no such export took place of any South African-produced Cactus system. It has been reported, however, that France and South Africa share the royalties of the project, which would mean considerable earnings for South Africa from the French export of Crotale.[23] This remains unconfirmed.

In 1981 it was revealed that South Africa had disposed of six Cactus systems, which were sold to Chile. In connection with this, the first information on export agreements in the original French–South African contract was also revealed—Matra undertook to buy back missiles that South Africa might want to sell. Thus, the Cactus missiles were shipped back to France and then sold to Chile from France. This was reported as a means of disposing of unwanted equipment.[24]

Armscor's executive manager F. J. Bell said in 1982 that South Africa needed to improve its northern air defence capabilities and its Cactus SAM. In 1984, reports appeared of a study to upgrade the Cactus SAM system with a TV tracking option, and to add features resulting from its in-service experience.[25]

One final indication that the French contract was terminated could be that when South Africa started on ship-to-ship missiles, it did not attempt a naval version of Cactus. Instead, the South Africans used the Israeli Gabriel.

Ship-to-ship missile systems

Skerpioen

Ship-to-ship missile technology was acquired with the first order announced in 1974 for Israeli fast attack gunboats of the Reshef-class, armed with Gabriel-2 missiles, also licence-produced. The Israeli Gabriel-2 missile is in turn based on the French Exocet. In South Africa, a version of this missile is being produced locally. Scorpion (usually designated by its Africaans name, Skerpioen) arms 12 Reshef-type fast attack craft, three Dvora-type fast attack boats and three other light attack craft, all of Israeli design.

As was the case with the Kukri AAM, various sources have noted resemblances with other systems of the same generation, notably the Taiwanese Hsiung-Feng missile.

The first six Israeli attack boats were delivered in 1978, but no mention of missiles occurred until 1980. The South African press then reported from a naval exercise called 'Operation Sanitary' the existence of a new, classified ship-to-ship missile. It was test-fired successfully against the decommissioned destroyer *Jan van Riebeeck*. The exercise was undertaken 'to launch the Navy into the missile era'.[26] The official yearbook of South Africa, 1982, presents Skerpioen for the first time. The actual identity of this missile is not quite clear—*Jane's Fighting Ships* says Skerpioen is *believed to be* the South African name for Gabriel 2. Skerpioen has also been described as a joint venture by Israel and South Africa, presumably based on Gabriel 2.[27]

Exocet version

In 1982, Armscor executive manager F. J. Bell announced that work had started on a new generation of anti-ship missiles, similar to the French Exocet range. This decision was taken after a preliminary study of the Falklands campaign. The new missile was to replace Skerpioen.[28] This is not the sole reason for interest in a new ship-to-ship missile; according to Armscor Chairman P. G. Marais, Armscor sees the key to many of South Africa's armaments requirements in the development of suitable missiles. Thus, a new ship-launched missile will replace the maritime surveillance aircraft and naval bombers that have become impossible to acquire from abroad. The concentration on new missile technology was also reflected in the development of the new Overberg missile testing range on the eastern Cape coast, at considerable cost to Armscor.[29]

Negotiations were completed in 1983 for a new missile test range at the De Hoop reserve in the southern Cape. The De Hoop range (or the Overberg range) will replace the St Lucia test site, which is considered to be too close to Mozambique.[30] Firing from the area would be mainly in an easterly direction with impact points on land and sea up to 100 km. According to Defence Minister M. Malan, the test site will be completed in 1990, and the cost in 1983 alone was R238 million. Tenders to private firms under Armscor management were first called for in 1984.[31] Obviously, this site will suit the testing demands of, for example, Exocet-type missiles.

From 1983 onwards, Western sources began to report on the same project within the context of what amounts to yet another fantastic story of clandestine arms technology smuggling. First, according to the Paris journal *Afrique-Asie*, Armscor managed to acquire the documentation for the MM-38 Exocet missile with the assistance of highly-placed French Government officials, but not directly from France.[32] The actual plans were handed over to agents in Indonesia and Singapore and then to the Armscor import directors in Amsterdam, where these plans plus one missile and a manual of instructions were examined. Also in 1983, US intelligence sources suddenly reported that South Africa was *co-producing* the Aerospatiale Exocet missile.[33]

Following wide publicity about the alleged delivery of South African-produced Exocet missiles to Argentina during the Falklands war, first reported by US diplomatic sources in Cape Town,[34] came official denials by Defence Minister M. Malan—and then silence. An Armscor spokesman refused to comment on the *Afrique-Asie* story,[35] saying that it was 'against Armscor's policy to react to reports on its activities'.[36] Interestingly, a piece of information appeared in *The Star*, quoting the price of the South African 'Exocet' at US $550 000.[37] It remains to be confirmed what the facts behind these reports are. However, it is certain that the new ship-to-ship missile project exists: in 1982, the first prototype was tested at the Youngfields navy base in Cape Town, and the missile was close to series production.

Whether this actually is a licensed production of the MM-38, or something else, is not clear. If, however, P. W. Botha was correct in his biography and South Africa actually financed the Exocet range R&D in France, then part of this missile is South African property, which poses a new dilemma in embargo contexts. In this case, the acquisition of Exocet know-how is more similar to the acquisition of the Cactus SAM than to the G-5 smuggling story.

The anti-tank missile project

From 1984, R&D work was started on South African anti-tank missiles. In an interview, the Armscor Chairman was not forthcoming about future projects but he did confirm that such work was going on.[38] A little more detailed information came in 1985, to the effect that Armscor was in the process of developing a long-range beam-riding guidance missile for use with the Ratel vehicle.[39]

Remotely-piloted vehicles (RPVs)

The Eyrie RPV

The existence of a South African RPV was revealed by journalists after a pilotless spy-drone was shot down over Maputo in Mozambique in 1983. That drone eventually turned out to be an Israeli Aircraft Industries Scout 2011, which for the first time proved that South Africa was one of the buyers of that system. A report to the effect that Scout was being licence-produced in South Africa has been impossible to confirm.[40] However, it was found that a private company in Durban was producing an RPV called Eyrie. This was discovered by a journalist team from the *Sunday Tribune*, investigating after the Maputo incident. The designer was Dr M. Reed, a member of the President's Council's Scientific Committee and Director of National Dynamics. This company had manufactured Eyrie since 1982, mainly for the export market, and sales were handled by an agent in FR Germany. Eyrie was the fourth generation RPV designed by the company. The company is not affiliated with Armscor—that is, production does not take place for the South African Defence Forces. Mr Reed stated that the only connection to Armscor was that they issued all export licences.[41]

Two prototypes of Eyrie existed in 1982, and the next year this RPV was offered for sale, for unique dual RPV operation, using a second drone to relay the programming signals to extend the operating range. In addition to cameras, Eyrie can carry up to four rockets for strike roles, and it has six hours' endurance.

Its origins are disputed. While the South African producer obviously claims design capacity, other sources noted a similarity with both the Lockheed Acquila (USA) and the Dornier Minidrohne (FRG). Some West German involvement might have been at hand in view of the National Dynamics connection to that country, but no more information is available, however.

One source describes Eyrie as 'one of the oddest looking RPVs currently flying', with a rhomboidal wing with one set of roots at the tail of the vehicle and another towards the front. The front and rear-mounted wings are joined at the wing-tips and have a span of 4.27 m.[42] Command guidance and control are by means of the Vega 6163 ground control system.

Jane's Weapon Systems describes Eyrie's potential missions as reconnaissance, surveillance, electronic warfare and countermeasures, artillery adjustment, rocket strike, SAR (search-and-rescue) duties and general survey tasks. It is, according to the same source, *not* similar to the Israeli Scout or Mastiff, which was used in the Lebanon in 1982.

In 1986, Armscor declared that work on a new RPV had begun.[43] This RPV, designated *Seeker,* was displayed at the FIDA air show in Chile in March 1988.

Notes and references

[1] *Flight,* 12 Dec. 1963.
[2] *Jeune Afrique*, 17 Nov. 1970.
[3] Cervenka, C., and Rogers, B., *The Nuclear Axis—Secret Collaboration between West Germany and South Africa* (Julian Friedmann Books: London, 1978), p. 233.
[4] Schissel, H., 'The Paris-Pretoria conspiracy', *Africa, no.* 65 (Jan. 1977).
[5] de Villiers, D. and de Villiers, J., *PW (Biography of P. W. Botha),* (Tafelberg: Cape Town, 1984), p. 294.
[6] *Jane's Defence Review,* vol. 4, no. 6, 1983, p. 513.
[7] *International Herald Tribune*, 11 Nov. 1971.
[8] *The Times*, 10 Oct. 1968.
[9] *International Herald Tribune*, 18 Dec. 1968.
[10] *Cape Times,* 10 Dec. 1982.
[11] *Flight International*, 23 Oct. 1982; Pretty, R. T., 'South African Kukri air-to-air missile' in *Jane's Defence Review*, vol. 4, no. 6, 1983. For a detailed account of this system, see for example *Défense et Armements*, no. 15 (Jan. 1983).
[12] For a detailed account of this system, see, for example, *Flight International,* 23 Oct. 1982; *Defense & Armament*, no. 15, Jan. 1983; and Pretty (note 11).
[13] *Jane's Defence Review*, vol. 4, no. 6, 1983, p. 519.
[14] *Flight International*, 22 and 29 Dec. 1984, p. 1683.
[15] *Air et Cosmos*, 21 June 1969.
[16] Gerdan, E., *Dossier A . . . Commes Armes* (Editions Alain Moreau: Paris, 1975).
[17] *Air et Cosmos*, 10 May 1969.
[18] *The Star,* 14 June 1969.
[19] *African Defence,* Apr. 1983.
[20] *Military Balance 1985–86* (IISS: London, 1986).
[21] Crotale advertisement, *Flight International,* 1 Oct. 1983.
[22] Statement to Parliament, 2 May 1969; *Cape Times,* 3 May 1969.
[23] *The Times*, 29 Oct. 1981.
[24] *Observer,* 6 Feb. 1981.

[25] *Flight International*, 22 and 29 Dec. 1984.
[26] *Rand Daily Mail*, 7 May 1980.
[27] *Defense & Armament*, no. 11 (Sep. 1982), p. 13.
[28] *Defense & Armament*, no. 11 (Sep. 1982).
[29] *Jane's Defence Weekly*, 13 July 1985, p. 98.
[30] *Daily News*, 21 March 1983.
[31] *Paratus*, Jan. 1984, p. 10.
[32] *Afrique-Asie*, July 1983; and *Die Burger*, 21 July 1983.
[33] *Aerospace Daily*, 28 Nov. 1983.
[34] *African Defence*, Sep. 1983; see also the section on South African arms exports.
[35] *Afrique-Asie* (note 32).
[36] *African Defence*, Sep. 1983, p. 35.
[37] Reuters, Johannesburg, 24 May 1982.
[38] *International Defense Review*, no. 10, 1984, p. 1567.
[39] *African Defence*, Feb. 1985, p. 20.
[40] *Noticias* (Mozambique) quoted by *Defence & Foreign Affairs Digest*, July 1983, and repeated by *Militärtechnik*, no. 8, 1983.
[41] *Sunday Tribune*, 5 June 1983.
[42] *Defence Attaché*, no. 1, 1986, p. 44.
[43] *Flight International*, 5 Apr. 1986. Note that RPVs are often described as remote-controlled reconnaissance aircraft.

Chapter 8. The warship industry

I. Introduction

The building of warships in South Africa did not start in earnest until 1978, when the Israeli Reshef-class missile boats began to be constructed. The Dutch East India Company built the first berthing facilities in Simon's Bay in 1768. The British naval base Simonstown was created in 1808 and later became the most modern naval dockyard in the southern hemisphere. Repair, maintenance and manufacturing support for the South African Navy are undertaken at the Naval Dockyard in Simonstown. The continuous expansion of the Simonstown dockyard illustrates the emphasis on upgrading and retrofitting existent ships. This expansion became essential after the embargo of 1977, which directly stopped delivery of large warships that had been ordered, such as the Aviso class corvettes from France, and new submarines.

One of the programmes for upgrading and modernizing the fleet that existed before the 1977 embargo was the modernization programme of the four British President-class frigates, worth R2 million each. In this way, their lifetime was considerably increased, pending the arrival of the first missile strike aircraft. In 1986, only *President Pretorius* still remained in service, having been recommissioned after a refit. Another example is the conversion done at Simonstown of the 10 British Ton-class minesweepers, delivered between 1955 and 1959. Two were converted into patrol minesweepers and two into minehunters, and the remainder were modernized. All remain in service. New management techniques have also been employed to cut down running costs and allow money for new vessels.

The second state-owned dockyard, managed by the Navy, is the Naval Dockyard Durban, on Salisbury Island. This dockyard has been expanded since 1980, in particular to provide maintenance for the new strike craft flotilla. (The naval base on Salisbury Island was reactivated in 1976.)

The first real expansion of the Simonstown Naval Dockyard, and also of the naval base, took place in connection with the purchase of the three Daphne-class submarines from France—to date the sole submarines of the South African Navy (SAN). While actual delivery took place in 1971 and 1972, the idea of a South African submarine flotilla dates back to 1961. The planning of the top secret 'project Daphne' began in 1964.

By that time it was clear that no submarines would be forthcoming from the UK and in the same year the first Daphne submarine was commissioned in France. In 1967, contracts were completed with the French Navy and the shipbuilders Dubigeon-Normandie. In France, training and education of the first South African submariners were undertaken. In 1970, trials began on the first vessel, *SAS Maria van Riebeeck*. In the Simonstown yard, a new submarine base complex was nearly completed by the end of 1970, including new jetties, a synchro-lift, workshops and support facilities. French advice and assistance in this expansion seems highly likely. Actual construction and building was, however, by a Danish building company, authorized by the Danish Government in 1969. The South African Defence White Paper of 1969 said it would cost US $20.3 million. The submarine headquarters were completed in 1971, and the flotilla was commissioned as *SAS Drommedaris* the same year, renamed *SAS Hugo Biermann* in 1974.

Since 1972, approximately 15 per cent of total Simonstown Naval Dockyard time has been spent on the submarines. They operate on a cycle which means a maintenance period every six weeks and a total refit every three years. It takes 4000 man hours/week with 120 men on the floor for a total of 18 months to return a submarine to the sea after a complete refit.

Nearly all spare and replacement parts are reportedly manufactured in the Simonstown yard, according to the SADF journal *Paratus*. There is no information on *what* parts need to be imported, however. The capacity of the Simonstown yard is of obvious interest concerning the plans to construct local submarines by the end of the 1980s—these are the only facilities in South Africa where such production could be undertaken.[1] In 1980, the P. W. Botha Tidal Basin with berths for 50 ships was opened. An entire Daphne-class submarine can be refitted.

From 1982 a new building project was initiated at Simonstown, which concentrates important electronic, mechanical and structural maintenance facilities in two buildings close to the refitting berths. This has greatly improved South African capacity to support some of the new sophisticated electronic and mechanical equipment which is entering service during the 1980s.

Private shipyards

The existing private shipyards of the 1950s lacked the capacity to construct larger warships. Shipbuilding was, during the 1960s, confined to one 220-tonne torpedo-recovery ship, *Flexible*, built by Dorman Long, Africa (later to become Dorbyl), in Durban in 1969. Dorman Long also completed the tug *De Mist* in 1978. By 1983 part of the Dorman Long yard had merged with another private yard and was called Dorman Long Swan Hunter. Two naval tugs, *De Neys* and *De Noorde*, were built by Globe Engineering Works in Cape Town in 1961 and 1969, respectively. Fred Nicholls in Durban in 1964 built a training vessel, *Navigator*. All of these ships are still in Navy service.

The 30 Namacurra-class harbour patrol vessels of only 5 tonnes full load are also reportedly of South African design, but there is a conspicuous absence of more detailed information on producer and completion dates. The same is true of the P 1558, a large patrol boat of 80 tonnes. It is described as built in South Africa, and was completed in 1976. This ship is reportedly armed with one 40-mm Swedish Bofors gun. The supplier of the gun remains unknown, as does the identity of the producer. If Sweden, or alternatively the UK, France or the FRG (where the Bofors guns have been licence-produced) supplied it to South Africa, it would constitute a direct violation of the embargo regulations. One other possibility is that the Bofors gun was moved from one of the British ships, now decommissioned, such as the anti-submarine warfare (ASW) frigates or seaward defence ships supplied in 1963.

The private yard, Krögerwerft of Rendsburg completed two rescue launchers of 87 tonnes in 1961 and 1962. These were the West German type FL9 SAR, presumably constructed under licence.

Change of SAN function

The role of the South African Navy has changed more radically than that of the Army or Air Force, although it has not been in the forefront of direct warfare. In the absence of new foreign-supplied large ships, maritime reconnaissance aircraft and naval bombers, its pre-embargo role as a blue-water navy responsible for the security of the Cape Route in an East–West strategic context, has changed into that of a coastal defence navy, with an emphasis also on counter-insurgency.

Defence Minister Botha announced publicly in 1978 that because of a lack of assistance from the West, his Government would no longer consider the protection of the Cape Route to be its responsibility. Coastal defence now called for a combination of missile strike craft, mine warfare vessels and submarines. Armscor Chairman P. G. Marais expressed this as follows:

In view of the fact that the Western countries are showing no active interest in supplying us with the type of aircraft required for air-sea rescue operations or for reconnaissance of the wide area of the Cape Sea route, we are certainly not going to do that for them any longer. We are looking after our own interests now.[2]

In 1972, the Yarrow African Maritime Consultancy—which acted as adviser to the Armaments Board and was connected with the British Yarrow Shipbuilders—announced that it had been instructed to investigate the country's potential for surface warship construction. Yarrow invited applications from interested shipyards, and Prime Minister B. J. Vorster promised a Government subsidy of up to 25 per cent of the expenditure for any ship built for the Navy. Durban was selected as the future construction centre, as it was the closest port to the country's major steel works.

The Dorbyl Marine Yard in Durban became the largest shipbuilder in the country, and here the Israeli Reshef-class missile boats were produced. In spite of reports of expansion and success for the South African naval industry, reports to the contrary have filtered through. In 1983, the chairman of Dorbyl said in his annual report to shareholders that depressed economic conditions at home and the world recession were threatening South Africa's shipbuilding industry. The future of the Dorbyl yard was even said to be in jeopardy due to lack of orders. Its labour force had dropped by 5925 persons to a total of 19 623 in 1983, due to plant closures and retrenchments.

In 1983, South African press reports underlined the problems for the future of the shipbuilding industry in general. One of these reports carried the heading 'Only war can save South African yards', and went on to say that:

Few industries in South Africa are more important in time of international upheaval than the marine engineering complexes of Durban and Cape Town, but they are suffering from thin order books and there is little assurance of improvement in 1984 . . . In the 1960s there were suggestions that South Africa would play a bigger part in building its own ships. But experience has shown that reliance on sub-contractors overseas endangers any delivery date. The cost of shipping out 70% of plant for ship building in South Africa is too high.[3]

This report concludes by stating that shipbuilding in South Africa would have to be conducted on the basis of patriotism and sentiment. Forthcoming military orders would thus seem to be of a vital commercial importance for the shipbuilding industry, in general.

Local construction of frigates, corvettes and submarines, announced several times over the years, remains to be undertaken in the future. Unreachable foreign technology still seems to be of crucial importance for such projects.[4]

In 1971 a programme was undertaken to expand the Navy from 30 ships to 45–50 ships, but the potential supplying countries withdrew under the influence of the embargoes, including first the UK, then Portugal and finally also France. Israel eventually became the sole supplier of naval technology between 1974 and 1977.

The last ships delivered to South Africa from the UK were the survey ship *Protea* (Hecla-class) in 1972 and two Fairey Marine Tracker-class rescue launchers in 1973. The last major new ships from France were the three Daphne submarines in 1970–72, while two Agosta-class submarines and two frigates were stopped by the 1977 embargo. Japan delivered the Mitsubishi-built Antarctic survey and supply vessel *Agulhas* in 1978. The official customer was the South African Department of Transport, not the Navy.

The pennant list in 1988 included only 32 ships plus the 30 small harbour defence boats, and has remained unchanged for a number of years.[5] The South African Navy possesses three French-supplied Daphne-class submarines; only one remaining ASW frigate of the President class (old British Type-12); eight Reshef-type Minister-class missile boats armed with Skerpioen missiles; three other missile boats also Skerpioen armed; 10 aged ex-British Ton-class minesweepers/hunters; four ex-British Ford-class large patrol craft; 30 new Namacurra South African-built harbour patrol craft; and one ex-Danish fleet replenishment ship, delivered in 1965.

The expenditure on maritime defence between 1975 and 1980 amounted to US $562 million. Much of that was taken up by construction of the Minister-class missile boats.[6] In spite of the expansion undertaken during the early 1980s, there have been alarm reports about the inadequacy of the South African Navy. In 1984 it got less than 7 per cent of the defence budget, and a special report claimed that the Navy was so weak that 'in fact, the country's enemies might be tempted to infiltrate arms and men by sea as this involved far less risk than crossing the country's border'.[7] However, the decision was taken to once again expand the South African Navy into an ocean-going force. Local construction of corvettes and submarines was included in this long-term plan.

II. Projects

The Minister-class fast attack missile boats

These were South Africa's first fast attack missile boats and are referred to as MOD-class by *The Military Balance* and Minister-class by various other defence yearbooks. The 1974 contract with Israel for the Reshef-class missile boats covered the acquisition of a total of 12 boats, of which the first three were built in Haifa and delivered to South Africa in 1978. Fast patrol boats are multi-mission vessels capable of filling both patrol and combat duties. These first South African fast patrol boats were tested on 25 March 1980 together with the South African-assembled Skerpioen missile in the classified naval exercise called Operation Sanitary. The Director of Naval Operations, Commander G. Syndercombe said on this occasion:

The acquisition of the FPB's (fast patrol boats) by the SA Navy in addition to our submarines, means we have entered an era where we can project a credible deterrent which every major naval force will have to take into account. Before, our naval strategy was based on providing naval bases and additional forces to complement the West's defence of the Cape sea route. Now we are totally committed to the defence of the waters and the marine infrastructure of the Republic of South Africa.[8]

It was further said that one such strike craft carried the same fire-power as a World-War-II light cruiser. The first of the South African-produced missile boats, *SAS Jan Smuts*, was launched in February 1977 and commissioned in July the same year. In December 1977, the second, *SAS P W Botha* was commissioned, followed by *Frederic Creswell* and *Jim Fouche* in 1978, *Franz Erasmus* in 1979, *Oswald Pirow* in 1980, *Hendrik Mentz* and *Kobie Coetzee* in 1983. The first three were built in Israel, the remainder in Durban by Sandock-Austral. Four more are reportedly under construction.[9] These ships make up the latest flotilla of the South African Navy, named SAS Scorpion. The ships each carry six Skerpioen surface-to-surface missiles, two 76-mm Oto Melara guns, two 20-mm Oerlikon AA-guns and four 12.7-mm machineguns.[10]

In Italy, the re-supply of the Oto Melara guns from Israel to South Africa caused a debate on Italian responsibility for breaking the 1977 embargo. The Minister class is generally described as a copy of the Israeli Reshef design (in turn a derivative of the French Cherbourgh class, which was based on a West German design by Lürssen). It is also assumed that the electronic warfare equipment is similar if not identical to the Israeli equipment, which in turn was derived from Italian technology, and supplied to Israel by the Italian company Elettronica.[11] One reporter wrote after a visit on board a Minister-class ship that such electronics equipment as radar screens or fire-control systems might have been South African copies of British or Israeli items, but that they bore no identifiable markings.

Namacurra-class harbour patrol boat

The Marine Corps was set up within the Navy organization in 1979 to deal primarily with COIN tasks. It is being equipped with the reportedly South African-designed Namacurra 5-tonne harbour patrol boat of which 30 were in service in 1988. Nothing more has been said about this product, not even the name of the producer. This in itself *could* point to a foreign supplier. On the other hand, the Namacurra is hardly an impossible task for the South African shipyards, being, so to say, at the other end of the scale compared to the sophisticated Minister-class boats.

The first seven Namacurra launches were built in 1979, to equip the first units of marines in Durban. Further such units have since been deployed in all parts of South Africa, and in Walvis Bay in Namibia.

Voortrekker-II ocean racing yacht

While not being a warship, *Voortrekker-II* is another of the few examples of indigenous naval design and development. It was launched in December 1981, and demonstrated to the public in 1983. Development took place at the Simonstown yard at a cost of R250 000.[12] It is in Navy service and is used for sail-training and ocean racing.

Shirley-T helicopter-carrier

In 1980, a prototype of *Shirley-T* was tested by the Navy. It is a turnhulled craft, designed by a private designer, Mr B. van Niekerk, and built by an unnamed Cape Town yard. The ship is reported to be of an unusual tunnel design, and carries helicopters and missiles.[13]

In 1985, US intelligence sources reported that a 7000-mile range helicopter-carrier was being developed in South Africa for Israel, in return for electronic equipment technology supplied by Israel.[14] This project may be identical with the *Shirley-T*.

Tafelberg conversion-armed helicopter carrier

The 1983–84 conversion of the fleet replenishment tanker *Tafelberg* has been described as a first move towards reviving the Navy's ocean-going capacity. In its new configuration, the *Tafelberg* was also to replace the grounded Avro Shackleton maritime reconnaissance aircraft for search-and-rescue duties.

Tafelberg was purchased from Denmark in 1965, the South African buyer being the Ministry of Transport. It served with the Navy, however, as a tanker.

In 1965 a first rehabilitation was done by Barendz Shipbuilders in Durban, and a helicopter deck was added by the James Brown & Hamer Yard, also in Durban, in 1975. A major refit took place in 1983–84 at a cost of several million rand, to convert *Tafelberg* into an armed forward-base ship. Sea trials were begun in 1984, after which the ship was recommissioned in its new role. Life expectancy was increased by 10 years, well into the 1990s. The refit was the largest such work undertaken by the Simonstown yard, and over 500 000 man hours were put into the project. A third deck was added and helicopter capacity was enlarged to include all three types of helicopters in South African Navy service, that is, Super Frelons, Alouette-3s, and Wasps.[15] Accommodation for 500 men was provided, and *Tafelberg* can also carry small boats up to the 5-tonne Namacurra size, plus six containers with fuel and various stores. The *Tafelberg* was in 1983 armed with the Skerpioen missile, and four new Swiss-designed 120-mm and 40-mm anti-aircraft guns.[16] Exactly how the Swiss Oerlikon guns were acquired by South Africa remains unknown, as in the case of the Bofors guns. The secret supply route for AA-guns to South Africa thus remains to be revealed.

The replacement of aircraft with a converted tanker illustrates one of the ways and means of coping with the effects of the arms embargo—new maritime aircraft had been found to be inaccessible for South Africa. The UK refused to supply the HS-748 maritime patrol aircraft and also Nimrod and Orion in 1980. The United States had in 1965 prevented the sale from France to South Africa of the *Breguet Atlantic*, containing US electronics.

Drakensberg fleet-replenishment vessel

In 1986, the naval industry could, like the aerospace industry, claim a major achievement for indigenous development with the launching of *Drakensberg* by Sandock-Austral in Durban.

The first reports of a new construction of a supply vessel to replace *Tafelberg* appeared in 1984, when the keel of the new ship was laid. This project was described as the biggest and most sophisticated warship to be built in South Africa. It is constructed to carry seaborne troops, two Puma helicopters, ASW torpedoes and depth charges.[17]

The 15 000-tonne *Drakensberg* was announced as the first naval vessel to have been designed and developed in South Africa, and the largest to have been built. It was commissioned in 1987. In addition to its replenishment role, *Drakensberg* will play a strategic role, partly taking over maritime patrol and surveillance tasks after the retired Shackleton aircraft.

During the 1987–88 investigation in FR Germany into the sale of submarine technology to South Africa, the West German shipbuilder IKL-Howaldtswerke was identified as a supplier to the *Drakensberg* project.

Future naval construction

With the above projects, the list of naval constructions actually undertaken in South Africa is exhausted. The future planning includes first of all corvettes, but also submarines.

In 1982, the retiring Navy Chief. Vice Admiral R. Edwards, declared that the South African Navy was planning for warships 'entirely ours from concept to completion', which would operate in the Atlantic and the Indian Oceans by the end of the decade. The ageing frigates (of which only the recommissioned *President Pretorius* was left by 1988) would be replaced by corvettes, and the Daphne submarines would be replaced by a new submarine built in South Africa.[18] He also said, however, that 'the Navy is not yet large enough to support a shipbuilding industry on its own'.[19] This could be interpreted as a veiled reference to international partners, particularly for the submarines. Numerous Western press reports keep referring to Israel and/or France as the most plausible partners in shipbuilding. The South African press also contains such hints.

Corvettes

The corvette planning, revived in 1982, actually dates back to the naval expansion programme which commenced in 1971. Then, under the name of 'Project Taurus', South Africa had arranged to purchase six Joao Coutinho-class corvettes of West German design, licence-produced in Spain, from Portugal. This deal never went through, due to the fall of the Portuguese regime in 1974. It remains quite clear that South Africa's access to corvette technology was effectively hampered from this time.

The subsequent order for two Type-69 corvettes from France was in turn cancelled by France after the 1977 UN embargo. All this having failed, there were occasional references to an intention to build this type of warship in South Africa until 1982, when the frigate *President Kruger* was lost in a collision. This accident signalled a new effort to create a corvette fleet to replace the now practically non-existent frigate fleet.

Vice Admiral R. Edwards declared at a news conference following the accident that this move had become necessary due to the large gap in the Navy's defences after the sinking of its flagship.[20] Durban was selected as the centre for corvette construction, apparently with a certain hesitation. This was expressed by the Vice-Admiral: 'The Durban shipbuilding effort has been— and to be objective and brutally frank—comparatively modest. . . . Whether Durban is going to provide this total facility—and by total I mean the whole vessel down to the engines—is another issue'.[21] He went on to say that the model for the South African Navy was a small—but potent—force on the lines developed by Israel.

Israel has been linked with the South African corvette programme, *inter alia* by the SADF journal *Militaria*. This source speculated that the South African

Navy might acquire an Israeli corvette design, or a combination of a French and Israeli design. The Israeli type mentioned was the SAAR-5 class, and it was said that a 'hybrid' of this and the French A-69 would be best suited to SAN requirements.[22] A joint South African–Israeli corvette began to be discussed in connection with the deal for the licensed production of the Reshef-class missile boats. One study claims that such a joint project was actually begun, with South African financing and Israeli technology. The result is called the 'Q9' 850-tonne missile guided corvette, and the first keel was to have been laid in 1981, in Israel.[23] However, the usually well-informed reference yearbook *Jane's Fighting Ships* claimed that this design was not yet in production in Israel due to financial problems (the project was named QU-09-35).[24] It can thus be speculated whether South African financing was involved or whether such financing was eventually turned down, due to mounting international obstacles in dealing with South Africa.

New missile boats will—according to Adams[25]—be produced in South Africa. There will be a successor to the Reshef class in Israel known as Aliyah class, for which a licence agreement was allegedly concluded in 1984. This information also remains to be confirmed.

Submarines: a Type-209 copy?

Like the corvette project, a local submarine project has been planned since the cancelling of the order of two Agosta-class submarines from France in 1977.

In 1968, Minister of Community Development and Public Works B. Coetzee said that plans to build indigenous submarines were already 'on the drawing board'.[26] That may have been so, but such construction at the time must have been technically out of the question. The submarine base at Simonstown did not yet exist, for example. In 1981, a rumour was spread that South Africa and Israel were secretly building a *nuclear* submarine at Simonstown. This was a direct result of the Israeli Defence Minister's visit to South Africa in 1980. The source quoted 'one individual closely involved in the project', on which no further information, positive or negative, had come forth by 1988.[27] A joint Israeli-South African submarine design is said to exist.[28] The expansion of the submarine facilities of the Simonstown naval base indeed supports reports of such construction, if not the existence of a joint project with Israel. Simonstown can hold submarines of up to 3000 tonnes, which is well in excess of the needs of the Daphne class now in South African service.

In 1983, the Spanish journal *El Pais* claimed that South Africa had requested submarine technology from Spain worth US $300 million, which was turned down by the Spanish Government, in spite of the financial difficulties threatening the Spanish Bazan Shipyard. This was said to include a refit of the three Daphne submarines in Spain, which was subsequently denied by the South African Navy, since the Simonstown yard is capable of complete refitting work.

In 1986, it was revealed that the future submarine may be a local construction of the West German Type-209, for which the blueprints had already been delivered by South African diplomatic mail in 1985. The criminal proceedings and parliamentary investigation that began in late 1986 revealed that the South Africans had been negotiating for these blueprints since 1983. South Africa finally paid out US $57 million for the construction plans to the state-owned Howaldtwerke of Kiel and a construction firm in Lübeck. The affair was ostensibly conducted entirely by the industries without formal Government participation, despite accusations to the contrary in FR Germany. The work of the special parliamentary submarine committee that was set up in FR Germany to investigate the Type-209 affair, came to a standstill during 1987. The key witnesses failed to appear in court, and companies involved were able to refuse to show documents that would reveal commercial secrets. A political row between the coalition government and the opposition further obstructed the work of the committee, and the situation remained unclear in mid-1988.

The initial investigations revealed that electronic equipment for the operating of submarines had also been delivered to South Africa from the West German subsidiary of the US company Litton Industries—Litton Technische Werke of Freiburg. The customer was the private company Hubert Davies in Johannesburg.

In August 1986, the Johannesburg press wrote about 'speculations' that the work on a local successor to the Daphne-class submarine had reached an advanced stage.[29] It was also said that South Africa now had 95 per cent of the know-how needed to build her own submarines, but that manpower and costs posed problems. The replacement of one Daphne submarine was estimated to cost R120 million.

If a South African Type-209 submarine materializes, previous speculations about co-operation with Israel in submarine construction might also emerge. Israel has operated the same type since 1970. On the other hand, Israel finds itself under mounting pressure from the United States to stop its military collaboration with South Africa. From what has been published about the Type-209 blueprint affair, it seems to have followed a typical embargo-defying pattern. It could take place mainly due to initiatives taken at the industrial level, to the ensuing confusion between governmental departments, and to the impact of economic interests in the selling country. Finally, this deal also illustrates the significant Armscor contact net among European industries.

Notes and references

[1] Details of the Daphne contract and of the Simonstown capacity were reported in 'The submarine flotilla, Hunter-killers of the SAN', *Paratus*, June 1984, p. 34–9.
[2] *International Defense Review*, no. 10, 1984, p. 1567.
[3] Young, G., 'Business Day/Shipping', *Rand Daily Mail*, 5 Dec. 1983, p. 16.
[4] *Argus*, 22 Dec. 1983.
[5] *Jane's Fighting Ships 1985–86* (Macdonald: London, 1986).
[6] *Financial Mail* (South Africa), 20 Mar. 1981.
[7] Campbell, R. K., Special Report for the Institute for Strategic Studies at Pretoria University, quoted in *The Citizen*, 29 June 1984.
[8] *Rand Daily Mail*, 7 May 1980.

9 *The Military Balance 1985–86* (IISS: London, 1986), and *Jane's Fighting Ships 1985–86* (Macdonald: London, 1986).

10 'Watchdog with razor-sharp SA Navy teeth', *Paratus*, Dec. 1984, p. 10–11.

11 Timmerman, K. R., 'South Africa's attack craft', *Defense & Armament*, no. 49 (Mar. 1986), p. 23.

12 *Rand Daily Mail*, 20 Oct. 1981.

13 *South Africa, Official Yearbook of the RSA 1982*, Department of Foreign Affairs and Information (Chris van Rensburg: Johannesburg, 1983), p. 871.

14 *Washington Daily*, 4 May 1985.

15 *Paratus*, Aug. 1984, p. 49.

16 *Daily Telegraph*, 27 Nov. 1984.

17 *Sunday Tribune*, 23 Sep. 1984.

18 *Rand Daily Mail*, 25 Sep. 1982.

19 *Rand Daily Mail* (note 18).

20 *The Star*, 23 Feb. 1982.

21 *Sunday Tribune*, 25 July 1982.

22 *The Star*, 8 Mar. 1982.

23 Adams, J., *The Unnatural Alliance—Israel and South Africa* (Quartet Books: London, 1984), p. 123.

24 *Jane's Fighting Ships 1985–86* (Macdonald: London, 1986).

25 Adams (note 23), p. 123.

26 *The Times*, 1 Dec. 1968.

27 *8 days*, 28 Feb. 1981.

28 Adams (note 23), p. 123.

29 *The Star*, 19 Aug. 1986.

Chapter 9. Infantry weapons and small arms

I. Introduction

Given the strategic situation in southern Africa, the South African Government has, ever since the guerrilla wars began in the Portuguese colonies in 1961, seen the main role of the SADF as the defence of borders. This task has gained importance over the years as white rule in neighbouring states has ceased. The South African troops first assisted the Portuguese and the white Rhodesian armies. Later, they made incursions into Mozambique and Angola, and kept in constant pursuit of SWAPO guerrillas in Namibia. This has been an infantry war, demanding infantry weapons of a basic kind, such as rifles, machineguns, grenades and mines. This is mirrored in the buildup of the arms industry, which is geared, first of all, to provide the Army with all necessary equipment.

The small arms industry is the oldest branch of South African military production. It remains the most comprehensive, the most thoroughly developed and in that respect also the most 'successful'. Self-sufficiency was first claimed in small arms and ammunition. Of the 127 foreign licences acquired by 1961 almost all were for the local production of ammunition, small arms, bombs and so on. Among these, the most well-known types were the Israeli Uzi sub-machinegun, sub-licensed to South Africa from Belgium, and the FN 7.62-mm standard NATO gun, also supplied from Belgium. Both licences were apparently formally revoked after 1963, but production in South Africa continued, presumably under the same policy described above. That is, South Africa considered itself free to use licence-supplied technology after a formal abrogation of such licences. This illustrates one well-known phenomenon from the field of trade in technology—once supplied, there is no way for the supplier to reclaim the know-how, or to force the buyer to forget the knowledge.

II. The producers

The main producing companies are Lyttleton Engineering Works (machineguns, rapid-fire ammunition and rifles), Pretoria Metal Pressings and Naschem (heavy calibre ammunition and grenades), and Somchem, originally attached to the African Explosives and Chemical Industries (AECI).

Somchem

Somchem, today an Armscor subsidiary, represents the oldest South African munitions and mining explosives industry, dating back to 1896 when the first dynamite factory was founded in the Transvaal. In 1924, AECI was created by the South African industrialist Sir Ernest Oppenheimer and Lord McGowan of Nobel Industries (created by Alfred Nobel, who later purchased the Bofors cannon factory in Sweden).[1] Lord McGowan later created the Imperial Chemical Industries (ICI) in England, which was to become one of the giant chemical and explosives multinational industries.

During World War II, AECI was an important supplier of munitions and propellants to the Allied forces. It remains one of the biggest industrial companies in Africa, but it sold its munitions interest in 1962 and after that no longer made any kind of arms. Munitions, propellants and other military explosives were handed over to Somchem, created in 1962 as a sub-section of AECI. In 1971, Somchem was incorporated into Armscor as a full subsidiary and now manufactures a wide range of rockets, propellants and explosives for the SADF.

In 1981, a new chemical factory owned by Somchem was opened at Krantzkop. This plant produces rockets and explosives for bombs for the SADF. At the opening ceremony, it was said that two countries had assisted South Africa in setting up certain of the manufacturing processes, but those countries were not named. It was also said that one of the processes employed is functional in only two other countries in the world. Construction of the new plant began in 1979, necessitated by the rapidly growing demands on Somchem's first factory at Somerset West.[2]

Naschem

Naschem, also an Armscor subsidiary, is one of the largest ammunition manufacturers in the southern hemisphere. Naschem's first ammunition plant, the Lenz plant, began operating in the late 19th century and was up to its closure in 1986 based on a labour-intensive production line, with hand-filling of mortar shells and detonators. In order to keep the core of a semi-skilled work force employed, 20-year-old French proximity fuses were being rebuilt at Lenz. But the total number of employees was cut from 6500 in 1980 to 1600 in 1985. All filling activities were transferred from the Lenz plant to the Boskop plant, opened in 1979, while Lenz was mothballed. According to the Armscor plan, in times of crisis the Lenz plant can be put back into production within a month, recruiting black labour from neighbouring Soweto on short notice.[3]

The Boskop plant immediately began specializing in base-bleed 155-mm ammunition for the G-5 howitzer using the equipment clandestinely acquired from Rheinmetall in FR Germany; from 1985 its filling line was wholly automated, run from a central control room using video terminals. New technology rounds are currently being developed, including bunker-breaking munitions and armour-seeking sub-munitions. Technology and munition-related equipment has also been exported from Boskop.

In May 1983, Armscor publicly unveiled its latest pyrotechnics factory, designed to make South Africa totally self-sufficient in this field. Military correspondents were shown a new Naschem plant in Cape Town and a third range of these new products, all claimed to be locally designed.

PMP

Pretoria Metal Pressings (PMP) produces 7.7-mm (.303) ammunition (the technology of which originated from Vickers, the UK), 7.62-mm ammunition for the FN rifle (Belgium), the 5.56-mm ammunition for the R4 rifle (Israel); 20-mm ammunition (the UK), 30-mm ammunition for DEFA 552/553 guns (France) and 35-mm ammunition for Oerlikon anti-aircraft guns (Switzerland). In 1974, Manurhin of France delivered new machinery to the PMP factory.

Pretoria Metal Pressings opened a new plant in 1981. The expansion programme was completed in 30 months at a cost of R90 million. The new plant is able to manufacture most sophisticated types of rapid-fire ammunition.

III. Ammunition and explosives

The supply of ammunition was especially affected by the 1977 arms embargo, after which all official suppliers preferred to stop the trade. As Armscor Chairman P. G. Marais said at the opening of Naschem's second munition plant, after 1977 the goal was to become 100 per cent self-sufficient in munitions since regular imports in a clandestine way were virtually impossible. 'Ammunition is made to be used and every item consumed must be replaced. Therefore Armscor has given priority to the production of ammunition'.[4]

By 1981, according to P. G. Marais, Armscor was able to supply the entire ammunition needs of the South African Defence Forces and 141 types of ammunition were produced in the country: 'These factories will be in production for several generations and long-term financing has therefore been utilized so that the next generation will also contribute towards the repayment of the investment'.[5] He also said that during the 1981 Operation Protea in Angola, ammunition worth millions of rand had been used.

The current ammunition production in 1981 involved a total work-force of 3000, employed with 110 different contractors and in 13 enterprises supplying related equipment.[6] Between 1977 and 1981, Armscor spent R628 million on expansion of its production facilities, much of this on ammunition manufacture.[7]

Defence Minister Botha declared in Parliament in 1970 that 'considerable progress' had been made in manufacturing *naval* ammunition.[8] In 1983, local ammunition was tested for the first time for the 76/62-mm Italian-supplied Oto-Melara compact guns arming the Minister-class missile craft. It may thus be inferred that up to then such ammunition was supplied from Israel or Italy. By 1985, this 76-mm naval ammunition was among those items offered by Armscor for export. Armscor could by then offer the following equipment: (*a*) pyrotechnics: a full range for army, air force and navy, from thunderflash, smoke canisters, rocket flares, trip-wire flares and coloured signals, to anti-missile decoys and an 81-mm smoke generator for combat vehicles; (*b*) a comprehensive range of hand grenades of offensive, defensive, smokers and riot-control types; (*c*) 5.56-mm and 7.62-mm rifle grenades of high explosive and red phosphorous smoke types; (*d*) non-metallic, anti-personnel and anti-tank mines; and (*e*) demolition equipment for various purposes.[9]

Included in the Armscor advertisements during 1985 was the M57B base-bleed 155-mm ammunition (in South Africa arming the G-5 and G-6 howitzer), amalgamating US, Canadian, Swedish and Belgian technology purchased secretly. The 155-mm ammunition was available in a series of ballistically similar projectiles including an HE (high-explosive) shell, standard or with base-bleed; red phosphorous smoke and illuminating types, and also an M107 HE shell.[10] Armscor offers a 90-mm range of ammunition for export, including a novel cannister round for tanks and armed personnel carriers. It also offers for export ammunition for the 155-mm gun arming the Olifant tank (see chapter 6).

Grenades

Grenades and grenade launchers are commonly used in the operational area by the SADF infantry units. Only two types of explosive grenades are used, one being of Portuguese origin.

A large number of all types of hand grenades are being manufactured locally using technology gained under licence, further developed according to war-fighting requirements. These include explosive and phosphorous combat grenades, smoke grenades for positioning and targeting, and irritants for clearing bunkers and ground shelters. The standard hand grenade in the South African army is a virtual copy of the US M26 and the British L2AI. A new South African-designed hand grenade was shown in 1983. It is capable of killing and injuring with a blast of needle-sharp white hot fragments.

The older types of anti-personnel rifle grenades have been produced in two models. The first is a South African combination of the US M26 design and the old Mecar design, which can be fired from both 7.62-mm and 5.56-mm rifles. Among the few rifle grenades of local design is one resembling a small mortar bomb, which is fired from a 7.62-mm rifle, and the 'Zulu' rifle grenade, which is used in standard infantry units.

The tactical role of grenade launchers has been tested along the borders of Angola and Mozambique. Armscor in 1984 presented a new local single-shot 40-mm launcher. This model fires the US designed 40-mm fragmentation grenade developed for the M79 manufactured by a large number of countries, apparently including South Africa. This weapon was reportedly designed to fill the gap between the maximum-range of a hand-thrown grenade and the minimum range of a platoon mortar.

In 1985, a six-shot semi-automatic 40-mm launcher for COIN and conventional combat use was presented by Armscor. This weapon was then about to enter production. Another new development was the single-shot Stopper 37-mm grenade launcher, presented in 1984 and intended for police anti-riot units. It is identical to the 1984 40-mm launcher except for the cartridge.

Another project is the 75-mm rifle grenade designed by Naschem, presented as a uniquely South African development, believed to be the only one so far developed which is fired pyrotechnically.

Bombs

Ammunition for all kinds of mortars—mortar bombs—has since 1964 been produced in South Africa, originally to French designs acquired with the mortars. Important modifications have been done to incorporate experience from the combat zones. So, for example, all mortar fuses have been re-adapted to better suit the climatic conditions. One example of modification to suit the climate is the South African smoke bombs which use titanium tetrachloride instead of white phosphorous. This reduces the danger of setting large tracts of bush on fire during the dry season.

A new development demonstrated at the pyrotechnic plant in Cape Town in 1983 was a South African redesignation of the old limpet bomb, which can be stuck to any surface like the magnet-operated bomb. In addition to modifications, South Africa has succeeded in producing many indigenous designs in this field.

In 1983, a new locally-produced fuse was introduced—the Merlin proximity/ impact fuse, which can be used with any calibre of mortar bomb. The NVSD (near vertical slope detection) circuit was locally designed. It also incorporates a frequency-agile transmitter which reduces the likelihood of failures due to electronic countermeasures.

The Valkiri has a new fuse developed and produced for Armscor by the Fuchs electronics concern. It is powered by an internal wind turbine generator. Naschem's second factory, opened in 1980, with the slogan 'Naschem makes a dream come true',[11] produces artillery projectiles and aerial bombs.

In early 1986, Armscor officially released details of three new types of bombs developed in South Africa. The first was a 450-kg cluster bomb, called CB470 or Alpha MK-2, which had been first tested in May and October 1985 on the Mirage F-1 fighter. It was said that the CB470 was already in service with the South African Air Force and another, unnamed air force (suspected to be Israel).[12] It was designed according to demands which arose in the war in Angola to produce high-density uniform fragmentation patterns over a large ground area. (Alpha-1 was originally developed by the Rhodesian Air Force in the early 1970s.) The Alpha bombs are also used with the Canberra aircraft, which release large numbers from sealed boxes each containing 25 bombs. The second new bomb was a 120-kg shrapnel bomb, and the third was a 250-kg practice bomb for use with aircraft.[13] The 120-, 250- and 450-kg bombs are fitted with the NATO 500 suspension lugs for mounting on an aircraft. The source of this equipment has not been revealed. These three types of bombs were by 1983 available for export. A bunker bomb has also been reported in production and use.

Landmines

The use of mine warfare against guerrillas has been practised in several cases. Two original South African landmines have been developed by Armscor and presented as 'mines born of the war experience'.[14] These mines are produced by Naschem. One is a high-explosive 3.7-kg anti-personnel mine. The second is a 7.4-kg anti-tank mine. Armscor also produces a third mine, the shrapnel mine no. 2, which is an exact copy of the US M18A1 mine, including the firing mechanism, test set and carrier bags. If, when and how any production licence was acquired from the USA remains unknown. These three mines are standard in the SADF infantry units.

The main company producing demolition equipment in South Africa is Swartklip Products in Cape Town. It produces a range of charges, snout switches and various forms of firing devices including pull, pressure, release and combination pull/release types.

Armscor has also demonstrated various other items of equipment to the public, including booby-trapping devices, a range of anti-riot devices and a stun grenade to use in hostage situations. At the Piraeus arms exhibition in 1982, an indigenous aircraft-mounted chaff and flare chute was first shown available for export, and designated the Hide system.

IV. Small arms

Rifles

R1 7.62-mm

In 1961, a licence was negotiated with the Belgian Fabrique National (FN) at Herstal for the NATO standard weapon, the FN FAL of 7.62-mm calibre. More than 300 000 have been produced by Lyttleton Engineering Works. In South Africa the rifle was designated R1. It replaced the old British Bren and Vickers .303 type. But the South African army was not satisfied with the performance of this rifle, as it was not found suitable for close engagement in bush terrain. After 1963, Belgium revoked this licence in compliance with the voluntary arms embargo, but production continued. However, repair and replacement posed a problem due to the embargo.

In 1976 a smuggling affair was disclosed, involving three shipments from Spain to South Africa consisting of 7.62-mm cartridges. (The long lifetime of small arms was also illustrated by another smuggling case discovered in 1982, involving the shipment of spare parts from Britain for the pre-war Bren and Vickers .303.)

R4 5.56-mm

From 1970, Army and Armscor engineers were searching for a replacement of the R1, and eventually opted for the best offer available—the Israeli Galil rifle. The R1 had been found wanting in comparison with the Soviet AK-47 Kalashnikov used in Angola and Namibia—and the Israeli Galil is modelled on the AK-47. In South Africa, the licence-produced Galil was designated R4. It was offered for export in 1979. By 1985–86, the R4 was to have completely replaced the R1 in the South African Army.[15]

The R4 is 1005-mm long as against Galil's 979-mm. It is virtually identical to Galil, except for some minor modifications. For the R4, there is a special piece of South African-made equipment—which illustrates how intensely the SADF has studied all information derived from wars elsewhere. The army soldiers use a webbing which fastens to the chest, containing six 35-round magazines, an automatic pistol, two grenades and a small signal flare launcher. This lashing was copied from the version used by the FNL troops in Viet Nam for their Kalashnikovs. A special nightsight called Gogga (insect) was developed for the R1 and R2 rifles, and shown for export at the FIDA arms show in Chile in 1984.

A commercial counterpart, the LM4, has been produced and sold on the civilian market by the Armscor subsidiary Musgrave Manufacturers and Distributors.

Finally, it may be pointed out that the various reports about Soviet Kalashnikovs in South African use could well have resulted from a confusion with the R4—a South African copy of the Israeli copy of the Soviet Kalashnikov.

R5 5.56-mm

From 1983, Lyttleton Engineering Works began the study of a shorter version of the R4, according to standards set by the SADF. This version, called the R5, was to be used exclusively with the Ratel armoured personnel carrier (APC). The R5 is 15 cm shorter than the R4, and weighs less than half the R1. It has been referred to as the SADF's 'Saturday Night Special'[16] and it was developed to counter the new Soviet small-calibre version of the AK-74, which appeared in the operational area from 1982.

In 1984, Musgrave Manufacturers offered a commercial counterpart of this rifle also designated the LM5, at a price of around R1000. The LM5 was presented as aimed for use by the security industry and farmers.

Machineguns

FN 7.62-mm and MG4

The standard machineguns since the 1950s have been the Belgian FN MAG 7.62-mm, and the British Browning M1919A4. Both were licence-produced from 1960. The South African Browning was designated the M-G4. It is primarily a vehicle-mounted weapon arming Eland and Ratel. Extensive modifications were done to the South African version. It was re-bored to 7.62-mm NATO calibre.[17] The MG-4 is available in two versions—the MG-4CA co-axial machinegun, and the MG-4AA for infantry support. The feed and trigger mechanisms have been redesigned in South Africa.

Uzi

In 1960, in addition to production licences for the FN MAG and the FN FAL described above, South Africa also purchased from Belgium the licence to produce the Israeli Uzi sub-machinegun. Belgium after 1963 claimed that both these licences, as well as other arms production licences, had been revoked and that all arms exports to South Africa had ceased. The Belgian Fabrique National had acquired the licence for Uzi from Israel in 1955. Uzi remained for many years a standard weapon with the SADF, but it has not been offered for export by Armscor. Production may have ceased after the development of the indigenous SS-77 described below, but in 1985 it was reportedly still in use with the South African Railways Police special task force.[18]

SS-77

The SS-77 was first presented by Armscor in 1985 and was to enter series production in 1986. The weapon was conceived in 1977, hence its designation as a direct result of the mandatory arms embargo. 'SS' indicates the names of the designers Smith and Soregi. The reliance on the previous imported types had become too hazardous, considering the fact the SADF had to rely on 'outside sources for supplies and parts',[19] and work on the SS-77 was under-taken according to SADF specifications. At its presentation in 1985 Col. A. Sarides, Deputy Director of Projects for the South African Army, stated that the Army was basically an infantry army and that the main fire-power of the infantryman on foot was from a rifle and a light machinegun.[20] The SS-77 uses the NATO 7.62-mm cartridge. Its development was in South Africa hailed as yet another proof of Armscor's capacity: 'With the unveiling of the SS-77, South African arms industry has again proven its ability to circumvent the total United Nations embargo imposed on the country'.[21]

The SS-77 was designed by Armscor, working jointly with the Army, and no reports have so far appeared of any foreign design, help or participation. It has been described as a conventional design, in some respects based upon the machinegun already in service with the SADF (the Belgian 7.62). In some respects, the SS-77 is also similar to the Soviet Goryunov SG43.

The Minister of Defence allowed Lyttleton to reveal the existence of the weapon only at the very last moment before entering production.[22] Colonel Sarides also disclosed at the introduction of the SS-77 that the final production price would be about one-third lower than the cost of importing a weapon of similar quality.

New equipment related to the machinegun programme has also been locally produced: in 1985 a new mounting design called the Rattler was announced, which can be used for the SS-77, the FN 7.62 and the MG-4 Browning types. The mounting can be used on all armoured vehicles, cupolas and naval vessels, and was primarily designed for anti-aircraft use.

GI-2 20-mm

The GI-2 20-mm quick-fire cannon is one of many examples of an extensive upgrading by Armscor. This gun is based on the French F2, and was purchased under licence in 1974 to equip the first Ratel armoured cars. The South African Army was never satisfied with the performance of this type, and demanded a replacement in 1982. Then, Lyttleton Engineering redesigned certain features of the F2, using laser-hardened steel which had previously been unavailable. In 1985, the re-named GI-2 gun was being offered for export along with the total product support package. It was one of the strongly promoted new South African-made weapons at the FIDA-84 arms exhibition in Chile. It is constructed for use in helicopters as well as armoured cars.

GA-1 20-mm

The GA-1 20-mm multi-purpose automatic cannon was announced by Armscor in 1986, when series production was begun. It is based on the Messerschmidt MG-751 of World War II origin, and includes a hydraulic sight, using recuperated French optics dating from the 1960s. Armscor claims that the GA-1 is 'the smallest gun in the world that can fire armour-piercing shells'. It is mounted on armoured vehicles, and is also intended for the new generation of attack helicopters, still at planning stage. The GA-1 was also one of the major exhibits in Chile in 1986.[23]

BXP-9

The BXP 9-mm Parabellum sub-machinegun was reported as an indigenous South African design of conventional type, first presented by Armscor in 1984. According to Armscor, the simple design makes it easy to maintain and economic to produce.

Machinegun mounting

Sterling sub-machineguns (UK) are still widely used. One example of indigenization of related equipment is a mounting design for machineguns introduced in 1984. The mounting fits all the types of machineguns in use, and can be adapted on all army vehicles, cupolas and naval vessels.

Pistols and shotguns

The pistols in military use remain mostly of foreign origin: the standard Browning GP-35 (FN of Belgium) and the Spanish Star 9-mm (UK and Spain). One indigenous product, the 9-mm Mamba is also in use, but is not widely distributed. Despite the embargoes, imported pistols for the commercial market are widely available in South Africa. For example, more than 20 years after the first embargo, Musgrave advertised in a South African journal six new Beretta models from Italy, and a private US company 'Florida Arms' offered Beretta, Star, Smith & Wesson and Colt with a 10 per cent discount for SADF and SAP personnel.[24] In total, over 100 types of small firearms are available on the market.

In addition, the SADF is to develop a new pistol.[25]

Striker

The commercial company Armsel, Johannesburg, announced in 1983 that its Striker semi-automatic 12-bore shotgun was about to enter production for military and police use. It was locally designed and developed from 1980.

A number of companies appeared in South Africa during the 1970s promoting commercial small arms, but none stayed in business for long. Armsel claims the capacity and intention to change this pattern, by ensuring strict adherence to international standards and by having every weapon proofed under the South African Bureau of Standards.

The Striker is described as a specific anti-riot weapon, and its idea originated in the Rhodesian bush war. According to the managing director of Armsel, Mr A. Hoffman, his company had already in 1983 received many orders from—as usual, unnamed—overseas dealers and security organizations.[26]

Mortars

The mortars in use with the South African Army are all produced under originally French licences. Mortars are reported to be particularly useful support weapons in the type of warfare which takes place along South Africa's borders. The SADF uses 60-mm, 81-mm and 120-mm mortars of French Hotchkiss-Brandt design. The first batches were imported from France in 1960, and licence-produced under a 1964 agreement. Local manufacture has continued ever since, even after expiry of the licences.

The 60-mm M1 originated with the Brandt model of 1963. Some minor local changes have been made to the design in light of combat experience, and in order to suit South African manufacturing capabilities. From the early 1980s, the M1 was being replaced by a locally developed version, the M4 series (see below). The M3 81-mm mortar is identical to the French Brandt MO-81-61 and is the standard company support mortar of the army. The M5 120-mm patrol mortar is the Brandt MO-120-60. In South Africa, it is used as a light artillery helicopter-transported weapon and is not handled by the infantry. The M4 60-mm mortar was developed in South Africa according to specifications from the infantry. It is based on the French M1, but upgraded according to the experiences from the combat zones. The M4 was first announced in 1983 as being available in two versions, one which uses drop firing and the other, a trigger unit. They are deployed with infantry units of the army.

The standard Ratel-20 armoured vehicle mounts a French M693 20-mm cannon in its turret and carries the 60-mm patrol mortar plus also a number of ex-Soviet RPG-7 rocket launchers.[27] The Ratel-60 is armed with yet another derivative of the original Brandt mortar; a 60-mm gun mortar. The Ratel-90 is armed with a South African derivative of the French F1 DEFA gun, and its ammunition is also based on the associated French designs, production having been continued after the licences expired. A smoke shell for this gun was completed in 1984, illustrating continuous upgrading and manufacture.

Notes and references

1 This connection to one of the first multinational arms companies of the world perhaps accounts for the fact that there is a 'Bofors Street' in Johannesburg.
2 *Rand Daily Mail*, 16 Oct. 1981.
3 *Defense & Armament*, no. 47, Jan. 1986.
4 *Paratus*, Nov. 1980, p. 25.
5 *The Star*, 18 Sep. 1981.
6 *Paratus*, Nov. 1981, p. 7.
7 *Milavnews News Letter*, Nov. 1981.
8 *The Times*, 7 Mar. 1970.
9 Armscor advertisement in *International Defense Review*, no. 12, 1984, p. 1809.
10 Armscor advertisement in *Jane's Defence Weekly*, 16 Mar. 1985.
11 *Paratus*, Nov. 1980, p. 25.
12 *Milavnews News Letter*, 29 May 1986.
13 *Flight International*, 5 Apr. 1986, pp. 10, 11.
14 *Defence Today*, no. 72, Apr. 1984.
15 *Jane's Defence Weekly*, 25 Feb. 1984.
16 *Paratus*, Mar. 1982, pp. 5–6.
17 *Defense & Armament*, no. 24, Nov. 1983.
18 *Paratus*, Dec. 1985.
19 *Paratus*, July 1985, p. 32.
20 *Paratus* (note 19).
21 *Paratus* (note 20).
22 Lenaerts, J., 'SS-77 GMPG from South Africa', *International Defense Review*, no. 6, 1985, p. 981.
23 *Defense & Armament*, no. 49, Mar. 1986; *Paratus*, Apr. 1986.
24 *Paratus Sports Supplement*, June 1981; and *Paratus*, Oct. 1984.
25 *Jane's Defence Weekly*, 25 Feb. 1984, p. 291.
26 *The Star*, 23 Sep. 1983.
27 Among other types of artillery weapons in service, a number of Soviet RPG-7 rocket launchers can be seen, as well as large stocks of ex-Portuguese G-3 assault rifles captured in Angola. In reply to questions about such arms, the SADF asserts that they were 'donated by SWAPO'. For participants in a war this is by no means an unusual means of acquiring weaponry, well known both from the Viet Nam and the Middle East experiences. In South Africa's case, this is yet another way of countering embargo effects. The RPG-7 has become the basic anti-tank weapon of the South African Army, in an upgraded version, pending completion of an indigenous anti-tank missile.

Chapter 10. Military electronics and communications equipment

I. Introduction

In the case of electronics, the mandatory embargo of 1977 coincided with the South African drive to take over this strategic industry, much like the case with the motor industry. The pullout of the largest US multinational companies, which began in earnest in 1982, further aided the South African indigenization programme. This pullout came too late for embargo purposes, since the initial know-how was already there. Furthermore, the South African takeover of the foreign subsidiaries did not, in practice, mean a cutoff of contacts with the foreign mother company. Hence, access to know-how remains unchanged and it is merely the ownership structure that has changed. A secondary effect of the combination of the US multinationals' withdrawal and the South African take-over is that information about turnover and operation of these strategic companies became even more scarce after 1982 than it was before.

Furthermore, European and Japanese companies were able to profit from the US pullout by remaining in South Africa (with some exceptions), which further undermines any prospects of a successful embargo implementation.

The electronics industry in South Africa, of crucial importance for the development of sophisticated weaponry, was established via large multi-national companies with subsidiaries in South Africa. Access to US, British, French, West German and Israeli know-how enabled the initiation of local industries. Foreign know-how remains indispensable, and access is facilitated by the fact that electronic components are practically impossible to define as either military or civilian.

The British corporations Plessey, Racal Electronics, General Electric Corporation (GEC), Marconi, Decca and EMI Electronics have all been involved in production for Armscor. Their subsidiaries later provided the basis for new South African companies. This has also been the case with International Telephone and Telegraph (ITT), Sperry-Rand and IBM (USA), and the West German-based Siemens and AEG-Telefunken.

The field

The field of military electronics covers such a wide area of equipment that any heading by necessity becomes very crude, and conveys a rather diffuse image of what type of equipment is actually covered. Roughly, the sectors of military electronics include: (*a*) the military semi-conductor and integrated circuits industry (computers); (*b*) C^3I (Command, Control, Communications and Intelligence) programmes; and (*c*) the microwave industry. (The vital part played by electronic equipment in modern weapon systems is illustrated by the extended operations of the COCOM embargo from the 1970s. Most reported breakages of this embargo concern high technology and advanced computers.)

The products of these industries include electronic warfare (EW) systems, such as avionics, radar and telecommunication systems; lasers and navigational optronics or electro-optics, and systems for training and simulation. All of this is computer-based science, and high-technology computers thus form the basis for all these sectors.

EW equipment of some kind is integrated into every existing or planned modern weapon system. Passive EW techniques are used to obtain intelligence-communications links. Radars, infra-red detectors, lasers, television cameras and sighting devices all use some portion of the electro-magnetic spectrum for their respective operations. Active EW techniques are employed to prevent enemy use of this spectrum—noise or deception jamming disrupts enemy C^3 networks and radar systems. Chaff, infra-red flares and smoke are used to disrupt radar seekers.

Several of these devices are already in production in South Africa, as will be shown below, mostly of identifiable foreign origin. Typical examples of military electronics application would be the helmet-guided Kukri air-to-air missile and the G-5 howitzer with its A580 fire-control system, which is based on a 16-bit computer with a 64-kb memory.

The leading weapon producers of the world, for obvious reasons, lead in EW technology, but some others, such as Japan, Israel, Korea, Singapore and Taiwan, are also important. South Africa, although a producer of military electronics, has not yet become as big an exporter as the above mentioned producers.

In South Africa, the military are among the largest customers of the rapidly growing electronics industry. In 1976, for example, it was decided to establish a specialist electronic warfare section for the Navy. In 1982, the Electronic Warfare Training Section was opened in Simonstown. Prior to this, EW training had been done at the Signal School in Simonstown. Even in the midst of the 1975–78 economic recession, *computer* sales rose at an annual rate of 25 per cent. Sales of electronic equipment and telecommunications grew at the same rate from 1980.

In 1981, it was estimated in one report that total sales of electronic equipment in South Africa (items imported complete as well as locally manufactured) would amount to R2000 million. This was the same size as the motor industry, except that the local content in electronics was still very much lower. According to the same report, US $250 million a year was spent by the SADF on electronic equipment in weaponry. The electronic component industry was valued at US $150 million per year.[1] South African efforts to export military equipment have met with the greatest success in the field of electronics and communication equipment; much more so than with the attempts to sell the G-5, armoured cars or other weapon systems.

II. From investment to disinvestment

More than any other branch of the military industry, the buildup of production know-how in military electronics and communication equipment in South Africa has benefited from the corporate network of multinational companies operating in the country. Virtually all ensuing local production has been based on foreign licences or, indeed, the takeover of entire foreign companies already in the country, enabling further indigenous developments and the general expansion of the industry. This, in turn, generated a new move from the early 1980s to bring the whole military EW industry under Armscor; previously, it was spread among a large number of private companies, including the foreign subsidiaries.

In 1984, the South African Government appointed a special committee to carry out Government strategy to support indigenous electronics development. This strategy is two-pronged: first, state buying power should be mobilized to increase the local content of electronic products, and, secondly, state aid should be provided for R&D of electronic systems.

The committee was made up of the IDC, the CSIR, Armscor, Escom and Nucor, and some other departments. The aim was to reduce dependence on imports of electronic equipment with strategic value, and to stimulate the manufacture of high-technology products with export potential. In connection with the setting up of this committee, several warnings were also made concerning the inherent dangers and costs of trying to achieve self-sufficiency in a 'siege' economy: concern was, for example, expressed by some members of the electronics industry that, although the use of import protection would promote the development of a local electronics capability, it would cause the sector to *develop in isolation from technological advances internationally*.[2] Concern was also expressed that the cost of 're-inventing the wheel' in the field of electronics would prove prohibitive: 'The idea of going so far as to set up a facility for the manufacture of integrated circuits is absurd'.[3] Finally, a note of warning about the manpower shortage in this field was voiced by Professor L. van Biljon, head of the Pretoria University's Electronics Department. He said that there were fewer than 1000 electronics engineers in South Africa, and that at least twice as many were needed.

Production of some electronic equipment in South Africa began during World War II with British aid. After the war, the first investors in such industries were US companies, such as IBM (from 1952). After 1960, considerable expansion occurred, inspired both by the growing importance of electronics in modern weaponry, general industrial development, and the drive towards military self-sufficiency.

By 1970, full manufacture under licence of foreign—mainly US—equipment was well under way. Some of the leading US companies had been operating in South Africa for more than a decade; for example, IBM, Burroughs and Hewlett Packard. But competition for this market was intense. European-based multinationals did their utmost to conquer a larger share of this lucrative market in South Africa. The British International Computers Ltd. (ICL), Plessey, Hawker Siddeley and Marconi were competing with Siemens and Motorola of FR Germany. The Dutch-based Philips electronics concern, French firms like the Fuchs subsidiary to Thomson-CSF, and Hasler of Switzerland all entered the competition and set up South African subsidiaries. In addition, the advanced Israeli electronics industry is also represented in South Africa by such companies as Tadiran and Atir. Access to Israeli know-how in the electronics field has been reported since 1972. Direct sales of such equipment took place from 1966. In 1980, Control Logic (belonging to the Anglo-American Corporation of South Africa), set up a new company jointly with the Eltron group of Israel, called Conlog, to operate in both countries. From 1983, Taiwan was added to this list of foreign investors in the electronics industry. All these foreign companies have figured in the documentation of the various anti-apartheid organizations in connection with breaches of the arms embargo, both as concerns direct sales of equipment to South Africa, and production in the country.

In addition, in the field of electronics yet another, unforeseen, method of circumventing the embargo was applied from 1977; namely, investing in overseas companies. One example of this is a South African-based multi-national corporation founded in 1984, Bromain Holdings, which owns Salton Incorporated (USA) and 51 per cent of the Israeli electronics firm Atir. Other examples are General Mining, which has shares in Siemens (FRG), and Sanlam, which has shares in Plessey (UK).

The Carter Administration's firm decision to adhere to the 1977 UN embargo resulted in new US regulations of 1978. These explicitly prohibited the sale by US-owned companies of computers, related equipment, or software to any South African government branch enforcing apartheid. These restrictions were immediately exploited by European and also Japanese manufacturers, and US computers were replaced by ICL, Siemens, Olivetti, Hitachi and others. In 1976, Plessey (UK) helped with the construction of a new factory for integrated circuits used in weapon systems.

In the wake of the 1977 UN embargo, the South African Government founded a group to study future access to electronic equipment. The move reflected concern over the embargo, the burst of growth in military demand due to weapon technology development in general, and also the demand from commerce and industry.

The goal decided upon was to achieve South African control of the strategic electronics industry. Two methods were used—first, many of the foreign-controlled companies in the country were taken over by South African capital, entirely—or at least up to 50 per cent. Second, new local producers were established.

In South Africa, as in Europe and Japan, concern was expressed about the heavy dependence on US technology, in particular. According to one important South African producer, Barlow Electronics, 'the transfer of technology will have to take place in all fields of electronics. Local manufacture may still be in its infancy, the country's first microchip factory is not yet in full production, but selective development of the local industry has already given the country a working level of strategic self-sufficiency'.[4]

By 1981, South African companies were producing such equipment as wide-range capacitors, solid state inverters, printed circuit boards and telephone capsules. Six companies were producing mini-computers and intelligent terminals. Local content was estimated at up to 70 per cent. But it was recognized that dependence on foreign sources for processors and memories for main-frame computers would remain for the foreseeable future.[5]

Radios, mine detectors and other classified electronic equipment have been locally designed and manufactured. By 1984, Armscor sales advertisements in overseas journals included: manpack and vehicle radio sets; transmitters, receivers and transceivers; airborne, ground-to-air, air/sea and maritime communications systems; walkie-talkies, line-of-sight equipment, telegraph converters, antenna systems, field telephones and a hand-held data entry terminal.[6]

Since 1976, Israeli Tadiran Electronics Industries has contributed to South African know-how acquisition—one of the first joint projects was the establishment of a dry battery plant, specializing in nickel-cadmium products and batteries for military use. The factory was operational in 1977, with a labour force of 120. A second project was begun in 1977, when a new electronics company, Consolidated Power, was set up at Rosslyn, Pretoria, to produce military communication equipment based on Israeli technology. Consolidated Power is jointly owned by the Calan group of South Africa, and Tadiran of Israel. The first plant is producing batteries and all electronic components for the Skerpioen missile (ex-Gabriel), and Consolidated Power produces the guidance systems for Skerpioen under licence. These have replaced the imported systems, reported to have cost US $90 000 each.[7]

Among the remaining non-US foreign-controlled electronics companies operating in South Africa by 1986 were ICL (South Africa) of Britain, and Hasler (South Africa) of Switzerland. But, in January 1988, ICL announced that it was selling about half of its 93 per cent holding in its South African subsidiary to a Johannesburg industrial holding firm called Malbak. The details of this deal may serve as a good illustration of how foreign capital manages to 'pull out' of South Africa without actually pulling out.

ICL, which in turn is part of the US-based Standard Telephone and Cables (STC) group, declared in this announcement that it would form a new holding company together with Malbak, with ICL still the controlling shareholder. The South African Mutual Life Assurance has a 7 per cent holding in ICL (South Africa), which it will retain. ICL began its involvement in South Africa in 1968, but it has not published its financial results there. The company's annual reports lump together the turnover in the whole of Africa and the Middle East.

This sale is the first major disinvestment by a British company after Barclays Bank sold its South African subsidiary in 1986. By comparison, over 140 US companies sold out their South African interests between 1984 and 1987. The largest of these were IBM, Ford, General Motors and General Electric, which all announced their withdrawal in 1986 and completed the sales of their subsidiaries in 1987. Most of the companies that have disinvested retain substantial business connections through distribution, licensing or technology agreements—the latter will be particularly important to the military sector in South Africa.

In the case of General Electric, for example, the parent company first sold its subsidiary Genwest Industries to its local South African managers. Then it negotiated 42 distribution agreements covering the entire range of electrical, electronic and industrial products it used to sell through Genwest. According to Genwest's managing director, 95 per cent of the company's sales are still made up of General Electric products and parts.[8] Around 40 per cent of the US companies that had left South Africa by 1987 had reached similar types of agreements ensuring future business.

No *military* producer has so far been identified among those companies that have abstained from further engagement. It has even been reported that many of the disinvestment sales specify that the parent company can buy back its former subsidiary at a future date.[9] Thus, the process of disinvestment has so far, in practice, developed in a way that was not foreseen by its proponents.

III. South African producers

Altech

The first electronics company created was Allied Technologies (Altech), South Africa's fastest growing electronics and communications group, based on British and French know-how. To circumvent the mandatory embargo, ITT—the British division of the giant US-based electronics and communications corporation—sold its 33 per cent stake in Altech in 1977. The ITT shares were bought by Altech's holding company, Altron. Altech in 1977 also gained control of the French STC company, which had been operating in South Africa. The goal was to create a major South African producer to compete with the multinational electronic giants, both in South Africa and, for a limited range of products, in overseas markets. Local content of the Altech group was reported at around 80 per cent by 1980.[10] Altech's work has been reported as 'pioneering and of greatest military importance'.[11]

Grinel

Another company that has established itself in this field through the takeover of a foreign company is Grinaker Electronics (Grinel), which bought up the British-owned Racal (South Africa) in 1978. In 1973, Commandant General G. Bierman stated that 'South African forces have learnt through the years that they can rely on Racal'.[12] Racal Electronics (UK) was at the time the leading world supplier of radio packs and tank radios. Well over half of Racal's South African production went directly to the armed services.

Grinel is thus partly based on British technology. The company has also benefited from French electronics know-how—in 1980, the Grinel subsidiary Secom (Security Communications) conducted an agreement with Silec DSI of France to become exclusive distributors of the French company's products in South Africa. Grinel has, according to its own advertisements, developed into 'specialists in the design and manufacture of advanced military communications and associated electronic equipment'.[13]

South Africa's first HF (high-frequency) radio was developed by Grinel in 1978 (based on the Racal TRA-931 manpack radio), and work started in 1963 on the next generation, called the TR-178. The new model incorporated a locally designed combat antenna, and the unit price was quoted as US $8000.[14]

Grinel's development engineers work closely with the SADF, gearing production to the needs that emerge in actual combat.

Tactel

Tactel, one of South Africa's major communications companies, is the product of a number of mergers and a restructuring of the electronics industry, which began in 1961. Through these mergers it took over a contract to re-equip the South African Army with locally manufactured Thomson-CSF TRC-3000 radios (French technology) and a major production contract with the Army for Danish-designed VHF (very high frequency) equipment.[15]

As in the case of Grinel, Tactel production has evolved from a very close interchange between the SADF and development engineers, based on actual combat experience of various products. It produces, as does Grinel, high-frequency hopping radios, which were held forth by Armscor in 1982 as one of the main South African export items.

Barlow Electronics/Reunert

Barlow Electronics, owned by the big industrial concern Barlow Rand, is another electronics company which has secured access to foreign technology by acquisition of foreign companies. In 1977, it acquired 50 per cent of the local Marconi (South Africa), a subsidiary of the British Marconi company. Barlow Rand also purchased the French-owned Fuchs Electronics in 1977.

In 1983, Barlow Rand set up a new electronic and power engineering group through the restructuring of its subsidiary, Reunert Electronics. On the Johannesburg Stock Exchange, the new Reunert was transferred from the engineering sector to the electronics sector. Several wholly or partly owned Barlow companies were sold to Reunert in exchange for new shares and Reunert's motor division. Barlow Rand owns 89.49 per cent of the new Reunert Electronics. The wholly Barlow-owned companies moved into Reunert were: Barlow Communications Telerama-Rediffusion Holdings, Impectron Sales, HESA, Barlow Heavy Engineering and Werat. The partially Barlow-owned companies moved in under the Reunert umbrella were: Heinemann Electric

South Africa (US-based), Barlow Data, Barmarc Holdings, and General Electrics Corporation South Africa. The new Reunert was planned to have assets of R450 million and annual sales of R800 million. The objective of this restructuring was to 'develop business of strategic importance to the country'.[16] It was also stated in connection with the reorganization of Reunert that the new group would be able to co-ordinate increased expenditure on research and development. In 1983, expenditure on R&D by Barlow's Electronics Division amounted to about 8 per cent of annual sales. The new Reunert would spend about 5 per cent of sales, directly and indirectly, on research and development.[17]

Further, it was declared outright that the new Reunert company would give Barlow access to leading overseas technologies from the USA, Europe and Taiwan through its long-term know-how agreements with a number of foreign suppliers. Among these suppliers, specific mention was made of Hitachi of Japan, the General Electrics Corporation (UK), Marconi (UK) and Heinemann (USA). Reunert was a tangible result of the call by Defence Minister M. Malan of 1981 to take the electronics industry into South African hands.

Eloptro

In the early 1970s, the SADF was totally dependent on imports to meet its requirements for optical and electro-optical devices.

Eloptro was set up in 1974 as an Armscor subsidiary, with 70 employees, to undertake the manufacture of optical components for various weapon systems. In 1979, Eloptro became an independent business unit of Kentron. All of Eloptro's work is for the SADF and covers five main areas: research and development; manufacturing; maintenance; rebuilding and modification of existing equipment; and consultation.

Production of optical devices began in 1976. Also in 1976, Eloptro started work on the sight for the 155-mm G-5 howitzer. This work was essentially an updated and metricated version of the British sight used on the 5.5 inch gun already in Army use. The same sight was used on the 127-mm Valkiri rocket launcher.

In 1977, licensed production of night-vision equipment started, either with an Israeli licence, or based on ITT technology available through its South African subsidiary. In 1981, development of the mini-nightsight known as Gogga started, and also a night driver's scope and a compact laser rangefinder. This equipment was introduced into the Army in 1984, and also put up for show at the arms exhibitions in Chile in 1984, 1986 and 1988 as particularly suited for export. By 1986, over 1200 units of the Gogga nightsight had been produced. It is applied to the 7.62-mm R1 and the 5.56-mm R4 rifles, but can also be mounted on the AK-47, M16 and G3 rifles and the Bren and Vickers machineguns. Eloptro provides all of the optical devices for the Ratel and the Eland armoured cars, and contributed to the helmet-sight system in the Kukri missile.

Around 50 per cent of the total contents of its products are made within the company, 45 per cent are made by subcontractors in South Africa, and 5 per cent are imported.[18]

Between 1974 and 1977, Eloptro's production was almost exclusively based on foreign licences. In 1986, it claimed that 99 per cent of its production originated in its own designs.[19] Of the 373 employees at that time, 240 worked in production and 60 exclusively on R&D. By 1990 the company hopes to *export* 50 per cent of its total production, of which the gunnery sights for the G-5 and G-6 howitzer is to account for half. Eloptro is one of the few Armscor companies still operating at close to 100 per cent capacity, not affected by the mounting financial problems for the defence industry at large. A third generation of a light intensification cathode tube is under development.

Trivetts-UEC

Trivetts-UEC (United Electronics Corporation) of Durban has produced sonar electronics and action-information organization (AIO) equipment for the French-supplied Daphne submarines since 1981. The company has drawn on French technology and on the expertise accumulated during the servicing of the Daphne submarines, as well as on the experience of the Reshef-class programme. The updating of the sonar electronics for the submarines included the addition of computer-aided target-motion analysis, using a single computer to process sensor data, feed them to the torpedo system and drive two displays. The update further included a new navigation sub-system and new sonar systems to replace those originally supplied from France. Equipment for updating the medium-range active and intercept sonars was delivered in 1984, and a passive tracker and underwater telephone followed in 1985. This new sonar system was originally specified by South African engineers and developed by French industry. After the 1977 embargo the further development of the system was transferred to South Africa.

Apart from sonar electronics, Trivetts-UEC is engaged in programmes in such areas as semi-automatic analysis of low-frequency noise, transducer and array design and anti-torpedo countermeasures. It specializes in electronic and electrical engineering and also carries out the repair of electrical machinery. It has a long history of co-operation with Armscor and the SADF, and it has built up a special department for electrical and electronic aspects of shipbuilding.

PTI

Protea Telecommunications Industries (PTI) is another major supplier of electronics to Armscor, and one of the oldest producers. In 1972, the company gained a major contract for supplying field telephones to the SADF, and by 1975 it was supplying transformers and power supplies to the armed forces. In 1977, new field switchboards designed by PTI were introduced in the SADF.

PTI is also capable of conducting calibration tests on electronic test equipment, much of which is used in military applications.

Other producers

A wholly South African-owned computer company, Datakor, was launched in 1977. The company specializes in communications.

In the area of military communications equipment, a radiosonde ground check chamber designed and developed in South Africa was reported to be extensively deployed under operational conditions and in regular army service. The producer was given as Diel, Plumstead.[20]

The bulk of the antenna systems are produced by the South African company Jasco. Jasco manufactures a range of products that are modifications of those produced by international companies. Among other electronics companies producing for the SADF, Pekor Electronics specializes in sophisticated security equipment.

IV. Electronic products

A comprehensive description of all electronic equipment and military com- · munications equipment in production in South Africa would be an unreasonable undertaking. The following is, therefore, merely a sample of such equipment produced.

Computers

By 1985, the South African computer market had grown to R1500 million. The IBM disinvestment in 1986 left the way open for Japanese competitors, which because of lower prices had already gained an inroad. (Hitachi began to sell computers to South Africa in 1979 and during the period 1982–85 far exceeded IBM sales, being 30 per cent cheaper.) In September 1988 the information processing industry was valued at R3000 million by *South African Panorama*, which stated that 98 per cent of the computer equipment was imported and that the computer population was growing at a rate of 30 per cent a year.

Among South African developments, one system offered for export by Armscor is the AS-80 computer-controlled artillery fire-control system. The system is produced by ESD, and consists of a 16-bit digital mini-computer, a terminal unit with a keyboard, a printer, and visual display facilities. All programs and data are retained in memory even when the power is switched off.

In 1983, a computerized mobile inventory system for spare parts allocation for military vehicles was first introduced in the Army during 'Operation Askari' in Angola. This system is called 'Project Tiffy' and comprises an air-conditioned shelter with a computer keyboard. The producer has not been named. In 1982, a computerized digital air navigation simulator was taken into use at the SAAF base Langebaanweg. The system had been developed and manufactured in South Africa since 1980, and replaced an obsolete imported simulator.

Optronics

Kentron's development of the helmet-mounted sight linked to the weapon-aiming computer for the Kukri missile has been mentioned above. The origins of this know-how are open to speculation. In 1986, the Israeli electronics firm Elbit announced the development of a strikingly similar helmet-sighting system.[21] One study claims that Israeli electronics firms have been supplying large amounts of equipment to South Africa since 1973.[22]

Equipment designed to improve night sight has been of special interest to the SADF, since night-time, in principle, offers advantages for guerrilla forces. The Eloptro company's nightsight projects might also be based on foreign technology—as early as 1974, Dr L. L. van Zyl of the NIDR visited the Dutch company Oude Delft, which produced nightsights and air surveillance equipment. Gogga, the mini-nightsight used with the R1 and R4 rifles, is also produced by Eloptro.

Armscor announced in 1983 the local development of a laser range-finder based on combined transmitter/receiver and sighting telescope optics. The applications are fire-control for mortars, artillery and armour; target ranging for missiles and light anti-tank weapons, and air-to-ground ranging. The NIDR representative mentioned above also visited during his 1974 tour the West German company Eltro Engineering in Heidelberg, which produces laser range-finders.[23]

Radar

The Plessey Electronics Corporation (UK) was the first supplier of radars and radar technology know-how to South Africa. A Plessey subsidiary was set up in South Africa in 1963. That company also developed a distance-measuring instrument—the MRA5—jointly with the CISR, primarily for military purposes. This device has been extensively exported to Third World countries from South Africa through a Plessey subsidiary in the UK, Tellurometer of Chessington.

In a TV interview in July 1982, Armscor executive director F. J. Bell said that preference had to be given to the indigenous development of radar in South Africa because of its increasing importance in modern warfare. He said that the country's current radar capabilities were one of its shortcomings, and that 'South Africa needs to develop the same ability and self-sufficiency in radar as in related electronic fields'.[24] Three years later, local development by Armscor was announced of the EMVA MK-10B muzzle velocity radar analyser. The producer was given as Global Chemicals, Cape Town.[25]

The NIDR emissary to West European arms producers, L. L. van Zyl, also visited the Royal Radar Establishment (RRE) in the UK during his October 1974 tour to discuss procedures for placing research contracts. The RRE did secret work on electronic materials; infra-red detectors, thermal energy, laser research, infra-red and radar reconnaissance, airborne radar and guided weapons. Dr van Zyl proceeded to Thomson-CSF in France, where radar, electronics and countermeasure systems are developed.[26] Contacts with foreign high-technology industries have been frequent. In the majority of cases, it has not been possible to determine exactly what sales were made—whether of equipment or technology.

Communications equipment

Military communications is another field where South African industry has developed considerable know-how. Armscor sales advertisements list frequency-hopping radios, manpack and vehicle radio set transmitters; receivers and transceivers for base-station and strategic applications; airborne, ground-to-air, air/sea and maritime communications systems; walkie-talkies, line-of-sight equipment, telegraph converters, antenna systems and field telephones.[27] To armed forces engaged in armed warfare, secure radio communication is, of course, indispensable, and hence the determined effort to increase local production in this field. This effort began in 1977 against all economic arguments—at one stage, it was reported that some communications equipment was costing the armed forces *nine* times the price they would have paid for imported equipment.[28] Other obvious applications are in border protection—in 1979, the SADF Headquarters announced that a radio communications network known as MARNET (Military Area Radio Network) was being installed, first in the Northern Transvaal and Natal, and subsequently along all borders to the north and north-west. The system was designed to keep the various local armed forces commands in constant communication with their headquarters, and also with individual farmhouses in the border areas. The connection between the 1977 arms embargo and the progress of this industry has been explained as follows:

While there can be no doubt that the United Nations' arms embargo has presented, and continues to present some major problems to the South African Government, its imposition has not been totally negative from a South African viewpoint. The country's thriving military communications industry, for example, owes its very existence to the embargo which created an almost perfect protectionist environment in which the then new and vulnerable electronics companies could become established. While the embargo was sufficiently 'leaky' to allow the embryo companies to acquire some technology, generally they were forced to innovate and seek their own technical solutions to produce equipment to meet the particular requirements of the South African Defence Forces (SADF). These requirements were considerable as the SADF embarked on major procurement programmes to ensure the country's security against what was seen as a growing threat to its borders.

Today the two major industrial groupings in the military communications field, plus a number of smaller producers of ancillary equipment, are beginning with increasing confidence to attack world markets with a proven range of products. Backed by the resources of the government-run Armaments Corporation of South Africa (Armscor) these companies are looking for export business worth an annual US $100 to 150 million within the next few years. Isolated as South Africa is, the salesmen are well aware of the task before them, but there are signs of the emergence of willing customers for whom the South African equipment offers a good and cost-effective means of meeting their requirements.[29]

That the above is a gross overstatement of the 1977 embargo effect, and rather represents one particular source's anti-embargo sentiments than actual reality, will be shown below, since the chronology of the South African electronics and communications industry is rather different from that presented above.

The fact is that the communications industry dates back to the same period as indeed the entire military industry; that is, the early 1960s. By 1970, full manufacture of foreign-designed equipment under licence was under way, and by 1975, the engineering capability of the local producers had expanded sufficiently to permit the complete development of radio equipment. Up to 1960, the main suppliers of military communications hardware to the SADF were the British company Plessey, and the Dutch-based multinational Philips. Plessey, Racal and Marconi (also British) in turn played a large role in promoting South African technology acquisition in this field.

In the late 1960s, South Africa began to operate its first modern military communications network, the Advokaat Telecommunications System, contained at the Silvermine control centre at the Simonstown naval base. This sophisticated C^3 centre was designed under the Simonstown Agreement with the UK to protect Western shipping in the South Atlantic and the Indian Ocean. The hardware was supplied by Telefunken of FR Germany. Marconi's parent company, General Electric Corporation, equipped both the South African national communications and telephone network, and the military Troposcatter C^3 network.

Notes and references

[1] *Financial Mail* (SA), 13 Feb. 1981.
[2] Jensen, M., 'Promoting electronics—no easy task', *Rand Daily Mail*, 8 June 1984, p. 15.
[3] Jensen (note 2).
[4] *Financial Mail* (SA), 13 Feb. 1981, quoting Barlow Rand director Derek Cooper.
[5] Simon, B., *Financial Times*, 26 May 1981, p. XII.
[6] *International Defense Review*, Dec. 1984, p. 1811.
[7] *Los Angeles Times*, 6 Feb. 1977.
[8] Hammonds, K. H., 'US firms keep a foot in the door', *International Herald Tribune*, 19 Aug. 1986.
[9] Sampson, A., 'Can they be sure of Shell?', *Africa Analysis*, 5 Sep. 1986, p. 4.
[10] *Financial Times*, 28 Nov. 1980.
[11] *Sunday Tribune*, 7 June 1981.
[12] Quoted in *Peace News*, 11 Feb. 1977, p. 7.
[13] Advertisement in *Paratus*, Nov. 1979, p. 53.

[14] *International Defense Review*, no. 10, 1984, p. 1501.

[15] *Jane's Defence Review*, vol. 4, no. 9, 1983, p. 830.

[16] Mulcahy, J., 'Barlows sets up high-tech group', *Rand Daily Mail*, 9 Aug. 1983, p. 11.

[17] Mulcahy (note 16); this piece of information means that the expenditure on R&D will be facilitated through economies of scale and should *not* be interpreted as meaning a smaller investment in R&D.

[18] Foss, C. F., 'Eloptro in search of latest weapons systems', *Jane's Defence Weekly*, 26 Apr. 1986, p. 770.

[19] Timmerman, K. R., 'The South African armament industry', *Defense & Armament*, no. 47, p. 47.

[20] *Jane's Weapon Systems 1985–86* (Macdonald: London, 1986), p. 275.

[21] *Jane's Defence Weekly*, 1 Feb. 1986, p. 166.

[22] Adams, J., *The Unnatural Alliance—Israel and South Africa* (Quartet Books: London, 1984), p. 92–3.

[23] *Observer*, 9 May 1976.

[24] *The Star*, 10 July 1982.

[25] *Jane's Weapon Systems 1985–86* (note 20).

[26] Wilson, A., 'South African arms chief in secret visit', *Observer*, 9 May 1976.

[27] Armscor advertisement in *International Defense Review*, no. 12, 1984, p. 1811.

[28] *Defence*, Jan. 1984, p. 24.

[29] Ragget, B., 'South African milcom comes of age', *Jane's Defence Review*, vol. 4, no. 9, 1983, p. 829.

Chapter 11. The CBW industry

I. Introduction

By its very nature, concrete information on chemical and biological weapons (CBW) production in South Africa is hard to come by. Reports are impossible to corroborate, in particular on biological weapons—and are often inconclusive. This, indeed, tends to be the case with chemical and biological weapons projects generally. Because of the secrecy surrounding the field of CBW weaponry, one of the main methods of establishing the existence of production facilities is to observe their actual use in warfare. Such use—at least of chemical weapons—has reportedly occurred in several regional wars since 1945. The South African Army has repeatedly been accused by Angolan authorities of using paralyzing gases during invasions into the country.

II. Chemical weapons

AECI—jointly owned by the British-based multinational ICI and de Beers, South Africa, dominates the chemicals market. Other producers are Sentrachem (South Africa), and Hoechst (South Africa), based in FR Germany. Only AECI, however, is connected with military/police application of chemical products.

AECI produces tear gas, widely used in riot control in black areas, nerve gas and defoliants. The UK began supplying tear-gas for riot control in 1912, which continued until the first embargo in 1963. By then, local production had already started at one of the AECI factories at Modderfontein. In 1963, Professor A. J. A. Le Roux of the CSIR disclosed that work was being carried out on developing the poison gases Tabun, Soman and Sarin.

According to the London-based South African committee of military resistance, the SADF used chemical agents in 1978 against 600 Namibian refugees at the Kassinga camp in Angola. In 1981, SWAPO President Sam Nujoma again accused South Africa of using napalm and chemical warfare in Angola; for example, 'knock-out gas' bombardment of the Kassinga camp in 1979.[1] In 1983, the Angolan Ministry of Defence claimed that the South African Army had been using chemical weapons with paralyzing effects and tear gas against civilians and government troops in southern Angola. In mid-July 1987, the official Angolan news agency reported an SADF attack with napalm on a town close to the Namibian border.

The use of defoliants in Namibia had been confirmed by South African authorities—the Kavango war zone on the Angolan border was defoliated in 1983. A similar defoliation programme was undertaken in the Ovambo war zone some years earlier.[2]

The London-based *Resister*, quoting a South African army officer, reported that Armscor was designing the 155-mm artillery shells for the G-5 and G-6 howitzers with two compartments containing pure liquid chemical substances which fuse on explosion, capable of poisoning a vast territory. This work was being carried out at the Institute of Medical Research of the South African Air Force in Pretoria. If it exists, this shell is a copy of the binary shell with nerve gas which was developed in the USA in 1977. The Soviet journal *International Affairs* has quoted a statement by A. J. A. Le Roux, reportedly confirming that South Africa was in 1983 doing research on improving nerve gases: 'Such substances can be equated to an atom bomb in their killing capability. Missiles and airplanes can deliver them over considerable distance'.[3]

R&D on chemical weapons has been reported to take place at the Institute for Aeromedicine in Pretoria, in particular, on the poison gas Sarin. In 1978 a secret company in the Orange Free State was allegedly producing chemical weapons, according to a report in the Zimbabwean newspaper *People's Voice* in September 1978.

In the northern Transvaal, a secret research institute has reportedly been set up to experiment with chemical and bacteriological weapons. The South African Naval School in Simonstown conducts similar research. This information comes from the newsletter *Resister*.[4] The journal *Africa Now* in 1983 referred to 'recent allegations' of research being carried out for the production of chemical and biological weapons.[5] Such reports have not been confirmed.[6]

As is the case with alleged nuclear weapon production, South Africa makes—apparently deliberately—ambiguous statements on the matter of CBWs. For example, Defence Minister Botha's reference in a speech of 1966 to 'a secret weapon' has been interpreted to mean either a nuclear weapon or a biological weapon. No hardware had been presented by 1988, however.

III. Bacteriological weapons

Research and testing of an 'ethnic' weapon against white South Africa's enemies has been widely rumoured and reported, presumably a mixture of fact and fiction. Apparently, these reports originated from Namibian refugees reporting in 1984 to the United Nations Committee on Decolonization. According to these reports, the SADF had already begun testing special types of viruses and bacteria, harmless to whites but lethal to non-whites. The testing had allegedly been conducted on political prisoners in South Africa. The centre for bacteriological weapons research was allegedly the secret biological laboratory at the SAAF base Louis Trichardt in the Transvaal. According to these reports, active research in this field was also being carried out by the South African Navy's School for Chemical, Biological and Radiological Defence, located at Red Hill Mountain close to the Simonstown naval base.

Various press reports in black Africa have taken up this subject. In 1983, the SWAPO representative in Brazzaville said that all the components necessary for the manufacture of chemical and bacteriological weapons were being produced in South Africa, originally under licences acquired from the United States and some NATO countries.[7] The Ghana journal *Weekly Spectator* at the same time carried a report that such work is being done in South Africa jointly with Israel, based on 'scientific data' from the Pentagon originating from the Viet Nam War. These weapons were to be tested on the black or Arab prison population in the two countries.[8] The Angolan state news agency, ANGOP, has taken up the same charges. In February 1983, South African newspapers carried daily reports on cholera cases among the black African population in the north of the country. Then the epidemics spread from the Transvaal to some neighbouring states, in particular Swaziland. The Mozambique weekly *Domingo* accused South Africa of having caused this epidemic through tests of bacteriological devices. *Resister* has further reported that after receiving 'documents' from Israel, Armscor introduced certain corrections into the design of the Olifant tank, making it fit for use in areas contaminated with pathogenic bacteria.

But as is evident above, there is a conspicuous lack of corroboration from other independent sources. According to the World Campaign, the original reports about bacteriological weapons were never confirmed and are no longer considered so reliable.[9]

Towards the end of 1987, reports about alleged co-operation between US and South African scientists in the field of bacteriological weapons reappeared. The *Ghanaian Times* wrote that development of binary shells for the 155-mm G-5 howitzer was taking place at an air base near Pretoria.[10] It also claimed that a leading South African geneticist, on 5 September 1986, visited the Fort Detrick Laboratory in the US, which engages in the development of bacteriological weapons as well as genetic engineering and its military applications. It would thus seem premature to rule out the existence of some kind of research programme for this type of weaponry.[11]

Although fiction heavily outweighs the facts of the case, there remains one point to consider. In the psychological climate in southern Africa, reflecting a growing polarization between black and white, there is apparently no limit as to what the South African regime is expected to do in order to preserve white supremacy.

Notes and references

[1] *The Star*, 3 Apr. 1981.
[2] *Rand Daily Mail*, 19 Oct. 1983.
[3] Kosova, M., 'Chemical weapons in South Africa', *International Affairs* (Moscow), Oct. 1983, p. 157.
[4] Quoted by the Angola News Agency, ANGOP, 2 Mar. 1983.
[5] *Africa Now*, Feb. 1983.
[6] For example, Szelowski, D. W. of the US Marine Corps, in *Marine Corps Gazette*, Mar. 1985.
[7] *Strategic Analysis* (IDSA, New Delhi), no. 6 (Sep. 1984), pp. 555–59.
[8] As quoted by *Krasnaya Zvezda*, 17 Aug. 1984.
[9] This information was obtained by personal communication with Abdul Minty, director of the

World Campaign against military and nuclear collaboration with South Africa. However, when considering the physical impossibility of a weapon capable of 'killing only non-whites', it is worth remembering the wishful thinking of Nazi doctors in the concentration camps in Europe during World War II.

[10] Quoted in *Soviet Weekly*, 16 Jan. 1988, p. 4.

[11] In October 1988, a US chemical weapons expert was convicted of spying for South Africa. According to the US Department of Justice, the expert had between 1979 and 1983 delivered a large amount of classified information to South African diplomats in the US (*Svenska Dagbladet*, 12 Oct. 1988).

Chapter 12. Nuclear technology

I. Introduction

When the mandatory embargo of 1977 finally banned nuclear co-operation with South Africa, this measure amounted to no more than a blow in the air. It is inconceivable that the Western powers involved were unaware of this. In fact, it rather seems as if South Africa's achievements in the field of nuclear technology were a precondition for the eventual acceptance of the embargo. When, in 1977, the Carter Administration stopped the supplies of enriched uranium to South Africa, the indigenous South African enrichment plant had already been working for two years. In 1976, one year ahead of the embargo, South Africa managed to secure a contract with France for the building of nuclear power stations. Furthermore, it was reported that in 1976 a secret agreement was reached with Israel for nuclear weapons co-operation. What has been delivered to South Africa from the West is not a nuclear bomb but definitely the capacity and know-how to produce such a bomb.

South Africa is one of the most advanced countries in the world in the field of civilian or peaceful nuclear technology. Its possession of nuclear weapons remains an open question, but its capacity to produce such weapons is equal to that of almost any industrial nation in Europe.

The first stage of its nuclear development programme resulted from the West's scramble for uranium which began during World War II. The United States and Britain invested in uranium processing facilities in South Africa, where the first processing plant was opened in 1952.[1] The United States imported more than 40 000 tonnes of South African uranium oxide valued at US $450 million between 1953 and 1966, when US Government purchase contracts ended. In 1957, South Africa and the United States signed a 20-year agreement under the Eisenhower Administration's Atoms for Peace programme. The agreement covered the purchase of a research reactor from the USA and the enriched uranium needed to run it. It also covered the education of South African scientists in the USA. The uranium resources also gave South Africa access to French technology for the development of nuclear energy, and to West German technology for uranium enrichment. Finally, it is more than likely that South African uranium was the hardware paying for military co-operation with Israel and Taiwan.

In 1985 a total of 11 African states (Algeria, Egypt, Gabon, Ghana, Kenya, Libya, Morocco, Nigeria, South Africa, Tunisia and Zaire) possessed nuclear power installations in some form, but of these countries, South Africa was the only one suspected of running a nuclear weapons programme. The prospect of an 'Afrikaner nuclear bomb' has since the early 1960s caused more international attention and concern than South Africa's conventional armaments buildup. In 1961, the UN General Assembly called upon all states to consider and respect the continent of Africa as a nuclear weapon-free zone, and also called for the termination of any nuclear collaboration with South Africa.[2] In 1964, the General Assembly and the Organization of African Unity (OAU) adopted the Declaration on the denuclearization of Africa, endorsed by the Assembly in Resolution 2033 of 3 December 1965.

The Security Council decided in Resolution 418 of 1977, which established the mandatory embargo on exports to South Africa, that all states should also refrain from any co-operation with South Africa in the manufacture and development of nuclear weapons. The unanimous adoption of Resolution 418 by the Security Council members was in itself a consequence of the detection by satellite in 1977 of a suspected test site for a nuclear explosion in the Kalahari desert (further described below).

The question whether South Africa aims at a nuclear weapons capacity still remains unsolved. This debate has been conducted in the various international fora, in the relevant literature, and in the international press, in a highly emotional climate. This is understandable, but it has, however, not facilitated judgement about South Africa's nuclear intentions. The high-water mark of the reactions caused by the prospect of a nuclear-armed South Africa was perhaps the call by the OAU in 1984 on its member states to develop their own nuclear weapons capability to counter the threat from South Africa—a recommendation which has since been withdrawn, however. When presenting what is known about South Africa as a near-nuclear weapons country, or indeed—as some have it—a country already secretly possessing nuclear weapons, it is of value to separate facts from fiction as far as possible. Technical evidence is confined to the civilian sector of nuclear technology. The facts are:

1. South Africa possesses the second largest uranium reserves in the Western world—uranium reserves in Namibia and South Africa amount to approximately 17 per cent of the world total. The United States imported uranium from South Africa until 1971. France, FR Germany, Israel, Japan and the UK are all large importers of South African uranium. Belgium, the Netherlands and Switzerland are also among the importers. Although Taiwan imports uranium from South Africa, since this is enriched in the United States, trade statistics do not reveal its origin. All information on uranium exports is classified in South Africa.[3]

2. South Africa has since 1975 operated a pilot uranium enrichment plant at *Valindaba*, capable of producing c. 50 tonnes of commercial-grade uranium a year. Access to enriched uranium enables the development of nuclear explosives.

3. At *Pelindaba* (both these names are in the Zulu language, implying 'top secret') uranium hexafluoride (UF_6) is manufactured. This is required in the process of turning uranium into reactor fuel or nuclear explosives. This know-how was apparently, according to a US report, provided by the UK.[4] The plant started operating in 1978.

4. South Africa has, since 1952, possessed several plants for manufacturing uranium oxide (U_3O_8), which represents the first stage in the nuclear fuel cycle.

5. South Africa has operated a nuclear research reactor—Safari-1 (*South African Fundamental Atomic Research*) since 1964 at the Pelindaba site.

6. South Africa operates two nuclear power reactors—Koeberg-1, since 1982, and Koeberg-2, since 1985.

Such a programme could be achieved only with the active co-operation of a number of foreign countries, notably the USA, the UK, France and FR Germany. A number of other countries have also been involved, including the neutral countries Sweden and Switzerland.[5] None of the technology transfers indicates that South Africa actually has a nuclear weapons programme. However, if such a programme materializes in the future, it will be quite correct to state that it was the result of the foreign supply of nuclear technology.

The assumption that a secret nuclear weapons programme exists in parallel to the civilian undertakings is based mainly on two events. Firstly, in August 1977, Soviet satellite photography discovered what was reported as a site for testing a nuclear weapon in the Kalahari desert. Secondly, on 22 September 1979, a US Vela satellite identified a double flash, indicative of a nuclear test, over the South Atlantic—close to South African waters. Although a scientific inquiry found the evidence inconclusive, the event was reported *inter alia* by the CIA as a joint South African–Israeli nuclear weapon test.[6]

The existence of a nuclear weapon programme has also been inferred from South Africa's refusal to co-operate in the nuclear non-proliferation area, and from ambiguous official South African statements on nuclear weapons. South Africa has refused to sign the Non-Proliferation Treaty (NPT). (On the other hand, so have Angola, Mozambique, Niger, Uganda, Tanzania, Zambia and Zimbabwe.) Furthermore, the Valindaba uranium enrichment plant is not open to International Atomic Energy Agency (IAEA) inspection, while Pelindaba and the Koeberg power stations are accessible to the IAEA by contract. In the absence of firm evidence, the matter remains a subject for interpretation and as such, is dependent on the subjective views of the interpreter.

II. The nuclear research programme

The South African uranium resources provided the foundation for the country's entry into the nuclear age. Before the end of World War II, in 1945, South African Prime Minister General Jan Smuts ordered a secret survey to be undertaken of his country's potential uranium resources. This was done at the request of the UK, and directly related to the fact that the US and the UK were embarking on nuclear weapon programmes for the future. In 1948, the Atomic Energy Act was passed in South Africa, under which the Atomic Energy Board (AEB) was set up in 1949. By 1981, nearly 2000 persons were employed by the

AEB, most of them at Pelindaba. The AEB took over control of uranium production and export. In 1950, an agreement was concluded between the Combined Development Agency, a British–US institution, and the AEB on uranium mining. By 1955, 19 mines were in operation.

In 1954, increased interest in basic nuclear research was illustrated by the creation of a physics unit within the AEB. South Africa joined in the formation of the IAEA the same year.

The CSIR took an early interest in nuclear physics—in 1955 it began to operate a cyclotron, imported from the USA. In the mid-1950s nuclear physics research was also initiated at the universities of the Witwatersrand and Potchefstroom, later also at the universities of Stellenbosch, Pretoria and Cape Town. In 1959, the South African Government took the decision to approve the AEB plan for the creation of a National Nuclear Research Centre located at Pelindaba.

A reorganization was undertaken in 1982, when the Atomic Energy Corporation (AEC) of South Africa was set up under the Ministry of Mineral and Energy Affairs. The Uranium Enrichment Corporation (Ucor) and the Atomic Energy Board were re-established as full subsidiary companies of the new AEC. Further, the AEB changed its name to become the Nuclear Development Corporation of South Africa (Nucor). The AEB president, Dr J. W. L. de Villiers, became the first chairman of the AEC.

In 1983, Nucor announced its plan to build a new nuclear research centre within five years (1988) at Gourica in the Riversdale area of the Cape. By 1993 some 300 scientists, engineers and support staff are expected to work there, according to Nucor chairman de Villiers. The research station is necessary since Pelindaba cannot be expanded further, and it will be part of a multi-billion rand establishment called the 'high-technology triangle', one side of which stretches from Cape Agulhas, through Mossel Bay to Cape Town. The facilities include—in addition to the planned research centre—the Koeberg reactor site, the Gamoep nuclear waste dump, the Parow Valley nuclear casualty treatment facility, the Beaufort West uranium mine, the Faure nuclear accelerator, the Cape Agulhas missile site (the Overberg site) and the Wellington rocket fuel plant.[7]

Foreign staff have been involved in nuclear research throughout this period. In 1984, South Africa's state-owned power company Escom hired some 40 US atomic reactor operators, and similar recruitments have also been reported from the UK. Between 1980 and 1982 five export licences from the USA to South Africa for nuclear programme equipment were approved. This included computers, multi-channel analysers and vibration test equipment. In particular, the Cyber 750/170 computer which was delivered to South Africa can be used in nuclear weapons research.[8]

Safari-1

In 1957, South Africa signed an agreement with the United States under the 'Atoms for Peace' programme. This agreement was subsequently amended to expand its scope and duration in 1962, 1967 and 1974, then extended up to the year 2007. According to the agreement, the US corporation Allis Chalmer in 1961 supplied South Africa with the first research reactor, known as Safari-1. It is an 'Oak-Ridge'-type reactor, and began operating in 1965. Other firms were also involved in this construction, notably Krupp of FR Germany, and some French firms. It has a capacity of 20 MW (thermal rating) and is used only for research purposes. In 1962, under the same agreement, the United States undertook to supply the enriched uranium from Fluor Corporation, USA, needed for Safari-1. By 1976, the agreed 104 kg of enriched uranium had been supplied to South Africa. These supplies were thus not disturbed by the switch in the United States policy towards South Africa which became noticeable from 1975. Opposition grew against supplying uranium usable for weapons programmes to a country that had not signed the NPT. From 1976, the USA required cancellation of pre-existing contracts and the refund of South African deposits. In 1977, the Carter Administration effectively stopped further shipments of enriched uranium to South Africa, and in 1978 a new law was passed, prohibiting the supplies of enriched uranium to all countries which have not signed the NPT. Under the Reagan Administration, restrictions on the supply of dual-use equipment for the nuclear industry were relaxed between 1980 and 1985. During this period, the US government granted export licences for the sale to South Africa of helium-3, vibration test equipment, multi-channel analysers and a hot isostatic press. But in each case, an assurance was demanded that the item would not be used for military purposes. The ban on the supply of enriched uranium was never relaxed, however.

This means that the agreement of 1957 is no longer valid. The US ban did have some effect on the work of Safari-1, since the South African AEB was forced to reduce markedly the operating power of the reactor to stretch the existing fuel, pending full-scale operation of the indigenous uranium enrichment plant at Valindaba. The success of this plant has since made the effect of the embargo null and void and, furthermore, it turned out that South Africa was able to import enriched uranium from Europe to cover the needs for its nuclear power reactors at their initial stage.

Safari-1 was from the outset covered by IAEA safeguards. According to official US and UK sources, the uranium sent to South Africa has been adequately accounted for and thus not diverted to any secret nuclear weapons programme.[9] But unrelated to the uranium issue, the Safari-1 reactor could be used for experiments in weapons technology such as the generation and control of neutrons. This would have been relevant for the future development of a tactical nuclear weapon such as an artillery shell.

Pelinduna-zero

South Africa's second nuclear research reactor, Pelinduna-zero, began to operate in 1967. It is usually reported as having been constructed in South Africa, and was part of the intensive research on reactor physics. Very likely, this was also a part of the drive towards independence from foreign suppliers in all strategic technologies. However, reports appeared in 1970 that an agreement had been signed in 1961 with Krupp of FR Germany for the delivery of an experimental nuclear reactor to the Pelindaba site.[10]

This has never been denied or corroborated, but it certainly seems improbable that South Africa, with its relatively limited reactor experience at the time (Safari-1 began working in 1965), would have been able to construct a wholly indigenous reactor. Financial constraints forced the South African Government to choose between this programme and uranium enrichment technology, and the latter got priority. The research on the reactor Pelinduna-zero was thus phased out. This reactor was never covered by IAEA safeguards. The enriched uranium was supplied by the US, fabricated into fuel elements in the UK, and then shipped to South Africa. Heavy water was supplied by the US.

These research programmes provided South Africa with the technological infrastructure for future nuclear research, and also with valuable training of South African scientists. The USA played the main part in this, followed by the UK. In 1958, US nuclear tests in the South Atlantic were monitored by a joint US-South African team; in 1967 a joint British-South African team participated in the monitoring of French nuclear tests in the Pacific Ocean. Since 1966, France has supplied technical expertise in nuclear physics as well as staff to South Africa, and has trained South African scientists.

III. The Ucor uranium enrichment process

Research on the enrichment of uranium began in 1960 under the direction of the AEB, according to a programme drawn up in 1958. The existence of this research was kept secret until 20 July 1970, when Prime Minister B. J. Vorster announced to the South African Parliament that South African scientists had succeeded in developing a new and unique process for uranium enrichment. Funds were authorized to construct a pilot enrichment plant at Valindaba and, simultaneously, the Uranium Enrichment Corporation, Ucor, was set up to handle further developments. Valindaba began to operate in 1975.

This history illustrates that the South African investment in nuclear technology dates back to the same time as the general investment in military R&D, and the buildup of the defence industry in general. Strategic independence from the West has occupied a position of first priority in South African planning ever since 1960. It must have been clear to the South African Government that the supplies of enriched uranium and other assistance from the United States and the UK would be in jeopardy, considering the calls for an embargo against South Africa. An indigenous uranium enrichment plant would escape IAEA inspection, should such secrecy be wanted.

The collaboration with FR Germany in the field of uranium enrichment technology has been extensively publicized,[11] and it remains unclear how indigenous the South African process really is. According to material released in Bonn in 1977 by the banned opposition organization, the African National Congress (ANC) of South Africa, an agreement for such co-operation was in force between 1962–77. Under this agreement, the West German concern STEAG (involved in commercial use of uranium) issued a licence to the South African AEB and Iscor, giving them the know-how for at least part of the latter's uranium enrichment process at Valindaba. The Valindaba plant was operating from its inception with licence-produced equipment from the STEAG concern, until the expiry of these licences in 1976. In this context, it is of interest to note that in 1977 as many as 17 West German nuclear sector subsidiary companies were operating in South Africa. The machinery concern MAN (Maschinen-Fabrik Augsburg-Nürnberg) exported compressors to the Valindaba plant.[12] The Swiss company Sulzer also supplied equipment to Valindaba.[13]

Construction of the Valindaba plant was completed by March 1977, and it soon reached the capacity of producing 10 tonnes SWU/year (separate work units). Ucor originally planned to construct a commercial enrichment facility in addition to this pilot plant, which was to begin operation in 1984, producing 5000 tonnes SWU/year. These plans were, however, shelved, for financial and technological reasons, indicating yet another direct effect of the Western embargo policy on this programme. Instead, Ucor undertook to expand the pilot plant's capacity to 200–300 tonnes SWU/year by 1987.[14]

The enriched uranium from Valindaba is needed first of all for the Koeberg nuclear power reactors. Almost 200 tonnes SWU/year is needed. The Valindaba uranium is also needed to supply the Safari-1 research reactor, for which fuel is also no longer available from the United States. But Safari-1 needs only 14 kg enriched uranium per year, which means that *if* the Valindaba plant produces as much as 300 tonnes SWU/year, a surplus capacity is created that could allow for the secret supply of enriched uranium for a weapons programme.

The laboratory facilities for uranium enrichment have not been opened to IAEA inspection. Ostensibly, this has been done to guard the South African enrichment process from industrial espionage. But, on the other hand, South Africa stated its willingness to accept IAEA safeguards on any future *commercial* enrichment facilities, including the very same enrichment process. Valindaba has thus, through its very existence and operation as a secret establishment and its inaccessibility to inspection, become widely seen as a concrete proof of the existence of an equally secret nuclear weapons programme.

Over the years since the announcement of the South African uranium enrichment technology, numerous speculations have appeared as to its military use. For example, a UN report of 1981 reasoned as follows:

Depending on the design sophistication, the minimum of high enriched uranium required for a 20 kiloton device may range in practice from 15 to 25 kilogrammes. Consequently, by August 1977 South Africa could have had sufficient material to make one or, at the most, two fission bombs. In turn, again depending on the sophistication of the weapon design, sufficient material could have been available by mid-1979 for making upwards of seven or eight fission bombs. Thus it cannot be doubted that, had it decided to do so, South Africa by mid-1979 could have produced sufficient weapon-grade uranium for at least a few nuclear weapons. Current plans call for the expanded uranium enrichment facility being built by South Africa to have a capacity of 200–300 tonnes SWU/year. If designed and operated for that purpose, this additional capacity could produce about 1,000 to 1,500 kilogrammes of high enriched uranium per year, enough for making several dozen fairly sophisticated fission bombs. But even without using the extra capacity of the expanded pilot plant to produce high enriched uranium, South Africa by 1985 still could have produced sufficient high enriched uranium for making 15 to 20 fission bombs.[15]

The issue remained unsolved by 1988. Even *if* a nuclear weapons capacity *was* at hand by then, it still remained unclear whether the fissile material had come from Valindaba.

IV. The nuclear energy programme

Nuclear *energy* became an obvious South African priority after the oil boycott declared by the OPEC countries in 1973. The cost of the indigenous Sasol method of producing oil from coal is reportedly enormous and hence, nuclear energy was seen as a cheaper alternative to solve the energy problem.

In 1974, the South African Government was negotiating with a multinational consortium, which was headed by General Electric of the US and included Dutch and Swiss companies. Negotiations had advanced far enough for a letter of intent, and in 1975 an agreement was signed with the US Energy R&D Agency for the supply of enriched uranium for two power reactors up to 1992.

However, this deal was stopped by the US policy from 1976, and also by anti-apartheid pressure on the Dutch Government. Instead, the French-based consortium Framatome won the Koeberg contract and signed the agreement with Escom in August 1976. Work on the site began the following month.[16]

When South Africa in 1976 succeeded in acquiring French co-operation for its nuclear power programme, this immediately multiplied speculations about a future weapons capacity. In 1977, for example, US government officials declared that South Africa could develop nuclear weapons by 1981.[17]

The following presentation contains the typical argumentation that links reactor technology to weapons technology:

It is not, in fact, true that Koeberg would add nothing to South Africa's military nuclear capacity. The plutonium which the reactors will produce could, if South Africa were to develop its own chemical reprocessing plant, be used for the manufacture of nuclear weapons. Together with uranium from the Valindaba plant after its expansion in 1981, this would transform South Africa's situation from being able to produce a very small nuclear arsenal to being able to produce an arsenal which, within a few years, could number above 300 weapons.[18]

Upon the signing of the Koeberg deal with South Africa, the French Premier Raymond Barre expressed yet another view, totally devoid of the more usual anxiety concerning South Africa's future nuclear plans. He stated that South Africa already had a military nuclear capacity to which the Koeberg reactors would add nothing.[19]

Framatome supplied the two reactors, of Westinghouse design, while fabrication of the uranium into fuel rods was undertaken by the Belgian-French company Eurofuel, under a contract which lasts to 1994. As much as 82 per cent of the finance for Koeberg was put up by a group of French banks, headed by the state-owned Credit Lyonnais. France also trained 100 South African technicians for one year. Equipment for Koeberg was supplied also from Alstrom of France, Hitachi, Mitsubishi and Toshiba of Japan, Combustion Engineering USA, and Babcock & Wilcox, USA. The Framatome consortium is owned 51 per cent by Creusot-Loire (France-Belgium), 30 per cent by the French parastatal Atomic Energy Commissariat, and 15 per cent by Westinghouse of the USA.

The two Koeberg reactors could produce 400 kg plutonium per year, or one equivalent to a Nagasaki-size atomic bomb per week. In addition, Nucor chairman Dr de Villiers told an energy seminar in Pretoria in 1983 that a few more 'nuclear power stations of Koeberg's size will probably have to be built before the year 2000'.[20]

While speculations continue to be presented as to the possible use of the plutonium produced in the Koeberg site, it is still a fact that a trilateral safeguards agreement between the IAEA, France and South Africa entered into force on 2 January 1977. There were two IAEA visits to Koeberg in 1978 and 1979 to verify the construction. The agreement between France and South Africa specifically excludes the reprocessing in South Africa of spent nuclear fuel from this station, and requires that all plutonium extracted in the course of reprocessing of that fuel be stored *outside* South Africa. The spent fuel is being shipped back to France for reprocessing, and thus not left to accumulate in South Africa. This in practice means that the Koeberg power station cannot provide the plutonium needed for a nuclear weapons programme.

South Africa does not have a fuel fabrication or a reprocessing facility. Dr A. J. A. Le Roux (first president of the AEB and later Chairman of Ucor) has furthermore declared that South Africa for financial reasons does not intend to fabricate its own fuel elements.[21]

Koeberg-1 began working in March 1984. The second reactor, Koeberg-2, was started in July 1985. The total cost was estimated as R1801 million at 1982 prices.[22] France was to supply the enriched uranium needed for the two reactors, according to the 1976 sales agreement.[23] With the completion of the Koeberg programme, however, it looked as if France's participation in South

Africa's nuclear technology acquisition would come to an end, due to inter-national pressure and UN demands. After the United States banned the sale of enriched uranium to South Africa for the power station Koeberg-1 in 1977, there was speculation on the source of supply, since imports continued. According to the Hong Kong based *Far Eastern Economic Review* China provided the uranium needed, marketed through a Swiss firm. Instead, it turned out that two US uranium brokers acted as intermediaries between Eurodif in France and the AEB. Eurodif was in a position to sell the desired fuel to South Africa via Switzerland. Eurodif in turn is jointly owned by France, Italy, Spain, Iran and Belgium. The enriched uranium, which in spite of the US embargo reached South Africa, is, however, subject to IAEA safeguards, according to the agreement signed between France and South Africa for the Koeberg reactors. And at any rate, this import was temporary, pending the full operation of Valindaba.

V. A 'nuclear Frankenstein in Africa'?[24]

The resource factors presented above could have resulted in a theoretical South African production of 20–300 nuclear weapons. Taken together with the events described below, a nuclear weapons programme seems highly probable. These events were the discovery of the Kalahari 'test site', and the mysterious flash over the South Atlantic.

The Kalahari test site incident

A definite confirmation of what was really under construction in the Kalahari desert in the mid-1970s may well have to await disclosure by the South Africans themselves. Based on satellite information, Soviet diplomats in August 1977 informed the Western governments that work was nearing completion in South Africa on a nuclear weapons test site, and that testing was imminent.[25] Upon this, US satellite photography confirmed the existence of what was widely interpreted to be a nuclear weapons test site—the pictures showed a hole suitable for an underground nuclear test, a tower, and other structures usually associated with nuclear weapons testing.

In mid-August 1977, the governments of the USA, the USSR, the UK, France and FR Germany joined forces to stop such an undertaking, and threatened to break diplomatic relations with South Africa. The South African Government denied the reports, but, on the other hand, it never allowed any inspection of the area in Kalahari. (It did take journalists on a flight over the desert, but there was no confirmation that this was over the area in question.)

At any rate, the strong reaction by the Western powers must have made it clear to South Africa that any atomic explosion would be too much for the rest of the world to accept. This attitude is illustrated by an official French statement on the issue, which also declares that South Africa was planning a 'peaceful' nuclear explosion.

> . . . we did indeed receive information that South Africa was preparing for an atomic explosion, which, according to the South African authorities, was for peaceful purposes. We know what a peaceful atomic explosion is; however, it is not possible to distinguish between a peaceful atomic explosion and an atomic explosion for purposes of military nuclear testing. We therefore warned South Africa that we would regard such testing as endangering all the peaceful processes under way and as having potentially serious consequences with respect to our relationship with South Africa.[26]

If South Africa was indeed preparing for a 'peaceful' atomic explosion, this places it very close to actually possessing a nuclear weapon capability.

The South Atlantic flash on 22 September 1979

On 22 September 1979, a US Vela satellite (placed in orbit in 1970 to monitor compliance with the 1963 partial nuclear test ban) observed a double flash of light consistent with that caused by a nuclear explosion. It occurred on or near sea level in the South Atlantic close to South Africa's coast. The Vela recording created a public row between the Administration and the scientific community in the US. There was also a lack of consensus within the intelligence community on the issue. The initial presumption was that a nuclear explosive device with a yield of 2–4 kilotons had been detonated by South Africa. An *ad hoc* panel, convened by the Carter Administration in late 1979 reviewed the evidence for two months and came to the following conclusion:

> Based on lack of persuasive corroborative evidence, the existence of other unexplained zoo events (signals of unknown origin) which have some of the characteristics of signals from nuclear explosions, and the discrepancies observed in the September 22 signal, the panel concludes that the signal was probably not from a nuclear explosion. Although we cannot rule out the possibility that this signal was of nuclear origin, the panel considers it more likely that the signal was one of the zoo events, probably a consequence of the impact of a small meteoroid on the satellites.[27]

Other experts claimed that the panel had dismissed corroborating evidence of a nuclear explosion. A radio telescope in Puerto Rico registered an ionospheric disturbance at the same time as the Vela recording, for which no natural explanation could be found. A detailed study by the US Naval Research Laboratory (NRL) analysed a hydroacoustic signal at the same time as the flash, and concluded that the pulse could only be compared to signals produced by earlier nuclear tests in the Pacific.[28]

The CIA initially declared that acoustic evidence from widely scattered listening posts indicated a nuclear explosion. But later the agency decided that background noise could have been responsible. A classified Defense Intelligence Agency report concluded, however, that the Vela had recorded a nuclear explosion.[29]

In 1985, Congressman John Conyers (and the Washington Office on Africa

Education Fund) published a new report based in part on 500 pages of previously classified documents from the NRL entitled 'The September 22 1979 mystery flash: did South Africa detonate a nuclear bomb?' The report, written by Dr R. Walters of Howard University, concludes that a weapon test had been conducted, and that a joint South African-Israeli nuclear weapons programme exists:

This report unveils additional compelling evidence that a nuclear explosion did in fact occur off the South African coast on September 22 1979. Despite denials by both the Reagan and Carter White House, the evidence presented, including hydroacoustic data, independent tests indicating ionospheric disturbances at the time of the blast and evidence of radioactivity in Australian sheep at up to six times the detectable level, was so persuasive as to convince the U.S. Naval Research Laboratory, the Defence Intelligence Agency, the Los Alamos Scientific Laboratory and individuals in the Department of State as well as the Department of Energy that a nuclear bomb was detonated off the South African coast. The summary dismissal of this evidence by both the Carter and Reagan Administrations raises numerous questions yet to be answered.[30]

The NRL documentation also included a CIA judgement that South Africa and Israel were jointly responsible for the 1979 nuclear flash. This documentation was apparently put aside by the US government in favour of the negative conclusion by the special panel quoted above, because of the political motivation of the Carter Administration: a covert South African–Israeli test would have had grave policy implications for Carter's non-proliferation policy. Also, the timing for a show-down with South Africa was inopportune because of the ongoing Lancaster-House negotiations for the independence of Zimbabwe, in which South Africa had just been persuaded to co-operate with the Western powers. Furthermore, a positive finding would have proved embarrassing because the United States had played a crucial role in providing South Africa with nuclear technology, relying upon its peaceful intentions. Last but not least, it could have damaged US-Israeli relations.

According to a book by two Israeli journalists, Eli Teicher and Ami Dor-on, it was *Israel* which had been allowed to use South African waters in 1979 to test a nuclear device. The book, called 'None shall survive us! The history of the Israeli nuclear bomb,' was completed in 1980 but stopped by the Israeli censors. However, its contents were leaked to the mass media.[31] According to these authors, nuclear co-operation started between Israel and South Africa in the mid-1950s, with South Africa exporting uranium in return for importing nuclear technology.

In September 1982 a study entitled *Two Minutes over Bagdad* by Israeli nuclear experts was published in London.[32] The authors—Professor A. Perlmutter of the Johns Hopkins University and Dr M. Hendel and U. Bar-Joseph of the Hebrew University in Jerusalem—supported the long-held rumour of co-operation between South Africa, Israel and Taiwan in nuclear technology. The authors suggested that the low yield of the suspected device tested in 1979 indicates a *neutron bomb*, or a nuclear artillery shell fired from a cannon. A neutron bomb test would explain the low yield of the weapon and the absence of radioactive fallout. Their presentation and argumentation was on the whole perceived as logical and plausible, and has been widely quoted. But it should be pointed out that the sole source given by the authors of this book is US columnist Jack Anderson.[33] It should also be said that Prime Minister Begin of Israel denied any nuclear links with South Africa.

Scattered press reports over the years in various countries provide, when put together, a picture—although confused, of a long-standing Israeli connection in nuclear co-operation. For example, a UPI report from Washington on 29 December 1977 was the first to mention a joint programme by South Africa and Israel, with Iran as the third partner. *Newsweek*, 12 September 1977, reported on a joint South African-Israeli nuclear weapons development plant.

Nuclear delivery systems

Even *if* a nuclear explosion in 1979 had enabled South Africa to complete a nuclear weapon, it would still need the delivery means. Ever since the Kalahari venture, South Africa's various conventional weapon systems have been scrutinized with this aspect in mind. Mention has been made of its Mirage F-1s, Mirage-3s, Canberras, Buccaneers and Shackleton aircraft, all of which in principle 'could carry a first or early generation fission weapon of 450–1100 kg. Larger nuclear weapons *could* be carried by commercial aircraft or military transports'.[34] Technically, it is, of course, possible to arm the Mirage fighters with a nuclear device. As for the Buccaneers, Shackletons and so on, they were all grounded by 1985. But with the acquisition and construction of the long-range G-5 howitzer, a modern nuclear delivery system may actually have been achieved. A nuclear capability of the G-5 155-mm howitzer is plausible. The neutron bomb is a nuclear artillery shell, and South African ambiguity regarding the nuclear capability of the G-5 has encouraged these rumours. It was revealed during the 1980 US investigation of the G-5 affair that a 155-mm nuclear shell delivers a 2-3 kiloton blast—the yield estimated from the observations of the US Vela Satellite in 1979. (No nuclear shells were delivered, but the G-5 could fire such shells.) On the basis of such findings, the ITV television report that in 1980 presented the G-5 story stated explicitly that the 1979 flash was a nuclear explosion caused by joint South African–Israeli testing of an extended-range 155-mm shell.

Further fuelling suspicions about the G-5's place in South African nuclear ambitions is the strange coincidence that the SRC representative, the seller of the 155-mm shell for the G-5 howitzer, happened to be in South Africa precisely at the time of the explosion. Reports have also appeared speculating on a future South African development of 'either short or intermediate range ballistic or cruise missiles for delivering nuclear weapons'.[35] In the 1982 study *Two Minutes over Bagdad*, U. Bar-Joseph, a former Israeli Air Force officer, alleges that South Africa, in collusion with Israel and Taiwan, has developed a nuclear missile with a range of 2400 km.

Speculations concerning South Africa's nuclear intentions rose again in 1986, this time connected to the reports of South African plans to build a military base on Marion Island, 2000 km south of the Cape of Good Hope. The British Foreign Secretary, Sir G. Howe, moved a resolution at the UN, calling on South Africa not to become involved in nuclear testing on Marion Island.

South Africa's nuclear intentions

All the technical and circumstantial evidence and indicators taken together suggest that South Africa's *potential* for becoming a nuclear weapons power cannot be dismissed:

There is virtually no doubt that South Africa has the capability to design, produce and deliver a small nuclear weapon. There is an equally high probability that the Kalahari complex was designed to be, or appear to be, a nuclear test site. This clearly implies that the weapons option has played a part in South Africa's nuclear strategy and calculations.[36]

In the light of the Conyers Report it also seems possible that a nuclear *explosion* took place in 1979.[37]

Probably, both technical and economic constraints for a nuclear weapons programme can be regarded as irrelevant. The cost of a nuclear weapon programme is not an intimidating factor, compared to the costs of conventional weapons production. According to one expert, South Africa could spend R100 million per year on a nuclear weapons programme, excluding required elements that would already be funded by other allocations, by diverting hardly more than five per cent of the military budget allocation for conventional weapons procurement.[38]

The political intentions and calculations of the South African Government have also been extensively analysed in the literature.[39] This study will not further elaborate what South Africa would use nuclear weapons for, against what targets, and in what scenario. This has been done extensively elsewhere. These scenarios share a common element with nuclear war scenarios involving the US and the USSR: in all of them nuclear weapons are a 'last resort', the consequences of which may be unimaginable.

The question whether the Government would use it at all has been taken up in connection with the more psychological matter of the ideology of Afrikanerdom.[40] Adelman and Knight emphasize that 'the critical factor in such a decision will not be technological but rather psychological, namely, the politico-strategic perspectives of the rulers'.[41]

The key concept of the total onslaught has been inspired by the special Afrikaner notion of a potential apocalypse, part of the special destiny of the Afrikaner people in its fight against evil forces. The most outspoken proponents of possible use of nuclear weapons against South Africa's enemies are at the same time the politically most rightist elements, represented by the

Broederbond organization. Several statements by National Party representatives over the years seem ominously to reflect the Afrikaner notion of the unavoidable apocalypse; for example, Information Minister Connie Mulder's declaration in 1977:

Let me just say that if we are attacked, no rules apply at all if it comes to a question of our existence. We will use all means at our disposal, *whatever they may be.* It is true that we have just completed our own pilot plant that uses very advanced technology, and that we have major uranium resources.[42]

One spokesman of the South African ruling establishment, in particular, has come to be regarded as providing an insight into high-level thinking on nuclear strategy. This is Dr L. D. Barnard, appointed to the key post of Director of the Department of National Security (the security police, formerly known as BOSS) in 1978. In the extensive writings of Dr Barnard (including his 1975 dissertation) the Afrikaner ideological heritage stands out as a main theme. For example, he maintains that a Christian state, strictly under the authority of the kingdom of God, must be militarily prepared and must not recoil from waging necessary and just war as the occasion arises. His writings are filled with Biblical allusions to 'the sword of God', and also with outright contempt for the weak and defensive West. His main piece on South African nuclear strategy is entitled 'The deterrent strategy of nuclear weapons', written in Afrikaans in the mid-1970s. The proposals made in this paper are to a striking extent concomitant with several of the actions undertaken by various South African governments. Barnard proposed that South Africa should no longer try to rely upon the West for its security, since the Western states were pathetically defensive in the face of communism. He also stated that obtaining nuclear weapons would not add to South Africa's already considerable isolation in the world, and thus, the costs would be politically unimportant in this respect. He advocated preparation, including developing a nuclear weapons capability immediately, for when the onslaught came it would be too late to prepare. Finally, he declared that 'the value of nuclear weapons lies in their deterrence. This in turn relies upon the perception of that capability. Hence, South Africa must not only develop nuclear weapons, but must also announce to the world and convince the world that it possesses such capability'.[43]

An urge not to overlook the psychological factor was expressed also by the South African poet Breyten Breytenbach in a 1986 interview where he said: 'The Europeans underestimate the machiavellian side of the whites in this country'.[44]

In light of this, at least two theories on the South African strategy present themselves, in particular as concerns the purported Kalahari test site. First, the absence of camouflage, coupled with the South African denial of any foreign inspection of the territory fits well into the Barnard recommendation of making the world see the extent of the South African nuclear capability. But this is still short of an outright confession of weapons capability, which might be considered too demonstrative even for the South Africans.

Second, it *could* also be that, while still following the Barnard prescription, the Kalahari test site was merely intended to make the world believe in a South African nuclear weapons capability. This would mean that there was no real test site but just a modern-day 'Potemkin front'; the erection of a tower and the excavation of a hole in a desert area would in that case have been a very easy method to achieve an international reputation as a 'near-nuclear' country (indeed, an undertaking on a much smaller scale than the real Potemkin fronts were at their time). On the other hand, they may just have used the opportunity to create ambiguity:

South African officials may not have staged the 1977 'bomb-scare' or the 1979 flash! But no doubt, they have benefited from them, for they thereby avoided as blatant an act of proliferation as India a few years ago, yet sparked a cacophony of rumours which accomplished real results. Afrikaner hardliners were consoled in their belief that the government has the capacity to create a nuclear bomb, if not possessing the weapon already. Western leaders were handed a shock in return for all the rhetorical shocks they have doled out to the Afrikaners.[45]

This view is also expressed in the following: 'comparable ambiguity still characterizes the official position in Pretoria'. At the very least that suggests that South Africa's leaders may be tempted to exploit the expression that South Africa may be a latent nuclear-weapon state.[46]

What more than anything else seems to support the notion of a faked weapons programme—although the technological competence in itself is certainly no fake—is that it is in keeping with the South African stance with regard to the rest of its military production projects. No opportunity is ever missed to emphasize how far South Africa has advanced in military know-how, and an exaggerated view of its indigenous capacity has been presented on numerous occasions. It lies very much in South Africa's interests to create the impression that it is indeed on the verge, or already there, of becoming the world's sixth nuclear weapon nation.

Finally, there are other strands in the South African environment which may contradict the apocalyptic scenario of a nation prepared and willing to disappear following a nuclear strike against its enemies. The Afrikaans-speaking Dutch descendants make up some 60 per cent of South Africa's white population. A good number of these, together with the rest of the white population, are unlikely to share any kamikaze ideal. There is, for example, a growing number of conscientious objectors who refuse to do military service. For example, in just one year (1984–85), this number increased from 1500 to 7500.[47]

The UN General Assembly in 1980 concluded that 'many analysts believe that the South African government will stop short of openly testing and deploying nuclear weapons, relying instead on the psychological deterrent created by the widely-held belief that the threat existed'.[48]

A nuclear Opec leader

South Africa's uranium enrichment programme could well be what the spokesmen for the 'peaceful' line claim it to be: a programme aimed at making South Africa one, if not *the* most important uranium exporter in the Western world. In May 1974, the Vice President of the AEC, Dr L. Alberts, emphasized that South Africa, with one-quarter of the uranium resources of the non-socialist world, *was in a bargaining position equal to that of any oil-rich Arab country, in terms of the world's energy crisis.*[49]

Such a strategy, coupled with economic motivation, could well be a central theme in South Africa's nuclear ambitions rather than the production of weapons-grade material. The US Uranium Institute has called South Africa the world's most reliable uranium producer and estimated that South Africa will supply some 14 000 tonnes per year by 1990, compared to its 1980 production level of just under 9500 tonnes. World demand was estimated at around 67 500 tonnes by the mid-1990s, and some 90 000 tonnes in the next decade. A Stanford Research Institute report concludes:

As explained in our previous report in this area, its large uranium reserves could permit South Africa to become a leader of a nuclear 'pariah nation' network. For it can supply uranium ore currently and possibly enriched uranium subsequently to other nations without having to place these shipments under IAEA controls. *The prospect of South Africa becoming head of a nuclear OPEC cannot be lightly dismissed.*[50]

In other words, South Africa's refusal to accept IAEA inspection and safeguards on the Valindaba enrichment plant could be seen as part of a long-term, essentially *economically* motivated plan for a future uranium export to any customer—without interference. But in early 1984, the South African Government announced that South Africa would export nuclear technology and material *only* to recipients who guaranteed placing these items under IAEA safeguards.[51] Simultaneously, the South African Government also assured the US government that it will administer its nuclear affairs 'in line with the spirit, principles and goals of the NPT and the nuclear suppliers' group guidelines'.[52] When this declaration was made by Nucor chairman J. W. L. Villiers in Pretoria on 30 January 1984, he added that South Africa was prepared to resume discussions with the IAEA on its (non-existing) semi-commercial enrichment plant, but still not on its pilot enrichment plant at Valindaba.

What, for the sake of argument, might provide additional support for this theory, is the fact that South Africa has after all signed the Partial Test Ban Treaty (PTBT) of 1963. While much has been made of South Africa's refusal to sign the 1970 Non-Proliferation Treaty, its acceptance of the PTBT has been surprisingly neglected. This treaty prohibits nuclear tests in the atmosphere. Should South Africa have tested a nuclear device over the Indian Ocean, this would constitute a clear violation of a treaty which at the time was willingly accepted. This could indeed point to a nuclear programme aimed not at nuclear weapons but at making South Africa a leading uranium exporter, with the hope of gaining some political leverage in a future global energy crisis.

Assessment

In the absence of a demonstrated nuclear weapons capability, the confused picture presented by the South African establishment might indeed represent a marriage between the fact of a concrete peaceful nuclear energy and uranium enrichment programme, and the deliberate fiction of a possible nuclear weapons programme.

To this it can be added that a nuclear technology programme such as South Africa's, including the existing basic resource factors and the expanding nuclear *energy* programme, in itself enables the switch to a nuclear *weapons* programme in the future, if so decided. This is so, since, in the words of a contemporary nuclear expert, 'nuclear energy is the Siamese twin brother of nuclear weapons'.[53]

However, the official South African policy seems of late to have swung towards reassuring the rest of the world of the non-existence of a nuclear weapons programme. On 21 September 1987, Prime Minister Botha announced for the first time that his government was prepared to discuss the possibilities of signing the NPT—thereby opening up all its nuclear facilities to IAEA inspection.[54]

It is interesting that *The Observer* carried a report from its correspondent in Luanda, Angola, to the effect that Cuba was seeking Soviet approval for a formal declaration of war on South Africa. This report also included the statement that, according to Cuban intelligence, South Africa '*does not as yet have a nuclear weapons capability*, which would be another reason to attack before they do'.[55] This diverges from the usual Soviet and socialist bloc view of South Africa as a covert nuclear weapon power.

From the above presented overview, it is clear that there is forceful argumentation *for* the existence of a South Africa nuclear weapons programme as well as *against* its existence.

On balance, it is here concluded that the existence of a weapons programme is more probable than the theory of a mere fictional creation. Circumstantial evidence rather than technical proof leads to this conclusion—the South African Government's determination to survive and remain in power renders unlikely the idea that these authorities would devote time and finance to the creation of an illusion when they could just as well conduct a real nuclear weapons programme in secrecy.

It would, further, seem at least plausible that such a programme could concern *nuclear artillery*, considering the acquisition of an adequate delivery platform—the G-5 or G-6 long-range howitzer. The development of a nuclear shell, and maybe also the development of a nuclear-armed or nuclear-powered submarine, seems more plausible than the construction of Hiroshima-type bombs which would be carried by obsolete bomber aircraft.

Thus, to summarize, it has in the end to be concluded that South Africa is at least technically capable of nuclear weapons development, beginning with an artillery shell, and has maybe co-operated with Israel in such a venture. Whether any weapon has actually been completed and deployed remains an open question, however.[56]

Notes and references

[1]   Betts, R. K., 'A diplomatic bomb for South Africa?' in *International Security*, no. 4, 1979, p. 94.
[2]   UN Resolution 1652, 24 Nov. 1961.
[3]   UN Document A/Conf. 107/2, 17 Apr. 1981.
[4]   Adelman, K. L. and Knight, A. W., 'Impact upon US security of a South African nuclear weapons capability', SRI (Stanford Research Institute) Project 1200, Apr. 1981, p. 7.
[5]   In 1982, an independent Swedish journal *ETC* (no. 1, pp. 5–7) accused Sweden of assisting the South African nuclear programme by the sale of three isostatic high-pressure presses from the company Carbox to a South African buyer called Deochem. Deochem is one of c. 160 secret companies which do not appear on any official publications in South Africa. In 1980 the US nuclear centre Los Alamos purchased such presses from the Swedish state-owned company. A few months later, Deochem contacted Carbox and negotiations continued in 1981 for Deochem to become the representative in South Africa for the Swedish presses. (Carbox was later bought by the large Swedish concern Asea, which also has a subsidiary in South Africa.) See also *Rand Daily Mail*, 26 July 1984.
[6]   This was alleged in a press release, 21 May 1985, from the Washington Office on Africa by Congressman John Conyers entitled: 'New evidence on South Africa's nuclear explosion'.
[7]   *Argus* (SA), 13 July 1983; *The Star*, 22 June 1983.
[8]   *The Times*, 20 May 1982.
[9]   Statement by N. Sievering, US Energy Research and Development Administration, June 1976, to US House of Representatives International Relations Committee, quoted in Cervenka, Z., and Rogers, B., *The Nuclear Axis: Secret Collaboration between West Germany and South Africa* (Julian Friedmann Books: London, 1978), p. 245. Safari-1 is covered by IAEA safeguards.
[10] 'L'Appareil Militaro-represif de Pretoria', *Jeune Afrique*, no. 515, 17 Nov. 1970, p. 27.
[11] See, e.g., Cervenka and Rogers (note 9).
[12] Disputed information, from the World Peace Council, Helsinki 1975, *Imperialist Military Collaboration with South Africa*, pp. 32–4; Colchester, N., 'Bonn denies South African nuclear deal', *Financial Times*, 27 Sep. 1975.
[13] See for example *The Nuclear Axis* (note 9). The licence agreement with STEAG is also mentioned in: 'Verdeckter Rüstungstransfer, Beiträge der BRD zur militärischen Stärkung der Republik Südafrika (II)', in *Blätter für deutsche und internationale Politik*, no. 8, 1976, pp. 931–32.
[14] *Afrique Defense*, vol. 56, p. 32, Apr. 1985.
[15] Onwumechili, C. A., 'South Africa's plan and capability in the nuclear field', *Disarmament Study Series*, no. 2, UN, New York, 1981, pp. 20–1.
[16] The Koeberg site is located 30 km from Cape Town, and the nuclear power station was erected right across a rich Stone Age archaeological site. Since Afrikaner propaganda has no desire to add credibility to non-white claims to the land, a Stone Age site was not deemed worth saving and permission was not given for an archaeological survey.
[17] *Washington Post*, 16 Feb. 1977.
[18] Smith, D., 'South Africa's Nuclear Capability', World Campaign Against Military and Nuclear Collaboration with South Africa, UN Center Against Apartheid, Feb. 1980, p. 24.
[19] *International Herald Tribune*, 18 Feb. 1977; it remains a fact, however, that the agreement from the outset included IAEA safeguards, precluding any military use of the plutonium from the Koeberg reactors.
[20] *Rand Daily Mail*, 4 Feb. 1983.
[21] 'Talks continuing on US uranium for South Africa', *Financial Times* (UK), 19 July 1979.
[22] *The Star*, 17 Mar. 1982.
[23] *Le Monde*, 27 July 1985.

[24] Epithet used by Dan Smith (note 18), p. 7.
[25] Statement by TASS, quoted in *Pravda*, 1 Aug. 1977.
[26] Statement made by the French Minister of Foreign Affairs, Mr de Guiringaud, on French radio, 'France-Inter', 22 Aug. 1977, quoted in Onwumechili (note 15), p. 40.
[27] Onwumechili (note 15), p. 32.
[28] Kramish, A., 'Nuclear flashes in the night', *Washington Quarterly*, summer 1980.
[29] *Science*, 1 Aug. 1980, p. 572.
[30] Source: Congressman John Conyers (note 6).
[31] This information was quoted in *New Outlook; Middle East Monthly*, Mar./Apr. 1983, p. 34; and in Subcommittee on the Implementation of United Nations Resolutions and Collaboration with South Africa, 'The development of South Africa's nuclear capability', UN General Assembly Document A/AC.115/L.602, 25 Oct. 1983.
[32] *Two Minutes over Bagdad* was published by Vallentine, Mitchell & Co. Ltd: London.
[33] Perlmutter, A., Handel, M. and Bar-Joseph, U., *Two Minutes over Bagdad* (Vallentine, Mitchell & Co. Ltd: London, 1982), p. 51.
[34] Onwumechili (note 15), pp. 22–3.
[35] *The Military Balance 1970–80* (IISS: London, 1980).
[36] Jaster, R. S., 'Politics and the "Afrikaner Bomb"', *Orbis*, vol. 27 (winter 1984), p. 834.
[37] This was alleged in a press release, 21 May 1985, from the Washington Office on Africa by Congressman John Conyers entitled: 'New evidence on South Africa's nuclear explosion'.
[38] Betts, R. K., 'A diplomatic bomb for South Africa?', *International Security*, no. 4, 1979, p. 97.
[39] See for example: Spence, J., 'South Africa: the nuclear option', *African Affairs*, vol. 80, no. 321, 1981; and Betts (note 38).
[40] See for example: Adelman and Knight (note 4), p. 10; Jaster (note 36); and Steward, A., *The World, the West and Pretoria* (David McKay Company: New York, 1977).
[41] Adelman and Knight (note 4), p. II.
[42] Quoted in Jaster (note 36), p. 843.
[43] Barnard, L., 'The deterrent strategy of nuclear weapons', *Journal for Contemporary History and International Relations*, vol. 2, no. 2 (Sep. 1977), pp. 74–97.
[44] *Le Monde*, 14 May 1986, p. 2.
[45] Adelman and Knight (note 4), pp. 16–17.
[46] Onwumechili (note 15), p. 29.
[47] Quoted in *Dagens Nyheter* (Stockholm), 6 Dec. 1986.
[48] Report in *The Star*, 16 Oct. 1980.
[49] Quoted in Väyrynen, R., 'South Africa: A coming nuclear-weapon power?', *Instant Research on Peace and Violence*, Tampere Peace Research Institute, no. 1, 1977, p. 43.
[50] Adelman and Knight (note 4), pp. 40–41.
[51] *Argus*, 1 Feb. 1984.
[52] *Rand Daily Mail*, 31 Jan. 1984.
[53] Prof. Hannes Alfvén, Stockholm, quoted on numerous occasions in the context of the nuclear energy debate in Sweden.
[54] Battersby, J. D., 'South Africa says it may soon sign atomic agreement', *New York Times*, 22 Sep. 1987, p. 1.
[55] *The Observer*, 24 Nov. 1985.
[56] It is possible to advance an entirely different interpretation of the above-described events. South Africa could be aiming to launch an intelligence-gathering satellite which would explain the early involvement of the STEAG satellite research company and the space research activities of the RKI and Tsumeb institutions.

Chapter 13. South Africa's arms exports

I. Introduction

The field of South Africa's arms *exports* was until 1982 completely protected from insight. No information whatsoever on weapons or customers was ever provided by the responsible authorities; nor were comprehensive figures revealed as to the value of military exports, except very rarely. Similarly, the terms of credit, contracts and financing were never even referred to by official sources. This is still the basic state of affairs today, although Armscor with its plunge into the arms export market in 1982 had to reveal one hitherto secret subject—namely, the individual *weapons* it wanted to sell on the international market. Identification of customers and orders remain a closely guarded secret, however. (Other arms-producing industries do not differ in this respect—information is seldom volunteered, and then only when requested or demanded by higher state authorities. Publicity in advance of an arms export deal is rarely deemed to be in the interest of either the seller or the buyer, for *commercial* if not for political reasons.)

South Africa has exported certain types of military equipment and armaments since the 1960s. This equipment has often been exported through intermediaries, in roundabout ways, to avoid announcement of the origin of the goods, parallel to the growing international calls for a boycott of South African goods. (Such tactics were also used in fruit exports from South Africa; one way was to send the consignment to Swaziland and then resell it to European or US importers, now labelled 'Packed in Swaziland'.) An example of the devious methods used in exporting South African equipment came to light in 1984 when the Plessey Electronics Corporation's subsidiary, Tellurometer (UK), was brought to court and fined for having disguised the South African origin of a distance-measuring instrument. The device, called the MRA5, was developed in South Africa jointly by Plessey and the CSIR for military purposes, and had been in production since 1964. It was re-exported from the UK to a number of Third World countries, including India, Nigeria and Pakistan, with invoices and certificates of origin stating that the instruments were 'British'.

The South African communications equipment producer, SMD, developed a high-frequency manpack transceiver, called the B16, which was manufactured by Racal, UK, under licence as the Racal Squadcal. This radio achieved world-wide sales of more than 12 000 units. A similar pattern was followed in 1980 to export both hardware and software developed by the South African company Datakor. ICL (South Africa), a subsidiary of the UK-based ICL concern, signed a co-operation agreement with Datakor, under which ICL obtained the right to market all Datakor's products outside South Africa.

In addition to the UK, FR Germany has provided opportunities for export of South African equipment—a subsidiary in South Africa for many years exported diesel engines to the FRG and from there they were re-exported to a number of foreign customers. The South African-made Eyrie RPV is being marketed from FR Germany to an unknown number of unidentified clients.

Common to all these cases is that the buyers remain unidentified; it is plausible that the South African origin of quite a number of products is kept unknown to the ultimate buyer.

If South Africa receives revenue from the French export of Crotale—the South African-financed missile—this too makes up a clandestine export of sorts, where the ultimate buyer is unaware that he is supporting the South African arms industry.

Finally, Israel also appears to provide an outlet for South African exports: in 1980 a joint South African–Israeli electronics company was set up, called Conlog. Conlog is owned by Control Logic, a subsidiary of Anglo-American, and the Israeli Eltron group. South African technological know-how was reported to be used in the manufacture in Israel of Control Logic's industrial controls and automated electronics.

Even the USA has imported South African-made equipment for military use. In 1980, the Durban-based Non-Ferrous Metals group (not formally connected to Armscor) launched the Universal Solder, capable of soldering any metals together. The US Department of Defence then contracted a substantial order for this new solder, on behalf of the US Navy.[1]

Of course, products such as those described above are nowhere classified as specifically 'military' equipment, and even less as 'arms'. This illustrates the issue of the trade in dual-use equipment, which is practically out of reach of any arms embargo regulations. It can be added that the volume of South African exports of such equipment cannot be established. Individual cases appear now and then, often brought to light by the anti-apartheid movements in Europe. The same is the case with South African exports of small arms, ammunition and other military items that are possible to conceal, and where the origin is not immediately clear.

When it comes to major weapons, it is not possible to conceal exports indefinitely, although, as will be shown below, confusion as to both customer and weapon may occur. The bulk of South Africa's arms exports to date is, however, not made up of major weapons but of other types of armaments and equipment. The following presents what little is known about South Africa's arms customers, in chronological order, without any claim to being exhaustive. Rather, the missing data are certain to exceed by far the existing data.

II. The flow

Arms exhibitions

In 1982, Armscor, then one of the most secretive arms enterprises in the Western world, unexpectedly stepped forward with its presentation of South African-made armaments for export at the arms exhibition Defendory 82 in Piraeus, Greece. Its appearance at this fair created what was widely described as a shock effect among the arms dealers of the world: 'From the defence journalist's point of view Defendory '82 was a show full of news and interest. The biggest surprise, which almost overshadowed some other news items, was the attendance in force of the South African Armscor, complete with a G5 gun and a range of radios and other equipment'.[2]

Another report expressed the same surprise:

We are now accustomed to watching the slow unfolding of weapons developments over a period of time by the major powers and their manufacturers . . . It comes as a shock, therefore, when a country suddenly appears in the international arena complete with an outfit of modern weapons which no-one has foreseen and of which no-one had the slightest inkling until the finished product was laid before them.[3]

The *Rand Daily Mail* of Johannesburg wrote that Armscor's performance in Greece 'created a Big Bang effect'; Armscor Chairman P. G. Marais described it as 'our big coup'; and the Afrikaans language newspaper *Beeld* stated that 'South Africa has extended its war fist to Athens'.[4]

South Africa's sudden participation in Defendory 82 indeed contained some elements of a coup—Armscor was invited through private arms industry connections in Athens only 10 days before the event. A South African C-130 Hercules transport brought in 15 tonnes of armaments for the exhibition, which included the G-5 base-bleed howitzer, the Kukri missile with its sighting helmet, 140 types of ammunition, electronics and radio equipment, and Eland and Ratel vehicles.

The Greek agent for Armscor failed to report the proper country of origin for the Armscor display, and the Greek socialist Government was presented with a *fait accompli*. On the second-to-last day of the week-long exhibit, Armscor was expelled from Greece, but P. G. Marais was jubilant nonetheless, stating: 'We expect good business. And it was especially satisfying that our first international show took place in a NATO country'.[5] After this 'breakthrough', little information has appeared as to possible concrete sales, however. At least, no confirmed orders for such high-technology weapon systems as the G-5 howitzer and the Kukri missile have appeared.

The timing of this Armscor performance was, according to P. G. Marais, due to the wish to be able to present two 'world leader' products: the G-5 howitzer and the frequency-hopping radio. These were ready just in time for the Piraeus exhibition and the aim was to impress the armaments business community.

Behind the decision to enter the export market were, of course, the very same economic and industrial dynamics that force *all* armaments industries to export. P. G. Marais explains the need to export thus:

It is impossible for a country to have an arms industry tailored specifically for its own needs. Firstly, you run into capacity problems. Secondly, private industry is looking for a proper return on the capital that it has invested. With the general trend towards restraint on defence spending, exports are part and parcel of the industry.[6]

One revelation of the expected usefulness of arms exports is found in the missile producer Kentron's export policy: company officials describe themselves as 'technological followers, not leaders'.[7] To broaden the company's financial as well as technological base, Kentron is actively pursuing foreign partners for whom it could develop new missile systems. 'If this strategy works, the SADF will be offered the new system the same as any other client', says one company executive.[8]

The next occasion for Armscor to show off its products was at the international air fair FIDA-84 in Chile in March 1984. The Kukri missile was one of the chief exhibits on this occasion. But no orders have become known after the Chile fair and the results of Armscor's appearances at the FIDA-86 and FIDA-88 arms exhibitions, also in Chile, are as yet unknown. The Armscor slogan at FIDA-84 was 'Third World Weapons for Third World countries', and according to company spokesmen, a number of orders for South African weapons were signed in Chile.

The volume of arms exports

At the Defendory 82 exhibition in Greece, Armscor presented itself as the world's tenth largest weapons producer. Without access to the basis for such a valuation, the claim is difficult to judge.

Armscor is not *one* company, but a corporate umbrella organization encompassing a large number of different enterprises. Hence, the rank as the tenth largest weapons producer in the world is probably best understood as a sales promotion argument, not a statistical fact. Armscor's turnover has been reported as in excess of R1500 million per year.[9] For example, a turnover of US $1800 million in 1981 was quoted.[10]

By comparison, in India—another leading new arms producer—arms production amounted to US $2000 million in 1983–84, engaging a total work force of 283 000 people (more than 10 times that of Armscor). It is not disputed that Armscor is one of the largest producers in the world. But a comparison with individual companies, in the United States, for example, makes Armscor's self-appointed rank incredible. A Department of Defense listing of the 100 largest prime contract companies in the US in 1984 contains 13 companies with a higher turnover than Armscor.[11]

The US Arms Control and Disarmament Agency (ACDA) in 1979 ranked South Africa as 24th world-wide, on a par with Brazil and Spain. After Rhodesia's independence and the loss of this arms customer for South Africa, arms exports went down sharply. In 1981, Armscor's own report quoted a figure of R10 million.[12] In 1982, P. G. Marais of Armscor declared that current arms exports reached only US $9 million, but that the goal was to increase this to US $150 million per year within the decade. That goal still remains to be achieved.

Arms export figures are still not published, however, and official statements remain confined to the size of the market that is to be conquered in the future. For example, in 1987 the Executive General Manager of Armscor, Johan van Vuuren, declared at an arms symposium in Pretoria that the time has come for South Africa *to enter* the international weapons market purposefully.[13]

Armscor's customers

The declared export policy from 1982 has been to aim at the arms markets of Africa, Latin America, the Middle East and the Far East. It is also in these regions of the world that South Africa's military customers are found (with a few exceptions). Some reports suggest that South Africa may already be exporting to more than 30 countries, including many of its black African neighbours.[14]

Africa

Among the early direct importers of armaments was Portugal; the use of South African equipment in the wars in Guinea-Bissau, Mozambique and Angola was often mentioned up to the collapse of the Portuguese colonial power in 1974. 'South Africa has entered the ranks of arms exporting nations—in Africa, the second nation after Egypt to do so . . . South African-assembled jeeps are being used by Portugal in her guerrilla war in Guinea, on the West coast of the continent, and a number of armoured cars have recently been sent to Mozambique'.[15] The same author mentions also Madagascar, Malawi, Rhodesia and Israel among probable buyers of South African armaments.

SIPRI's arms trade registers include a DC-Dakota transport aircraft supplied to the Portuguese forces in Mozambique in 1972. Malawi in 1972 also received six second-hand Ferret (ex-British) armoured cars from South Africa.

Rhodesia (now Zimbabwe), was the largest single customer until the end of white rule in 1980. Throughout the period 1972–76, the total value of South Africa's arms exports amounted to R18 million, most of which went to Rhodesia, in the form of small arms and security equipment, and also major weapons.[16] In 1967, Rhodesia received 12 AL-60 ex-Italian light transport aircraft and four Alouette-3 helicopters from South Africa, and in 1973, a first batch of some 30 Eland armoured cars was delivered along with Puma helicopters. In 1971 a further seven AL-60s plus seven AM-3C light planes were transferred to Rhodesia. In fact, South African military support for Rhodesia's armed forces from Ian Smith's declaration of independence in 1965 until 1980 was such that it enabled Rhodesia to survive in spite of the complete economic and military sanctions declared by Britain and the United Nations.

When this arms customer disappeared with the creation of independent Zimbabwe, South Africa's arms exports fell from an estimated R9 million in 1979–80 to a mere R1.4 million in 1981.[17]

Since the time of South Africa's emergence as an arms producer, it has been said that other African nations are importing South African armaments. South Africa has sold some equipment to Botswana, Lesotho and Swaziland.[18] Mozambique in 1984 purchased certain security equipment to guard its section of the Cabora Bassa power line.

A reported military co-operation and sales agreement with Somalia in 1984 caused the same uproar and denials as the alleged export of the G-5 to Iraq described below. *The Observer* in April 1985 presented an account of a secret meeting in Mogadishu in December 1984 between Somali president Siad Barre and the South African Foreign Minister R. Botha. Based on sources from Somali opposition forces, the article alleges that Somalia agreed on airbase rights for South Africa in exchange for spare parts for Soviet weapons. The Somali Government protested against this report, calling it disinformation. It maintained that the purpose was to 'confuse international opinion and to help South Africa by false information about improved relations between South Africa and Black African nations'.[19]

The possibility of *deliberate* disinformation—in addition to accidental misinformation—must, of course, be taken into account concerning South African arms exports, just as in the case of the nuclear programme and the so-called ethnic weapon. In reality, considering the consistent anti-apartheid policy voiced by all the OAU member states, it would seem to be an odd political move for any African nation to enter into what would resemble close military ties with South Africa.

Latin America

Central and South American countries have constantly been reported as an important target area for the Armscor salesmen. In that region, South Africa has managed to maintain far better relations with a number of countries than in any other part of the world. Both Argentina and Brazil have, at various times, showed some interest in the South African initiative to create a SATO organization.

Argentina, mentioned as one of South Africa's arms customers in 1979, was again alleged to be a customer during the Falklands war in 1982.[20] US 'diplomatic sources' in Cape Town claimed to have identified a consignment of ship-to-ship missiles in the docks, which were being shipped to Argentina at the height of the war. The consignment apparently included Exocet, Skerpioen and Gabriel missiles. These were allegedly being loaded on to a Uruguyan DC-8, labelled 'tractor spares'.

Following US and UK protests, the South African Government first repeated its standard statement on such occasions, namely, that South African policy is to never comment on arms deals. Later, however, Defence Minister Malan stated definitely that South Africa had never sold any missiles to

Argentina.[21] In another unusual departure from the policy of 'no comments', the SADF reportedly considered suing the Argus newspaper group for having initiated the reporting about the alleged missile deal with Argentina. In the end, the British Government accepted South Africa's denials, and the South African view seems to have been one of regret (that no such deal actually took place), mingled with pride over the allegation. Armscor chairman P. G. Marais expressed this view:

The whole flare-up over the Falklands was very complimentary for us. In a way it hurt to have to deny the allegations. But we could not do otherwise because it would not have been true. It is interesting, though, that now that the war is over Britain has captured vast quantities of arms, German arms, American arms, French arms, but so far, not a word about South African arms.[22]

In fact, a UN report in 1984 stated that it was Israeli arms that were being shipped to Argentina via South Africa during the Falklands war.

While the exact composition of any arms sales to Argentina remains unknown, somewhat more is known about such deals with Chile—another of the Latin American customers. From 1981, the Chile Army Day has been celebrated in South Africa. On the second such occasion, Brigadier A. Rodrigues, Chilean Military Attaché to South Africa, expressed his country's affinity to South Africa with the following words: 'There are many ties between our two countries, and the defence forces share not only common ideals but are both fighting the same enemy—international Marxism and the terrorism and chaos that it heeds'.[23]

It is known, at least, that Chile was the first customer in 1980 for an Altech product known as the SOR-18 system (enabling 18 simultaneous conversations on telephone party lines). Further orders for this system reportedly came from Argentina and Colombia. The market for SOR-18 was expected to be worth R5 million a year. Another export success in Latin America is made up of telephone transmitter and receiver capsules, of which Altech produces 1.2 million units per year.[24]

In 1981, South Africa sold six of its Cactus surface-to-air missile systems to Chile via France. Under the original sales agreement with France, the French company Matra agreed to buy back the missiles from South Africa (which financed most of the R&D costs for the development of Cactus/Crotale) at a later date. A French Foreign Ministry spokesman at the time declined to deny or confirm this transaction, but stated that there was no ban on arms sales from France to Chile. In that respect, this deal was another example of South African arms exports through an intermediary country.

In 1985, the South African shipbuilder Sandock-Austral formed a joint company, Astilleros Cabo de Hornes, together with the Chilean Navy's Asmar shipyard. This new enterprise participated in the construction of a port at Punta Arenas in Chile, and in a Navy project for a new sinker lift facility. South Africa has contributed US $13 million to the project. There are also high level relations between the two countries. The Chilean Defence Minister P. Carvajal and a delegation of military officials visited South Africa in the period 13–22 October 1985, to 're-establish a relationship of mutual co-operation between Chile and South Africa on matters relating to defence'.[25] The delegation visited the Operational Area (Namibia/Angola), Armscor, the Simonstown naval base and the Silvermine C^3 centre. No further details on arms exports are known, however, but the visit of this delegation followed on the South African 'success' at the FIDA-84 arms exhibition in Chile the year before. Early reports from this exhibition stated that South Africa was prepared to extend 'technical aid' to Chile, presumably in the military field. Although South Africa participated again in the FIDA shows in 1986 and 1988 the major arms deals hoped for remain unconcluded. According to an Armscor spokesman, South Africa had pushed very hard to sell its Minister-class fast attack boats to Chile, but in vain, as it was in direct competition with Israel—marketing the same vessel.

Guatemala and Paraguay also keep up relations with South Africa in defence matters: South Africa plays a major role in advising the Guatemalan Army on how to resettle the Indian population in so-called model villages to cut them off from leftist guerrillas. In 1983, Guatemalan officers visited Namibia to study the South African programme to deny guerrillas access to the civilian population. It is thus plausible that the Guatemalan regime has imported South African-made COIN equipment, police equipment and small arms, but no further details are known. In 1982, the Israeli State Television reported in a news broadcast that Israel and South Africa were *jointly* involved in 'supporting the regime in Guatemala'.[26] In 1984 it was reported that Paraguayan pilots were being trained in South Africa.

The Middle East and North Africa

Armscor has succeeded with some sales in the Middle East region, and to one north African country—Morocco. Oman is said to have purchased armoured cars in 1979, in a deal not recorded by standard arms trade sources.[27]

Morocco received a large number of Eland-5 and Eland-6 (AML-90) armoured cars at the end of 1979, accompanied by eight South African instructors. Polisario forces later captured some 30 of these vehicles from the Moroccan Army after a battle in the Sahara. The Polisario headquarters in Algiers confirmed this, according to *Le Monde*, and offered photographic proof.[28]

Following Armscor's revelation of its G-5 howitzer at the Piraeus arms exhibition in 1982, an immediate order of 100 units from Iran was reported.[29] Delivery was to take place in March 1985 by ship, and the deal was worth about R1000 million, the largest ever by Armscor. Payment was to be made partly in crude oil. However, the G-5 has not been observed with Iranian forces. In addition, later sources reported *Iraq* as the buyer.[30] The Iraqi government issued a formal denial to the United Nations in July 1985. In September 1985, the Iraqi representative at the United Nations also conveyed to the Security

Council a memorandum denying alleged imports of flame-throwers from South Africa.

No further information has emerged as to the identity of the buyer of the equipment. However, a deal with Iraq would first of all be a direct violation of South Africa's own official arms export rules: its stated policy is *not* to sell arms to potential enemies. A huge arms deal with Iraq would, furthermore, not be in line with South Africa's close relations with Israel. On the other hand, a deal with *Iran* would not endanger the relationship with Israel.[31] Persistent rumours that Iran is one of Armscor's secret customers in exchange for oil gained credibility in connection with a smuggling investigation in 1987, involving a private Swedish arms dealer, a Caribbean air freight company and a Greek firm. According to a well-documented UPI report, the Greek firm was a typical example of a South African 'cover company', wholly controlled by South African capital and systematically used since 1984 to acquire armaments in exchange for oil. This does not, of course, confirm the G-5 deal. There is the possibility that the reports from Iran have simply confused the Austrian-supplied howitzer with Armscor's G-5.

Israel is the closest contact for South Africa in the Middle East. South Africa has supplied large amounts of hardware to Israel. In 1967, for example, South Africa was the chief supplier of spare parts for the Mirage fighters of the Israeli Air Force. It seems reasonable to assume that technology co-operation in military R&D has taken the place of direct arms exports since the Israeli arms industry is more advanced than the South African. In 1982, P. G. Marais of Armscor confirmed in an interview that both Israel and Taiwan played a role as intermediaries for South African arms exports.[32] Theoretically, an arms deal with Iran could have been negotiated through Israel, just as a deal with Thailand could have been arranged through Taiwan.

Asia

Armscor's sales promotion is, in principle, directed towards the Third World regions, or developing countries. Some intrusion on the Asian market has been achieved, mainly in the form of developing a technological co-operation with Taiwan. Since Taiwan is developing its own arms industry, sharing of technology and R&D costs would logically receive priority over direct arms imports. Both Taiwan and South Korea appear among those nations which have publicly decorated senior Armscor executives and South African defence officials (the others being Argentina, Chile, Paraguay and Israel).

In February 1985, the *Bangkok Post* quoted 'military sources' as saying that Thailand was looking for long-range howitzers, and that the weapons competing for the order were the Austrian GHN-45 and the South African G-5. In addition, an advertising campaign for South African weapons had been organized in Thailand through a Hong Kong-based company. According to South African sources, a Thai military team visited Pretoria to examine the G-5.[33] Eventually, however, the Thai government chose the Austrian weapon, avoiding any conflict with the UN, and in accordance with the 1984 UN call for an embargo on all arms imports from South Africa—an early example indicating a difficult future for direct arms exports from South Africa.

In 1982, an apparent piece of disinformation appeared concerning the G-5 howitzer: the *Rand Daily Mail* reported, quoting an anonymous Armscor spokesman, that China had shown interest in the G-5.[34] After 1982, no further mention was made of this. But even if China wanted to buy the G-5, such a sale would certainly violate South Africa's arms export rules, as in the Iraqi case.

Arms to guerrilla movements

A special part of South African arms exports is to the anti-government movements UNITA in Angola and MNR in Mozambique. These arms are, in principle, ex-Soviet arms, once captured by South African forces or purchased on the illegal market. This clandestine trade is now and then highlighted through the arrest of individual salesmen. In 1982, for example, such a deal was revealed at a trial in the UK. This concerned Vickers and Bren machinegun parts and Belgian FN rifles, intended for UNITA rebels in Angola. *The Guardian* commented that the trial at the Old Bailey was 'one of the rare occasions when the veil was lifted from South Africa's huge and clandestine efforts to maintain the efficiency of its defence force and to arm anti-government guerrillas in neighbouring black African states'.[35]

In 1987, formerly classified documents made public in the United States revealed an abortive plan of 1984, under which the Nicaraguan rebels—the 'Contras'—would have received training and equipment ultimately paid for by South Africa.[36]

III. Armscor's sales organization

In 1980 new legislation was passed, for the first time thoroughly formulating and regulating South Africa's arms export policy. By a decree from the Ministry of Defence a new sales and marketing department, Nimrod, was created to handle all exports within Armscor.

According to a list in the Government Gazette on 6 December 1981, the following goods cannot be exported or marketed inside South Africa unless covered by a permit issued by Armscor: 'Warships designed or adapted for offensive or defensive military action, armoured and mine-protected vehicles, vehicles equipped with weapon mountings, all other vehicles designed or adapted for military use, and aircraft with fixed or rotating wings designed or adapted for military use'.[37] It also included a large number of other items of military equipment.

At the same time, official guidelines for armaments export were established: South Africa is, according to P. G. Marais, prepared to sell to any customer because of its independent production of weapons and equipment. Therefore, no resale restrictions apply to weapons produced in South Africa. The sole consideration is the national interest in not selling to potential enemies; that is, primarily communist countries.[38]

Sales promotion

The first task of the Nimrod sales organization was reportedly to train a team of salesmen to prospect the market in Latin America, the Middle East, the Far East and African countries. The special South African demands on weapons systems are considered particularly suitable for 'Third World conditions' rather than for the European market. Armscor is apparently aiming at those Third World customers which are considered for one reason or the other unfit for the usual big salesmen of the West. The advertisements promise product support, individualized instruction and confidential service.

From 1982 Armscor has, however, managed to appear in only four large international arms shows—the Piraeus exhibition in Greece, which ended with the expulsion of the South Africans, and the three FIDA air shows in 1984, 1986 and 1988 in Chile. Thus, Chile stands out among the 50 or so Western nations that arrange yearly arms exhibitions as the sole country willing to provide a shop window for Armscor's products. In South Africa, the participation in Chile has been presented as a triumph for the local arms industry: 'ARMSCOR's appearance at the FIDA International Air Show in Chile this week may be short-lived. But the mere fact that it is there, which alongside private sector suppliers makes SA one of the biggest exhibitor nations, should provide the pro-sanctions lobby with food for thought'.[39]

Asked in 1982 whether Armscor had been hiring experienced Western arms salesmen for its new marketing branch, Chairman Marais replied: 'I won't say that's out, but we would want them to be a part of our organization. We are not very keen to work through gun-runners and agents'.[40] On the same occasion, P. G. Marais noted that Armscor's experience on the procurement side meant that it was more than a beginner in arms traffic. He also confirmed a report in the Johannesburg weekly *Financial Mail* that South Africa might sell its wares through third parties (such as Israel or Taiwan), to avoid embarrassment for the clients. In other words, there would seem to be no reason why weapons could not be smuggled *out* of South Africa just as they can be smuggled in.

Armscor advertising and media coverage

Another particular activity of the Armscor salesmen has been to try to persuade the established Western military and technological journals to give good coverage to the Armscor weapons. Here, notable successes could be seen from 1982, at least up to 1985, beginning with the first exalted reports from the Piraeus fair quoted above. Naturally, this type of journal rarely deals with politics, concentrating on the state-of-the-art in modern weaponry. Nevertheless, the completely apolitical reporting on South Africa's advances in weapon technology is often remarkable to a politically informed reader. In particular, this is so in the case of the well-known journal *Jane's Defence Weekly*, published by the same concern as the classical series of *Jane's* defence yearbooks.[41] This source has repeatedly published reviews on various South

African weapon achievements in a tone of open admiration (even recommending that NATO start importing South African wares, as mentioned above), coupled with open criticism of the West's boycott of military imports from South Africa.

In October 1983, Armscor launched an international advertising campaign and, in addition to an advertisement in *Jane's Defence Review,* managed to place a four-page display of its weaponry in *International Defense Review* (IDR), one of the world's leading arms publications.[42] The IDR is published in four languages and is distributed to subscribers in 135 countries. This journal was invited to visit Armscor's factories after the show in Piraeus. Since then, the IDR has, together with *Jane's Defence Weekly,* appeared as South Africa's chosen advertising and publicity vehicle. At one point in 1984, Armscor actually stood out as the largest single advertiser in IDR.

Apparently, this state of affairs became embarrassing for the journal, which in January 1984 carried an editorial to the effect that the publication does not accept any political responsibility for its technical articles.

This journal has not been backward in seeking and publishing new information about developments in the equipment made by South Africa's defense industry, which has not escaped the attention of some who would have us stop. IDR can not and does not provide a political platform for any particular group or government and a free press does not accede to a request for it not to cover developments in certain areas. We report on military developments in the East and West, North and South, countries communist and non-communist alike. This does not mean that we agree necessarily with the politics of any governments concerned.[43]

While this declaration of an apolitical stance contains an element of dissociation, nothing of the sort has appeared in the *Jane's* publications. On the contrary, from January 1986, *Jane's Defence Weekly* has produced a two-page feature in *Paratus* called 'World defence news'.[44]

Another well-known technical journal which has carried well-informed and detailed reports on South Africa's arms industry is the French *Defense et Armements,* albeit without any political recommendations.

In April 1984, the Irish Anti-Apartheid Movement reported that two Armscor representatives visited the Dublin-based magazine *Strategy and Defence* and offered the editor £10 000 in return for a favourable editorial line in the journal.[45]

In its advertisements, Armscor's weapons are introduced with the wording 'Born of necessity, tested under fire'. The description 'combat-proven' is the central sales argument for South African weapons, and the buyers are even offered the opportunity to inspect the products 'under operational conditions' in Namibia and Angola.

A concerted effort is made to export the most sophisticated armaments to maintain the domestic industry. A marketing executive of Armscor has explained this: 'Export products are chosen for their value in maintaining our high-technology capability, because this is the industrial sector that will remain vital in the future. Exporting large quantities of low-technology items is not a priority'.[46]

The 1984 UN embargo on arms imports from South Africa, although not mandatory and thus not binding for its member states, nevertheless seems to have thwarted Armscor's newly launched export drive. At least, such seems to be the case with the sales of the large, identifiable and visible—and most valuable—weapon systems. The G-5 howitzer was in 1982 reported to be an 'export success', but it has so far not been exported. (Should the reported large deal with Iran—or Iraq—have taken place, the fact remains that these weapons have not been seen and were not used in the Iran–Iraq war.)

The Western press is increasingly sceptical as to Armscor's prospects on the international export market: 'The South African development of their G-5 howitzer was a major step, though subsequent political developments make it unlikely that they will find a major export market for some time to come'.[47]

For all practical purposes, the G-5 has so far lost out to its main competitor (also of Space Research origin), the Austrian Voest-Alpine GHN-45 howitzer, of which over 200 units were eventually sold to Thailand and Iraq via Jordan. *The International Defense Review*, when reporting on the Thai search for a new howitzer, foresaw the defeat of Armscor for political reasons:

In Thailand's howitzer competition, Austria is a neutral country which, like others of its kind, has an exporting arms industry. South Africa has undoubtedly developed a weapon which can compete with the best in performance and price, but as a direct result of an attempt to debar acquisition of such a weapon from elsewhere. The Thai government will doubtless take its membership of the UN Security Council into consideration in making its final choice.[48]

South Africa has admitted that there are problems for its arms export drive. In 1984, Armscor Chairman Marais claimed to be 'very satisfied' with Armscor's penetration of the international arms market, saying that South Africa has achieved in four years what he thought would take ten. However, he did admit that 'the expanded embargo will . . . create some difficulties for ARMSCOR.' He went on to emphasize that Armscor would have to increase its export activity to prevent the loss of expertise as a result of declining demand from the SADF, which faces budgetary restrictions.[49]

A most significant problem indicator is still the fact that no export figures have been revealed after the 1982 US $9 million—if Armscor has indeed achieved some real successes, the most obvious proof of this would be an increased export figure. Finally, two differing opinions from independent Western sources will conclude this section. One forecast presents an optimistic view of Armscor's chances, noting that the South African industrial management

conveys a definite impression of being more pragmatic than dogmatic and is in the forefront of social change. The prognosis is therefore more favourable than South Africa's detractors might suggest is the case, and certainly the isolation forced upon the Republic by the arms embargo has led to a most remarkable display of innovation and self-sufficiency.[50]

The following statement in *Newsweek* in November 1982 was made by one of the rare observers who was not impressed by Armscor's appearance in Piraeus: 'The export drive is a smokescreen and a way to pick up a little extra cash (says one Washington-based defence analyst). Armscor's most important overseas business will continue to be *acquiring* advanced weapons and technology, by whatever means'.[51]

Armscor has hardly as yet achieved its desired position as a leading arms exporter on the world market. What it has achieved is rather a position as a willing exporter to a number of nations which for one reason or another are cut off from military business with the leading Western arms producers. But the big deals with sophisticated weaponry like the G-5 or missiles are not likely to materialize, considering the political stigma on products labelled 'made in South Africa'.

Notes and references

1   *Sunday Times* (South Africa), 1 Mar. 1981.
2   'Defendory Exposition 1982', *Jane's Defence Review*, vol. 4, no. 1, 1983, p. 85.
3   Cross, N., 'Weapon Development 1983: Land', *Brassey's Defence Yearbook 1984*, p. 285.
4   Quoted in *Der Spiegel*, 25 Oct. 1982, p. 208.
5   'South Africa, making weapons for export', *Newsweek*, 29 Nov. 1982, p. 22.
6   Reed, J., 'ARMSCOR—Defence talks to Commandant P. G. Marais', *Defence*, Jan. 1984, p. 24.
7   Timmerman, K. R., 'The South African armament industry', *Defense & Armament*, no. 47, Jan. 1986, p. 45.
8   Timmerman (note 7), p. 47.
9   *African Defence*, Nov. 1983, p. 51.
10   *Défense et Diplomatie*, 29 July 1981.
11   '100 companies receiving the largest dollar volume of prime contract awards fiscal year 1984', Department of Defense, Washington, DC, 17 Apr. 1985.
12   *Financial Times* (UK), 14 Sep. 1982; *Financial Mail* (SA) 17 Sep. 1982.
13   *Defense & Economy World Report*, 2 Nov. 1987, p. 5976.
14   *Défense et Armements*, no. 47, Jan. 1986, p. 40.
15   Venter, A. J., 'South Africa's Military/Industrial Complex', in *International Defense Review*, Dec. 1971, p. 547.
16   Frankel, P. H., *Pretoria's Praetorians—Civil-Military Relations in South Africa* (Cambridge University Press: Cambridge, 1984), p. 89.
17   *African Defence*, Oct. 1982, quoting the *Financial Mail* (SA).
18   *South Africa, a country study*, Foreign Area Studies, Washington, DC, 1980, p. 348.
19   Message from Somalia's embassy in Stockholm to *Dagens Nyheter*, 3 May 1985.
20   See, for example: *Frankfurter Allgemeiner Zeitung*, 25 May 1982; *Défense et Armements*, no. 13 (Nov. 1982), p. 64; and *African Defence*, Sep. 1983.
21   *Rand Daily Mail*, 23 Nov. 1983.
22   *Sunday Times* (SA), 11 July 1982. See also: United Nations Centre Against Apartheid, Special Issue, 'Alliance Between South Africa and Israel', p. 78.
23   *Paratus*, Dec. 1982, p. 29.
24   *Financial Mail* (SA), 13 Feb. 1981.
25   *Paratus*, Dec. 1985, p. 59.
26   Beit-Hallahmi, B., 'Israel and South Africa 1977–1982: business as usual and more', *New Outlook, Middle East Monthly*, Mar./Apr. 1983.
27   The US Arms Control and Disarmament Agency (ACDA), the International Institute of Strategic Studies (IISS) and SIPRI.
28   *Rand Daily Mail*, 31 Mar. 1980.
29   *African Defence*, Jan. 1983, p. 22.

[30] *Africa Confidential*, vol. 26, no. 8 (10 Apr. 1985).
[31] One possible explanation of the confused report may even be that one or more sources mixed up Iran and Iraq, out of the same kind of Eurocentrism that has resulted in a widespread misuse of the 'Third World' concept.
[32] *New York Times*, 5 Dec. 1982.
[33] *Africa Confidential*, vol. 26, no. 16 (31 July 1985).
[34] Quoted in *Afrique Défense*, Oct. 1982.
[35] Pallister, D., 'Trade that keeps Pretoria fighting', *Guardian*, 19 Oct. 1982.
[36] *International Herald Tribune*, 21 Aug. 1987.
[37] *The Star,* 7 Dec. 1981.
[38] Quoted in *African Defence*, June 1985, p. 52.
[39] *Paratus*, Apr. 1986, p. 39.
[40] Lelyveld, J., 'South Africa tries to sell its arms', *New York Times*, 5 Dec. 1982.
[41] See, for example, *Jane's Defence Weekly*, 27 July 1985 and 26 Apr. 1986; see also *Jane's Defence Review*, vol. 4, no. 4, 1983.
[42] *International Defense Review*, no. 3, 1983, pp. 268–71.
[43] Gilson, C., Editorial, 'Logic of the Day', *International Defense Review*, no. 6, 1985, p. 845.
[44] See, for example, *Paratus*, Mar. 1986.
[45] *Irish Press*, 4 Oct. 1984.
[46] Timmerman (note 7), p. 39.
[47] Stone, W., 'Current trends in artillery' *Defense*, no. 1, 1985, p. 511.
[48] Gilson (note 43).
[49] *Defence*, Nov. 1985, p. 50.
[50] Reed (note 6), p. 26.
[51] *Newsweek*, 29 Nov. 1982, p. 22.

Part IV.
Implementation and disimplementation

Chapter 14. Embargo implementation

I. Introduction

From the factual account of the establishment of South Africa's arms industry presented in parts II and III, it is clear that this industry, such as it has developed to date, owes its very existence to the access to foreign technology. Western military know-how, acquired by various ways and means, laid the foundation for the aircraft industry (Italy, France, the UK, the USA and Israel, in that order), the military vehicle industry (France, FR Germany, Japan, USA and Canada), the rocket and missile industry (FR Germany, Israel and France), the naval industry (Israel and FR Germany), the small arms industry (Belgium, the UK, the USA, Israel and France), the electronics industry (the UK, the USA, France, Israel, the FRG, Austria and the Netherlands), the nuclear industry (the UK, the USA, France and FR Germany) and the CBW industry (the UK and the USA). Related technologies, such as for the development of special steel which is of obvious military importance, have been acquired from an even wider range of producers in the West, including companies in Sweden and Switzerland.

The arms embargoes declared by the United Nations are international measures, undertaken to put political pressure on South Africa. But these measures are *not* accompanied by any mechanism for international implementation or law enforcement. The sole international control organ is the Security Council's Special Committee, set up after the passing of the mandatory arms embargo in 1977 (by Resolution 421, 22 December 1977) and consisting of all 15 members of the Security Council. The main task of this Committee was confined to 'studying ways and means by which the mandatory embargo could be made more effective against South Africa and to make recommendations to the Council'. But the Committee enjoys no special powers to demand information from the individual industries concerned—it has to rely on official replies to enquiries by the various governments, and it relies extensively on information from non-governmental organizations to monitor adherence to the UN embargo. The Committee also has no powers to impose penalties for breaking embargo regulations, and there is no international court which can deal with such an issue. Thus, all aspects relating to the implementation of the embargo against South Africa remain within national jurisdiction.

In a national context, the first problem to solve is the *definition* problem— there is no internationally agreed comprehensive list of armaments and there is certainly no agreement on what constitutes military technology. Military technology is defined in the UN documents as 'equipment and materials for the manufacture and maintenance of arms and ammunition'.[1] While the intent was clear, this definition was far too vague for practical purposes; for example, for application by customs offices in the exporting countries, as is evident from the continued import of technology by South Africa. Most countries have found it impossible to ban the export of equipment which can also be used for civilian production, whether this is 'dual-use', 'dual-purpose', 'grey-area', or 'non-lethal' equipment. Classified as civilian material, components of various kinds, machinery, engines, computers and electronic equipment of the most vital importance to military production are exported to South Africa without *formally* violating the national embargo legislation. When broken down to individual items, the 'nuts and bolts', the magnitude of the definition problem is quite clear: a modern combat aircraft is made up of over 100 000 parts; a tank consists of tens of thousands of parts. The production lines for the weapons consist in their turn of machinery comprising hundreds of thousands of parts, and so on.[2] Exactly how military technology is defined remains unknown to the public. While lists containing categories of weapons are openly documented, there are no corresponding lists of technology—with the notable exception of the USA.

By comparison, the COCOM embargo initiated by the United States (and applied by NATO and Japan to prevent military supplies to the USSR and the socialist bloc) operates with an arms list that is the most comprehensive to date. The COCOM list is based on the US Export Control List, which by 1985 numbered some 300 000 items. In addition, the COCOM embargo also covers 'critical technologies', based on a 700-page document drawn up by the US Department of Defense. This so-called Military Critical Technologies List contains a virtually comprehensive description of modern military technology, and its very existence effectively contradicts the arguments sometimes voiced in connection with the South African embargo that it would be too complicated a task to try to define all possible 'military technologies'.

The fact remains that none of the countries involved with the COCOM embargo applies the COCOM criteria to the embargo on military equipment to South Africa—clearly illustrated, for example, by the VAX affair of 1984 (discussed further below). The disparity between the detailed COCOM regulations applied to the East and the national embargoes against South Africa are of special interest here, since the very countries involved in COCOM have been the main suppliers of military technology to South Africa. Arms export regulations in general in the United States and within the NATO group began after World War II with the COCOM embargo. National legislation in the UK, France and subsequently in the other European arms-producing nations was modelled on the COCOM lists, although it varies from country to country. The COCOM embargo was a function of the cold war climate, and the goal was, and remains, to prevent all military supplies to the socialist bloc countries. When arms export regulations had to be applied to anti-communist regimes like South Africa, the entire ideological basis for applying these strict regulations no longer existed. Together with the pressure from the national arms-producing industries to be allowed to export—a pressure at work also in connection with COCOM—this created bureaucratic dilemmas within the government agencies responsible for embargo implementation. The method chosen by the NATO member countries was to apply *part* of their existing arms export regulations when dealing with South Africa, as will be exemplified below. The variations between the legislation of individual countries, based on national definitions of arms and arms technology, represent a serious complication in the implementation of the arms embargo against South Africa.

The South African embargo application, by definition, becomes an issue which does not readily fall into one category of government responsibility. It may be regarded as primarily a foreign policy issue, but also a trade sanctions issue; thus different government agencies are involved in its implementation. Responsibility is spread, shared or divided among a number of government agencies whose interests may run counter to one another. For example, while a foreign affairs department may regard the prevention of the export of military related equipment to South Africa as a priority, a department of commerce may see as its first task the promotion of exports, not the prevention. These priorities have varied over time, reflecting the growth of international pressure against South Africa. In the 1950s, it was openly considered to be in the interests of the West to supply anti-communist states.

Finally, none of the countries which are of most interest as military suppliers to South Africa has set up any special monitoring and policing agency to supervise adherence to the embargo. Cases of breaches or loopholes are discovered by chance after the deals have been made and the goods have been delivered. In this case, too, a comparison can be made with the COCOM embargo, where the United States undertakes monitoring and imposes penalties on those companies which are caught delivering embargoed goods to the East. In the South African case, no comparable individual watchman exists, and the task is dealt with practically only by anti-apartheid organizations and individual journalists in Europe and the USA. The national governments, furthermore, lack the jurisdictional right to pursue investigations of cases of smuggling outside their own territories.

These aspects of national embargo implementation go a long way towards explaining *how* military equipment has been exported to South Africa, although all governments concerned claim adherence to the embargo. There is, in fact, no nation in the world that has openly stated that it is willing to support the South African military. Some examples of embargo implementation in the most important supplier countries will illustrate how these aspects have been dealt with. These examples are presented chronologically according to their entry on the South African military production scene, beginning with the UK and the USA, the EEC countries and Japan, and last, the so-called 'pariah' group including Israel and Taiwan. These examples also show how the British-US embargo implementation from 1963, in spite of all the loopholes and inadequacies, influenced Armscor's future import policy and technology acquisition.

II. The UK

Legislation

British implementation of the arms embargo against South Africa has been affected by mutually conflicting pressures—the necessity to accommodate to the demands voiced by the Third World Commonwealth members, counterbalanced by considerations with regard to Western defence policies and such pro-South African lobby groups in the UK as the South Africa Committee of the British National Export Council and the UK-South Africa Trade Association.

Successive British governments have been formally committed to implementing the arms embargo ever since 1964. The official Government posture, as presented to the UN in 1985, is that the UK is operating an effective embargo through the Export of Goods Control Order of 1970 (as amended) and that it has not sold any arms, with the exception of certain paramilitary police equipment, to South Africa. An Order in Council also prohibits licensing arrangements for the use in South Africa of patents and other information on arms.

At the same time, however, the history of the British embargo implementation shows how this very legislation, its interpretation and the definition of armaments, coupled with the traditional economic ties with South Africa, has provided for a great number of exceptions to the arms embargo. This has been illustrated by numerous reports of military equipment exported from the UK to South Africa.[3]

The legislation of relevance to arms exports to South Africa from the UK is ultimately based on the general arms export regulations formulated under powers conferred by the Import, Export and Customs Powers (Defence) Act of 1939. In connection with the UK's adherence to the COCOM embargo in 1949, the arms export regulations included a listing of military equipment divided into three groups. These lists contain the official British definition of military and strategic equipment, and have been continuously updated and changed. The Export of Goods Control Order of 1970 was replaced by a new Order in 1978, another in 1981, and then by the current Order of 3 June 1985, where a fourth group of equipment was added. The four groups are:

Group 1. Military aircraft, arms and related material; ammunition, military stores and appliances and security and paramilitary police equipment.

Group 2. Atomic energy minerals and materials, nuclear facilities, equipment and appliances.

Group 3. Metal working machinery and associated equipment, chemical and petroleum equipment, electrical and power generating equipment, general industrial equipment, aircraft compasses, gyroscopic apparatus, servomechanisms and photographic equipment, metals, minerals and their manufactures, chemical, metalloids and petroleum products, and synthetic rubber.

Group 4. Goods, technologies and processes in respect of which the export of technological documents, other than documents generally available to the public, are prohibited to any destination in any country specified in Article 2.

Each of these groups, in turn, includes a list of individual headings of items taking up 140 pages of the 1985 Export Order. There are two general points to stress regarding these 140 pages listing military equipment: these items are not subject to a general export prohibition, but are subject to a prohibition to export without a government licence. Further, and most importantly, the specific countries referred to are made up exclusively of the socialist bloc countries. The significance of the COCOM embargo for British arms export policy, as compared to the embargo against South Africa, was made very clear in an explanatory note from the Foreign and Commonwealth Offices to the British anti-apartheid movement; the note explained why a range of items belonging under groups 2–3 in the export control lists could be exported without a licence to South Africa:

These arrangements operate to control supply of items of military and strategic significance to the Chinese and Soviet blocs and to guard against diversion to these blocs via third countries. Under these arrangements, while military and atomic energy equipment and highly sensitive items have been subject to export control to all destinations, the export of other items in the COCOM industrial list are not controlled to a number of countries including South Africa where there is no significant risk of diversion to the bloc countries.[4]

For the growth of the South African arms industry, access to industrial equipment, dual-purpose goods and items not directly classified as arms was, of course, of vital importance. This access was further secured by the many subsidiaries of relevant British companies operating in South Africa.

The Export Orders and listings of military equipment make up the UK's *general* arms export legislation. There was no legislation specifically dealing with the embargo against South Africa until 1977. During the period of the voluntary arms embargo, from 1963 up to the mandatory embargo of 1977, there was no official declaration of how the 1970 Export Order was being applied to military exports to South Africa, apart from statements made in connection with the Simonstown Agreement.

The distinction between 'weapons for external defence' and 'weapons for internal use' was introduced by the British in 1955, when the Simonstown naval base was handed over to the Government of the Union of South Africa. This distinction allowed for the delivery of four anti-submarine warfare frigates, ten coastal minesweepers, and four seaward defence boats—including their armaments—between 1955 and 1964. It also allowed for the delivery of naval Wasp helicopters to arm the frigates and the Buccaneer naval bombers after renegotiations in 1961, when South Africa was compelled to leave the Commonwealth. The South African understanding of the British definition of arms which could no longer be imported from the UK after the ministerial talks of June 1961, prolonging the Simonstown Agreement, was expressed as follows:

Supply of arms and ammunition. Provided the supply of small arms and ammunition were excluded, there should be no serious difficulty about supplies. In principle, there was no objection to licensing agreements for production in South Africa. There might, however, be certain items which could give rise to political difficulties.[5]

The precise arms-supplying obligations under the Simonstown Agreement were debated with furore during the 20 years of the treaty's existence, until it was finally abrogated by South Africa in 1975.

The Conservative Government in power at the time of the 1963 UN embargo continued to apply a distinction between weapons for external defence and counter-insurgency weapons, but the Labour Government that came into power in late 1964 decided on a complete embargo on all armaments to South Africa, although existing contracts were to be honoured.

There are many concrete examples of the immediate embargo implementation in the UK: the embargo of November 1964 declared by the Wilson Government meant immediate business losses worth £90 million pounds. Over a 10-year period, the value of cancelled orders, including spares and follow-up contracts, had grown to £200 million.[6] Among individual weapon systems embargoed were 16 Buccaneer naval bombers, 15 Shackleton maritime reconnaissance planes, 6 HS-125 transport aircraft, 4 Tribal-class frigates, Sea Dart ship-to-air missiles, and radars.

The Simonstown Agreement nevertheless laid the foundation for South African naval industry development, since the agreement provided for 20 years of access to British know-how. One well-informed source described the implications of this treaty with Britain thus:

South Africa could see the writing on the wall. It would not be long before other countries, even possibly France, refused to negotiate arms sales with South Africa. It was essential therefore for South Africa to become much more self-reliant in the field of arms supplies. *It was here that the generous help in previous years from the Royal Navy and the excellent facilities at the Simonstown base stood the South African Navy in good stead.* Virtually any spares were becoming obtainable—even such items as non-magnetic anchors etc. Carefully the SAN began to build up a store of technical knowledge that almost defied imagination. All those mundane items that one never really considers important were inspected and measured and dies of the parts carefully taken so that when replacement became necessary the SAN was able to manufacture the part herself.[7]

Thus British embargo regulations up to the mandatory ban of 1977 did not prevent technology transfer; nor were there any end-use or 'no-resale' clauses in sales contracts, which meant that British equipment could arrive in South Africa through a third country. The production licence for the Rolls-Royce Viper engine, re-exported by Piaggio of Italy to Atlas Aircraft Corporation in the early 1960s, represented a typical example of more than one 'loophole'. Such a deal could go through observing the *legal* obligations of the British embargo, although hardly the intent of the UN embargo of 1963. Besides, for direct purchases of major armaments other than the naval vessels included in the Simonstown Agreement, the South Africans had already diversified their sources of supply before 1963. When the debate about resuming arms supplies flared up again in 1967 in the UK, with the Conservatives in favour and Labour, in principle, against, *The Economist* summed up the general view of UK observers regarding the South African arms trade in the headline: 'South Africa: the arms market we had already lost'.[8] The main argument used in favour of resuming arms supplies to South Africa centred on South Africa's importance for Western defence, coupled with economic considerations—with respect to possible huge arms export contracts to South Africa. The Labour cabinet was split on the issue. However, the embargo was adhered to with the exception of the supply of four Wasp naval helicopters. This was stated in a White Paper published in 1971, containing the last investigation of British obligations under the Simonstown Agreement before its cancellation in 1975. The law officers who had conducted a six-month investigation concluded that the UK had a continuing legal obligation to supply replacements for the initial equipment, stores and base reserves for four frigates and other vessels supplied but, apart from that, the Simonstown Agreement did not cover any more arms supplies.

The Parliamentary debate from 1967 to 1971 was the last heated debate in the UK on the South African arms issue, and contained all the classic moral argumentation from both sides: Labour representatives countered the economic argument in favour of arms exports by pointing out that the campaigners against the slave trade in the 18th century were constantly told that the UK could not afford to end it. The economic dependence on the slave trade was compared to the economic dependence on supplying arms to South Africa. The leader of the Conservatives, Mr Heath, argued that South Africa was a critical part of the South Atlantic defence and, at the same time, the UK's third biggest overseas customer. Subsequently, the list of armaments sought from the UK by South Africa but *not* supplied became long: South Africa did not manage to acquire 14 additional Buccaneer naval bombers; the export licence for 7 Wasp helicopters (in addition to 6 delivered in 1963) was revoked; a British veto stopped the sale of the British-French-produced Jaguar fighter in 1969; a £20 million contract for the Bloodhound missile placed before Labour came to power in 1964 was cancelled; and the Beagle 206 was vetoed in 1967.

The overriding British interest in securing world-wide support for its embargo against Rhodesia also figured among the reasons why the UK should observe the South African embargo; if it had continued to supply South Africa, its competitors on the arms market could have chosen to supply Rhodesia.[9]

However, a whole series of commercial dealings during the 1970s illustrate the loopholes in the embargo regulations. Communications equipment, electronics and radar, for example, were not subject to government prohibition. In 1975, the South Africans ordered a computer-controlled communications network called the Tropospheric scatter system from the Marconi company, representative of the grey area between military and civilian equipment. While not definable as a 'weapon', it was essential for computer-controlled warfare and the electronic battlefield.

One expert on the arms trade summarizes the effect of the British embargo thus: 'The British embargo continued to be rather less rigorous than it appeared; one defence salesman boasted to me that he had actually exported more arms equipment under the Labour government after 1974, than under the Conservative'.[10]

The detected cases of outright smuggling or illegal export deals from the UK, in particular after 1977, reveal that South Africa concentrates on obtaining high-technology components rather than complete weapons. Examples of components smuggled in are high-pressure gas cylinders and cooling devices, spare parts for the Centurion, magnetrons for radars and artillery components.

The regulations did not cover the operations of the British companies in South Africa. A report in 1977 identified 36 British arms manufacturers operating in South Africa.[11] Only after the mandatory embargo of 1977 was specific legislation concerning military equipment to South Africa enacted. The embargo on the supply of arms was enforced through Statutory Instrument 277 of 1978, labelled 'The South Africa (UN Arms Embargo, Prohibited Transactions) Order 1978'. The British Government issued a note to the UN Security Council on 28 April 1978, where it for the first time explicitly stated the measures applied under the voluntary embargo of 1963, and the new measures undertaken to enforce the mandatory embargo.[12] The underlying arms export legislation was still the Export of Goods (Control) Order of 1970, but as amended by Statutory Instrument No. 277 of 1 March 1978, where five items of paramilitary police equipment were added to the list of arms in Group 1 of the list of categories of military equipment. The note listed all items in this group, and explained for the first time officially how the Export Order was applied to South Africa by saying that all goods to which the UN Security Council Resolution 418 of 1977 applied were included in Group 1:

It prohibits persons from entering into any licence arrangements for the use in South Africa of patents, registered designs of industrial information or techniques specially designed for the manufacture or maintenance of arms or equipment specially designed for military or paramilitary police purposes.[13]

The above definition adequately explains continued export of dual-use or grey-area items and equipment, since such items are not explicitly designed for military purposes. For purposes of technology transfer, by the mid-1980s, the dual-use items can be said to have taken the place of the exclusively military equipment.

There is, furthermore, nothing explicitly stated in the British legislation concerning South Africa in 1978 that corresponds to the UN embargo's call to revoke all existing production licences with South African firms. No official list of production licence agreements has ever been published, and likewise, the applications for export licences by individual exporting companies in the UK are treated as commercial secrets and never published.

For example, in April 1984, the Department of Trade refused a request by a Member of Parliament to publish the number of licences granted yearly since

1977 for exports to South Africa and Namibia. Thus, the factual basis for an objective assessment of the implementation of the embargo is not available. The Export of Goods (Control) Order was amended again in 1981, through Statutory Instrument No. 1641, but South Africa and Namibia still did not appear in the annexed list of countries to which the strongest restrictions should apply. (These countries were still the socialist bloc nations.)

In July 1985, the latest Export of Goods (Control) Order brought substantive changes insofar as the letter of the law is concerned: according to this Order, *all* the items specified in Groups 1–3 now became subject to control to *all destinations*. The Commonwealth countries and South Africa and Namibia, which up to then enjoyed a special favoured status for equipment listed in Group 3, are thus no longer exempted from automatic licence probation for all equipment.

A Group 4 was added to the list of strategic equipment with the purpose of controlling the export of technology. However, these controls reflect the COCOM revival of the 1980s and the US concern about high-technology transfer to the East. They apply only to 15 countries, all within the socialist bloc. Although South Africa and Namibia are not on the above-mentioned annexed list, the export of production licences to these two recipients is still controlled by the 1978 legislation.

The implementing agencies

Theoretically, three ministries and three government agencies are involved in the granting of export licences to South Africa: the Department of Trade, the Foreign and Commonwealth Office, the Ministry of Defence, the police and other security agencies, and Customs and Excise. The licences exclusively concern exports from private companies in the UK, since no government sales from, for example, the Royal Ordnance Factories (once the exporters of Centurion tanks to South Africa) took place after the 1977 mandatory embargo.[14]

The main actors are the Department of Trade, whose Export Licence Branch grants the licences, and Customs and Excise, whose task it is to ensure that items leaving the UK have the appropriate licences. The other ministries and agencies act in a consulting capacity, generally to decide on the definition problem from case to case. Investigations of suspected violations of the export rules are known to have been initiated mostly by Customs and Excise and the Foreign and Commonwealth Office, often after first having been alerted by non-governmental actors such as workers' organizations, journalists, television companies or the anti-apartheid movement. (As an example of trade union involvement, in June 1977, the Rover Consolidated Shop Stewards banned the export from British Leyland of Landrover parts for assembly in South Africa. Although this export was formally legal, the equipment had a military application.)

One aspect which further illustrates the complications involved in the implementation of the embargo is that the Defence Ministry office involved appears to be the Defence Export Services Organization. This office was set up in 1966 with the explicit task of *promoting* British arms exports, not preventing them. The prevention of exports is, by definition, also contrary to the usual tasks of the Department of Trade.

Recipients

Unlike the US legislation presented below, British legislation does not define which recipients are on the black list; in other words, it does not identify Armscor agencies, the Defence Ministry, the SAP, and so on. But the practice is to issue export licences to civilian customers only. Plessey radar equipment, first sold to South Africa in 1974, and again in 1978, totalling US $65 million, was consequently first defined as intended for civil use; the official customer was a civilian air traffic company.

The contract first caused a row in 1979 when it was revealed that Plessey had been training three SADF members to operate the equipment. At the time, the British Foreign Secretary, in addition to the definition arguments, also used the 'pre-1977 argument' which was to become so common: the export was legal, since the contract had been signed before the 1977 mandatory embargo.[15] An example presented in the South African press as a potentially valuable military acquisition was the export in 1984 from a London-based British firm, Airship Industries, of an airship to a South African private company, Placo, entirely unknown for any Armscor connections.[16]

In 1985, some presumably common disagreements between various implementing agencies were revealed in the debates about a South African request to buy the Edgley Optica surveillance aircraft. The South African customer was named as National Airways Corporation, which belongs to Lonrho and is not, apparently, connected with Armscor. In 1985 the Foreign Office declared the contract null and void, but the Trade Department claimed that Optica needed no licence if exported without its communication equipment. The Department also protested officially against what it regarded as a breach of 'commercial confidentiality'.[17]

Penalties

All the Export Control Orders referred to above include details of the penalties for breaking the export regulations. These penalties have remained identical over time, and involve a maximum fine of £1000 and up to two years imprisonment. Individual agents (persons or companies) can also be brought to trial for offences against the Customs and Excise Management Act of 1979, provided not more than three years have passed since the time of the offence.

Breaking the customs law is also punishable by fines or imprisonment but, in addition, one case is known of a compounded settlement (the offender is allowed to settle the case by paying an agreed amount out of court).

Two cases concerning the illegal export of arms or equipment to South Africa have been resolved since 1979. The first in 1980, involving five companies and five individuals, was settled by Customs *compounding proceedings* under their statutory powers. It is not the Commissioner's practice to reveal details of compounded settlements. The second case in 1982 involved three individuals who were prosecuted and convicted, one receiving nine months imprisonment with six months concurrent and £1000 fine, and the others receiving six and three months imprisonment, respectively.[18]

In this connection, the British anti-apartheid movement has reported that the secret sum agreed on in the compounded settlement of 1980 was £193 000, whereas the value of the armaments smuggled to South Africa was £2 million.[19] The second case illustrates the psychological barrier in the West against prohibiting the legal government of South Africa from importing arms, whereas it comes more naturally to prohibit arms shipments to the socialist bloc or to revolutionary movements. The presiding judge said in summing up the 1982 case: 'I also bear in mind, as I must, that these things were supplied, *not to revolutionaries or insurgents*, but to the Republic Government'.[20]

The case referred to above illustrates yet another complication also experienced by US and European government authorities: the lack of co-ordination between various departments. The three convicted arms dealers were arrested by Customs officials following an investigation by Customs and Excise. The Home Office was apparently not involved at all, since the three persons were able to get their licences to act as arms dealers renewed on a routine basis between their arrest and trial. The South African Armscor representatives were under no travel restrictions. Furthermore, the Foreign and Commonwealth Office only became aware of the case when it appeared in the press, 16 months after the arrests.

III. The United States

Legislation

The United States has presented the world's most extensive and detailed legislation for regulating arms exports, including arms exports to South Africa. Theoretically, if the letter of the law had been strictly followed, it would have been possible to stop the export of all types of US equipment to South Africa. Nevertheless, such equipment was exported.

In 1954 Congress passed the Mutual Security Act, which established policy for the exchange of technical defence-related information and military hardware with foreign countries. The thrust of this legislation was to ensure military exports to allied countries and prevent the same to socialist bloc countries. That act was replaced by the Arms Export Control Act of 1976, but its operative principles remained. The Export Control Act and its implementing set of regulations—the International Traffic in Arms Regulations (ITAR)—provide the statutory/regulatory basis for controlling the export and import of arms. The arms are listed in the Munitions List under 21 categories, and any item for export must be licensed by the Office of Munitions Control of the State Department. The Munitions List, which thus contains the relevant definitions of 'arms, ammunition and implements of war', is controlled, checked and updated by the Departments of State, Energy, Defense and Commerce, and contains hundreds of items ranging from automatic weapons to sophisticated communication devices. As pointed out earlier, US legislation and policy initiated and maintain the multinational COCOM embargo. All items, the export of which are forbidden to the East under the COCOM embargo or under the more comprehensive US export controls, are specially marked in the Munitions List. However, these items are not automatically included in the embargo on exports to South Africa.

The 21 categories on the US Munitions List designated as 'arms, ammunition and implements of war' are as follows:

Category I. Firearms
Category II. Artillery Projectors
Category III. Ammunition
Category IV. Launch Vehicles, Guided Missiles, Ballistic Missiles, Rockets, Torpedoes, Bombs and Mines
Category V. Explosives, Propellants and Incendiary Agents
Category VI. Vessels of War and Special Naval Equipment
Category VII. Tanks and Military Vehicles
Category VIII. Aircraft, Spacecraft and Associated Equipment
Category IX. Military Training Equipment
Category X. Protective Personnel Equipment
Category XI. Military and Space Electronics
Category XII. Fire Control, Range Finders, Optical and Guidance and Control Equipment
Category XIII. Auxiliary Military Equipment
Category XIV. Toxicological Agents and Equipment and Radiological Equipment.
Category XV. Reserved
Category XVI. Nuclear Weapons Design and Test Equipment
Category XVII. Classified articles not otherwise enumerated
Category XVIII. Technical data
Category XIX. Defense services
Category XX. Submersible Vessels, Oceanographic and Associated Equipment
Category XXI. Miscellaneous Articles[21]

According to information obtained by NARMIC under the Freedom of Information Act, US $8.6 million worth of Munitions List items were exported to South Africa by US companies; that is, in commercial deals, during the entire period from 1950 to 1980. This tallies with other general information to the effect that direct arms transfers from the United States to South Africa have been relatively few—the USA was never among the main suppliers of complete weapons. After 1980, applications for export licences of Munitions List equipment dwindled, although not explicitly prohibited.

The reason why exports could continue to South Africa is found in the country list attached to the Munitions List, dividing up all countries of the world according to their suitability as receivers of US military equipment. South Africa is placed under category V, 'friendly non-allied countries', which reflects the fact that US arms export policy is, above all, a function of its foreign policy towards the socialist bloc.

In addition to the Munitions List, there are two other lists containing the official US definition of strategic goods which, after 1963, have been of more relevance to the South African military industry. Those are the Commodity Control List (CCL), handled by the Commerce Department and based on the Export Control Act, and the Military Critical Technologies List (MCTL), handled by the Department of Defense. The CCL essentially comprises dual-use or grey-area equipment not included in the Munitions List. The MCTL, classified until 1984 (when it was finally published with secret parts deleted), is a catalogue of modern technologies with military application. Restrictions of sales to *non-communist* countries were by definition not the first priority when implementing the MCTL List.

The implementing agencies

The US Government agencies that handle the arms embargo against South Africa are the Departments of State, Commerce and Defense, and the Customs. The US experience presents a catalogue of examples of inter-departmental controversy, both as to the definition of military equipment, and as to who is responsible for maintaining the embargo. In addition, the Export–Import Bank also represents government involvement in military exports to South Africa, insofar as it assumes the risk for loans provided by local banks for these exports. The Eximbank during the 1970s financed the sale to South African customers of several aircraft that were officially classified as civilian (Beechcraft-55 and -58 in 1973, Helio Super Couriers in 1976, Beechcraft Bonanza, Cessna light planes, Piper light planes and Mitsubishi Mu-2s produced in the USA. All these are, according to South African law, also enlisted with the SAAF).

Under the authority of the Export Administration Act of 1979, the Department of Commerce administers the export administration regulations which control the export of technology for items on the Commodity Control List. Scheduled to be re-enacted before it expired on 30 September 1983, the Export Administration Act of 1979 was the largest issue of deep controversy between the Commerce and Defense Departments. Because of the absence of a Congressional consensus the Act expired in October 1983. President Reagan had to invoke his executive powers to prevent export controls from lapsing while Congress continued to work on re-enactment. Part of the controversy was attributed to Congress, which insisted on bringing 'irrelevant' issues into the debate, such as human rights and anti-apartheid policy regarding South Africa.

By internal delegation of functions and authority within the Department of State through the Under Secretary for Security Assistance, Science and Technology, and the Director of the Bureau of Politico-Military Affairs, the Director of the Office of Munitions Control (OMC) is responsible for controlling the *commercial* export of defence articles and services. OMC prescribes applications of the ITAR regulations in Title 22, Code of Federal Regulations.

The official investigation of the Space Research case, the sale of the G-5 155-mm howitzer technology to South Africa, led to the conclusion that the lack of co-ordination and co-operation between various US foreign policy and other governmental agencies was such that arms exports to non-communist countries was enhanced, in general, and in particular in the case of South Africa: 'The causes of the Government's failure to adequately implement the arms embargo *were structural rather than accidental in nature'.*[22] The report goes on to state that the OMC was incapable of enforcing arms licensing regulations due to a lack of resources: 30 000 licence applications per year were handled by seven officers, and there was a lack of technical experts capable of adequately defining weapons components. The Army's share of responsibility in the SRC case—allowing the production of 155-mm shells for South Africa in an Army factory—was due to the absence of control procedures about end-use; and the CIA's involvement was due to a preoccupation with the need to move arms into Angola and a negligence regarding the larger US policy of enforcing the arms embargo against South Africa.

Monitoring and penalties

The thorough investigation of the SRC case, cited above, also came to the conclusion that the main default in the embargo implementation lay in the fact that collecting information about this was not high on the list of any agency's priorities. No procedures existed for sharing and centrally assessing relevant information and, above all, there was no clear delineation of organizational responsibilities for obtaining relevant intelligence, evaluating it, and acting upon it.

The conclusion was that there is a 'non-system' operating to implement the US embargo against South Africa, in spite of the existence of extensive export regulations. Initiation of investigations by the OMC and Customs have mostly taken place after alerts from non-governmental organizations, mass media or, as in the SRC case, workers' organizations.

The penalties for violating US military export regulations are part of the legislation that governs all exports. Violations of the Export Administration Act are punishable by a maximum fine of not more than five times the value of the illegally exported goods, or a maximum of US $150 000. Wilful violations are punishable by up to US $1 million in fines and imprisonment of up to 10 years. Fines and imprisonment are also prescribed for violations of the Arms Export Control Act and ITAR regulations. Lesser penalties for illegal exports may include seizure of the commodity, and the withdrawal of export privileges. There are relatively few instances in which individuals or companies have been prosecuted for South African arms embargo violations.

Implementation

Most importantly, there is no comprehensive legislation that can really reach the operations in South Africa of US-based multinational companies. US policy has rather been to ask industry for co-operation in implementing the embargo. Evidence of such co-operation is not impressive. However, one example was the General Motors decision of 1986 to stop selling vehicles to the South African police and military authorities. This move was largely prompted by *shareholders'* pressure, and it came only after a growing number of US companies had decided to withdraw from South Africa altogether. The reason for this, in turn, was generally given as lack of profitability due to political uncertainty about South Africa's future, and thus unrelated to embargo implementation. In the General Motors case, the official embargo implementation had resulted in a ban from 1978 on US components in the vehicles. Instead, these components were then supplied by General Motors from its other overseas companies and exported to South Africa.

The US arms embargo against South Africa began in 1962. The United States voted in favour of the voluntary embargo in 1963, unlike Britain and France, which abstained from voting on Resolution 181. This was facilitated by the fact that, unlike Britain, the United States was not burdened by any traditional military relationship or responsibility for South Africa, although it was one of its largest trade partners and investors. In addition, there was, and also remains, the constant pressure against apartheid, evident among the public as well as in Congress and within the Administration. This pressure has strong national roots, specific to US society, and makes up one additional factor working against military as well as economic ties with South Africa. The US arms supplies to South Africa in the 1950s—including 150 T-6 Harvard trainers, eight Shackleton maritime patrol aircraft and five Sikorsky naval helicopters—followed upon South Africa's participation in the Korean war and were related to Western defence interests.

From 1963 to 1977, the USA formally observed the voluntary embargo. When it together with Britain and France in 1977 finally accepted the long-voiced demand for a mandatory embargo, this was a very important *political* stance against the white South African regime.

During the period of the voluntary embargo, the US Customs seized 10 shipments, illegally destined for South Africa. In 1978, the United States, under the Carter Administration, unilaterally expanded the embargo, and imposed a total ban on all export of goods and technical data to the South African police and military. Thus, the Carter policy introduced the definition of the *customer,* in addition to the definition of military goods. But later, Kissinger's formulation of what became the US policy towards South Africa, known as 'constructive engagement'—the Tar Baby Option—was reflected also in the embargo implementation. In March 1982, export became permitted for five previously restricted categories of goods and data to the military and police which 'would not contribute significantly to military or police functions'.[23] The regulations governing aircraft sales were also relaxed: foreign— third country—suppliers would, from 1982, no longer have to seek US licences to sell to South Africa equipment incorporating *less than 20 per cent* of US- made components. Among the goods available to the military and police from 1982 were industrial equipment and chemicals not rated as being of 'national security concern': food, non-military clothing, calculators and personal computers. While the anti-apartheid lobby in the United States and elsewhere condemned what was generally labelled the relaxation of the US embargo, the revised regulations were not entirely unequivocal. In 1981, the US Ambassador to the UN, Mrs J. Kirkpatrick, stated that the USA would not permit third-country sales of military equipment which contained US components, and that this ban explicitly included the Israeli Kfir jet fighter. This signalled the Reagan Administration's upholding of a major element in the arms embargo against South Africa. It has, moreover, been unique to the US legislation and has had a negative effect on the development of South Africa's *aircraft* industry in the 1980s. At the same time, the Administration's reasons for relaxing the ban on non-military sales in the future were described thus: there have been complaints to the US Commerce Department that the ban has cost US companies extensive orders which have merely gone to their European competitors, particularly to West German companies. According to the electronics corporation Burroughs, orders to the value of R1200 million for electronic medical equipment for military hospitals had been lost to the West German Siemens concern.[24]

The value of US computer exports to South Africa rose from US $147 million in 1964 to US $185 million in 1982, which was more than the value of sales from the UK, Japan, FR Germany and Italy combined.[25] The implications of this for South Africa's defence industry can hardly be exaggerated, given the utter dependence of any modern high-technology enterprise and of the weapons themselves on computer techniques. Concerning sales of arms and arms equipment contained in the Munitions List, it is also evident that the Carter Administration's policy brought a downturn of US exports during the period from the start of the mandatory embargo in 1978 until 1980, in which year no export licence at all was issued by the State Department. In contrast, the State Department, during the years of 'constructive engagement' in 1981–83, authorized sales of more than US $28 million worth of dual-use equipment to South Africa. According to the formulation of the NARMIC organization 'the arms trade with South Africa is now conducted by US corporations under a shroud of commercial secrecy: *it has become privatised and invisible*'.[26]

In the autumn of 1985, however, the Reagan Administration yielded to pressure from Congress and the public and enacted new restrictive measures. Nuclear exports to South Africa were banned, as were all computer sales to the South African security forces and 'apartheid-enforcing agencies'. Although still under fire as being too permissive, this strengthening of the embargo against South Africa may be seen as indicative of the determination in Congress to further disassociate the USA from the South African regime.

However, an entirely different explanation of the 1985 restrictions is possible. The Reagan Executive Order of 9 September 1985, which banned computer sales to the agencies 'enforcing apartheid', nuclear commerce, and the *import* of South African-produced armaments, was in fact the direct result of a US inter-departmental conflict and the VAX computer smuggling case further described below. In January 1985, President Reagan authorized the Department of Defense to review the licensing of high-technology products in 15 non-communist countries, settling a long-running dispute between the Pentagon and the Commerce Department over export-control responsibilities. The list of the 15 restricted countries is classified, but according to US press reports, the list was said to include Finland, Sweden, Austria, Switzerland, *South Africa*, Hong Kong, Taiwan and Singapore, all regarded as conduits for illegal export of strategic goods to the Soviet Union. The VAX affair, which changed South Africa's status from 'friendly non-allied country' to one of the 15 countries considered by COCOM as a possible third-country route for military goods to the East, involved the following. In 1982, the US Commerce Department considered the application from Digital Equipment Corporation of New York for an export licence to ship a VAX 11/782 computer to a private company, Microelectronics Research Institute (MRI), in Cape Town. The MRI was unrelated to Armscor, but related to a Swiss firm which operated as middleman for strategic goods to the Soviet Union. Between 1982 and 1983 US $8 million worth of computer equipment was shipped to the South African company—then reshipped to Europe and intercepted in German and Swedish ports before transfer to the Soviet Union. The US authorities were, ironically, first alerted about these transhipments by the South African Police. Through this turn of events, it became possible for the US Administration to accept stronger restrictions on the export of computers to South Africa, although the VAX affair involved private agents and was of no benefit to the official South African establishment.

In other words, a larger part of the COCOM list of prohibited goods was applied to South Africa almost by chance.

IV. France

Legislation and implementation

Like the other leading European arms-producing nations, France introduced its first arms export regulations in 1939. Article 13 of this law, on which the present regulations are based, laid down the principle that war material and related items require export licences authorized by the Government. A special decree, also from 1939, established a list of equipment requiring such licences. The same decree provided for exemptions for certain types of equipment—civil aircraft, spare parts and material in transit. The war material list was then constantly updated and changed over time, but these initial detailed exemptions enabled the continued deliveries to South Africa of much essential material after the 1963 UN embargo. These exemptions can be suspended for exports destined for certain countries, but considerable time passed before France applied this to the South African exports. The 1939 law in its entirety, plus the invocation of the decree to stop export of military-related equipment, add up to the embargo legislation. The exporting companies are also requested to place a deposit to guarantee the final destination of armaments exports and prevent its re-export to prohibited destinations. For the export of dual-use equipment, a customs declaration is sufficient to guarantee the end-use. These controls were finalized in connection with the setting up of the COCOM machinery in Paris, and first applied exclusively to the socialist bloc countries.

Implementing agencies

Formally, the export licences are issued by the Ministry of Finance, after approval by the Minister of Foreign Affairs, the Minister of the Interior, the Minister of War, Navy or Air, and the Minister of Defence. Export promotion, negotiations and the acceptance of orders must also be authorized by the ministers of foreign affairs and defence. Also in cases where negotiations have been approved, the administration may later refuse an export licence.

In 1949, this control network was further tightened by the establishment of the inter-ministerial war material export committee. Its function was to handle all requests for authorization to produce and export war material, and to study the policy that should govern the production of war material for foreign countries. A second decree of 1953 made this commission directly responsible to the President of the Council—later the Prime Minister. The commission includes the ministers of defence, foreign affairs, and finance and economic affairs; but, in practice, the power is centred on the Ministry of Foreign Affairs. Finally, in practice, the embargo against South Africa is handled by the President, and laid out in presidential decrees.

The French arms export control system is thereby centralized to a much higher decree than the British and US structures, and allows for strict governmental supervision. There is little room for inter-ministerial disputes and even less for any 'non-system' on the US pattern, which allows arms exports to a prohibited destination due to inter-ministerial confusion.

This means that virtually all the large arms and military technology sales to South Africa from the 1960s up to 1978 took place with the full approval of the French Government, at the same time as the respective governments claimed to observe the UN embargoes. The French record further shows very few cases of interception of smuggling compared to the British and US experience. And even then, for example, in the Danish trial in 1986 concerning illegal arms shipments including aircraft material from Aérospatiale to South Africa in 1981–82, the Danish shipowner accused claimed that the French President had given a tacit approval of the shipments leaving Bordeaux.[27] The official answer to this accusation was that the Government indeed authorized the export at the time, but that the destination had been given as Argentina.[28]

Implementation policy

To state simply that the French arms export policy with regard to South Africa has been subordinated to various national interests does not explain the French intrusion on the South African market from 1963. A more detailed scrutiny of the nature of these national interests is necessary. Further, it may be argued that an explanation of the *initiation* of a policy is of particular value. Once the French arms-exporting industries had achieved their South African connections, it is possible to regard later contracts as a follow-on phenomenon.

The military co-operation with South Africa reflected an official French foreign policy that completed an almost full circle from 1960 to 1986. From practically no relations with South Africa, the two countries were in 1978 described by P. W. Botha as having relations close to a military alliance;[29] then came the downgrading of the connections and withdrawal of the French ambassador from Pretoria in 1985, and the trade sanctions of 1986.

The mounting tension in South Africa during the latter half of the 1950s, leading up to the shootings at Sharpeville in March 1960, did not have the same impact in France as, for example, it did in the UK and the USA. The French *rapprochement* with South Africa dated from 1958 when General de Gaulle again came to power. The decision to build up an independent nuclear force and the necessity to improve the economy and modernize the industrial infrastructure brought South Africa into the picture as a supplier of gold and uranium, and as a customer for French armaments. At the time of Sharpeville, the apartheid issue was not a priority for the French Government or the public. France was entirely absorbed by what many view as a national catastrophe and trauma—the Algerian war. From the outset, France was condemned by the entire non-aligned world, and increasingly also by both public and official opinion in Western countries. The sole state on the African continent that supported France was South Africa, and South African officers were invited to Algeria to study counter-insurgency warfare and to inspect French-produced weaponry. The first arms deals were finalized during 1961, including a number of production licences for small arms, and for the Panhard armoured cars that were to become the Eland.

The Algerian war was also taken up by the UN General Assembly, and resulted in the long-standing French policy of 'preventing the United Nations from interfering in the internal affairs of a state using the pretext of safeguarding human rights'.[30] On the basis of this thinking, France did not uphold the UN's rights to deal with the apartheid policies of South Africa or the

Namibian question. This anti-UN intervention trend continued up to the mid-1970s.

The French distinction between weapons for external defence and anti-guerrilla weapons was made before the 1963 embargo, in the Presidential circular of 10 September 1962. Like the UK, France abstained from voting on the first UN resolution of 1963, but adhered to the 1964 resolution with the proviso that the voluntary embargo should cover only weapons for anti-guerrilla warfare; that is, light mortars, machineguns, grenades and napalm bombs. Production under licence of all of these had already begun in South Africa. Thus, the French embargo explicitly did *not* cover weapons for conventional warfare, needed to defend the country against a foreign invasion, that is, aircraft, armoured cars and naval equipment, and it did not cover replacement parts and spare parts for orders concluded before 1964.[31] Between 1960 and 1968, Armscor became, for example, the third largest customer of the French aerospace industry (after Israel and the USA), with orders worth a total of Fr. 1571 million.[32]

All the first 20 Mirage-3 aircraft contracted in 1961 were already delivered by December 1963, and the consistent French justification of this sale continued to emphasize partly the timing, and partly the definition of Mirage as a 'conventional armaments' type. The much-publicized arms-for-uranium deal was signed in 1964, and it has also been reported that part of the military contracts were paid for in gold.[33] In 1970, President Pompidou personally ordered a ban on the sale of French arms, notably armoured cars and helicopters, to countries which could use them against insurgents. This move was a response to 'African friends of France', according to official sources, and became an irritant for the ongoing British internal debate about the sale of the Wasp helicopters to South Africa.[34] But France had already sold over 90 helicopters, and the Eland was in full production in South Africa. Regardless of armaments imports, the South African arms industry had been consolidated and continued to benefit from its access to French technology—up to 1977, France did not adhere to the December 1963 UN embargo on technology. Among the military deliveries was much industry-related equipment: for example, in March 1968, 250 engines for the Eland armoured car were exported; gun parts for field weapons were sold in 1969 and shipped via Switzerland; Atar engines and replacement parts were sold in 1969 for Mirage fighters and so on.[35]

Protests mainly from African governments against the sale of assembly rights for the Mirage F-1 mounted in 1971, but led only to an official reiteration of the argument that France adhered to the 1963 embargo by not selling weapons for internal repression. It could not refuse to sell weapons for South Africa's external defence.[36]

During his electoral campaign in 1974, Giscard d'Estaing indicated that France would stop selling arms to countries where the rules of democracy were not respected. His competitor, the socialist candidate François Mitterrand, explicitly promised to ban all weapons to the South African Government. Once in power, President Giscard d'Estaing did tighten up further the original decree of 1962 by extending the embargo also to land and air armaments. Naval arms were still excluded. The timing of this extension is interesting insofar as the Mirage fighters were already being assembled in South Africa, and new orders covered only two Aviso-class corvettes and a further two Agosta-class submarines for delivery in 1978–79. No restrictions were yet placed on the continued manufacture of arms under licence in South Africa. On the contrary, there were reports at the time quoting 'sources in Paris', to the effect that the South African authorities accepted the new French anti-apartheid line and tightening of the embargo in the light of assurances of help to continue building up the domestic military industry:

Sources here said that South Africa had been carefully prepared for Mr Giscard d'Estaing's announcement. According to these informants, South Africa knew that every care would be taken to cushion the repercussion on its military capacity. That was South Africa's price, the sources said, for not retaliating by reducing its nonmilitary imports from France, currently worth more than US $235 million and growing.[37]

While this alleged horse-trading has so far been impossible to corroborate, the fact remains that France's record as a military supplier to South Africa supports the claims made by the above article. Its embargo on exports to South Africa has progressively been extended to cover various items at the same pace as the South Africans have managed to start their own production of the same items. The French connection with South Africa, military as well as economic, and to a certain extent also political—France strongly supported South Africa's abortive 'dialogue policy' with black Africa—developed unquestioned in France. The exceptions were confined to trade unions, and the socialist and communist parties. The same can hardly be said for independent Africa, and France became increasingly criticized both in the UN framework and by the OAU for its ambiguous South Africa policy. Particularly during the period from the fall of the Portuguese colonial regime in 1974 up to the UN declaration of the mandatory arms embargo in 1977, the French Government came to realize that continued military support of South Africa meant losing political leverage in the rest of Africa.

France had decided to join the other main Western military powers—the UK and the USA—in not vetoing the forthcoming mandatory embargo. Already before the formal UN Security Council declaration of November 1977, President Giscard d'Estaing announced an extension of the French embargo. This announcement was made during a visit to Mali in February 1977, and the new element was that the embargo now also covered the supply of spare parts for the Mirage fighters, helicopters and missiles already delivered to South Africa. As mentioned above, naval equipment was still not affected by the ban. Defending the sale to South Africa of the two 922-MW nuclear power generators for Koeberg, Prime Minister Raymond Barre said that South Africa 'already has a nuclear military capability' and the reactors would add nothing to it.[38] The broadening of the embargo was generally considered as unlikely to affect South Africa's military capacity much. Nevertheless, reports appeared in 1979 that the SAAF had had to ground its entire fleet of 48 Mirage F-1s due to lack of spare parts, in particular, for the radar and the engine.

It became clear to France that its position of allowing certain direct armaments sales while claiming to adhere to a mandatory embargo would be untenable. The Security Council declaration of the embargo on 4 November 1977 was followed on 7 November by an official French declaration that the two Aviso corvettes and the two Agosta submarines would not be delivered. South Africa had already paid 70 per cent of the purchase price for the corvettes, the first of which was undergoing sea trials at the time. At the same time, the Defence Ministry declared that a review was being made in the areas of sub-contracting, licensing, and supply of dual-purpose equipment to South Africa. The mandatory embargo regulations came into force in 1978, and in effect signalled the end of public military contracts with South Africa. Military exports continued, according to several later reports, even after the socialist Mitterrand regime came into power in 1980,[39] but the military trade was slowly becoming privatized, commercialized or outright illegal as in the United States and Britain, even if tacit Government acceptance was possible.

In 1983, Sam Nujoma, the President of SWAPO of Namibia, accused France of still allowing French technicians to work in South Africa with the production of the Eland armoured cars and the Mirage aircraft (or the future Cheetah redesign). In reply to this, the French President's adviser on African affairs, Mr Guy Penne, declared in Luanda that 'Paris does not supply arms, spare parts or technical expertise to the South African regime'.[40]

In 1985, France was the first major Western power to call for Security Council economic sanctions against South Africa, and the French ambassador was recalled from Pretoria.

V. FR Germany

Implementation and legislation

FR Germany was, like France, able to enter the South African military market at considerable profit, at the same time benefiting commercially from this new market in the wake of the British-US adherence to the embargo from 1963. But unlike France, the FRG has kept a low political profile in the region, and its main interest has been of an economic nature. The West German industrial input is found in the armoured and military vehicle industry in South Africa, in the rocket and missile industry, in electronics and communications equipment and in the nuclear industry.

This input has largely concerned dual-purpose military equipment, machinery and components, and no entirely West German-produced weapon system is actually in use with the SADF. This enabled the respective West German governments to claim strict adherence to both the 1963 and 1977 UN embargoes against South Africa. But for FR Germany, as for the other main Western military suppliers to South Africa, it holds true that strategic goods impossible to export to the Soviet Union, for example, have been given export licences for South Africa.

The arms export *legislation* of the FRG was conditioned by its political situation after 1945. Arms production was prohibited until 1955, then progressively the restrictions were lifted but export rights were confined to NATO countries. Hence, the expanding West German defence industry by 1960 concentrated its export efforts on the sales of equipment not defined as 'military' according to West German law, and on the sale of licences and investments in South Africa regarding such equipment. Most of this industry in FR Germany is privately owned. Commercial sales of equipment are handled by the state-owned Vebeg agency or by private firms acting as intermediaries. In addition, the export from the FRG of armaments produced jointly with a foreign company, or incorporating foreign parts or design, requires approval from the foreign partner. The first West German arms export control law was passed as late as 1961—the War Material Control Act—which regulates production, ownership, handling and sales of weapons. Weapons are defined under a number of headings first contained in the 1961 *Bundesgesezblatt*.[41]

Of more relevance to exports to South Africa are the guidelines for the granting of export licences for other strategic goods not defined as arms. These are stated in paragraph 7 of the Foreign Trade Act, which stipulates that export licences must *not* be granted where such exports endanger the security of the Federal Republic or disturb 'peaceful coexistence' or West German foreign relations. An end-use certificate is always demanded from the customer.

Export licences for the commercial sales of equipment are issued by the Ministry of Finance, on the recommendation of the Ministry of Foreign Affairs. The sales to South Africa have been commercial and the equipment has not been defined as weaponry. According to the Weapons of War List, weapon platforms such as vehicles are not included, which enabled Magirus to sell 3000 military trucks to South Africa and three West German companies to build an engine factory in Cape Town.

Unlike the practice in the UK and the USA, there is a restricted use of the end-use clause in cases of collaborative military projects—which have been undertaken mostly with French industry. According to a 1972 agreement with France, the end-use clause can be invoked only if there is a danger of losing a know-how monopoly.[42] The Foreign Trade Act does not include dual-purpose items, and the wording of the definition, in fact, legalizes all such export to South Africa. The West German trade regulations further actually make state intervention quite risky: in order to intervene in the free trade of commodities, the Government has to prove its case, and a negative decision can be the subject of appeal at special administrative courts.[43] Thus, embargo implementation in cases of exports of goods other than those on the weapons list and the strategic goods list is largely left to the discretion of the exporting companies.

The definition point was emphasized by the Parliamentary Secretary of State of the Ministry of Economics in response to a parliamentary enquiry concerning the shipment of trucks for the South African Army:

The export of military vehicles is subject to the requirement of a permit according to §5, sentence 1 of the Foreign Trade Act in connection with item 0006 section A part 1 of the export list, an appendix to the Trade Act. Item 0006 refers according to the title to tanks and other vehicles *specifically designed for military purposes.* Letter b of the item referred to above mentioned vehicles where *the adaptation of weapons is prearranged.*[44]

All trucks and licensed production rights for trucks exported to South Africa have, in fact, concerned vehicles possible to designate as civilian, and all military adaptations have been carried out by Armscor in co-operation with the West German subsidiaries in South Africa. During the 1970s, parliamentary as well as non-governmental opposition to the West German arms export policy to Third World countries in general—and South Africa in particular—grew steadily. While still in opposition, the Social Democratic Party introduced on three occasions proposals to Parliament aimed at significantly tightening the export controls. After a long and controversial public debate, new guidelines were finally formulated by the Social-Liberal government in May 1982. The most significant change for South Africa's access to know-how was the inclusion of licences and machinery to produce weapons used in warfare as items to be controlled under the arms export policy. The definition of prohibited designations was also changed from the previous 'area of tension' to encompass countries where the danger of an outbreak of armed conflict exists. The 'inner situation' of a country was also to be considered—as a concession to human rights proponents.

So far, no attempts have been made in FR Germany to design special regulations to prevent military-related equipment from being exported to South Africa specifically. There are precedents to show that such a move is possible—in the case of Rhodesia a special additional list was added to the Foreign Trade Act, and in the case of Iran after 1979, the Foreign Trade Act was temporarily altered. The absence of a special South Africa list of prohibited goods according to the pattern above illustrates, among other things, the fact that embargo implementation is a political question.

The *implementing agencies* in the FRG concerning the embargo against South Africa are concentrated in an inter-ministerial council—the Federal Security Council. It consists of high-ranking representatives of the Office of the Chancellor, the Ministry of Foreign Affairs, the Ministry of Finance, the Ministry of Defence and the Ministry of the Interior. However, as emphasized above, few applications for export of sensitive goods to South Africa reach this Council. The licensing of equipment defined as non-military is handled by the Ministry of Finance. Moreover, the practice is that a potential exporting company tables an unofficial inquiry with the section in charge at the Ministry of Finance in advance. Export licences are sought only for equipment which already has been approved for export to South Africa.

There is no special monitoring agency that follows the implementation of the embargo. But in FR Germany, a strong anti-apartheid movement was established during the 1960s and 1970s, and a large part of the South Africa debate has actually concerned cases of military shipments revealed by this movement.

Items covered by the Foreign Trade Act are routinely controlled by the Federal Agency for Commercial Economy under the Ministry of Finance. In the 1986 court case against the Rheinmetall company, charged for illegally selling an assembly line through Paraguay to South Africa for G-5 production, some information on the operation of these export controls was revealed. A Federal Agency officer reported that the usual procedure for a manufacturer exporting prohibited equipment was to separate the components and file export applications for each single part. In cases of doubt, the policy was to regard the need to export as a priority.[45]

VI. Italy

While ranking far behind industries in the countries presented above as suppliers of military technology to South Africa, the Italian arms industry nevertheless played an important role in initiating the South African aircraft industry in the early 1960s. Italy has also functioned as an intermediary in the supply of technology—US technology in particular—and it has enabled so-called third-country sales, for example of the Oto Melara cannon, and the Selenia radar mounted on the Israeli Reshef-class gunboats, which were delivered through Israel. The long production run of the Atlas Impala counter-insurgency aircraft and the assembly of the Bosbok and Kudu light planes for use in the operational areas resulted in a considerable strengthening of South Africa's military capacity. This export of military technology to South Africa from Italy also focused attention on Italy as a country willing to supply items previously embargoed by the UK and France. Atlas Aircraft tried first to buy the production rights for the British Miles trainer aircraft and then for the French Fouga Magister, but did not succeed after the 1963 UN embargo. The Italian Government, closely following the practice within the NATO community, ceased even before the adoption of UN Resolution 181 on 7 August 1963 to release licences for the sale to South Africa of arms especially suited to support the policy of apartheid.[46] The sale by the Macchi company (later Aermacchi) of the production licence for the MB-326 was negotiated during 1964, and the contracts were finalized in 1965.

It has been suggested that political control over arms exports in Italy may be more lax than in other European countries. However, a trainer such as the Impala was not defined as a weapon system, and even less as a counter-insurgency weapon, and was hence treated as a normal commercial export of civilian goods. Secondly, there were national economic pressures at work in the early 1960s when the Italian domestic defence industry was expanding. This expansion, with the full support of the Government, also included support for exports of military equipment wherever such exports could be made, competing in a market dominated by the USA, the UK, France and also FR Germany. Previously excluded from the arms market, Italy relaxed controls in particular over its aircraft companies, Fiat, Macchi and Piaggio, of which the latter two entered the South African market.

The Italian arms export legislation is similar to that in other European nations. It is based on two Ministerial Decrees of 1939 which prohibited the export of aircraft, ships, vehicles and firearms without a government licence. There are also analogous import restrictions, which were applicable to the UN embargo of 1984 on imports from South Africa. The list of items requiring an export licence is continually revised and follows closely the practice in other nations and the COCOM lists. The prohibited destinations include, in addition to the socialist bloc countries, nations involved in conflict and nations subject to a UN embargo.

In 1972, the Italian Parliament amended the arms export regulations to prohibit the export also of civilian aircraft without government authorization to South Africa. No further such export has been recorded since then. Italy has also reported, in response to a request by the Special Committee on Embargo Implementation of the Security Council, that since 1972 no licences have been granted for the export of aircraft spare parts to South Africa.

The implementing agencies include the Ministry of Foreign Trade, the Finance Ministry, the Ministry of Internal Affairs and the Ministry of Defence. The actual decision on a particular transaction is made by an inter-ministerial committee composed of representatives of those ministries. Reported frequent inter-departmental rivalries have facilitated exports to South Africa.

The Italian regulations include an end-use clause whereby the importer can be prevented from re-exporting Italian-produced military equipment. This was not invoked in the case of the cannon and radar re-exported via Israel to South Africa.

VII. Japan

The Japanese entry on the South African market indirectly benefited Armscor's defence industry buildup. For example, the Japanese are half-owners of the Magnis truck enterprise, producing entirely for the South African Army, and are active in the electronics industry. This has been achieved while the official Government position has been to support the 1963 UN embargo.

In 1970, the Japanese Ambassador to the UN denied a charge by Zambia that Japan was selling arms to South Africa: 'As has been frequently stated by representatives of Japan, the Government of Japan is faithfully observing the arms embargo against South Africa in compliance with the decision of the Security Council and has never authorized the export to South Africa of arms or other military goods prohibited by those decisions'.[47]

The above statement corresponds to reality, but the South African arms industry has sought and received high-technology equipment rather than armaments from Japan. The Japanese arms export legislation is, like that of FR Germany and Italy, formally restrictive. Japan is also a party to COCOM, and applies the COCOM embargo lists against socialist states. There are no arms export legislation or formalized regulations at all. But the restrictive practice was begun after a brief peak of arms and military equipment deliveries to the US forces during the Korean war. In 1967, the Japanese Government announced the 'three principles' of arms export. No export licence is given (*a*) for exports to communist countries of items on the COCOM list, (*b*) to countries subject to a UN embargo, and (*c*) to belligerents, or suspected future belligerents. These principles were further expanded in 1976, when the Government announced that, in the future, all arms exports would be discouraged, even to those nations not covered by the first three principles. This, in fact, amounts to a complete ban on arms exports. This policy has been guided by the identity of the customer. The definition of weapons has varied: prior to 1976, several separate definitions were used within various agencies. So, for example, one definition was used by police, another within the Ministry of Trade, and yet another in connection with arms export affairs, and so on. The current government definition of 'weapons' remains customer-oriented, defining 'weapons' as 'items used by military forces in combat'. None of the automobile industry products, the truck components or the electronic components of computers supplied to South Africa could be defined as weapons, according to this practice.

Considering Japan's adherence to the COCOM embargo, there is reason to assume that the equipment sold to South Africa could not have been sold to the Soviet Union, since it does fall under the category of 'strategic goods' as applied by COCOM. But there is a notable reluctance, or a structural problem as in the industrialized Western nations, in controlling trade in strategic goods other than armaments to non-communist destinations. An indication of this was given during the visit to Japan of a mission from the OAU in 1972, asking for Japanese support of liberation movements in Africa and a reduction of Japan's trade with South Africa. The Japanese Foreign Minister stated that Japan was 'a free trade nation and not a socialist state, and its government was not in a position to control trade by private firms'.[48]

From 1964, Japanese companies were prohibited by law from investing directly in South Africa. But it was only after the mounting international sanctions debate in 1985 that Japan introduced new legislation to bar the sales of computers to the South African Defence Force and Police.

VIII. The Third World arms producers

Implementation and legislation

In principle, information about any government's policy on individual arms or military deals is a classified matter not automatically accessible to outside observers. The possibilities of access to such information are not the same in all countries and can actually be ranked on a falling scale. The structure of the US system, with special legislation like the Freedom of Information Act, allows the most insight into the operation of an existing embargo, although this is by no means complete. In Europe, secrecy is greater than it is in the USA. The UK differs considerably from the United States in this respect; France and FR Germany in turn protect their governmental decisions to an even higher degree than the UK. Outside Europe and the United States, in the new arms-producing nations, access to any information whatsoever is scarce, and the respective political systems do not provide any official information channel for this kind of information. The nations of relevance to the South African embargo case comprise what is loosely defined as the 'pariah alliance': nations which for one reason or the other find themselves isolated from other national groupings. Israel and Taiwan figure prominently as suppliers of military technology or as partners in military research and development with South Africa. They also figure as recipients or transit nations for South African-made equipment, thus counteracting the 1984 import embargo.

Some Latin American countries can be added to the 'pariah' group—Chile, Paraguay and Guatemala—but they are probably more relevant as arms customers of South Africa than as military suppliers. Membership of the pariah alliance varies as governments fall or are ousted; and as a solution to South Africa's technical isolation, co-operation with these states must be regarded as a short-term, uncertain policy. The terminology used in the literature to describe this informal alliance reflects its shaky foundations. For example:

Slyly, over recent years, an odd grouping has formed—odd because none of its members really wanted to join. It resembles nothing so much as a lonely hearts club—dejected souls seeking fellowship in an inimical world, banding together to avoid total banishment. Despite its pathos, however, there is little of permanence or clout to the group. The so-called pariah state network consists primarily of Israel, South Africa, South Korea, and Taiwan; some Latinos (Uruguay, Paraguay, Argentina, Chile) participate sporadically and tangentially. Each of the four prime members suffer acute trepidation, possibly diagnosed as paranoia were the threats less severe . . . For the world community shuns if not slanders the pariahs. Taiwan is officially recognized by a mere handful of nations, Israel and South Africa by no more than a third. The four feel themselves estranged from the First World (Western democracies), blasted by the Second World (the communist states), yet barred from the Third World.[49]

Crudely, what this group of nations has in common is isolation from the West, and also from the Third World, coupled with a fear of communism. South Africa's attempts to utilize these states represent a frantic effort to break its isolation, illustrated by the series of state visits undertaken to the Far East in 1985–86 in an effort to pre-empt the expected international economic sanctions. It is unlikely that this network of odd nations will, in the future, be able to provide South Africa with technology and supply a market for its military products. Israel is the sole technologically capable partner, and the future of the Israeli connection seems doubtful.

Israel

The relationship between South Africa and Israel has indeed allowed for a continued flow of high-technology equipment unobtainable from more traditional suppliers since 1977. The military technology co-operation developed during the 1970s—similar to the co-operation one decade earlier with France—and reached a stage where it was often described in terms of an informal military alliance. The connection involved not only technology sales but other types of co-operation, such as the recruitment in Israel of skilled workers and scientists for Armscor. In 1977, three Israeli companies—Tadiran, Elbit and IAI—supplied South Africa with the equipment for an electronic 'wall' that was erected along part of its northern borders. South Africa imported from Israel, in return for exporting special steel, its new armour plate used for the Olifant tank, night-vision equipment and other equipment later described as having been developed in South Africa.

This connection has generated a vast number of special investigations and reports about the scale and scope of deliveries of military equipment from Israel. Many authors and observers share the notion that this relationship amounts to something 'unnatural', 'abnormal' or even 'incomprehensible'.[50]

Implementation policy

History goes some way to explain at least the *initiation* of the relationship. As was demonstrated in the case of France, an industrial relationship once established is not easily dismantled.

General Jan Smuts, who at the time was a statesman of international standing, was a personal friend of Dr C. Weizmann, the first President of Israel. South Africa received many Jewish refugees from Europe during the 1930s and 1940s. This Jewish community (which now numbers approximately 200 000), later became a direct link with the new state of Israel. In 1948 South Africa was one of the first nations to recognize Israel. The positive relationship continued also after the National Party came into power in South Africa in 1949. The first National Party Premier, Dr D. F. Malan, was in 1953 the first head of state to visit Israel. South Africa provided military aid to Israel in the June War of 1967—and again in the Yom Kippur War of 1973, this time even including Mirage fighter aircraft and pilots who were reserve officers from the Jewish community in South Africa. But on the political level, relations deteriorated from 1960 up to the Yom Kippur War. Israel followed the other Western powers in opposing apartheid in international fora. In November 1961, the Israeli Government voted in favour of the first UN proposal to apply arms sanctions to South Africa, and took this stance again in 1962 when it also broke diplomatic relations with South Africa.

Within a month of the declaration of the UN voluntary embargo in August 1963, Israel informed the UN Special Committee on Apartheid that special measures had been taken to ensure that no arms, ammunition or strategic equipment would be delivered to South Africa. Israel claimed to have cancelled the production rights for the Uzi sub-machinegun which was being produced in South Africa under a Belgian sub-licence. However, production know-how was already so advanced in South Africa that it could continue irrespective of formalities. During the rest of the 1960s, relations with South

Africa were kept at consular level, and this was also the period of Israeli *rapprochement* with a number of African countries such as Zaire and Uganda. This involved military aid programmes.

The Yom Kippur War had an effect on the future of South Africa's military industry. After 1973, 27 African states broke off their diplomatic relations with Israel, which then embarked on a policy of strengthening its connections with South Africa in the fields of finance and technical and military co-operation. In 1974, diplomatic relations were raised to ambassadorial level, and Israel ceased to vote against South Africa in the United Nations. Trade increased by 400 per cent between 1973 and 1978, and much of the South African exports to Israel consisted of strategic goods such as special hardened steel (for the construction of which South Africa seems to have employed Swedish know-how according to a 1986 report[51]), uranium, diamonds and gold. In return, South Africa obtained access to naval technology with the licensed production agreement for the Reshef-class missile gunboats and the Gabriel ship-to-ship missile (which came off their respective production lines in South Africa as the Minister-class and the Skerpioen missile). Prime Minister B. J. Vorster visited Israel officially in 1976, which is generally assumed to be when a new technical co-operation agreement was signed, covering nuclear co-operation and probably also the adoption of Israeli technology for the Mirage redesign—the Cheetah fighter. The significance of the 1976 agreement was emphasized by South African Government spokesmen and widely commented on by the South African press at the time: 'This agreement has acquired for South Africa a public friend, an avowed ally, at a time when this country confronts an increasingly aggressive black Africa'.[52]

Between 1973 and 1977, South Africa was reported to be one of Israel's largest markets for *small arms*, in addition to being a partner in technical co-operation.[53] On top of the political factors favouring this military connection, there was also pressure from the Israeli arms industry to export, in turn regarded as vitally important for Israeli security and the capability to supply its own armed forces. This was also the period when Israel developed into the leading new Third World arms producer, and was conquering a substantial share of the international arms market, hitherto dominated by the traditional producers in Europe and the USA.

The political conditions began to change while the industrial connections continued to build up a momentum of their own. Apparently, Israel followed the United States closely in its policy towards South Africa. Contrary to what is often claimed, the Israeli Government formally adhered to the mandatory UN embargo of 1977, and declared this policy in advance of the actual embargo declaration: according to a Foreign Ministry spokesman in Jerusalem, 'Israel conducts its relations with South Africa on a legal basis and if there is a Security Council resolution, Israel will not violate it'.[54] In a letter of April 1978 to the UN Secretary-General, Israel confirmed its embargo adherence.

Since 1977, there have been no known *orders* or *contracts* for the direct sales of armaments or military technology. A confirmation of sorts came from

Armscor chairman P. G. Marais, who in an interview in 1982 said that co-operation with Israel in the ground-equipment sector virtually ceased after 1977.[55] This statement might also suggest, however, that technical co-operation on a fighter aircraft project was still considered legal. In 1979, a Johannesburg radio report predicted closer defence technology co-operation with Israel, assuming this to be a result of a recent visit to South Africa and Armscor by an Israeli delegation of technical experts.[56]

In 1980, a PLO (Palestine Liberation Organization) source reported an unconfirmed contract with Israel for 36 Kfir fighter aircraft at a price of US $430 million. This report was obviously not correct, as the Kfir was never delivered, but it *could* have referred to a co-operation agreement to update the South African Mirages to the Cheetah standard.[57] The Cheetah programme in South Africa remains to materialize—only future developments will solve the question of whether the programme only amounts to a refit of the SAAF's existing Mirage fighters once acquired from France, or if new production will actually be undertaken.

In 1980, Israel began to adhere to a renewed policy of *rapprochement* with black Africa, which by 1985 had met with a certain success in terms of a 'return to bilateral co-operation'.[58]

Concerning military contacts, in 1982 there were reports about continuing co-operation. Israeli officials were quoted as saying that South Africa was a leading recipient of Israeli-made weapons, and also that Israel was acting as a proxy for exports of US-made equipment to South Africa.[59]

By 1985, however, the political tide had turned. Prime Minister S. Peres, in a cabinet speech on 11 August, declared that Israel was against apartheid; and the Knesset Commission for Foreign Affairs and Defence also condemned it. At the same time, what was labelled the 'myth' of vast economic and military relations with South Africa was denied. It was pointed out that exports to South Africa—excluding military goods which do not appear in the statistics—were less than 1 per cent of total exports. According to Professor N. Hazan of the historical faculty of the Hebrew University of Jerusalem, the military exports to South Africa were by 1985 not more than 5 per cent of all Israeli military exports sales.[60] This may be compared to the general situation: Israel was exporting arms to 50 countries, and arms exports made up 20–25 per cent of its total exports.[61]

As to the alleged nuclear weapons co-operation, it is also a fact that after the suspected nuclear flash over the Atlantic in 1979, there have been no more incidents which would confirm an ongoing programme.

Finally, in a report to the UN in 1985, the Israeli Government announced that it had called on industry to take measures to terminate licensed production agreements with Armscor, and that it would not approve any applications for their renewal or extension. Thus in Israel, as in the USA, Britain and Italy, in particular, embargo implementation has been partly handed over to the export industry.

It should be remembered that over the years many reports have appeared on alleged sales of military technology to South Africa which have not materialized. It has, for example, been claimed that the Israeli Lavi fighter was to be licence-produced, and that South Africa would produce a nuclear submarine in co-operation with Israel. Likewise, according to one source, South Africa has financed the Q9 guided missile corvette project in Israel, and was to receive this vessel after 1984 as well as the Israeli Aliyah-class guided missile patrol vessel.[62]

However, in October 1988 a new contract for high-level military co-operation was reportedly signed in Pretoria. According to *Africa Analysis*, the estimated US $500 million/year military trade between the two countries comprises mainly South African funding for military R&D in Israel.[63]

Legislation

Israel's arms export policy does not seem to be based on any formal legislation. It is apparently not even covered by a foreign trade act.[64]

The arms export policy is instead based on the guidelines formulated in 1958 by Prime Minister D. Ben-Gurion, which still remain in force, apparently unchanged over time:

No sale of arms should be made to any country without the Prime Minister's prior knowledge and consent; the Prime Minister will not decide before consulting the Foreign Ministry; there must be complete co-ordination of the arms sales policy, as the sale of weapons is a diplomatic fact, not just a financial and economic one.[65]

In January 1983, the Minister of Industry and Commerce, G. Patt, enumerated three principal considerations governing decisions on arms exports, in addition to the guidelines above:

1. *No arms are exported to an enemy country.* Under this regulation, approximately 80 per cent of Israel's own designs, technology and indigenous military products remain classified and are not eligible for distribution or sale overseas. To facilitate arms exports, certain equipment has been modified by removing ultra-sophisticated and secret devices, such as the Kfir version offered for export.

2. *Export is avoided of arms designed specifically for use in suppressing domestic disturbances.* According to this rule, certain types of arms were denied to the Shah of Iran, for example, and to South Africa after 1977.

3. *Export is prohibited of certain types of lethal or inhumane weapons* generally described as 'weapons of ill repute'.[66]

4. A most relevant Israeli export rule, regulation or principle was for the first time disclosed by Mr Patt, namely, the principle self-imposed by Israel *not to authorize the sale of weapons to any country denied arms from the United States, Canada, France and Great Britain.*

In retrospect, however, it is evident that these regulations did no more than ban the export of items which were no longer being exported to South Africa.

After all, Israel's export of complete weapon systems has been minimal compared to its export of technology and know-how, in particular after 1977.

The renewed US engagement in embargo implementation from 1986 resulted in pressure on Israel to end this kind of co-operation with South Africa. In March 1987, US Secretary of State G. Shultz handed over a State Department report to Congress where it was stated that in 1986 alone, Israel delivered US $400–800 million worth of military technology to South Africa. Later the same month, the Israeli Government pledged not to enter into any new military deals with South Africa.

In September 1987, Prime Minister Y. Shamir further declared the imposition of 10 specified sanctions intended to reduce ties with South Africa in line with the actions of other Western governments. These sanctions included a ban on new investments, and the limitation of economic and scientific ties with South Africa. If implemented to the letter, this would close the last major route of access to foreign military technology by South Africa.

Implementing agencies

Thus it is clear that the arms export policy, and the policy regarding implementation of the arms embargo against South Africa, remain ultimately controlled by the Prime Minister, reflecting the degree of centralization within the Israeli political system in general. Second to the Prime Minister, there is a Ministerial Committee on Weapons Transfers, which comprises the highest policy-making group within the Cabinet. But this committee meets infrequently, and then only to review the arms export programme. The actual handling of export licences is conducted at ministerial level, where the Defence Ministry and the intelligence service, Mossad, play the most important part. The Defence Sales Office within the Defence Ministry is the highest administrative agency with authority over military exports. Its mandate is, however, basically to *promote* Israeli arms exports; thus, it is singularly ill-suited to implementing an embargo. A certain inter-ministerial competition is, not surprisingly, reported between the Defence Ministry and the Foreign Ministry, where it can be assumed that the Foreign Ministry is more likely to see a necessity to restrict arms exports for political reasons.

Monitoring agencies

There is no statutory requirement in the Israeli political system for consulting or even informing Parliament about planned or existing arms transactions. Neither Parliament nor public opinion has enough access to data to be able to put pressure on the Government for embargo implementation.

Taiwan

Proceeding along a falling scale of access to information, Taiwan as a military supplier to South Africa provides so few hard facts that the Israelis, by comparison, provide substantial information. By 1988, South Africa had diplomatic relations only with Taiwan and South Korea in Asia. The Association of South-East Asian Nations (ASEAN) maintained a general trade boycott against South Africa. There are no known weapon projects or technology contracts between Taiwan and South Africa. Nevertheless, there are many reports about military-technological co-operation based on circumstantial evidence; the sources, such as they are, often harp on the 'pariah' concept, and differ markedly from the usual analytical studies in international relations literature. One example describes the South African connection with Taiwan using a dense jumble of metaphors:

But such exchanges must now draw to a close as Israel pledges to abide by the 1977 mandatory UN arms embargo against South Africa. Pretoria may consequently turn to the Asian pariahs Taiwan and South Korea—who are excluded from the UN and thus may not be legally bound to honor its embargo. This must be part of the flirtation between Taiwan and South Africa that has blossomed of late. Never have two medium-sized nations 900 miles apart had such a strange affair. It began in the late 1970s when South Africa as usual swam against the world tide and opened full diplomatic relations there just as other nations were closing the shop.[67]

Commercial trade between South Africa and Taiwan grew at an average rate of 37.5 per cent yearly between 1973 and 1978. In 1975, the two nations granted each other 'most-favoured-nation' benefits (refused to Japan, for example, by South Africa). In 1976, Taiwan raised its diplomatic strength from consular to ambassadorial level in South Africa. After the mandatory embargo, there were reports in the South African press that, during a 1978 visit to South Africa, Taiwan's Vice-Foreign Minister promised field artillery, machineguns, automatic rifles and missiles to South Africa. In May 1979, co-operative projects on atomic energy were agreed on.

The arms deals reported above remain unconfirmed and seem unlikely in view of the fact that the weapon types listed are among Armscor's own long-standing products, and also considering the comparatively low level of the Taiwanese arms industry.

However, in May 1980, during the South African visit of Taiwanese Prime Minister Sun Yun-Suan and the Chief of Staff, a contract was signed for 4000 tonnes of uranium from South Africa worth US $400 million. The agreement runs from 1984 to 1990. The uranium is shipped to the USA from South Africa for enrichment, and then supplied to Taiwan, hence not appearing in Taiwanese-South African import statistics.[68] Later in 1980, Defence Minister P. W. Botha visited Taiwan. In May 1981, a Taiwanese training cruiser visited South Africa, and South African officers have visited Taiwan for training in 'political warfare'.

From 1983, prospects for wider military co-operation seemed to increase, as Taiwan was increasingly being refused access to more sophisticated US weapon systems (due to US concern about China). In June 1983, the Taiwanese Chief of General Staff of the Armed Forces, General Hau Pei-Tsun, together with a number of high-ranking military officers, visited South Africa. He inspected a number of SADF installations as well as the operational area in Namibia. The

General publicly suggested closer military co-operation, saying that the South African experience 'in fighting foreign forces have proved valuable resources for the Republic of China'.[69] At the same time, 'military analysts in Taipei' were quoted as confirming that Taiwan was co-operating with South Africa on research in advanced weaponry.[70]

Taiwanese industry has been credited with developing *jointly* with Israel the second-generation version of the Israeli ship-to-ship missile, Gabriel 2, known in Taiwan as the Hsiung Feng. The Gabriel 2 is also licence-produced in South Africa, as is the Skerpioen missile. Several sources reported a direct connection between Taiwan and South Africa in this missile project, but there is no confirmation whatsoever, and the reports are confused. It has even been suggested that Taiwan has *imported* the Israeli-designed missile from South Africa. This link, in particular, as well as military collaboration in general, has been refuted by Taiwanese Government spokesmen: 'That is somebody's invention to further isolate the three countries' (Taiwan, Israel and South Africa).[71]

In 1986, under the mounting threat of general economic sanctions against South Africa, Prime Minister P. W. Botha toured Asia—in search of more trade outlets and strengthened ties, wherever possible. The first country to be visited was Taiwan; South Africa and Taiwan had shortly before achieved a new trade agreement, covering also scientific and technical co-operation in unspecified areas. In connection with reporting on this, however, it was pointed out that the general picture of trade with Taiwan was very modest; two-way trade was worth only US $500 million in 1985, and had fallen since the 1982 peak of US $600 million. There was also speculation that the South African Prime Minister would be asking Taiwan to keep open lines of supplies from future sanctioned markets and, further, that sophisticated computers comprised the single most important item.[72]

Summary

Table 14.1 gives a rough overview of the current arms export legislation in a number of countries which have been of importance for South Africa's buildup of its military industry. It is clear that the export and re-export of armaments, arms production technology and spare parts are a government responsibility in a majority of the countries listed. However, the limits to a legalistic approach lie in the fact that legislation in itself does not necessarily reflect a policy of restrictiveness. It rather reflects the extent of governmental *power* in a defined area of international trade. The USA and France, for example, are large arms exporters in spite of their comprehensive legislation in the field.

Consequently, for South Africa, the major chance of circumventing the arms embargo has been provided by benevolent government treatment. Also, industrial independence has been facilitated due to the lack of government controls in such smaller European countries as Belgium or the Netherlands. Finally, dual-purpose equipment belongs rather to the field of general eco-

Table 14.1. General arms export legislation in selected countries as of 1987

Aspects under government control	Australia	Austria	Belgium	Canada	France	FRG	Italy	Netherlands	Spain	Sweden	Switzerland	UK	USA
Export of arms, ammunition and war material	yes	yes	yes	yes	yes	yes	yes	yes	yes	yes	yes	yes	yes
Export of arms and ammunition, production licences and manufactured equipment	yes	no	no	no	yes	yes	yes	no	no	yes	no	yes	yes
Export of military technology, patents, etc.	yes	yes/no	yes	yes	yes	yes	yes	yes	no	no	no	yes	yes
Export of dual-purpose items	no	no	no	no	no	no	no	no	no	no	no	no	no
Export of dual-purpose technology	no	no	no	no	no	no	no	no	no	no	no	no	no
Spare parts	yes	yes	yes	yes	yes	yes	yes	no	yes	yes	yes	yes	yes
End-use clause	yes	yes	yes	yes	yes	yes	yes	yes	yes	yes	yes	yes	yes
Third-country sales of licence-production	no	no	no	no	yes	no	yes	no	no	yes	no	yes	yes
Jointly developed items	yes	no	no	no	yes	yes	yes	no	no	yes	no	yes	yes
Parliamentary involvement provided for	no	no	no	no	no	no	no	no	no	yes	no	no	yes

nomic sanctions. Since 1985, most of South Africa's major trading partners have also placed restrictions on economic dealings with that country, and many private foreign companies and investors have cut their ties. In the future, this may limit the access to equipment needed for the armaments industry to a higher degree than the arms embargoes ever did.

Notes and references

[1] UN Resolution 182, Dec. 1963.

[2] Point made in Document A.4: 'The arms embargo and national controls', conference paper, presented at the International Seminar on the Arms Embargo Against South Africa (The World Campaign Against Military and Nuclear Collaboration with South Africa and the UN Special Committee Against Apartheid), London, 28–30 May 1986.

[3] See, for example, 'How Britain arms apartheid', A memorandum for presentation to Her Majesty's Government, Anti-Apartheid Movement, London, 1985; First, R., Steele, J., Gurney, C. and Smith, T., *The South African Connection, Western Investment in Apartheid* (Temple Smith: London, 1972); and a number of UN reports.

[4] Note of 10 Nov. 1976 quoted in 'How Britain arms apartheid' (note 3), p. 32.

[5] *Republic of South Africa, Review of Defence and Armaments Production: Period 1960 to 1970*, Defence HQ (Government Printing Office: Pretoria, Apr. 1971), p. 10.

[6] SIPRI computerized arms trade registers.

[7] 'A young navy forging a future', *Navy International*, Jan. 1982, p. 776.

[8] *The Economist*, 23 Dec. 1967, in an article showing how the French and Italians had already taken over the South African arms market.

[9] *The Times*, 24 Jan. 1969.

[10] Sampson, A., 'The companies, the dealers, the bribes from Vickers to Lockheed', *The Arms Bazaar* (Hodder & Stoughton: London, 1977), p. 168.

[11] *Black South Africa Explodes*, Anti-Report no. 17, Counter Information Services, London, 1977.

[12] *Note Verbale*, UN Document S/12494/ADD 1.

[13] 'How Britain arms apartheid' (note 3), p. 30.

[14] The supply of Centurion spares was stopped, in principle, by the Labour embargo rulings of 1964. In 1976, it was revealed that Armscor had succeeded in importing £1 million worth of spare parts for Centurion tanks through a Jersey company which had given a fraudulent order. The case was brought to court and the company was fined.

[15] *Cape Times*, 1 May 1981.

[16] *Rand Daily Mail*, 23 Jan. 1984; *The Star*, 9 June 1983.

[17] 'The campaign against arms trade', *London News Letter*, no. 71 (25 Apr. 1985).

[18] *Hansard*, 13 Apr. 1984, written reply by the PM to question by Robert Hughes, MP.

[19] 'How Britain arms apartheid' (note 3), p. 37.

[20] Regina v. Hammond, Cherrett and Aspin, Court transcript Oct. 1982, quoted in 'How Britain arms apartheid (note 3), pp. 37–38.

[21] Source: Document B.7; Conrad, T., 'The UN arms embargo and US controls', conference paper presented at the International Seminar (note 2).

[22] *Enforcement of the United States Embargo Against South Africa*, Hearing before the Subcommittee on Africa of the Committee of Foreign Affairs, House of Representatives, 97th Congress, 2nd session, 30 Mar. 1982 (US Government Printing Office: Washington, DC, 1982), pp. 44–45.

[23] In *African Defence*, no. 29 (Jan. 1983), p. 18.

[24] *Rand Daily Mail*, 20 Apr. 1981.

[25] Schatz, W., 'South Africa: pulling the plug', *Datamation*, 1 Oct. 1985, p. 24.

[26] Quoted in *Africa Now*, Feb. 1984, p. 8.

[27] *Le Monde*, 22 Aug. 1985.

[28] *Le Monde*, 12 Jan. 1985.

[29] *Financial Mail* (SA), 6 Dec. 1978.

[30] *La France et l'O.N.U.*, Presses de la fondation nationale des Sciences politiques, 1979, p. 325.

[31] *Journal Officiel*, 9 Aug. 1969.

[32] *Le Monde*, 3 Apr. 1971.

[33] Schissel, H., 'The Paris-Pretoria conspiracy', *Africa*, no. 65 (Jan. 1977), p. 40.

[34] *International Herald Tribune*, 22 Oct. 1970.

[35] Legum, C., 'Secret French arms deals help Vorster', *Observer*, 18 Oct. 1970.

[36] Foreign Minister Maurice Schumann in radio interview, 12 July 1971, *International Herald Tribune*, 15 July 1971.

[37] Kaplan, B. D., 'France carefully cushions South Africa arms embargo', *International Herald Tribune*, Aug. 1975.

[38] *Milavnews News Letter*, no. 184 (Feb. 1977).

[39] *The Star*, 7 July 1981; *Daily News* (UK), 26 May 1981; *The Sowetan*, 21 May 1981.

[40] *African Defence*, no. 31 (Mar. 1983).

[41] Document B.4: 'The UN Arms Embargo and Federal Republic of Germany Controls', conference paper (note 2).

[42] Mann, S., in *Verteidigungspolitische Information für Politik und Presse*, no. 216 (5 Sep. 1974), p. 3.

[43] Document B.4: 'The UN arms embargo and Federal Republic of Germany controls', conference paper (note 2).

[44] Document B.4 (note 2), p. 5.

[45] Document B.4 (note 2), p. 8.

[46] *The Arms Trade with the Third World*, SIPRI (Almquist & Wiksell: Stockholm, 1977), p. 278.

[47] *Japan Times*, 2 Feb. 1970.

[48] *The Standard* (Tanzania), 27 Apr. 1972, 'Japan says NO to OAU's arms aid pleas'.

[49] Adelman, K., 'The Club of Pariahs: Israel–South Africa', in *Africa Report*, Nov.–Dec. 1980, p. 8.

[50] See, for example, Adams, J., *The Unnatural Alliance—Israel and South Africa* (Quartet Books: London, 1984).

[51] Isolera Sydafrika-Kommitten (*ISAK*), Stockholm, 1986.

[52] *Rand Daily Mail*, 14 Apr. 1976.

[53] Klieman, A. S., *Israel's Global Reach—Arms Sales as Diplomacy* (Pergamon-Brassey's International Defence Publishers: Washington, DC, 1985).

[54] *New York Times*, 3 Nov. 1977, quoting AP report from Jerusalem.

[55] *Military Technology*, no. 8, 1982, p. 54; see also: Goell, Y., 'A view from Jerusalem', *Africa Report*, Nov.–Dec. 1980, pp. 18–22.

[56] BBC Monitoring Report, 10 Feb. 1979, quoted in *ANC Weekly Report*, vol. 3, no. 6 (Feb. 1979), pp. 53–54.

[57] Briefing Paper, PLO Office, London, 1980.

[58] *Afrique Défense*, Feb. 1985.

[59] *New York Times*, 8 May 1982; *Financial Times* (UK), 18 Aug. 1982.

[60] *Le Monde*, 13 Aug. 1985.

[61] *Strategic Digest*, Sep. 1985, p. 1153.

[62] Adams (note 50), p. 123.

[63] *Africa Analysis*, 30 Sept. 1988, p. 5; If this is correct it would suggest that the Israeli adherence to a stricter sanctions policy is merely cosmetic.

[64] Klieman (note 53), pp. 92–122.

[65] Klieman (note 53), p. 108, translated from Hebrew. These guidelines were published in the Israeli Government Yearbooks, in the Defence Sales Directory 1983, and in the Defence Ministry publication *Guidelines for Coordination Between Exports of Military Products and Defence Technology and the Defence Sales Office*, Apr. 1983 (Hebrew).

[66] Klieman (note 53), p. 95. The wording of the definitions is a direct translation from Hebrew.

[67] *Africa Report*, Nov.–Dec. 1980, p. 10.

[68] *Africa Report* (note 67), p. 10; and BBC Monitoring Report, 17 Mar. 1980, quoting Johannesburg Radio, in *ANC Weekly Report*, vol. 4, no. 11 (Mar. 1980).

[69] *African Defence*, June 1983, p. 28.

[70] *Asia Research Bulletin*, 31 May 1983, p. 1049.

[71] *Far Eastern Economic Review*, 3 Mar. 1983.

[72] *The Times*, 8 Sep. 1986.

Chapter 15. Summary and conclusions

I. Introduction

The embargoes against South Africa have been in force for 25 years. During that period, South Africa has built up a military industry and remains the leading military power in the region. This in itself provides enough evidence that the embargo was not efficient.

The main aims of this study stated in the introduction were to present: *what* types of military technology South Africa has been able to import in spite of the UN embargoes, and from where; *how* this import has been possible; and *why* the sellers have been motivated to break the embargoes.

The first question was broadly answered by going through individual weapon projects. This account, which does not claim to be exhaustive, nevertheless shows that the South African arms industry owes its development to foreign input at different levels, in different forms and from a large number of suppliers. It was not the ambition to arrive at a listing of all imports. Such an endeavour would indeed not be possible, considering the fact that any major weapon system is put together from thousands of components, the exact origins of which may be unknown even to those directly working in the South African arms industries. It seems to be a safe speculation, however, that if it were possible to construct an all-inclusive list of the origin of all the 'nuts and bolts' of military equipment, an even larger share of foreign content would be found.

The main and obvious factor working against all embargo efforts has been the capacity and determination of the target regime. South Africa's resourcefulness and the priority given to investing in a domestic arms industry have throughout the period created immense problems for embargo implementation. Armscor has, so to say, managed to keep one step ahead.

This is illustrated by the chronology of events leading South Africa up the staircase of know-how acquisition. When the first UN embargo was eventually declared in 1963, South Africa had already laid the foundation of its arms industry and acquired new suppliers of the technology needed. The embargo thus marked the end of the import of complete weapon systems. In the new technology market, France, Italy and the FRG attracted most attention as technology providers, followed from 1972 by Israel. With the switch from arms import to arms production, a host of component industries based in the UK, the USA and other nations also became involved.

The mandatory embargo of 1977 in turn marked the end of the acquisition of production licences for weapon systems. But Armscor had already reached the stage where the need for licences had been replaced by the need for certain sophisticated high-technology items and for technical collaboration with foreign industries, which was easier to hide than the purchase of licences.

The current status of South Africa's military industry can now be presented as having entered into the weapon development loop, illustrated in figure 15.1.

This picture envisages the continuous development of ever more sophisticated weaponry as a dynamic process. Unlike the initial acquisition of military know-how, which is illustrated by the 'staircase' (figure 1.1) in chapter 1, there is no 'beginning' and no 'end'—the process advances through the stations of research, development, testing and evaluation (RDT&E), production, sales and new technology acquisition. The know-how and financial resources gained are in turn applied in RDT&E on a new weapon system or on a redesign which then enters production, is sold, and so forth. This is a stylized picture of the ideal state of the art for an arms industry, if allowed to work without interference by factors outside its control. In the real world, the process is constantly subject to various interferences. When one of these stations is seriously disturbed, the process may stagnate.

First, the RDT&E station may be disturbed by a cutoff of financial resources. This is not likely to happen in South Africa's case under the present regime. Another threat would be the lack of skilled manpower to continue development work. The shortage of electronic engineers has been observed with alarm in South Africa, and the ongoing emigration, in particular of skilled personnel, may in the future affect all branches of the military industry. But the greatest threat to South Africa's capacity in the field of military research and development would be a total cutoff from contacts with the outside world. This has been stated in connection with nuclear research, but it also holds true for all other military research.

The production station may be threatened by a lack of access to necessary foreign components and material, and also by a lack of skilled manpower and adequate financing. Production often turns out to be costlier than initially planned at the R&D stage.

Outside interference occurs mostly with the import and export stations. In

Figure 15.1. The weapon development loop

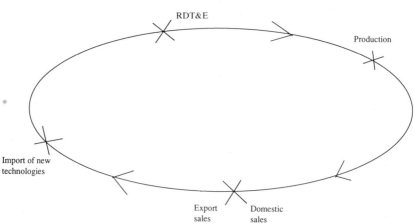

the technologically most advanced arms producing nations, the industries are practically free to import whatever they can afford. In South Africa's case, the possibilities to import have been severely disturbed by the embargo, although not completely squashed. It remains a matter of speculation how Armscor's production would function if the existing loopholes in the embargo were closed. Still, access to military know-how is difficult to trace and, once delivered, impossible to take back. For example, the sale of the West German submarine blueprints led to a fine against the seller in FR Germany, but the blueprints remain in South African possession.

The 1984 embargo on arms imports *from* South Africa has thwarted Armscor's efforts to become a major competitor on the international arms market. For political reasons, it seems unlikely that this situation will change under the present regime.

II. The methods of disimplementation

How the embargoes have been broken emerges from a summary of the development history of the South African arms industry.

The means used to circumvent the UN embargoes since 1963 have most often been presented as 'loopholes' in the embargo legislation. Here, they are presented as the methods of disimplementation—a concept which was constructed to enable the coverage of *all* the various routes used to bring military equipment into South Africa. Some of these measures are hardly, or just barely, open to legislative control; for example, the capture of Soviet-made weapons in Namibia and Angola, or the investment of South African capital in European military industries. The methods of disimplementation, as practised by the South African Government and its overseas industrial collaborators and as revealed in the description of the various weapon projects, resulted from the South African determination to acquire a domestic defence industry at whatever cost, as well as from the producers' readiness to sell. This readiness to sell was sometimes coupled with the respective government's willingness to ignore the identity of the buyer, and sometimes involved the deliberate deception of the government in the supplying country.

The study of the South African acquisition of military technology reveals the following methods of disimplementation.

Licensed production

The South African arms industry was started with the acquisition of foreign production licences. The *timing* of these acquisitions reveals, in retrospect, a high degree of co-operation between the South Africans and foreign companies, if not governments—most of the 127 foreign licences mentioned by Defence Minister Botha in 1963 were acquired just before the first voluntary arms embargo was declared. The agreement with France, for example, for the production of the Panhard armoured cars, was concluded in 1961. Likewise, all the subsequent production agreements were concluded before the mandatory embargo of 1977, including those for the assembly of Mirage fighters in 1972; the production of the Impala in 1964; and the Israeli Reshef-class ships and Scorpion missiles in 1972. In the case of France, it is even claimed that an agreement existed with Armscor to the effect that France would not agree to a mandatory embargo until such time as the South Africans were capable of a degree of indigenous production. To date, no detailed information has emerged about the terms of any licensed arms project. It can be assumed, however, due to the nature of the merchandise, that licence fees were considerable. This assumption is borne out by some indicators: for example, the *New African Yearbook 1980* gave the information that the payments for licences for all industrial projects involving foreign technology were a considerable burden to the balance of payments in South Africa; licence fees during the 1970s amounted to more than 50 per cent of the value of all goods exported.

This statement may also serve as a reminder of the general South African industrial dependence on foreign technology. Co-operation with foreign industries has in turn facilitated the connections with military industries—in particular in the 'grey-area zone' of dual-purpose equipment.

The UN mandatory embargo of 1977 called for a cancellation of all arms production licences. All were not revoked, however. The 1977 recommendation was even openly disputed by Italy, whose government claimed that a revoking of production licences would only benefit South Africa since Armscor would be able to continue production without paying the licence fees. The official South African viewpoint (often stated) is that the 1977 embargo did in effect cancel all licence agreements; this meant a net financial gain for South Africa, since production could continue without payment of licence fees: 'South Africa has no intention of halting the manufacture under licence of foreign weapons even if these licences are withdrawn', said Armscor Chairman P. G. Marais in 1978.[1]

The possibility of acquiring licences from overseas is the single most important explanation of how South Africa was able to build its military industry. Without access to foreign technology, the list of weapons produced would be very short.

The redevelopment work and the efforts put into redesigning such licence-produced weapons represent the largest share of South African input into its military industry. The extent to which redesigned or improved versions of an imported design—such as the various models of the French Panhard armoured car, or the Italian Impala COIN fighter—have required a renewal of existing licences remains company knowledge. There is, for example, no information on French licences for components for the Cheetah Mirage fighter.

The duration of contracts signed between Armscor and foreign industries likewise tends to remain a closely guarded secret. Only the increased US pressure in 1987 on Israel to cut off all military connections with South Africa, for instance, led to the revelation that many Israeli-Armscor contracts would run until the year 2000.

Once signed, contracts are hardly ever broken or cancelled. Hence, the acquisition of a foreign licence represents a real advance for the buyer. However, the unfavourable publicity in store for any industry selling to South Africa has limited Armscor's opportunities, as illustrated by the scandal caused by the discovery in 1986 of the West German submarine design deal.

Considering the general Western dependence on US high technology, the US policy on this issue may turn out to be decisive. A total stop to the existing input into the South African arms industry from various Western industries would leave Armscor on its own without alternative suppliers, except for the private arms smugglers, whose capacity remains limited by comparison. Armscor's import capacity is also affected by financial aspects—a military component no longer available from a foreign industry automatically turns into a black market component, with the consequent doubling or tripling of its cost.

The operation of multinational companies and banks

The second most important source of military technology to date has been the multinational (transnational) companies operating in South Africa, which provide components and material for Armscor industries particularly crucial to the electronics industry. The subsidiaries of the transnational companies (TNCs), have also been important for other dual-purpose industries, in the fields of the vehicle and light-engineering industries, for example. From around 1980, the TNCs started to leave South Africa, partly in response to the US and British disinvestment campaigns, but also to a large extent acting independently from any government policies—the growing unrest simply created a climate unfavourable to foreign economic interests. But the techno-logical know-how already built up remains intact, and can no more be revoked than can the production capacity be achieved through foreign licences. When a TNC pulls out of South Africa it is sold out to local industries. A report of 1980 on the disinvestment issue undertaken by the Anglo-American Corporation stated:

Once a company has made an investment in a country, the investment takes the form of fixed assets and cannot be withdrawn. All the owner can do is to sell his investment for what it will fetch—or, in the last resort, abandon it. The loss falls on the owner, not on the country where the investment is made.[2]

The tendency for foreign majority-owned or wholly owned subsidiaries in South Africa to become foreign minority holdings does not necessarily represent any political action. Some of these takeovers have rather cor-responded to South African interests, and have indeed been South African initiatives. In the section describing the development of the South African electronics industry above, it was, for example, described how the Govern-ment decided after the 1977 embargo to acquire local majority ownership of strategic industries.

Over time, South African legislation designed to counter unwanted actions by foreign-owned companies has been passed. The most significant such piece of legislation of relevance for suppliers to the military industry is the National Suppliers and Procurement Act of 1970. According to this Act, the Defence Minister can order any firm in South Africa (*a*) to sell part of its production to the South African Government; (*b*) to produce certain goods for the South African Government; and (*c*) to set up special production lines for products for the SADF. Thus, after 1970, it was no longer possible for a foreign-owned company to refuse to sell to Armscor or to the SADF. This Act was used for the first time during the incursion into Angola in 1976. A second Act of importance for the Armscor industries was the Protection of Business Act of 1978. This Act was designed to counter effects of the so-called Sullivan Principles (US) and the EEC Code of Conduct of 1977, demanding a certain anti-apartheid policy from US and European companies working in South Africa. The Act prohibits foreign subsidiaries from complying with orders or instructions from their overseas head offices without prior permission from the South African Government. Thus, after 1978, an order from abroad to a company in South Africa not to sell its products to the military could not automatically be complied with.

Foreign corporate investment has been an important source of capital, equipment and technological know-how for the South African arms industry. In addition, transnational banks have been a critical source of finance for the military sector as well as for the South African industry at large. For example, the Chairman of South Africa's second largest bank—the Standard Bank South Africa, owned by the London-based Standard Chartered Bank—was appointed to the Defence Advisory Board by Prime Minister Botha. Barclays Bank in London was in 1980 subject to an official investigation dealing with arms shipments from Colombia to South Africa apparently financed by its subsidiary—Barclays Bank South Africa. When Barclays withdrew from South Africa in 1986, it was generally interpreted as the beginning of a British withdrawal from the country, following the example of several US companies.

The withdrawal of international banks leaves no fixed assets for South African interests to take over, unlike the situation when a foreign enterprise pulls out and leaves its factories behind. The result is automaticaly an increased cost for the South African Government in procuring military equipment.

South African investment in overseas strategic industries

While there are a number of investigations and reports about the foreign companies in South Africa, less attention has been paid to South African investment in such enterprises overseas. One early example was the South African financing of, and participation in, the Cactus missile project in France. In the future, this method may take the place of local subsidiaries as an important conduit of technological know-how. One variation of this method may be seen in the purchase of shares in Western Europe and the USA—for example, most of those electronic companies that preferred to withdraw from South Africa rather than to accept local ownership have sold shares to South

African industries. Among such shareholders are: the General Mining Corporation, with shares in Siemens (FRG); Sanlam, which owns shares in Plessey Electronics (UK); and Barlow Rand, which owns 50 per cent of Marconi (UK). Thus, contact with and access to foreign technology can be maintained even when a strategic industry moves out of South Africa.

In 1984, the British anti-apartheid movement asked the British Government to change company law in order to stop South African penetration of local industries as a means to circumvent economic and arms trade sanctions. But even if such legislation were to be considered in the leading industrialized nations, a remaining obstacle would be to identify South Africa as the buyer, as illustrated by the next method of disimplementation—the setting up of 'dummy' companies.

Cover companies

The use of paper companies, dummy companies or cover companies with non-committal names has been practised by Armscor and by the South African Government for decades to hide imports to the South African military industry, or to the SADF.

Such companies have been set up inside South Africa as well as abroad. So, for example, it was possible to use the Armscor subsidiary Infoplan as the official buyer of equipment intended for Armscor from the United States at a time when the identity of the Armscor subsidiaries was not commonly known. The G-5 deal involved the construction of several cover companies in Belgium. This method is likely to be of increased use in the future, given the difficulties of revealing true ownership until after the respective deals have been effected.

The full extent of South African overseas possessions relevant to securing imports for its military industry is not known. A report covering the related field of transport companies appeared in 1984 by *Guardian* reporter Paul Brown, who had researched the subject for one year.[3] According to this report, South African industry and government have built up a world-wide network of transport companies and travel agencies to protect imports in the event of general economic sanctions. These companies, formally owned by paper companies that obscure South African ownership, have been established in London, Edinburgh, Jersey, the Netherlands, the Bahamas and Panama, and are linked together so that goods can be bought, transported and delivered anywhere in the world without outsiders being able to trace either the origin of the goods or their destinations. Linked with this network are the South African companies Safmarine, Anglo-American, Musgrove (which is one of the Armscor subsidiaries) and Freight Services of South Africa.

Dual-purpose equipment

The import of dual-purpose or grey-area equipment has been and will probably remain one of the most efficient means of circumventing embargo regulations.

The absence of a commonly usable definition of 'weapons' permits the selling party to claim that the exports have not been definable as arms. It is even more difficult to define arms technology. A large number of items, in particular components, electronic equipment, various types of vehicles and aircraft, have a dual capacity and have been exported as civilian goods. Such equipment is then turned into military versions in the South African industries. A variation of this method is to take over aircraft from civilian airlines, such as Boeing transports with a refuelling capacity, and light planes from flying clubs.

The supply of spare parts, support and maintenance equipment for existing projects

Business practice is apparently never to cut off such follow-on contracts to a licence deal. Monitoring by outside agencies is not possible.

The use of foreign manpower

Not least important for the buildup of South Africa's know-how in military technology has been the use of foreign manpower. The establishment of the Atlas Aircraft Corporation and its continued work provide an illustration of this. Foreign experts have been used to train and educate personnel in South Africa, and South Africans have also received training and education abroad.

Renting and leasing

Renting and leasing have, in particular, been used to get access to computer technology from foreign subsidiaries. This method of disimplementation was hardly foreseen in 1963 and is not likely to be more controllable in the future than in the past.

Third-country deliveries

South Africa has been able to purchase equipment needed for its military industry by means of third-country sales—Italian naval radar, US decoy launchers and West German high-speed demagnetized diesel engines from Israel, parts for Mirage fighters from Belgium, and so on. Efforts have been undertaken to demand end-use certificates to prevent re-export to South Africa, but there is little chance of the UN Arms Embargo Committee or other agencies' knowing about such deals in advance. Italy, Belgium, Israel and Taiwan are among those who have been willing to supply equipment from the major arms-producing nations. This has been of great importance for Armscor's establishment of military industries.

Smuggling

The importance of outright smuggling of arms and other military equipment to secure Armscor access to foreign technology has grown in congruence with the extent of embargo compliance. Military trade with South Africa has belonged, to a certain extent, to the category of smuggling or clandestine trade ever since 1963. So far, the smuggling cases that have ended up in court have mostly concerned shipments of armaments, but components and blueprints can also be traded on the black market. The G-5 deal, for example, contained all the ingredients of a typical illegal affair—a private seller, middlemen, cover companies, ships with false destinations and false labelling of the goods.

Standard methods include changing destination by secret orders at sea or in the air, forging the end-use certificates and stating a false buyer or even a false buying country. The arms are labelled 'agricultural machinery' or given other neutral descriptions and shipped through the key centres for this particular trade to South Africa.

Now and then a revelation is made which suddenly illuminates this particular trade and the exporters involved. An example of this is the trial in Denmark of a shipping company in 1984, where not only Western weapons were mentioned but also cargoes from Bulgaria and Czechoslovakia.

In 1981 a UN seminar held in London came to the conclusion that military equipment from 15 countries had reached South Africa during the preceding four-year period, in spite of the embargo. All attempts to stop the export of electronic equipment to South Africa were frustrated by agents in France, the UK and the USA. The UN Arms Embargo Committee, working under the Security Council, is constantly asking for statements from various countries where the embargo is broken by private dealers; for example, in 1980 such statements were demanded from the governments of Bulgaria, Denmark, the Netherlands, Portugal, and the USA. In fact, practically *all* the countries in Western Europe have at one time or another figured in connection with smuggling to South Africa. In 1982 an article in *El Tiempo* claimed that about 500 kg of weapons per month were being shipped to South Africa via the Madrid airport Barajas. The transports are handled by South African Airways, which flies twice a week between Madrid and Johannesburg, and the weapons are made up of fine-calibre guns and ammunition from the Eibat works at San Sebastian. The Spanish harbours and in particular the Canary Islands are vital smuggling centres.

Lisbon is another centre, according to the Portuguese journal *Expresso* (Portugal employs some 50 000 persons in its military industry and exports 90 per cent of its production).[4] Among the archetypal examples are the two British arms dealers who were arrested in Houston, Texas, in 1981 for an attempt to smuggle US $1.2 million worth of weapons out of the United States to South Africa. They had chartered a Boeing 707 from Montana Austria Airlines, and the consignment of 2000 weapons was intended for Sudan, according to a false export licence issued by the airline's Vienna office. The weapons were called 'steel products'.

Weapons from the Eastern bloc, according to disclosures made in connection with the trial of the Danish Trigon shipping company, are officially destined to a friendly nation or a liberation movement in Africa.

A large percentage of smuggling cases involve radar, electronics and other critical technology. (As to shotguns and other small arms not of obvious use for the South African armed forces themselves, there are many reports of their appearance with the UNITA forces in Angola or the MNR in Mozambique.)

If the embargo continues to be tightened, South Africa will have to rely more on black market imports, with obvious difficulties involved. High-technology smuggling is a more complex undertaking than the illegal shipping of old rifles from Colombia, and some equipment needed for the military industry may be practically inaccessible for a private dealer in the supplying country. The main problem with the black market is that it cannot ensure continuity of supply.

The South African arms exports

Like all other nations which have advanced up the staircase of acquisition of military production know-how and entered into the loop of weapons development, South Africa needs to *export* armaments. Those nations that are willing to import, disimplementing the UN embargo of 1984, thus contribute directly to Armscor's ability to keep up its own production—that is, to stay in the loop.

III. The motives for disimplementation

On each occasion when the *governments* in the respective supplying countries deliver military equipment to South Africa in spite of the embargo, one can find a combination of economic and political reasons for the decision. When *industries* sell military equipment, disguising it with civilian labels, the contradictory interests of industry and government come to the surface. Non-compliance by the strategic industries in Europe and the USA has been and continues to be a formidable obstacle to the operation of even such a large-scale undertaking as the COCOM embargo. Hence, the expectation that producing companies in the West will willingly agree to stop all export of their products to such a customer as South Africa seems over-optimistic.

National economic and political factors receive priority at all times, ahead of any desire to eventually bring down the apartheid system. The breakdown of actors into governments, industry and individual agents, and the further breakdown into different groups at each level, explains the difficulties of arriving at a workable control and monitoring system. Different government agencies work for different goals—one agency's task may be to promote arms exports, the other's is to stop illegal exports. The story of the G-5 deal shows a great confusion of responsibilities within the various US administrative agencies involved.

Given the non-monolithic structure of the Western states, the number of actors involved in organizing an export deal is considerable. This allows both for a genuine confusion as to which agency bears a final responsibility to stop a deal with South Africa, and also creates the possibility of deliberate confusion. No government has set up any specific South Africa control body within its general arms export control departments. The application of the UN embargoes is most often legally contained in a more general clause barring arms shipments to 'countries subject to a UN embargo'.

Above all, the disimplementation of the embargo is best understood when considering the fact that all arms export regulations in all Western countries after 1945 arose out of the cold-war situation, where the main issue remains to prevent the East from acquiring arms and militarily sensitive high technology from the West.

South Africa was not a 'natural' embargo case in this context, considering its historical ties to Britain, its anti-communist stance, economic resources and economic ties with all the major Western powers. The *initiative* to undertake the embargo, furthermore, did not come from the West but from the Third World nations in the UN. Over the years, it has been evident that priorities differ sharply between these groups of nations—the high priority accorded the UN embargo against South Africa demonstrated by the Third World representatives in the UN has not been matched by a similar engagement on the part of the major Western powers.

The UN Arms Embargo Committee in 1986 summarized its difficulties of working jointly with the respective national governments as follows:

Member states have not been helpful in reporting suspected violations to the Committee, although the Secretary-General had expressly asked them to do so on 3 April and 18 May 1978. We are aware of only one such report. All other information has come from other UN bodies, the press, and non-governmental organizations.

The standard procedure for dealing with information on suspected violations of the arms embargo is for the Committee to draw attention of the government concerned to the information giving rise to suspicion, to request further information, and to ask the government to comment. Governments often replied that the allegations were totally unfounded and refused to discuss the matter further. Other replies fall into the following categories:

1) The alleged violations are not within our jurisdiction
2) The alleged violations are within our jurisdiction but they are not punishable because they do not fall within the terms of resolution 418 (1977)
3) The alleged violations are within our jurisdiction and punishable, but there will be no prosecution because no criminal intent is in evidence, or because prosecution would serve no useful purpose
4) The alleged violations are within our jurisdiction and punishable. Criminal proceedings are under way.[5]

IV. Final assessment

The future of South Africa's military-industrial complex will depend largely on the future of the South African political structure. Presently, it looks as if an extreme government—whether of the present kind or radicalized—will bring further isolation of the military industry.

There is an element of truth in all the conflicting assessments to date, ranging from the opinion that the embargo created and benefited the buildup of South Africa's arms industry, to the opinion that the embargo has been of use as a selective measure to draw attention to the apartheid issue.

Self-sufficiency of a kind has been achieved in military production, but self-sufficiency is relative. In future, the stations in the loop of weapons development run the risk of disturbances which will then negatively affect the production capacity. A drain of educated manpower and a lack of contacts with other armaments industries may disturb the RDT&E capacity; production may be affected by an increase of costs and increased difficulties in achieving new designs and acquiring certain components and *matériel*; South African arms exports may for the foreseeable future be seriously hampered by a lack of more attractive customers—the leading industrialized nations—and by the difficulties of exporting the most sophisticated types of weapons; and imports may be further strangled, particularly if stricter economic sanctions are undertaken.

The South African embargo case provides a catalogue of disimplementation methods that ought to be taken into account if similar cases appear in the future. When trying to stop military exports to a resourceful country, special national legislation seems a basic requirement for (*a*) setting up a special supervisory office with far-reaching investigative powers; (*b*) defining in each case the type of goods to be considered 'military'; and (*c*) defining potential military customers in the target country.

The stated goal of preventing South Africa from acquiring and producing armaments and thereby changing the apartheid system has not been reached after 25 years of embargo implementation. On the other hand, no termination of the UN embargo is in sight. Such a termination would involve a Security Council agreement to lift the embargo. The debate during the past few years has rather gone in the opposite direction, demanding not only a strengthening of the military embargo but general mandatory economic sanctions. Since the chances of such an agreement are as remote as a termination, what remains is the more tedious work of improving the implementation of the present embargo.

The reasoning behind attempts to strengthen the embargo, instead of rejecting it because of its insufficiency, needs to be no more complicated than in other generally agreed fields of international co-operation. For example, no responsible person argues that international co-operation to curb the trade in narcotics should cease because results are unsatisfactory. In the case of South Africa, there have been many proposals in various countries for greater powers for customs and police to stop suspected shipments; and there is also the proposal from the Danish Seamen's Union that all ships bound for South Africa should have to report their cargo.

Over the years, the accusation of a secret collusion between the most involved Western powers and South Africa in circumventing the embargo has often been voiced. The frustration over South Africa's continuing military buildup, in particular on the part of the Third World representatives in the UN and in the OAU (and of the various anti-apartheid organizations) is easy to understand. It may help to clarify the substance of such accusations if the embargo issue is divided into two parts, *timing* and *implementation*. The timing of the mandatory embargo of 1977 coincides, in retrospect, with the achievement of enough contracts and know-how for the South African military industry to proceed with its work despite the embargo. This degree of self-sufficiency may have lowered resistance to the embargo in the supplying countries at the industrial, as well as the political, level. There would not even have been any need for formal agreements or 'collusion'.

National implementation of the embargo suffers, on the other hand, from documented inefficiency, as listed above. Such disorders can be corrected once they are discernible and subjected to scrutiny. A mobilization of forces to implement the embargo, involving a stronger element of international co-operation, could still affect the future of the South African defence industry, which after all needs access to high-technology arms developments abroad.

The execution of any policy can often be regarded as a learning process, creating a feedback into the policy itself. All legislation and regulations have to be interpreted before being applied. A lax interpretation of the embargo regulations in the South African case could result in a termination of the embargo for all practical purposes, even if a formal termination is never arrived at. A strict interpretation, implementation and control are essential.

Finally, the most notable effect of the embargo policy against South Africa is to be found in the realm of international politics. The embargo policy has over the years influenced the Western governments towards an increasing isolation of South Africa to a degree inconceivable in the absence of the embargoes. The legalistic framework created by the national embargo regulations has provided the means to criminalize military collaboration with South Africa. Without this framework, the powerful traditional ties between South Africa and the West would have continued to support the *status quo* unchallenged.

Notes and references

1 UPI report, in *The Guardian*, 12 Jan. 1978.
2 *The Star*, 8 July 1980.
3 'Apartheid's secret UK network', *Daily Mail*, 28 Mar. 1984.
4 *Le Monde*, 18 July 1981.
5 Source: Document A.3, 'All States shall cease forthwith, the Security Council and its Arms Embargo', paper presented at the international seminar on the UN arms embargo against South Africa, London, 28–30 May 1986 (The UN Special Committee Against Apartheid and the World Campaign Against Military and Nuclear Collaboration with South Africa), p. 11.

Appendix 1. Sources and methods

I. International sources of information

The sources used in this study are given in Appendix 3. In addition, much of the technical data on individual weapon systems delivered to, or in production in, South Africa have been obtained from SIPRI's computerized data base for major weapon systems (aircraft, armoured vehicles, missiles and warships). This in turn is based on a continuous search of the international defence literature, some 300 technical and military journals, and some 40 daily newspapers and relevant special reports such as US hearings and UN reports. Information on production and acquisition of military software and other weapon categories comes from the same sources. Due to the nature of the subject, the information presented here cannot claim to be absolutely correct or comprehensive. Rather, the presentation has to be made with a note of caution as to exact details, such as numbers of weapons actually produced, since there are no totally reliable sources. When the reporting is considered extremely unreliable, this is pointed out in the text or in a note.

Further, as is the case with military information in general, the information on South Africa's arms acquisition is often unsystematic and scattered, and sources are often found to repeat and quote each other. In particular, clandestine arms deals are, by definition, secret. This traffic is highlighted by the cases discovered and put on trial, and those cases are thus treated as samples allowing for general conclusions. The total amount of this trade can probably not be established.

II. South African sources

Extensive use has been made of the few available South African official sources, such as the Parliamentary Records and Defence White Papers, as well as press reports, mostly from the now defunct *Rand Daily Mail*, which broadly represented white English-speaking opposition to the ruling party in South Africa.

Information on military production is more difficult to find in South Africa than in most Western nations, because of a number of restrictions on such matters. By means of legislation, beginning with the Defence Act of 1957, section 118, and the Police Act of 1958, section 5, the right to publish information concerning the SADF has been progressively restricted and is totally prohibited in some fields, such as access to strategic materials. In March 1980, the so-called Steyn Commission Report further restricted mass media reporting on military matters, and in mid-1985 new legislation was passed prohibiting news reports concerning upheavals in black residential areas.[1] The

Steyn Report has the following to say about the need to protect the arms industry, in particular, from publicity:

This industry is one of the main sources of armaments and ammunition supply for the country's security forces. As a result of the arms embargo imposed over two years ago on the Republic by the UN, and the previous restrictions imposed on their own accord years ago against South Africa by various countries, including Western countries, the Armaments Supply Industry has played a steadily increasing role in the maintenance of law and order and in the preservation of national security, and is now unquestionably a key industry in the Republic. The prevailing conflict situation, of which subversion and sabotage are important facets, makes this industry a prime target in the conflict, both as regards its personnel and its premises and vehicles. The industry is divided into two sections: armaments manufacture and armaments procurement. It is particularly in the latter respect that actual danger to life is experienced by personnel, and a careless word or disclosure of activities can have fatal consequence. *Secrecy of information is thus even more essential here than in the case of the Defence and Police Forces,* and is required for the protection of the Armaments Supply Industry and the promotion of its interests. If this industry is disrupted, extremely serious consequences for the security and order of the country could ensue, and steps to prevent this are therefore in the highest national interest.[2]

On the recommendation of the Steyn Report, the Armaments Development and Production Act, No. 57, section 11, of 1968, was amended to include a prohibition on all information relating to arms production in South Africa unless authorized by the Defence Minister. The punishment for breaking this law is eight years imprisonment and/or a fine of R 15 000.

At least 150 companies in South Africa have been exempted by ministerial decree from disclosing information and are operating in secret. The files and company reports are removed from circulation and are not available to public scrutiny. According to the deputy registrar of companies, Mr H. Coetzee, many of these were major companies with subsidiaries, which pushes the figure of secret production even higher. The industries involved reportedly include those dealing with arms, petroleum and strategic minerals, and also companies working with sensitive trading partners. In terms of an amendment to The Companies Act of 1978, the Defence Minister may prohibit the disclosure of any given company's existence, and exempt the company from presenting any information on its activities. The Act states clearly that it is not in the public interest to make information on strategic trade public.[3] Consequently, there is no detailed information on Armscor to be found in South African sources, other than what the Defence White Papers choose to present. In particular, the identity of arms exporters to and importers from South Africa remains a closely guarded secret.

III. Implementation analysis

The theoretical framework for the approach taken in this study has been inspired by the current literature on policy analysis and, in particular, implementation analysis.[4] This means that the functioning of the arms embargo against South Africa is regarded as a policy process, involving the stages of initiation, estimation, selection, implementation, evaluation and termination. What is of most interest here is the actual *implementation* of the embargo decisions. This means that the stages of initiation, estimation and selection are not dealt with in any detail in this book. In fact, a comprehensive survey of the various initiatives, debates and negotiations and the pattern of voting in the UN, which preceded the final acceptance by the Western powers of the embargoes, merits a separate study. The last stage of the theoretical policy process, termination, is not yet relevant to the South Africa case.

The close scrutiny of the implementation of the embargo includes evaluation of how the policy has been executed. The concept of evaluation includes control and correction, in this study expressed in chapter 15 as methods of disimplementation and proposals for future changes.

This approach includes the assumption that, theoretically, the embargo resolutions of 1963, 1977 and 1984, respectively, were passed with a clear political intention and an expectation that they might result in some change in South Africa's internal racial policies and external policy in the region. Theoretically, the embargo resolutions are all-inclusive and comprehensive. In practice the reason for ineffectiveness lies in the implementation of the ensuing national embargo policies.

IV. Terminology

Disimplementation

A new explanatory concept is introduced by the use of the term of disim- plementation. Disimplementation is used as an umbrella concept, to cover all ways and means by which the arms embargoes have been circumvented, broken, ignored or openly defied, whether intentionally or unintentionally at governmental level. The mechanisms for practising disimplementation have been initiated both at the seller's end and at the receiving end. In particular, in the case of South Africa, the multinational companies operating in the country represent one of the main methods of disimplementing the arms embargoes.

Arms and arms industry

The term defence industry is used synonymously with that of military industry and arms industry, for the sake of variation; in a strictly technological sense these concepts otherwise describe somewhat diferent phenomena.

It is worth noting, also, that there is no 'defence industry' as such; instead there are a number of different industries producing the various categories of military equipment, such as aerospace, vehicles, warships and electronics. The complexity of the structure of what is nevertheless commonly called a defence industry is evident in the sheer number of participants—many thousands of defence-related companies produce equipment on military orders in any average-sized arms-producing nation. Most of these firms produce, in addition, a mix of civilian and military goods. Thus there is a world-wide trade in dual-purpose products for military use, found also in South Africa's case.

This study describes the most important defence industries in South Africa by weapon category, so far as these categories can be discerned. *Infantry arms, small arms* and *military electronics* are used as umbrella headings for what are in reality very differing ranges of products, in particular as concerns the category of electronic equipment.

Military electronics in this study includes the subcategories military computers, communications equipment and optronic equipment. The presentation is best regarded as a sample indicating the scale and scope of this branch of military industry. Practically all modern armaments contain electronic equipment of one kind or another. This is reflected in the increasing use of the term 'weapon systems' instead of just 'weapons'.

Military electronics is sometimes in the literature referred to as 'military software', which is, however, misleading, firstly because the computer sector in itself is divided into 'hardware' and 'software' (referring to the machinery and the programming respectively). Software, moreover, also normally covers *all* non-lethal equipment, such as instrumentation and raw material.

A distinction is sometimes made between 'consumer' electronics and military electronics. This refers to the end user of the equipment more than to any specific in-built military capacity of the equipment itself. Military electronics is, in general, an example of so-called dual-use equipment, where at least the components if not the complete devices can just as well serve civilian buyers. This in turn creates an unprecedented definition problem for embargo implementation, multiplying the difficulties in deciding whether the equipment is military or not.

Raw material and infrastructure needed for arms industry development are not treated comprehensively in this study but merely referred to in relevant contexts. This concerns such products as uranium, special steel, titanium or the construction of special testing facilities.

Third World

The familiar concept of the Third World is used occasionally in this study, for example, to classify South Africa as the militarily dominant power in a Third World region. However, while the Third World grouping may be a convenient one in many circumstances, it is a concept which often conceals more than it explains about nations. South Africa is not in the economic sense a Third World country. To call South Africa a Third World arms producer is equally misleading, which is why the term 'new arms producers' has been introduced here, pointing to the distinction between the established arms-producing nations—the USA, the USSR and European countries—and newcomers after 1945. The same kind of reasoning has been reflected in technical journals in recent years, for example, in the following statement: 'The new manufacturers which are now entering the market have the price advantage which enables widening their possibilities of potential customers'.[5] This article deals precisely with the competition between traditional military suppliers and what are more commonly called the Third World suppliers.

One South African analyst describes the situation of the country thus:

South Africa is not a typically Third World state, nor for that matter a typical state of Africa. The structural features of modern South Africa may not even fall into the Third World category, and its leaders claim to be part of the developed world. The military in South Africa is a key institution supporting the values and the interests of the white minority, the perpetuation of South Africa's racial state.[6]

The need to elaborate the Third World concept is seen from various studies devoted to Third World issues—for example, one recent study starts out by subdividing the concept into different groupings of nations. According to that study, South Africa cannot be classified as belonging among those poor Third World countries that are also classified as developing countries. South Africa is found in a second group of Third World countries. These are

referred to as the economic miracles, because of their expanding competition in electronics and manufacturing. These include Taiwan, Hong Kong, South Korea, Singapore, South Africa, Israel, Argentina and Brazil. Each of these countries has assembled a unique combination of resources, capital, discipline, and hard work to industrialize and modernize . . . Each of these countries has built an impressive industrial base, a modern infrastructure, and a respected educational establishment.[7]

This grouping makes particular sense considering that it brings together the leading new arms producers Israel, Brazil and South Africa, and also considering the military–industrial co-operation between South Africa, Israel and Taiwan.

The military-industrial complex

The concept of the military-industrial complex is used in this study, although it encompasses more than the actual military industries. The armaments industries represent the hardware sector of this concept.

Notes and references

[1] Report of the Commission of Inquiry headed by M. T. Steyn, *Reporting of Security Matters Regarding the South African Defence Force and the South African Police Force* (Government Printer: Pretoria, Mar. 1980).
[2] Steyn Commission Report (note 1), 'Armaments. 43, The Armaments Supply Industry', pp. 31–32.
[3] Source: *Rand Daily Mail*, 22 Mar. 1984.
[4] See for example Brewer, O. and de Leon, P., *The Foundation of Policy Analysis* (The Dorsey Press: Illinois, 1983); and Pressman, J. L. and Wildwavsky, A., *Implementation* (University of California Press: Berkeley and Los Angeles, 1973).
[5] 'High-tech suicide', *Defense & Armament*, no. 48 (Feb. 1986), p. 5 (Editorial).

[6] Frankel, P. H., *Pretoria's Praetorians, Civil-Military Relations in South Africa,* University of the Witwatersrand (Cambridge University Press: Cambridge, 1984), p. XIII.

[7] O'Hefferman, P., Lovins, A. B. and Lovins, H. L., 'The first nuclear world war—a strategy for preventing nuclear wars and the spread of nuclear weapons', *The Third World Superpowers* (Hutchinson & Co.: London, 1983), pp. 110–11.

Appendix 2. UN Security Council resolutions on the arms embargo against South Africa

Resolution 181 (1963) of 7 August 1963 (voluntary)

The Security Council,

Having considered the question of race conflict in South Africa resulting from the policies of *apartheid* of the Government of the Republic of South Africa, as submitted by the thirty-two African Member States,

Recalling its resolution 134 (1960) of 1 April 1960,

Taking into account that world public opinion has been reflected in General Assembly resolution 1761 (XVII) of 6 November 1962, and particularly in its paragraphs 4 and 8,

Noting with appreciation the interim reports adopted on 6 May and 16 July 1963 by the Special Committee on the Policies of *apartheid* of the Government of the Republic of South Africa,

Noting with concern the recent arms build-up by the Government of South Africa, some of which arms are being used in furtherance of that Government's racial policies,

Regretting that some States are indirectly providing encouragement in various ways to the Government of South Africa to perpetuate, by force, its policy of *apartheid,*

Regretting the failure of the Government of South Africa to accept the invitation of the Security Council to delegate a representative to appear before it,

Being convinced that the situation in South Africa is seriously disturbing international peace and security,

1. *Strongly deprecates* the policies of South Africa in its perpetuation of racial discrimination as being inconsistent with the principles contained in the Charter of the United Nations and contrary to its obligations as a Member of the United Nations;

2. *Calls upon* the Government of South Africa to abandon the policies of *apartheid* and discrimination, as called for in Security Council resolution 134 (1960), and to liberate all persons imprisoned, interned or subjected to other restrictions for having opposed the policy of *apartheid*;

3. *Solemnly calls upon all* States to cease forthwith the sale and shipment of arms, ammunition of all types and military vehicles to South Africa;

4. *Requests* the Secretary-General to keep the situation in South Africa under observation and to report to the Security Council by 30 October 1963.

Adopted at the 1056th meeting by 9
votes to none, with 2 abstentions
(France, United Kingdom of Great
Britain and Northern Ireland).

Resolution 182 (1963) of 4 December 1963 (voluntary)

The Security Council,

Having considered the race conflict in South Africa resulting from the policies of *apartheid* of the Government of the Republic of South Africa,

Recalling previous resolutions of the Security Council and of the General Assembly which have dealt with the racial policies of the Government of the Republic of South Africa, and in particular Security Council resolution 181 (1963) of 7 August 1963,

Having considered the Secretary-General's report contained in document S/5438 and addenda,

Deploring the refusal of the Government of the Republic of South Africa, as confirmed in the reply of the Minister of Foreign Affairs of the Republic of South Africa to the Secretary-General received on 11 October 1963, to comply with Security Council resolution 181 (1963) and to accept the repeated recommendations of other United Nations organs,

Noting with appreciation the replies to the Secretary-General's communication to the Member States on the action taken and proposed to be taken by their Governments in the context of paragraph 3 of that resolution, and hoping that all the Member States as soon as possible will inform the Secretary-General about their willingness to carry out the provisions of that paragraph,

Taking note of the reports of the Special Committee on the Policies of *apartheid* of the Government of the Republic of South Africa,

Noting with deep satisfaction the overwhelming support for resolution 1881 (XVII) adopted by the General Assembly on 11 October 1963,

Taking into account the serious concern of the Member States with regard to the policy of *apartheid*, as expressed in the general debate in the General Assembly as well as in the discussions in the Special Political Committee,

Being strengthened in its conviction that the situation in South Africa is seriously disturbing international peace and security, and strongly deprecating the policies of the Government of South Africa in its perpetuation of racial discrimination as being inconsistent with the principles contained in the Charter of the United Nations and with its obligations as a Member of the United nations,

Recognizing the need to eliminate discrimination in regard to basic human rights and fundamental freedoms for all individuals within the territory of the Republic of South Africa without distinction as to race, sex, language, or religion,

Expressing the firm conviction that the policies of *apartheid* and racial discrimination as practised by the Government of the Republic of South Africa are abhorrent to the conscience of mankind and that therefore a positive alternative to these policies must be found through peaceful means,

1. *Appeals* to all States to comply with the provisions of Security Council resolution 181 (1963) of 7 August 1963;

2. *Urgently requests* the Government of the Republic of South Africa to

cease forthwith its continued imposition of discriminatory and repressive measures which are contrary to the principles and purposes of the Charter and which are in violation of its obligations as a Member of the United Nations and of the provisions of the Universal Declaration of Human Rights;

3. *Condemns* the non-compliance by the Government of the Republic of South Africa with the appeals contained in the above-mentioned resolutions of the General Assembly and the Security Council;

4. *Again calls upon* the Government of the Republic of South Africa to liberate all persons imprisoned, interned or subjected to other restrictions for having opposed the policy of *apartheid*;

5. *Solemnly calls upon* all States to cease forthwith the sale and shipment of equipment and materials for the manufacture and maintenance of arms and ammunition in South Africa;

6. *Requests* the Secretary-General to establish under his direction and reporting to him a small group of recognized experts to examine methods of resolving the present situation in South Africa through full, peaceful and orderly application of human rights and fundamental freedoms to all inhabitants of the territory as a whole, regardless of race, colour or creed, and to consider what part the United Nations might play in the achievement of that end;

7. *Invites* the Government of the Republic of South Africa to avail itself of the assistance of this group in order to bring about such peaceful and orderly transformation;

8. *Requests* the Secretary-General to continue to keep the situation under observation and to report to the Security Council such new developments as may occur and in any case, not later than 1 June 1964, on the implementation of the present resolution.

Adopted unanimously at the
1078th meeting.

Resolution 418 (1977) of 4 November 1977 (mandatory)

The Security Council,

Recalling its resolution 392 (1976) of 19 June 1976, strongly condemning the South African Government for its resort to massive violence against and killings of the African people, including schoolchildren and students and others opposing racial discrimination, and calling upon that Government urgently to end violence against the African people and to take urgent steps to eliminate *apartheid* and racial discrimination,

Recognizing that the military build-up by South Africa and its persistent acts of aggression against the neighbouring States seriously disturb the security of those states,

Further recognizing that the existing arms embargo must be strengthened and universally applied, without any reservations or qualifications whatsoever, in order to prevent a further aggravation of the grave situation in South Africa,

Taking note of the Lagos Declaration for Action against *Apartheid,*

Gravely concerned that South Africa is at the threshold of producing nuclear weapons,

Strongly condemning the South African Government for its acts of repression, its defiant continuance of the system of *apartheid* and its attacks against neighbouring independent States,

Considering that the policies and acts of the South African Government are fraught with danger to international peace and security,

Recalling its resolution 181 (1963) of 7 August 1963 and other resolutions concerning a voluntary arms embargo against South Africa,

Convinced that a mandatory arms embargo needs to be universally applied against South Africa in the first instance,

Acting therefore under Chapter VII of the Charter of the United Nations,

1. *Determines,* having regard to the policies and acts of the South African Government, that the acquisition by South Africa of arms and related matériel constitutes a threat to the maintenance of international peace and security;

2. *Decides* that all States shall cease forthwith any provision to South Africa of arms and related matériel of all types, including the sale or transfer of weapons and ammunition, military vehicles and equipment, paramilitary police equipment; and spare parts for the aforementioned, and shall cease as well the provision of all types of equipment and supplies and grants of licensing arrangements for the manufacture and development of nuclear weapons;

3. *Calls upon* all States to review, having regard to the objectives of the present resolution, all existing contractual arrangements with and licences granted to South Africa relating to the manufacture and maintenance of arms, ammunition of all types and military equipment and vehicles, with a view to terminating them;

4. Further decides that all States shall refrain from any co-operation with South Africa in the manufacture and development of nuclear weapons;

5. *Calls upon* all States, including States non-members of the United Nations, to act strictly in accordance with the provisions of the present resolution;

6. *Requests* the Secretary-General to report to the Security Council on the progress of the implementation of the present resolution, the first report to be submitted not later than 1 May 1978;

7. *Decides* to keep this item on the agenda for further action, as appropriate, in the light of developments.

Adopted unanimously at the 2046th meeting.

Resolution 558 (1984) of 13 December 1984 (voluntary)

Adopted by the Security Council at its 2564th meeting on 13 December 1984[1]

The Security Council,

Recalling its resolution 418 (1977) of 4 November 1977, in which it decided upon a mandatory arms embargo against South Africa,

Recalling its resolution 421 (1977) of 9 December 1977, by which it entrusted a Committee consisting of all its members with the task of, among other things, studying ways and means by which the mandatory arms embargo could be made more effective against South Africa and to make recommendations to the Council,

Taking note of the Committee's report to the Security Council contained in document S/14179 of 19 September 1980,

Recognizing that South Africa's intensified efforts to build up its capacity to manufacture armaments undermines the effectiveness of the mandatory arms embargo against South Africa,

Considering that no State should contribute to South Africa's arms production capability by purchasing arms manufactured in South Africa,

1. *Reaffirms* its resolution 418 (1977) and stresses the continuing need for the strict application of all its provisions;

2. *Requests* all States to refrain from importing arms, ammunition of all types and military vehicles produced in South Africa;

3. *Requests* all States, including States non-members of the United Nations to act strictly in accordance with the provisions of the present resolution;

4. *Requests* the Secretary-General to report to the Security Council Committee established by resolution 421 (1977) concerning the question of South Africa on the progress of the implementation of the present resolution before 31 December 1985.

Adopted unanimously
at the 2564th meeting.

[1] Source: S/RES/558 (1984).

Appendix 3. Selected bibliography

I. Books

Adams, J., *The Unnatural Alliance—Israel and South Africa* (Quartet Books: London, 1984).

Adler-Karlsson, G., *Western Economic Warfare 1947–1967—A Case Study in Foreign Economic Policy*, Acta Universitatis Stockholmiensis, Stockholm Economic Studies, New Series IX (Almqvist & Wiksell: Uppsala, 1968).

Arlinghaus, B. E. and Baker, P. H., eds., *African Armies—Evolution and Capabilities* (Westview Press: Boulder and London, 1986).

Arlinghaus, B. E., ed., *African Security Issues: Sovereignty, Stability and Solidarity*, Westview Special Studies on Africa (Westview Press: Boulder, 1984).

Arlinghaus, B. E., *Military Developments in Africa—The Political and Economic Risks of Arms Transfers* (Westview Press: Boulder and London, 1984).

Arlinghaus, B. E., ed., *Arms for Africa—Military Assistance and Foreign Policy in the Developing World*, United States Military Academy (Lexington Books: Lexington, MA, 1983).

Arnold, G., *The Last Bunker—A Report on White South Africa Today* (Quartet Books: London, 1976).

Ball, N. and Leitenberg, M., *The Structure of the Defense Industry—An International Study* (Croom Helm: London and Canberra, 1983).

Barber, J., *South Africa's Foreign Policy 1945–70* (Oxford University Press: Oxford, 1973).

Berg, C., *Sydafrikas krig, ett hot mot världsfreden* (Afrikagrupperna i Sverige (AGIS): Stockholm, 1984).

Bissell, R. E. and Crocker, C. A., *South Africa into the 1980s* (Westview Press: Boulder, 1979).

Bissell, R. E., *South Africa and the United States—The erosion of an influence relationship* (Praeger: New York, 1982).

Callaghy, T. M., ed., *South Africa in Southern Africa* (Praeger/Holt-Saunders: New York, 1983).

Carter, G. M. and O'Meara, P., eds., *Southern Africa: The Continuing Crisis*, second edition (Indiana University Press: Bloomington, 1982).

Cawthra, G., *Brutal Force—The Apartheid War Machine* (International Defence & Aid Fund for Southern Africa (IDAF): London, May 1986).

Cervenka, Z., and Rogers, B., *The Nuclear Axis: Secret Collaboration between West Germany and South Africa* (Julian Friedmann Books: London, 1978).

Chaliand, G., *The Struggle for Africa: Conflict of the Great Powers*, Contemporary African Issues (Macmillan: London and Basingstoke, 1982).

Davidow, J., *A Peace in Southern Africa: The Lancaster House Conference on Rhodesia 1979*, The Center for International Affairs, Harvard University (Westview Press: Boulder and London, 1984).

de Villiers, D. and de Villiers, J., *PW* (Biography of P. W. Botha), (Tafelberg: Cape Town, 1984).

Edmonds, M., ed., *International Arms Procurement—New Directions*, Pergamon Policy Studies on Security Affairs (Pergamon Press: New York, 1981).

El-Khawas, M. A. and Cohen. B., eds., *NSSM 39, The Kissinger Study of Southern Africa (Secret)* (Lawrence Hill & Co: Westport, CT, 1976).

Ellings, R. J., *Embargoes and World Power—Lessons from American Foreign Policy*, Westview Special Studies in International Relations (Westview Press: Boulder and London, 1985).

First, R., Steele, J. and Christabel, G., *The South African Connection—Western Investment in Apartheid* (Temple Smith: London, 1972).

Foltz, W. J. and Bienen, H. S., eds., *Arms and the African—Military Influences on Africa's International Relations* (Yale University Press: New Haven and London, 1985).

Frankel, P. H., *Pretoria's Praetorians—Civil-Military Relations in South Africa* (Cambridge University Press: Cambridge, 1984).

Gansler, J. S., *The Defense Industry* (MIT Press: Cambridge, MA, 1980).

Geisler, W., *DM-Investitionen in Südafrika* (Gottfried Wellmer: Bonn, 1983).

Geldenhuys, D., *The Diplomacy of Isolation—South Africa's Foreign Policy Making*, The South African Institute of International Affairs (Macmillan South Africa: Johannesburg, 1984).

Gerdan, E., *Dossier A . . . comme armes* (Editions Alain Moreau: Paris, 1975).

Grundy, K. W., *The Militarization of South African Politics* (I. B. Tauris: London, 1986).

Heitman, H-R., *South African War Machine* (Bison Books: Greenwich, 1985).

Hufbauer, G. C. and Schott, J. J., *Economic Sanctions Reconsidered: History and Current Policy* (Institute for International Economics: Washington, DC, 1985).

Innes, D., *Anglo-American and the Rise of Modern South Africa* (University of the Witwatersrand, Johannesburg, June 1984).

Jones, R. W. and Hildreth, S. A., *Modern Weapons and Third World Powers*, Significant Issue Series, vol 6, no 4 (Westview Press: Boulder, 1984).

Klieman, A. S., *Israel's Global Reach—Arms Sales as Diplomacy*, Tel Aviv University (Pergamon-Brassey's International Defense Publications: Washington, DC, 1985).

Kühne, W., *Die Politik der Sowjetunion in Afrika, Bedingungen und Dynamik ihres ideologischen, ökonomischen und militärischen Engagements* (Stiftung Wissenschaft und Politik: Ebenhausen, Baden-Baden, 1983).

Landgren-Bäckström, S., *Southern Africa—The Escalation of a Conflict*, SIPRI (Almqvist & Wiksell: Stockholm, 1976).

Leyton-Brown, D., ed., *The Utility of International Economic Sanctions* (Croom Helm: London and Sydney, 1987).

Miller, S. E., *Arms and the Third World: Indigenous Weapons Production* (PSIS: Geneva, 1980).

Nelson, H. D., ed., 'South Africa, a country study', in *Foreign Area Studies*, The American University, Area Handbook Series (US Government Printing Office: Washington, DC, 1981).

Neuman, S. and Harkavy, R. E., eds., *Arms Transfers in the Modern World* (Praeger: New York, 1979).

Newby-Fraser, A. R., *Chain Reaction—Twenty Years of Nuclear Research and Development in South Africa* (Atomic Energy Board: Pretoria, 1979).

O'Hefferman, P., Lovins, A. B. and Lovins, H. L., *The First Nuclear World War—A*

Strategy for Preventing Nuclear Wars and the Spread of Nuclear Weapons (Hutchinson & Co.: London, 1984).

Ohlson, T. and Brzoska, M., *Arms Production in the Third World*, SIPRI (Taylor & Francis: London and Philadelphia, 1986).

Perlmutter, A., Handel, M. and Bar-Joseph, U., *Two Minutes over Baghdad* (Vallentine, Mitchell & Co.: London, 1982).

Sampson, A., *Black & Gold* (Hodder & Stoughton: London, Sydney, Auckland, Toronto, 1987).

Sampson, A., 'The Companies, The Dealers, The Bribes from Vickers to Lockheed', *The Arms Bazaar* (Hodder & Stoughton: London, 1977).

Seidman, A., *The Roots of Crisis in Southern Africa*, Oxfam America, Impact Audit, no. 4 (Africa World Press: Trenton, NJ, 1985).

SIPRI, *The Arms Trade with the Third World* (Almqvist & Wiksell: Stockholm, 1971).

Spector, L. S., *The New Nuclear Nations*, a Carnegie Endowment Book, Vintage Books (Random House: New York, 1985).

Steenkamp, W., *Borderstrike! South Africa into Angola* (Butterworths Publishers: Durban and Pretoria, 1983).

Thayer, G., *The War Business—The International Trade in Armaments* (Weidenfeld & Nicolson: London, 1969).

Tuomi, H. and Väyrynen, R., eds., *Militarization and Arms Production* (Croom Helm: London and Canberra, 1983).

Tuomi, H. and Väyrynen, R., *Transnational Corporations, Armaments and Development—A Study of Transnational Military Production, International Transfer of Military Technology and Their Impact on Development*, Tampere Peace Research Institute, Research Reports, no 22, 1980.

Van Zyl Slabbert, F. and Welsh, D., *South Africa's options—Strategies for sharing power* (David Philip: Cape Town/Rex Collings: London, 1979).

Viaud, P., *L'Afrique et la guerre nucléaire* (L'Harmattan: Paris, Apr. 1984).

Wallensteen, P., *Ekonomiska sanktioner* (Prisma: Stockholm, 1971).

Western Massachusetts Association of Concerned African Scholars, *US Military Involvement in Southern Africa* (South End Press: Boston, 1978).

Wulf, H., et al., Transnational Transfer of Arms Production Technology (Institut für Friedensforschung und Sicherheitspolitik (IFSH): Hamburg, 1980).

Wulf, H., *Rüstung als Technologie Transfer* (Weltfurumverlag: München, 1980).

II. Special reports

Adam, B., 'Le parlement et le gouvernement face au commerce des armes (1980–1981)', *Dossier 'notes et documents'*, no. 42, GRIP (Group de recherche et d'information sur la paix), Brussels, 11 Sep. 1981.

Adelman, K. L. and Knight, A. W., 'Monitoring nuclear proliferation: a case study on South Africa', Defense Intelligence Agency, Washington, DC, SRI Project 7552, SRI International, Arlington, Apr. 1979.

Albright, D. E., 'The USSR and Subsaharan Africa in the 1980s', *The Washington Papers*, no. 101, Center for Strategic and International Studies (CSIS), Washington, DC (Praeger: New York, 1983).

Anti-Apartheid Movement, London, 'How Britain arms apartheid, A Memorandum for presentation to Her Majesty's Government', 1985.

Berghezan, G., 'La puissance militaire de l'Afrique du Sud', *Dossier 'notes et documents'*, no. 94–95, GRIP, Feb. 1986.

Bunzl, J., 'Die Vereinigten Staaten, Israel und Südafrika: Eine Untersuchung ihrer Beziehungen Österreichisches Institut für Internationale Politik', Forschungsberichte FB 3 (Wilhelm Braumüller: Vienna, June 1981).

Counter Information Services (CIS), 'Black South Africa explodes', London, 1976.

Crocker, C. A., 'South Africa's defense posture: Coping with vulnerability', *The Washington Papers*, Center for Strategic and International Studies, Georgetown University (Sage Publications: Beverly Hills and London, 1981).

Davidow, J., 'Dealing with international crises: Lessons from Zimbabwe', Occasional Paper, no. 34, The Stanley Foundation: Muscaine, IA, Oct. 1983.

de Bock, W. and de Plaen, E., 'Deux affaires d'exportation d'armes vers l'Afrique du Sud et l'Uruguay', *Dossier 'notes et documents'*, no. 18, GRIP, 14 May 1980.

de Plaen, E., 'Le commerce des armes en Belgique: législation et règlementation', *Dossier 'notes et documents'*, GRIP, 3 Dec. 1979.

Enforcement of the United States Arms Embargo against South Africa, Hearings before the subcommittee on Africa of the Committee on International Relations, House of Representatives, 97th Congress, second session, 30 Mar. 1982 (US Government Printing Office: Washington, DC, 1982).

Evans, M., *The Front-line States, South Africa and Southern African Security— Military Prospects and Perspectives*, University of Zimbabwe (Irwin Press: Harare, 1986).

Foltz, W. J., 'United States policy toward South Africa: is an effective one possible?', ACIS Working Paper, no. 43, Center for International and Strategic Affairs, University of California, Los Angeles, 1983.

Geldenhuys, D., ed., 'The Role of multinational corporations in South Africa', Study group series, The South African Institute of International Affairs, Braamfontein, Dec. 1979.

Geldenhuys, D., 'South Africa's search for security since the second World War' Occasional paper, The South African Institute of International Affairs, Braamfontein, Sep. 1978.

GRIP, 'Afrique du Sud: la dernière guerre de l'apartheid', GRIP informations, no. 9, summer 1986, Brussels, 1986.

Grundy, K. W., 'The Rise of the South African security establishment—An essay on the changing locus of State power', *Bradlow Series,* no. 1, The South African Institute of International Affairs, Braamfontein, Aug. 1983.

Gutteridge, W., 'South Africa's defence posture', *The World Today* (The Royal Institute of International Affairs: London, 1980).

Hanks, R. J., 'Southern Africa and Western Security', Foreign Policy Report, Institute for Foreign Policy Analysis, Cambridge, MA., and Washington, DC, Aug. 1983.

Hough, M., 'National Security in the RSA—the strategic importance of South and Southern Africa: the Pretoria view', Institute for Strategic Studies, University of Pretoria, Pretoria, June 1981.

IDAF, 'The Apartheid War Machine', Fact paper on Southern Africa, no. 8, London, Apr. 1980.

IDAF, in co-operation with the United Nations Centre against Apartheid, London, 'Apartheid, the facts', June 1983.

Institute for Strategic Studies, University of Pretoria, 'The UN Arms embargo against South Africa', in *ISSUP Bulletin*, no. 2 (4 July 1984).

Jaster, R. S., 'Politics and the Afrikaner bomb', *Orbis*, vol. 27 (winter 1984), pp. 825–51.

Jaster, R. S., 'South African defence strategy and the growing influence of the military', in *Arms and the African—Military Influences on Africa's International Relations*, eds, W. J. Foltz and H. S. Bienen (Yale University Press: New Haven and London, 1985), pp. 121–52.

Jaster, R. S., 'A regional security role for Africa's front-line states: Experience and prospects', *Adelphi Papers*, no. 180 (IISS: London, spring 1983).

Jaster, R. S., 'South Africa and its neighbours: the dynamics of regional conflict', *Adelphi Papers*, no. 209 (IISS: London, summer 1986).

Legum, C., *After Angola. The War over Southern Africa—The Role of the Big Powers* (Rex Collings: London, 1976).

Løvbrœck, A., 'Can transnational corporations be controlled?', DERAP Working papers, Chr. Michelsen Institute, Bergen, 1982.

Millar, T., 'South Africa and regional security', *Bradlow Series*, no. 3, The South African Institute of International Affairs, Braamfontein, Aug. 1985.

Minty, A., 'South Africa's defence strategy', Anti-Apartheid Movement, London, 1971.

Moorsom, R., 'Walvis Bay—Namibia's Port', IDAF in co-operation with the UN Council for Namibia, London, Jan. 1984.

NARMIC/AFSC (American Friends Service Committee), 'Automating apartheid, US computer exports to South Africa and the arms embargo', Philadelphia, 1982.

NARMIC/AFSC, 'Circumventing the arms embargo—invisible trade with Pretoria', New York, Jan. 1985.

NARMIC/AFSC, 'Military Exports to South Africa—a research report on the arms embargo', Philadelphia, Jan. 1984.

NARMIC/AFSC, 'Investigating Apartheid', Philadelphia, 1984.

Näringslivets Internationella Råd, 'Sydafrika och svenskt näringsliv' (Rahms: Lund, 1983).

Reichel, U., 'Militär und Gewalt in südlichen Afrika', *Militärpolitische Dokumentation*, vol. 19, no. 4, Freie Universität: Berlin, Jan. 1980.

Smith, D., 'South Africa's nuclear capability', The World Campaign Against Military and Nuclear Collaboration with South Africa in co-operation with the UN Centre Against Apartheid, London, Feb. 1980.

South African Institute of International Affairs, 'NATO and South Africa', Braamfontein, Oct. 1969.

South African Institute of International Affairs, 'NATO and the South Atlantic', Braamfontein, Jan. 1970.

Spence, J. E., 'South Africa—the Nuclear Option', *African Affairs*, no. 321 (Oct. 1981), pp. 441–52.

Testimony for the United Nations Commission on Transnational Corporations by T. Conrad, in *Transnational Corporations in South Africa and Namibia*, Section B, Part 7, Information and Resource Kit, United Nations Non-Governmental Liaison Service, New York, Jan. 1985.

The Committee on South African War Resistance (COSAWR), London, 'State of war—Apartheid South Africa's decade of militarism', 1984.

Thom, W. G., 'Sub-Saharan Africa's changing military environment', in *Armed Forces and Society*, vol. 2, no. 1 (fall 1984), pp. 32–58.

Tjønneland, E. N., 'Økonomiske sanksjoner som verkemiddel i internasjonal politikk', in *Internasjonal Politikk* (Oslo), no. 1, 1986, pp. 49–69.

Total War in South Africa—Militarization and the Apartheid State (Allies Press: Rondesbosch, 1982).

United States–South Africa Relations: Arms Embargo Implementation, Hearings before the subcommittee on Africa of the committee on international relations, House of Representatives, 95th Congress, first session, 14 and 20 July 1977 (US Government Printing Office: Washington, DC, 1978).

Väyrynen, R., 'South Africa: A coming nuclear-weapon power?' in *Instant Research on Peace and Violence*, Jan. 1977.

Wahren, P. and Walan, M., 'Den svenska stenen, Om svenska företag i apartheids försvarsmur', Afrikagrupperna i Sverige, Stockholm, 1984.

'Weapon against apartheid?—The UN Arms embargo on South Africa', *Analysis and Debate*, no. 12, Southern Africa Research Group, Uppsala University, Department of Peace and Conflict Research, June 1979.

III. South African official reports

Reporting of Security Matters regarding the South African Defence Force and the South African Police Force (Steyn Commission Report), RP 52/1980 (Government Printer: Pretoria, 1980).

Review of Defence and Armaments Production, period 1960 to 1970, Republic of South Africa, Defence Headquarters, Pretoria, Apr. 1971.

'The Armaments Development and Production Act No. 57, 1968 (ARMSCOR)'; in *Statutes of The Republic of South Africa* (Government Printer: Pretoria, 1968).

The Report of the Commission of Inquiry into Security Legislation (Rabie Commission), RP 90/1981 (Government Printer: Pretoria, 1981).

'White Paper on Defence 1977', 'White Paper on Defence and Armaments Supply 1982', and 'White Paper on Defence and Armaments Supply 1984', Department of Defence, Cape Town.

IV. Yearbooks

Africa South of the Sahara (Europe Publications: London), annual.

Jane's All the World's Aircraft; Jane's Armour and Artillery; Jane's Fighting Ships; Jane's Infantry Weapons; Jane's Military Vehicles and Ground Support Equipment; and *Jane's Weapon Systems* (Macdonald: London), annuals.

Rusi & Brassey's Defence Yearbook, annual.

SIPRI Yearbook, World Armaments and Disarmament (Oxford University Press: Oxford), annual.

South Africa. Official Yearbook of the Republic of South Africa, edited by the Department of Foreign Affairs and Information (Chris van Rensburg: Johannesburg), annual.

The Military Balance (IISS: London), annual.

The Statesman's Yearbook, Paxton, J., ed. (Macmillan: London), annual.

World Military Expenditure and Arms Transfers, 1972–1982 (ACDA, Washington, DC, April 1984).

V. UN documents

Ainslee, R., 'Israel and South Africa, an unlikely alliance?', Department of Political and Security Council Affairs, *Notes and Documents,* no. 20, UN Centre Against Apartheid, New York, July 1981.

'Alliance between South Africa and Israel—Statements at the International Conference on the Alliance between South Africa and Israel, Vienna, July 11–13, 1983', *Notes and Documents,* special issue, UN Centre against Apartheid: New York, Feb. 1984.

Asmal, K., 'The arms embargo, international law and the struggle against apartheid', *Notes and Documents,* no. 23 (Aug. 1981), UN Centre Against Apartheid: New York.

Barnaby, F., 'Nuclear South Africa', UN General Assembly A/CONF. 107/2, 17 Apr. 1981.

Conlon, P., 'Analytical compendium of actions taken by governments with respect to sanctions on South Africa', *Notes and Documents,* no. 16 (Sep. 1986), UN Centre Against Apartheid: New York.

Houser, G., 'Relations between the United States and South Africa', *Notes and Documents,* no. 11 (Aug. 1984), UN Centre Against Apartheid: New York.

Militz, E., 'Bank loans to South Africa from mid-1982 to December 1984', *Notes and Documents,* no. 12 (Oct. 1985), UN Centre Against Apartheid: New York.

Onwumechili, C. A., 'South Africa's plan and capability in the nuclear field', *UN Disarmament Study Series,* no. 2, UN: New York, 1981.

Reddy, E. S., 'Review of United Nations Resolutions and action with respect to the arms embargo against South Africa', UN Centre Against Apartheid: New York, 1981.

Seidman, A. and Makgetla, N. 'Transnational corporations and the South African military-industrial complex', *Notes and Documents,* no. 24 (Sep. 1979), UN Centre Against Apartheid: New York.

Seidman, A. and Makgetla, N., *Notes and Documents,* no. 35 (Oct. 1978), UN Centre Against Apartheid: New York.

'South Africa's nuclear weapon capability', World Conference on Sanctions Against Racist South Africa, UNESCO House, Paris, France, 16–20 June, 1986, UN A/CONF. 137/CRP:2, 15 May 1986.

Subcommittee on the Implementation of United Nations Resolutions and Collaboration with South Africa, 'The development of South Africa's nuclear capability', A/AC.115/L.602, UN General Assembly, 25 Oct. 1983.

UN Centre on Transnational Corporations, 'The Activities of Transnational Corporations in the Industrial, Mining and Military Sectors of Southern Africa', ST/CTC/12, UN: New York, 1980.

UN Council for Namibia, 'The military situation in and relating to Namibia' (IV: 'Acquisition of arms and armaments', V: 'South Africa's nuclear weapons capability', Annex: 'Security force bases and units permanently stationed in Namibia'), Doc A/CONF/CRP:2, UN, New York, 15 May 1986.

UN Department of Public Information Division for Economic and Social Information, 'International focus on Transnational Corporations in South Africa and Namibia', UN: New York, 1985.

UN Economic and Social Council, Commission on Human Rights, Thirty-seventh session, Updated report prepared by Special Rapporteur E. M. Khalifa (list of banks, insurance companies, firms and other organizations active in South Africa and Namibia), E/CN.4/Sub.2/1984/8/Add.1, 10 July 1984.

UN Economic and Social Council, 'Examination of the activities of transnational corporations in South Africa and Namibia', E/C.10/AC.4/1985/1-10, Aug. 1985–Feb. 1986.

UN General Assembly, 'Special Reports of the Special Committee Against Apartheid', General Assembly Official Records, Fortieth session, supplement no. 22A (A/40/22/Add.1–4), UN: New York, 1986.

UN Non-Governmental Liaison Service, 'Transnational corporations in South Africa and Namibia: aid or hindrance to apartheid?' Information and Resource Kit, compiled as a service to interested non-governmental groups, UN: New York, Jan. 1985.

UN Security Council Committee (Arms Embargo Committee) Established by Resolution 421 (1977), 'Concerning the Question of South Africa', Reports, Letters and Notes Verbales, S/AC.20/1/38/Add.4, UN, New York, 30 June 1978–14 Mar. 1986.

UN Special Committee Against Apartheid, Special report, 'Recent developments concerning relations between Israel and South Africa', A/41/22/Add.2, UN General Assembly, Oct. 1986.

UN Unit on Apartheid, Department of Political and Security Council Affairs, 'Military and Police Forces in the Republic of South Africa', Documents A/AC.115/L.203–204, UN: New York, 1967.

Appendix 4. South Africa's major weapons industry: the dependence on foreign military technology

Table 4A. The aircraft industry

Type	Foreign military technology	Stage of know-how	Method of disimplementation
Impala series 1-3 COIN fighter/armed trainer	Italy/UK (MB 326)	*Stage 5:* From assembly to manufacture Programme completed 1986 400 units	Licence 1965 Sold as 'unarmed trainer'
Bosbok transport/liaison	Italy/USA (AM-3C)	*Stage 2:* Assembly of 40 units from imported components Programme completed 1975	Licence 1971 Sold as 'light plane'
C-4M Kudu transport/liaison	Italy/USA (AM-3C, AL-60)	*Stage 2:* Local modification 1973 25 units Programme completed 1976	Sold as 'light plane'
Mirage F-1C/A jet fighter	France (Mirage F-1C/A)	*Stage 2:* Assembly of 48 units Programme completed 1977	Sold for 'external defence' Licence 1971 Planned local production of 100 stopped by embargo
Cheetah jet fighter	France/Israel (Mirage-3)	*Stage 5:* Local redesign Prototype 1986	Unofficial technical co-operation for modification of 47 Mirage-3 still in service
Alpha XH-1 gunship helicopter	France (Alouette-3)	*Stage 5:* Local redesign Prototype 1986	Unofficial technical co-operation

Table 4B. The missile industry

Type	Foreign military technology	Stage of know-how	Method of disimplementation
Cactus surface-to-air	France (Crotale)	*Stage 2:* Assembly of sub-assemblies	Licence 1964 Developed in France with South African financing and South African specifications Sold for 'external defence'
Scorpion ship-to-ship	Israel (Gabriel 2)	*Stage 2:* Assembly	Licence 1974, to arm 12 Reshef patrol boats
Kukri air-to-air	France/USA/Israel (Magic, Sidewinder)	*Stage 5:* Local RDT&E from 1964 Previous V3 and Whiplash cancelled Kukri redesign 1980 In production 1984	Unofficial technical co-operation with Israel
Exocet ship-to-ship	France (Exocet)	*Stage 5:* Local redesign 1982 Under development Project unconfirmed	Unofficial technical co-operation
ATM anti-tank	France/FRG (Entac, Milan, SS-11)	*Stage 5:* Local redesign 1984 Under development Project unconfirmed	Believed based on types in use with Army

Table 4C. Armoured vehicles

Type	Foreign military technology	Stage of know-how	Method of disimplementation
Eland series 1-7 armoured car	France (Panhard AML-60/90)	*Stage 5:* From assembly to manufacture of 1600 units 1966–84	Licence 1963 Not defined as 'COIN' weapon Clandestine acquisition
Ratel series armoured car	Belgium/FRG (Sibmas)	*Stage 5:* Local redesign late 1960s	Continued use of imported technology
AC-100 armoured car	Belgium/FRG (Sibmas)	1500 units produced Programme continued	
AC-200 armoured car	Belgium/FRG (Sibmas)	Under development in 1986, based on Ratel	
Olifant main battle tank	UK/Israel (Centurion)	*Stage 5:* Local redesign 1982	Unofficial technical co-operation Modification of 250 Centurions originally imported from UK
Valkiri multiple rocket launcher	Israel	*Stage 5:* Local redesign of Israeli copy of 'Stalin organ' 1980 In production	Unofficial technical co-operation
G-5/G-6 self-prop. long-range howitzer	Canada/USA/Belgium/Sweden	*Stage 5:* Local adaption of foreign-designed concepts Production start 1977	Developed by Space Research Corp. in USA/Canada and Belgium according to South African specification Clandestine acquisition 1976

Table 4D. Military trucks/transporters

Type	Foreign technology	Stage of know-how	Method of disimplementation
Landrover, jeep	UK	*Stage 5:* From assembly to manufacture 1962–1980 (?)	Licence 1961; not defined as 'COIN weapon'
Trax, jeep	France/UK/USA	*Stage 5:* Local design In production 1976 (?)	Licensed engines from Chrysler, Leyland and Peugeot; to replace Landrover UK radio communication system
Samil series, trucks Over 70 variants including: Buffel APC Bulldog APC Rhino troop carrier	FRG/Israel	*Stage 5:* From assembly to manufacture Redesign based on Samil-20, Samil-50 and Samil-100	Licence 1964 Magirus-Deutz/Unimog Reported Israeli-designed armour plate Continued use of imported technology
Magnis series, trucks	FRG/Japan	*Stage 5:* In production 1984	Merger of Magirus/Nissan technology; to replace Samil
Sakom series, light trucks Sakom-50	FRG	*Stage 5:* Redesign base on Samil-50 1982	Continued use of imported technology
Casspir series transporter	Unknown	*Stage 5:* 1972	Reportedly developed in co-operation with Rhodesia
Hippo/Ribbok transporter	Unknown	*Stage 5:* 1976	Reportedly developed in co-operation with Rhodesia

Type	Foreign technology	Stage of know-how	Method of disimplementation
P 1558 large patrol boat	Unknown	Stage 5: One unit produced 1974–76	Armed with Bofors guns
Flexible torpedo recovery ship	UK	Stage 2: One unit produced 1969	Built by foreign subsidiary Dorman Long (Africa); probably licence
De Mist tug	UK	Stage 5: One unit produced 1978	Built by foreign subsidiary Dorman Long (Africa); probably licence
De Neys and De Noorde tugs	UK	Stage 5: Two units produced 1961 and 1969	Built by Globe Engineering Works
Navigator training ship	Unknown	Stage 5: One unit produced 1964	Built by Fred Nicholls
87-tonne rescue launchers	FRG	Stage 2: Produced 1961 and 1962	Probably licence 1961 FL9 SAR type built by Krögerwerft
'Namacurra'-class 5-tonne harbour patrol boat	Unknown	Stage 5: Reported as local design; 30 units produced 1979	
'Minister of Defence'-class missile-armed FAC	Israel/Italy	Stage 2: 12 units in production from 1978	Licence 1974 Armed with Oto Melara guns
Voortrekker-II ocean racing yacht	Unknown	Stage 5: Produced 1983	In Navy service
Shirley-T helicopter carrier	Unknown	Stage 5: Prototype 1982	Reportedly produced for Israel; Unconfirmed
Tafelberg armed helicopter carrier	Denmark/Israel/Switzerland	Stage 1: Conversion of aged tanker 1983–84 Purchased from Denmark 1965	Modification of imported civilian vessel Armed with Scorpion missiles and Oerlikon guns
Drakensberg fleet replenishment vessel	FRG	Stage 5: One unit produced 1984–86	Announced as the first naval vessel designed and built in South Africa
Submarine Type-209	FRG	First unit planned 1992	Clandestine acquisition of blueprints 1985 Reported technical aid also from Chile and Turkey

Index

China 5, 42, 94, 182, 224
cholera 151
chromium 22, 28
Chrysler 81
Chrysler engine 99
Churchill, Winston 38
coal 22, 39, 45, 160
cobalt 28
COCOM (Co-ordinating Committee)
    embargo 7–8, 121, 136, 192, 193, 194,
    195, 202, 207
Coetzee, B. 121
Coetzee, H. J. 19, 243
Colombia 179
Common Market see EC
Commonwealth 39, 41, 194
communications equipment 135–49
computers 51, 136, 138, 139, 143, 144–5,
    156, 206–7
Congo 5
conscientious objectors 168
Consolidated Power 139
'Contras' 182
Control Logic 138, 174
Conyers, John 163, 166
corpse transporter 98
corvettes 120–1
Council for Scientific and Industrial
    Research (CSIR) 24, 38, 49, 105, 149,
    156, 173
counter-insurgency (COIN) weapons 31,
    66, 67, 71, 82, 100, 118, 127
Credit Lyonnais 161
CR Jansen Aviation 78
Crotale missile 92, 103, 104, 106, 174
Cuba 26, 31, 32, 170
Cyrano-4 radar 72
Czechoslovakia 42, 237

Daimler-Benz 96, 99
Daisy, Operation 84
Daphne submarines 42, 52, 113, 116, 120,
    121, 143
Darter, 106
Dassault 70
Datakor 144, 173
Datsun-Nissan 81
de Beers 149
debts 58
Decca 135
Defence Advisory Board 47
Defence Council 45
Defence Ordnance Workshop 38
defoliants 149
De Hoop range 109
De Mist 114
De Neys 114
Denmark 114, 118, 237, 241
De Noorde 114

Department of National Security 167
depth charges 119
Deutz Dieselpower 100
diamonds 22, 27
Diel 144
Digital Equipment Corporation 207
Domingo 151
Dorbyl Group 54, 56, 57, 114
Dorman Long 54, 114
Dorman Long Swan Hunter 114
Drakensberg 119
Drommedaris 114
dual-use equipment 174, 192, 198, 203, 206,
    212, 213, 225, 232, 233, 235–6, 245
Duiker water tanker 82
du Plessis, P. 28
Dvora boats 108

Eaton Corporation 100
EC (Economic Community) 6, 234
Economic Development Corporation 100
Edwards, Vice-Admiral R. 120
Eisenhower, Dwight D. 153
Eland armoured car 44, 81, 82–3, 104, 131,
    177, 180, 209, 210, 212
Elbit 145, 219
electronics:
    exports 136
    foreign technology and 37, 137–8, 139,
        142, 146, 147, 191
    licences for 137, 143
    producers 140–4
    production 38, 135–47
    self-sufficiency 16
Electronic Warfare training Section 136
Elettronica 117
Eloptro 53, 54, 142–3, 145
Eltro Engineering 145
Eltron Group 138, 174
Emeraude, Pierre 65
EMI electronics 135
emigration 230
engines 99–100
    see also under names of
Entac missile 84, 104
Escom (Electronic Supply Commission) 45,
    48, 156, 160
Ethiopia 4, 7
Eurodif 162
Eurofuel 161
Exocet missile 52, 92, 104, 108, 109–10, 178
explosives industry 39, 52
Eyrie RPV 110–11, 174

Falklands War 6, 27, 109, 178, 179
FH-77 89
Fiat 69, 77
FIDA-86 arms exhibition 77
FL9 SAR 115
Flexible 114

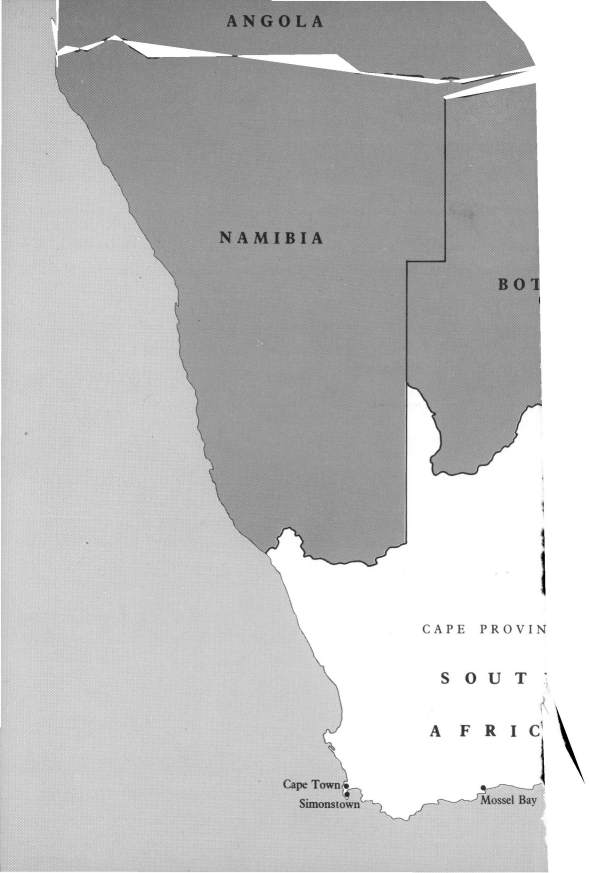